The Educational Role of the Museum

Second edition

Edited by
Eilean Hooper-Greenhill

Routledge
Taylor & Francis Group

LONDON AND NEW YORK

First published 1994
by Routledge
11 New Fetter Lane, London EC4P 4EE

Simultaneously published in the USA and Canada
by Routledge
29 West 35th Street, New York, NY 10001

Reprinted 1996

Second edition published 1999

Reprinted 1999, 2001, 2002, 2003

Routledge is an imprint of the Taylor & Francis Group

© 1994, © 1999 Eilean Hooper-Greenhill

Typeset in Sabon by The Florence Group, Stoodleigh, Devon
Printed and bound in Great Britain by TJ International Ltd,
Padstow, Cornwall

British Library Cataloguing in Publication Data
A catalogue record for this book is available from the British Library

Library of Congress Cataloging in Publication Data
The educational role of the museum / edited by Eilean Hooper-
Greenhill – 2nd ed.
p. cm. – (Leicester readers in museum studies)
Includes bibliographical references and index.
1. Museums and schools. 2. Museums – Educational aspects.
3. Museums and schools – Great Britain. 4. Museums –
Educational aspects – Great Britain. I. Hooper-Greenhill,
Eilean, 1945– II. Series.
LB1047.E38   1999
371.3'84–dc21
98–34491
CIP

ISBN 0–415–19826–7 (HB)
ISBN 0–415–19827–5 (PB)

The Educational Role of the Museum

Leicester Readers in Museum Studies

Care of Collections
Edited by Simon Knell

Collections Management
Edited by Anne Fahy

Interpreting Objects and Collections
Edited by Susan M. Pearce

Museum Management
Edited by Kevin Moore

Museum Provision and Professionalism
Edited by Gaynor Kavanagh

The Educational Role of the Museum: Second Edition
Edited by Eilean Hooper-Greenhill

Contents

Illustrations

PLATES

FIGURES

TABLES

Preface

Producing a second edition of this Reader has given me the opportunity to revise it thoroughly. The first edition has been well used, by those taking museum, heritage studies, leisure management and tourism courses, and by my own students in the Department of Museum Studies at the University of Leicester. Although the book has been useful to a broad range of readers, the primary audience remains those who are or intend to become museum professionals. Thus although some contextual cultural issues are addressed in some of the chapters, the main focus is on more narrowly defined professional matters. The educational role of the museum is again defined at its broadest, to include museum and gallery teaching, communication with museum and gallery visitors, and audience research.

The revision of the first edition has been rigorous, to reflect both developments in my own thinking and teaching, and developments within the academic field. The criterion for selection for this edition has been to retain those chapters that remain of contemporary interest, and of current use in teaching, and to drop those that are now out of date, such as the exhibition case-studies and the chapter on visitor patterns. One or two chapters have had to be dropped because of excessive copyright costs.

More than one third of the chapters are new. Some of them introduce issues of concern at the present time, such as constructivism, its context within postmodernism, and its application within museum and gallery exhibitions. Some are concerned with more sophisticated analyses than were available at the time of the first edition, especially within the area of audience research. Some of the new chapters are papers of my own. Museum education and communication are dynamic and rapidly developing fields, which present their own challenges to those of us who teach within them! My own ideas are undergoing some revitalization following an introduction to postcolonialism on an extended visit to Australia and New Zealand, and a subsequent turn to hermeneutics as a way of accounting for difference in processes of meaning construction. I am working on a book that develops this, which will be published by Routledge in due course.

Since 1994 the museum field has settled more firmly into patterns that emphasize the importance of successful relationships with audiences, and consequently the educational role of the museum has become even more significant. In addition to this, that role has changed. First, it has grown out of all recognition, and second, it has moved more firmly from the transmission of information to the enabling of the construction of personal relevance. Although these trends were becoming evident when I compiled the first edition, today they have become among the most compelling of issues within museums.

In 1998 we understand more clearly that education within the museum and gallery field is rarely about conveying factual information. This can be done elsewhere in a more competent way. A museum is not a book, or an encyclopaedia, although it has been compared with both; a museum is a complex cultural organization, which is made up of a site that is frequently spectacular, a body of people with rare and fascinating expertise, a collection of objects that in its totality is unique, and a range of values that are currently under intense scrutiny from within the institution, from the academy and from government. All of these elements are susceptible to study, and therefore present learning opportunities. The level of learning can range from early childhood education to postgraduate research.

Learning in museums is inevitably cross-disciplinary and can expose social and disciplinary classification systems. It is of value to a broad range of audiences, and can be of relevance within the spheres of formal learning, self-directed learning and family learning.

While the buildings, the sites and the analysis of museums as cultural organizations have great educational potential, much teaching and learning in museums and galleries focuses on the collections. Learning from objects can be uniquely holistic. It can encompass skills development (including those of literacy and numeracy); increase knowledge and awareness; offer experiences that illuminate personal relevance and that ground abstract concepts; and enable social learning.

Museums and galleries are particularly interesting in relation to large-scale cultural movements, and this has a direct bearing on their educational intentions. During the nineteenth century, and for much of the twentieth, education was mainly understood as the delivery of information to learners whose task was to absorb as much as possible. Knowledge was understood as objective, external to the knower, and transferable. In the museum, this led to authoritative, didactic displays, frequently arranged to illustrate conventional epistemological hierarchies and classifications. Today, we are coming to grips with learning theories that tell us that people are active in constructing their own particular interpretation of their educational experiences, according to their existing knowledge, skills, background and personal motivation. From this perspective, knowledge is relative, it will be subjectively reviewed and used, and learning is therefore unpredictable. The responsibility for learning falls more squarely on the learner, but the responsibility for the teacher is to prepare appropriate learning environments, to act as expert mentor, to help develop learning skills and to provide opportunities for testing and modifying individual meanings and interpretations.

Although the constructivist approach has been challenged, and the notion of personal learning does need to be tempered with an awareness of the constraints and possibilities that structure the communities of interpretation to which learners belong, these views have gained credibility in museums. As a result, museums and galleries are rapidly inventing new display methods that will encompass this shift in approach to education. Many of these new methods are indebted to teaching and learning approaches already very well established by museum educators, such as handling, questioning, offering alternative points of view, personalizing objects and references and using complementary images and sounds.

These broad shifts in learning theory and practice can be readily related to the cultural move from modernism, with its monolithic metanarratives (particularly evident in museum displays), to postmodernism with its more fragmented and diverse approach. The challenges and contests of the postcolonialism world are enacted daily in museums, especially those with ethnographic collections.

Thus, the educational role of the museum is becoming susceptible to analysis in new ways. As museums become more audience-driven, so they are changing to become more reflexive and self-aware. They are also, in some ways, becoming more unified, with a clearer view of how audiences and collections interrelate, and how patterns of collection use inform patterns of collection care and acquisition. The museum's educational role is becoming more integrated into its core identity, although this varies enormously from institution to institution and from country to country. However, there is no turning back: museums now depend on their audiences, and need to develop ever more sophisticated ways of understanding and providing for visitors' needs and desires.

Since 1994 a small number of important books have been published on the subject of the educational role of museums. Each in its own way responds to the changes outlined above.

George Hein's important monograph *Learning in the Museum* (1998) is an in-depth analysis of how visitors learn in museums, and how we can study this learning process. It covers both educational theory and visitor studies, putting both of these into detailed historical and theoretical contexts. Hein points out the challenges of researching and understanding learning, both in museums and elsewhere. He shows how different work-views held by researchers influence understandings of the nature of knowledge and the nature of learning. While he offers a thorough review of these from which to critique the learning and visitor studies he cites, he declares his own preference for a constructivist view of learning in museums, and a naturalistic approach to studying museums and visitors.

From Knowledge to Narrative: Educators and the Changing Museum by Lisa Roberts (1997) is in many ways a parallel volume. Although the approach taken is quite different, the basic mapping of the shifts in the educational role of the museum reviews the same landscapes and draws more or less the same conclusions about the major changes in museum education. Roberts uses the development of an exhibition on Linnaeus at the Chicago Botanic Garden as the central motif in a comprehensive discussion of the history and philosophy of museum education in America. The book seeks to show that the involvement of museum educators as forceful presences on exhibition teams has raised questions about the core values of museums, as museum education has been recast as less about facts and information and more about the enabling of personal meaning through narratives and experience.

However, museum educators in America (or some at least) appear to have some difficulty abandoning, or even reviewing, an educational function that prioritizes the didactic delivery of facts. In Britain, we take a different approach. Museum educators have been influenced by Dewey, Plowden, play and child-centred progressive educational methods, which have adapted very well into the museum environment. Our 'elders' Molly Harrison, Renee Marcouse and Barbara Winstanley showed us how to use workshops, drama, handling and practical creative sessions, in contrast to the information-based gallery tour. These methods adapt easily to the emphasis today on reinventing exhibitions as environments for creative learning.

A third book focuses directly on the educational role for exhibitions. *Developing Museum Exhibitions for Life-long Learning*, edited by Gail Durbin on behalf of the Group for Education in Museums (1996), is a Reader that has been compiled with the explicit objective of providing vital reading for museum educators who find themselves working as part of an exhibition development team. Sections cover learning theory, audience research, exhibition planning and case-studies, text and evaluation. This book is designed for pragmatic empirical use, although many of the readings deal with theoretical and philosophical issues in some depth. Many people, not only museum and gallery educators, will find this book extremely useful.

In Britain a major new report, *A Common Wealth: Museums and Learning in the United Kingdom* (Anderson 1997) has stimulated a great deal of professional interest in the development and significance of the educational role of museums and galleries. The report shocked many with its findings of the low esteem that many museums still accord to education. However, it must be remembered that when a general picture of museum provision is attempted, this includes a very large proportion of very small museums. Many of these very small museums are run by volunteers, are not open all the time, and are sometimes very under-resourced. Sometimes their roles are very limited and specific. Many museums such as these do not value their educational role as they might.

The report's brief was to 'review the current activities of museums in the United Kingdom as centres for formal and informal learning, and to identify how this function can be effectively developed'. This the report does very impressively. It identifies twelve targets for the development of museum education which, if they were to be accomplished, would indeed change the public role of museums. The report also presents a perceptive and thoughtful philosophical statement on museums as learning institutions. As such, it stands as a major contribution to the development of the educational role of the museum.

The study of the educational role of museums needs to cover a broad range of material, drawn from diverse but related fields. These include communication studies, cultural studies, sociology, educational theory and practice, and museum studies. However, it is difficult for students to appreciate the relevance of these fields of enquiry, if the writing is not related to museum and gallery work. Any course of study in this area, therefore, needs to work between theory and practice. Theory that cannot illuminate day-to-day responsibilities will not be useful to museum workers, and will not enable professional growth and development. On the other hand, it is not a great deal of help either to read in a descriptive way about the practices of other people, without being able to analyse from a critical and informed standpoint the approaches adopted and the results obtained. Many of the papers I have chosen for inclusion in this edition have either proved their worth to students, or are useful in that they draw on theory external to the museum field in such a way that relationships can readily be made.

The book has been restructured into four main sections: communication theories; learning in museums; developing effective exhibitions; and thinking about museum audiences. Each of these will be briefly introduced at its beginning. I have written a new introduction to the book, which places the sections of the book, and the issues each section addresses, in a contextual relationship; this is Chapter 1, in the first section. There are some suggestions for further reading in this introductory chapter and the reader is also referred to the bibliographies of the individual chapters that follow.

I hope the book will raise questions, stimulate debate, increase motivation to pursue these important issues further and, above all, be enjoyable.

Eilean Hooper-Greenhill
Leicester, 1998

REFERENCES

Anderson, D. (1997) *A Common Wealth: Museums and Learning in the United Kingdom*, London: Department of National Heritage.

Durbin, G. (ed.) (1996) *Developing Museum Exhibitions for Life-long Learning*, ed. on behalf of the Group for Education in Museums, London: HMSO.

Hein, G. (1998) *Learning in the Museum*, London: Routledge.

Roberts, L. (1997) *From Knowledge to Narrative: Educators and the Changing Museum*, Washington, DC and London: Smithsonian Institution Press.

Acknowledgements

Eilean Hooper-Greenhill, 'Communications in theory and practice', reprinted from Eilean Hooper-Greenhill (1994) *Museums and their Visitors*, London: Routledge. Eilean Hooper-Greenhill, 'Learning in art museums: strategies of interpretation', reprinted from Toby Jackson (eds) (1998) *Young Tate*, Liverpool: Liverpool University Press and the Tate Gallery, Liverpool. Robert Hodge and Wilfred D'Souza, 'The museum as a communicator: a semiotic analysis of the Western Australian Museum Aboriginal Gallery, Perth', reprinted with permission from *Museum* 31(4) (1979): 251–67. Copyright © 1979, UNESCO. Eilean Hooper-Greenhill, 'Museum learners as active postmodernists: contextualizing constructivism', reprinted from *Journal of Education in Museums* 18 (1997): 1–4. George E. Hein, 'The constructivist museum', reprinted from *Journal of Education in Museums* 16 (1995): 21–3. John Hennigar Shuh, 'Teaching yourself to teach with objects', reprinted from *Journal of Education* (province of Nova Scotia) 7(4) (1982): 8–15. Gail Durbin, 'Improving worksheets', reprinted from the *Journal of Education in Museums* 10 (1989). Jessica Davis and Howard Gardner, 'Open windows, open doors', reprinted, with permission, from *Museum News* (January/February 1993). Copyright © 1993, the American Association of Museums. All rights reserved. Joseph H. Suina, 'Museum multicultural education for young learners': this article is reproduced with the permission of Museum Education Roundtable. It first appeared in the *Journal of Museum Education* 15(1) (1990). Nina Jensen, 'Children, teenagers and adults in museums: a developmental perspective', reprinted, with permission, from *Museum News* (May/June 1982). Copyright © the American Association of Museums. All rights reserved. Charles F. Gunther, 'Museum-goers: life-styles and learning characteristics', reprinted from *Museums and Universities: New Paths for Continuing Education*, edited by Janet W. Solinger (1989). Used by permission of the American Council on Education and the Oryx Press, 4041 N. Central Ave., Suite 700, Phoenix, AZ 85012, USA. Jocelyn Dodd, 'Whose museum is it anyway? Museum education and the community': this article is reproduced with the permission of Museum Education Roundtable. It first appeared in the *Journal of Education in Museums* 13 (1992). Eilean Hooper-Greenhill, 'Learning from learning theory in museums', reprinted from *GEM News* 55 (1994). Mihaly Csikszentmihalyi and Kim Hermanson: 'Intrinsic motivation in museums: why does one want to learn?' by Mihaly Csikszentmihalyi and Kim Hermanson is reprinted, with permission, from *Public Institutions for Personal Learning: Establishing a Research Agenda*, edited by John Falk and Lynn Dierking. Copyright © 1995, the American Association of Museums. All rights reserved. Sam H. Ham, 'Cognitive psychology and interpretation: synthesis and application', reproduced from *Journal of Interpretation* 8(1) (1983): 11–27. Reprinted with permission of the author and the National Association for Interpretation, USA. Practical applications of the ideas outlined in this article are expanded in Ham's (1992) text,

Environmental Interpretation: A Practical Guide for People with Big Ideas and Small Budgets. Hank Grasso and Howard Morrison, 'Collaboration: towards a more holistic design process', reprinted from *History News* 47(3) (May/June 1992): 12–15 by permission of the publisher. Copyright © by the American Association for State and Local History. Communications Design Team, Royal Ontario Museum, 'Spatial considerations', reprinted from *Communicating with the Museum Visitor: Guidelines for Planning*, Toronto, Canada: Royal Ontario Museum, 1976. David Dean, 'The exhibition development process', reprinted from D. Dean, *Museum Exhibition: Theory and Practice*, London: Routledge, 1994. Margareta Ekarv, 'Combating redundancy: writing texts for exhibitions', from *Exhibitions in Sweden* 27/8 (1986/7), reprinted by permission of Riksutställningar. Translated from 'PÅ GÅNG i utställningssverige' 27/8 (1986/7), quarterly magazine published by Riksutställningar (Swedish Travelling Exhibitions). Elizabeth Gilmore and Jennifer Sabine, 'Writing readable text: evaluation of the Ekarv method', reprinted from *Museum Practice* 5 (2/2) (1997), Museums Association, London. James Carter, 'How old is this text?', reproduced from *Environmental Interpretation, the Bulletin of the Centre for Environmental Interpretation* (February 1993) by permission of CEI Associates, The Progress Centre, Charlton Place, Manchester, M12 6HS, UK. Helen Coxall, 'Museum text as mediated message', from *Women, Heritage and Museums (WHAM)* 14 (1990), reprinted by permission. Betty Davidson, Candace Lee Heald and George E. Hein, 'Increased exhibit accessibility through multisensory interaction', reprinted from *Curator* 34(4): 273–90. Copyright © the American Museum of Natural History 1991. Tony Bennett, 'That those who run may read: museums and barriers to access', from C. Scott (ed.) *Evaluation and Visitor Research in Museums – towards 2000: Conference Papers*, Sydney, Australia. Reproduced courtesy of the Powerhouse Museum, 1996. Reproduced courtesy of the Powerhouse Museum, Sydney, Australia. Eilean Hooper-Greenhill, 'Audiences: a curatorial dilemma', from S. Pearce (ed.) *Art in Museums*, New Research in Museum Studies, Vol. 5, London: Athlone Press. Sharon Macdonald, 'Cultural imagining among museum visitors: a case-study', reprinted from *Management and Curatorship* 11(4) (1992): 401–9. With permission from Elsevier Science. Rebecca McGinnis, 'The disabling society', reprinted from *Museums Journal* 94(6) (1994). Eilean Hooper-Greenhill, 'Museums and cultural diversity: a British perspective', paper written for the conference 'Cultural Diversity in Contemporary Europe', Cultural Traditions Group, Belfast, 8–11 April 1997. Phil Bull, 'A beginner's guide to evaluation', reproduced from *Environmental Interpretation, the Bulletin of the Centre for Environmental Interpretation* (February 1993). Articles from *Environmental Interpretation* have been reprinted courtesy of CEI Associates, The Progress Centre, Charlton Place, Manchester, M12 6HS, UK. G. Binks and D. Uzzell, 'Monitoring and evaluation: the techniques', reproduced from *Environmental Interpretation, the Bulletin of the Centre for Environmental Interpretation* (July 1990). Tim Badman, 'Small-scale evaluation', reproduced from *Environmental Interpretation, the Bulletin of the Centre for Environmental Interpretation* (July 1990). George E. Hein, 'Evaluation of museum programmes and exhibits', *Museum Education*, Danish ICOM/CECA, Copenhagen. Reproduced by kind permission of the author. Marilyn Ingle, 'Pupils' perceptions of museum education sessions': this article is reproduced with the permission of Museum Education Roundtable. It first appeared in the *Journal of Education in Museums* 11 (1990). Terry Russell, 'Collaborative evaluation studies between the University of Liverpool and the national museums and galleries on Merseyside', from P. Sudbury and T. Russell, *Evaluation of Museum and Gallery Displays*, Liverpool: Liverpool University Press, 1995. Anita Rui Olds, 'Sending them home alive': this article is reproduced with the permission of Museum Education Roundtable. It first appeared in the *Journal of Museum Education* 15(1) (1990).

Every attempt has been made to obtain permission to reproduce copyright material. If any proper acknowledgement has not been made, we would invite copyright holders to inform us of the oversight.

We would like to thank Jim Roberts for drawing the figures.

Part I
Communication theories

The chapters in this first section of the Reader indicate how ideas about museum communication have changed in recent years. They enable greater detail to be pursued in relation to some of the issues that are raised in Chapter 1, the Reader introduction.

Chapter 2 charts the development of museum audience studies and the approach to museum communication which is largely based on the transmission model. Chapter 3 offers a more cultural and interpretist approach to the understanding of communication. Chapter 4 presents a case-study of exhibition analysis. The analysis, which uses methods based in semiotics, exposes the exhibition as based on a transmission view of communication, both its subjects and its potential audience being ignored.

Museums have always been intimately interconnected to prevailing and changing views of what counted as truth, which itself emerged from contemporary structures of knowledge. Thus, as what counted as 'truth' changed across the centuries, museums and the interpretation of objects changed too.

Today we are at a further point of change. Some people call this a shift from the modern age to postmodern times. Others dispute both the names used and the nature and depth of the change. However, undoubtedly, museums are at a point of rapid and radical reinvention. Much of this change is to do with new ways of thinking about what counts as 'true' in museums today.

1

Education, communication and interpretation: towards a critical pedagogy in museums

Eilean Hooper-Greenhill

THE SIGNIFICANCE OF THE EDUCATIONAL ROLE OF THE MUSEUM

How should we study the educational role of the museum in the millennium? How can either 'education' or 'museum' be understood at this time? In many parts of the world, museums and galleries are reinventing themselves as they develop relevant identities for the complex present and the unimaginable future. Much of this development concerns new relationships with audiences,[1] both current and potential visitors, and real and virtual users. Today, it is seen more clearly than ever that it is the demonstrable and visible social use of museums that justifies support and financial investment, whether from government, sponsors or individual visitors. Value for money, which is demanded ever more loudly from museums, is perhaps more clearly demonstrated through the public face of the museum.

'Museum' is a capacious concept, and as a result museums are immensely varied, with a fluidity of organizational form that can be adeptly exploited to suit specific local circumstances. From large international urban cultural palaces to small homely displays of local life, and from the pungent pigsties of farm museums to the high-tech inter-active cyber-exhibits of science centres, each museum is unique. For all museums, however, their educational role is crucial.

The nature and range of the educational role of museums have changed and grown dramatically in recent years. Where, formerly, museum education was limited to providing specific provision for limited groups such as schoolchildren or adult tour-groups, the educational role of museums is now understood much more widely, to include exhibitions, displays, events and workshops. The work of the museum educator has correspondingly expanded, and now it might include working on exhibition devel-opment teams and carrying out visitor studies as well as managing and delivering educational sessions.

In grasping the complexity of the educational role of the museum, three words re-occur: education, interpretation and communication. There is confusion in museum circles as to what these words actually mean and how they interrelate. In some ways, this semantic confusion indicates a lack of a holistic view of the educational potential of the museum. There is still a tendency to see 'education' as taught sessions for schoolchildren, and there is still a failure to acknowledge that museum education must be seen in the context of the museum or gallery as a cultural organization within a contradictory and unequal social framework.

3

This introductory chapter brings together the themes that the chapters in the book present and shows one way in which they can be related to each other. Thus, I have tried to demonstrate, for example, how constructivist learning theory ties in with approaches to understanding communication, and how interpretation can become a more useful concept in the museum context if re-analysed from a perspective grounded in the philosophical approach know as hermeneutics.

The chapter covers a great deal of ground. It introduces and contextualizes the themes of the book, and it offers some suggestions for broader reading. The educational role of the museum, as it becomes more significant from both internal and external perspectives, moves into a sharper spotlight and is thereby susceptible to a more critical analysis. Placing this analysis within the field of cultural analysis in general raises questions about who uses museums, why and how. These are not new questions, but as we develop a more holistic approach to the public educational role of museums, they need to be asked more succinctly.

In the last thirty years, museum education professionals have focused on developing appropriate teaching methods for both face-to-face teaching (workshops, talks, drama) and distance learning methods (teachers' packs, loan boxes and kits), and on establishing a professional profile within the museum organization. Both of these ambitions have largely been achieved, with the result that the educational role of the museum has expanded and is now accepted as covering exhibitions and other aspects of public provision such as events and publications. The arena for educational work is no longer the 'education room', but the whole museum. With this shift to a broader scope for 'museum education', comes a necessity to accept a broader social responsibility. Museum educators, whether they are museum teachers, curators, volunteers or paid staff, must now acknowledge the cultural world beyond the museum classroom. The educational role of the museum has become part of cultural politics.

The rapid development of the scope and significance of the educational role of the museum has led to a need to broaden the theoretical analysis of educational practices. It is no longer sufficient to focus only on learning processes; broader social questions need to be asked. Educational theory needs to be supplemented by sociological and philosophical theory if we want to develop and articulate these broader themes. The concept of 'critical pedagogy', which analyses education in schools and colleges from a cultural perspective, has, I think, the potential for use within the museum.

A critical museum pedagogy is an educational approach that reviews and develops its methods, strategies and provision with regard both to educational excellence and to working towards the democratization of the museum. Current emphases within museums on access, on public value and on audience consultation, offer opportunities to work to address long-established relations of advantage and disadvantage, to enable new voices to be heard, and critically to review existing historical (and other) narratives. At the same time, cultural theorists and philosophers are producing new ways of working that can be of immense use in the development at both the conceptual and the practical level of a critical museum pedagogy (Fay 1996; Giroux 1992; Jordan and Weedon 1995). The development of a critical museum pedagogy that uses existing good practice for democratic purposes is a major task for museums and galleries in the twenty-first century.

MUSEUM AUDIENCE RESEARCH

In many ways it is the educational role that is leading museums forward, and one of the most significant reasons for this is the growing acceptance of differentiated responses to the museum experience. In recent years, museums and galleries have begun to research seriously the responses of audiences to specific exhibitions, and also to museums as a whole. Consequently, it has become clear that instead of a single unified reaction to museums, there are many different responses. These responses are both specific to the individual, and also susceptible to patterning according to the different expectations and requirements of museums held by different audience segments. As a result, the concept of the 'general public' is now replaced by the concept of a more differentiated audience.

This differentiated audience is beginning to be studied closely, both by some few museums and, in Britain, by national bodies such as the Museums and Galleries Commission (MGC). The detailed research, which takes the form of small-scale qualitative studies, although based on methods used by market research, is close to what sociologists would call ethnographic or naturalistic research (Glesne and Peshkin 1992). Much of the research is carried out through the use of focus groups. The qualitative studies stem from the fairly consistent findings of more quantitative studies of visitor patterns which are usefully summarized in Davies's *By Popular Demand* (1994).[2]

Studies suggest that approximately 40 per cent of UK adults visit museums at least once a year (Davies calls these 'regular visitors'), a further 40 per cent are occasional visitors and 20 per cent rarely visit museums. Although there is at strong core of committed visitors to all museums and galleries, the numbers visiting each vary enormously. The nineteen national museums account for about one third of all visits, with the British Museum claiming approximately 6 million visitors each year. Some very small museums, on the other hand, might receive only about 10,000 visitors or less each year.

The total number of museum visits in Britain is estimated by Davies at 110 million per year. He uses a very broad definition of a museum; a narrower definition of what counts as a museum results in a figure closer to 79 million. Figures for museum visiting, at least in Britain, are inadequate and frequently unreliable, and they tend to be used rather loosely. There is often no clear distinction made between 'visits' and 'visitors', which are clearly not the same thing; definitions of 'museum' vary enormously and may or may not include art galleries (either with or without collections), site museums such as railway heritage centres, historic houses, the built or natural environment, and archaeological sites. Concepts such as 'the arts', 'the heritage', 'the natural heritage' are used in conjunction with 'museums', and great care must be taken over evaluating any claims whatever in this area.

'FACTS' AND FIGURES: PLAYING WITH STATISTICS

The variable bases for data collection, combined with a general lack of awareness of an accurate picture of the museum field (and indeed the lack of such a picture itself) can lead to some interesting gamesmanship with figures.

For example, the arguments posed in articles in the *Times Higher Education Supplement* (7 November 1997: ii–viii) concerning class and culture were based on a range of statistics drawn from different population bases. One writer asserted that public funds of approximately half of £1.7 billion are expended on the arts and built heritage. She then went on to claim that less than a quarter of the population attend plays, art galleries, or exhibitions, and to query the value of public funding. 'Arts and built heritage' is a far broader category of analysis that 'plays, art galleries, or exhibitions'. Alternative sources (Merriman 1991) suggest that from 45 to 56 per cent of the adult population of Great Britain visit museums, arts and the built heritage. The nature of the category to be investigated has an effect on the nature of the findings.

A second writer also uses the statistics to suit her argument. Using the same figures (from Casey *et al.* 1996), she states that one fifth of the population visit museums and galleries, and that of the public funds available, 90 per cent supports collection-based museums and galleries to the detriment of artists and exhibition spaces. This, she protests, is manifestly unfair. She was writing from a base within the arts, including art centres, and this argument made her case.

Similar figures can be used to make another argument. Research Surveys of Great Britain, commissioned by the Arts Council in 1991, found that 48 per cent of the British public reported visiting museums, galleries, craft, photographic and exhibition galleries. Research surveys over time demonstrate that where museums and galleries are broadly defined, audiences include about 45 to 50 per cent of the British adult public in any one year (where the time-scale is longer, audiences are greater). The audience for art galleries and art museums, however, both in the UK and indeed internationally (Schuster 1995), is both much smaller (between one fifth and one quarter of the population of a country) and less democratic than that for museums.

It is possible to use the available statistics to demonstrate that about half the British public, and a reasonably democratic mix (especially in the North), use museums of all kinds, visit exhibition galleries of all kinds, and enjoy looking at castles, ruins and older buildings. However, a very small and considerably more elitist percentage finds art galleries attractive.

'Facts' about the uses of museums are slippery, and need to be treated with caution. This means reading around the figures quoted, and questioning the research carefully in relation to definitions, time-periods and purpose (Hooper-Greenhill 1994: Ch. 3). Given the diversity of museums and the lack of unity across the field, it is perhaps impossible to produce an entirely accurate picture of the use of museums.

THE VALUE OF NEW QUALITATIVE RESEARCH, AND TWO STUDIES ANALYSED

The very broad-brush picture of museum visitor patterns in Britain, which is really all we can rely on, suggests, first, that people from ethnic minority cultures, and particularly those from black communities, do not visit museums frequently;[3] and second, that children make up a much larger proportion of the audience for museums overall than had been previously considered. Such quantitative survey data has proved the springboard for more in-depth qualitative research that is designed to probe the attitudes and perceptions of these groups (as research study populations) to museums and what they do.

These two British research reports demonstrate the type of work that is currently being undertaken and, through a summary of their results, indicate the diversities and similarities of responses of two major audience segments: ethnic minority groups (made up of a range of ethnicities), and children (focusing on those aged 7–11 years).

MUSEUMS AND ETHNIC POPULATIONS IN ENGLAND

Cultural Diversity: Attitudes of Ethnic Minority Populations towards Museums and Galleries, commissioned by the Museums and Galleries Commission (Desai and Thomas 1998), set out to discover what perceptions of museums were held by England's ethnic communities. Focus groups were held in London, the Midlands and the North of England, where the concept of a museum, the experience of museum visiting, how museum visiting fitted into patterns of leisure time use, and how museums could better meet the needs of the participants were discussed.

This research illuminates issues of culture and representation from a museum perspective that are currently of enormous interest to students and theoreticians outside museums (Hall 1997; Jordan and Weedon 1995). These issues can also be seen as complementary to issues of access and culture that have been the subject of discussion outside Britain (e.g. Karp *et al.* 1992).

The main research method used was focus groups. Focus group members were all aged 25–50, all had children of school age, half were non-museum visitors (defined as not having visited a museum or art gallery within the previous twelve months) and half were museum or gallery visitors. The ethnic populations included in the research were black African, black Caribbean, Indian (Hindu and Sikh), Bangladeshi (Muslim) and Chinese men and women. A control group of white respondents of UK origins was also included to help with assessing the differences between minority communities and the general population. Group discussions were stimulated through a range of materials such as brochures and posters, and were structured through a topic guide. Each group was conducted by a researcher from an ethnic background similar to its members', drawn from the multi-ethnic, five-person team carrying out the research. The work with the Chinese and Bangladeshi groups was conducted in mother tongue (Cantonese and Sylheti). The research has been carried out in a highly professional manner and can therefore be relied upon. The findings confirm many of the general points that have arisen elsewhere, both in Britain (Trevelyan 1991) and in America (Walsh 1991) but also bring other more specific issues to the fore. Some matters are common to all museum audience groups, and some are specific to ethnic populations.

The image of museums was common across all ethnic groups. 'The Museum' is still the way that museums are perceived; an old building with an imposing appearance, like the British Museum. Typical contents include 'Kings and Queens, crowns, suits of armour, weapons, and "broken pots and rocks"'. The atmosphere in museums was described as quiet, reverential and unwelcoming to children. Not surprisingly, this rather unpleasant place was felt to be for intellectuals, and posh people. Art galleries were perceived as even more distant and elitist. There was a real fear that the displays would be too difficult to understand.

Black and Bangladeshi respondents were more likely than Indian and Chinese participants to perceive museums and galleries as 'white people's territory'. Ethnicity, class and educational level were all brought up as important factors in influencing the wish to visit. In addition, the actual experience of visiting was sometimes discussed, with some Bangladeshi women, for example, pointing out how uncomfortable and out of place they had felt in museums.

Curiously, given the strength of these negative attitudes, there was a general consensus across all groups that society needed museums. People were reassured by the existence of museums, even if they did not visit them. This feeling has also been expressed in other research, and does offer some comfort, in that it suggests that good-will does to some extent exist and that the potential to change attitudes remains. The research participants described the main roles for museums as preserving the past, educating (but mainly children), broadening horizons and increasing mutual tolerance, and offering places to engage emotionally with beautiful things. Some references are given to examples of successful good practice (and see also Selwood *et al.* 1996). Barriers to participation were investigated and reinforce findings of previous research (Merriman 1991; Susie Fisher Group 1990). They include lack of time, cost, lack of interest, lack of awareness, the need for effort, and the fear of not understanding.

The report brings out those issues that particularly relate to the perceptions of ethnic minority communities. Black, South Asian and Chinese people want to see things that relate to their own lives, cultures and histories. Where this has happened, they describe the sense of closeness, of personal relevance and personal interest which they experienced. Where exhibitions or events were perceived (in advance of visiting) to be related to their own culture, and especially their own religion, people were willing to make great efforts to visit.

However, a stronger theme to emerge was the disillusionment many people felt about the view of history that museums present (and see also papers in the first section of Hooper-Greenhill 1997). This was seen to be constructed from a white perspective that made little acknowledgement of the achievements of people or communities from ethnic minority populations. It is difficult, especially for those people who visit very infrequently, to separate the cultural representations to be found in museums from those in other mass communication media, and respondents tended to treat museums very much as part of a generalized mass communication system. It was felt, for example, that Africa is frequently represented as associated with dirt, disease and famine, and with few positive images. This is a general statement about the way that British society as a whole (as in the TV news, for example), represents Africa, but museum displays were perceived in the same way. A general dissatisfaction was expressed in relation to both the objects displayed, and their interpretation.

One theme that emerges extremely strongly from the research is the common perception that objects and material from outside Britain were looted from their countries of origin during the colonial period. Although in some cases this is of course true, it seems to be much more broadly assumed than might have been expected. The lack of accessible information about provenance enables these assumptions. For some, museums evoked images of colonial violence, domination and theft. However, where museums had indicated that collections had been purchased or donated, this was appreciated.

The potential of museums was perceived as enabling a greater awareness and a wider experience of the cultures of ethnic minority groups. This would be of value for families, who could take their children and show them their cultural heritage. The participants in the research did not want collections to be returned or repatriated, but did want more accurate information about provenance and background, greater recognition of the role that their cultures played in past and present British society, and greater acknowledgement of non-British perspectives on historical events.

This research raises some serious issues for museums. It shows clearly that cultural theory and postcolonial studies that are not always directly focused on museums and galleries nevertheless have a role to play in analysing the museum/audience relationship. It poses the kinds of questions that museums in Australia and Canada have been facing in relation to their indigenous people, questions that in Britain we have been less exposed to, and it underlines the importance of carrying out audience research in order to become aware of the attitudes to museums that are held by some of those who, through their taxes, pay for them. It is not until this awareness is in place that change can follow.

RESEARCHING THE NEEDS AND INTERESTS OF CHILDREN AND THEIR FAMILIES

A second report, also commissioned by the Museums and Galleries Commission, in association with the Arts Council of England, demonstrates both the similarities and differences that can exist between the different 'target groups'. Families, especially the very broad definition generally used in museums (adults with accompanying children under about 15 years), have similar child-rearing concerns whatever their ethnic origin, and some of the general issues to emerge in the previous report can be identified here too. However, those issues specific to ethnic groups, such as the concerns about the histories told in museums, do not recur. Instead, the special characteristics of the needs of children are highlighted.

Children as an Audience for Museums and Galleries (Harris Qualitative 1997) was also motivated by the findings of the earlier study largely based on quantitative data. Stuart Davies (1994) suggested that children make up about one third of museum and gallery audiences, and that less than one quarter of these visits are arranged through schools. In other words, and assuming that Davies is correct, about one quarter of all museum visits are made by children accompanied by their families. A market research company was commissioned to research the needs and attitudes of children and their accompanying parents/carers, in order to have a basis for increasing these informal visits by children.

Families with children aged 7–11 were the subjects of the research. The research brief was wide, to include both expectations and experience of visits, marketing information and the views both of those who had visited museums or galleries recently and of those who came less often. The findings are equally broad, and although they tend towards supporting existing 'common sense', do provide support for what was previously merely assumed.

The research was carried out by a well-established research company that specializes in qualitative work with children. From the details in the report, it would seem that the research was planned carefully to result in data that would be both relevant and reliable. This is useful, as much published museum research does not include children. The research methods used were qualitative, rather than quantitative; that is, the sample was small (fourteen groups/friendship pairs), and the focus was on in-depth meanings constructed by the participants. The methods are entirely appropriate for the research questions posed. As such, the report offers material that can be relied upon, that is as accurate as possible, and that can be used in museum and exhibition planning and development.

Both children and their parents/carers were interviewed in depth. Museum and gallery visits were discussed in the context of other leisure activities. In addition to this, stimulus materials such as brochures, photos, posters and leaflets were commented upon. The adults were asked how they made decisions about where to go with their children; if they had recently been to a museum, what they had experienced; if they had not been recently, why not; and how they compared museums with other kinds of outings. The samples were chosen carefully to give a range of experiences. As a small-

9

scale study, the people interviewed were restricted to the social segment regarded as being the most likely to attend museums with their children (BC1 social groups). People from both the north and the south of the country were interviewed.

All families were found to have busy, hectic life-styles, although there were significant differences of affluence between the north and south of the country. The 'attender' children came from the more middle-class and 'arty' families, were well travelled, computer-literate, involved in a broad range of activities, confident and articulate. Children from 'non-attender' families (defined for this study as those who visited less often, rather than not at all) tended to be from less middle-class families and were more mixed in their life-styles. Some tended to be less sophisticated in their attitudes, though they were equally bright and lively.

Family visits mainly took place during holidays and on Sundays. Many places including museums were visited. Interactivity and action were particularly important to the children. Choosing where to go was sometimes a challenge, when different agendas had to be reconciled. Children sometimes want to visit in connection with school projects, and sometimes this follows a successful school visit. 'Big ideas' (*Star Trek*, the Tudors) seem to attract both adults and children. A perception that the visit will be fun is crucial. The main success factors seemed to be experiencing history, effective experiments/interactives, computers, sophisticated simulations, tactile experiences, quiz sheets, drawing and making things, amazing buildings, and fascinating objects. Taking home a souvenir was important.

The main barriers to visiting seemed to be lack of information, lack of a frame of reference for museums (i.e. lack of experience), lack of time, perceptions that museums are/might be boring, expense, inaccessibility and expensive catering. Art galleries are seen as less interesting.

Recommendations for improving the experience for younger visitors include more accessible exhibits and interactives, better orientation, creative workshops, facilitation of shorter visits (people still expect to do it all), thematic displays and flexible ticketing.

The report emphasizes how busy families are, that museums are having to compete against other venues (with much larger and more visitor-aware marketing budgets), but also that there is a widespread positive feel about museums.

Both these research studies support the need to consider differentiated audiences for museums. They show clearly how museums need to be integrated into the personal agendas of visitors, and how these personal agendas can be conceptualized. They also illustrate that museum audience research needs to be reconceived.

NEW RESEARCH PARADIGMS: MARGINALIZING THE MUSEUM

We are accustomed to analysing the museum experience from a perspective that focuses on visitor behaviour, and on what the visitor does and what he/she says about it. This approach has a long history within museum work. It can be traced to pioneering work in the 1930s in America and through to work that was new in the UK at the Natural History Museum in the 1970s and 1980s (see Ch. 2). Much of the work is informed by a view of society that is overly consensual and, in the final analysis, functionalist, that is, with each individual playing a part within a group and each group playing its part to make the machine of society effective. This positivist approach to social and cultural analysis has underpinned the bulk of American social research work this century.

This assumed consensus about the nature and role of society is naive in its ignoring of groups that have been historically disadvantaged by social structures. It fails to see that museums might be problematic places for those who do not see themselves reflected within them, or who see themselves reflected to their disadvantage.

The gathering of data based on visitor behaviour represents an observation of bodies, and a drawing of conclusions from this. It fails to examine what the meaning of the behaviours is to the individuals concerned. Even where the observation of bodies is supplemented by data gathered through other means, such as visitor surveys and questionnaires, few of the studies have focused on the deeper meanings and interpretive processes that visitors followed.

In the past, audience research has been museum-centred: the museum has been the core organizing concept of the work, and people have been 'evaluated' as to how they have responded to that core (e.g. Loomis 1987). Looking out from over the museum ramparts has enabled the retention of the view that museums play a central role in people's lives. However, once research is conducted from outside the museum, in homes and places of work or recreation, it becomes clear how marginal museums are to most people's daily existence. The only people to whom museums are of central concern are those who work in them. For everyone else, museums must be fitted into their busy schedules, their personal and social identities, their interests and agendas. For everyone except museum workers, museums are at a distance, out there, one of a range of social institutions that can be used or avoided at will. In fact, of all social institutions, museums are one of the easiest to avoid.

A new approach to museum audience research is becoming established which is pushed forward partly by those who wish to democratize the museum, and partly by the general cultural shift towards postmodernism and postcolonialism. Part of this cultural shift is seen in the reworking of concepts of education and learning (see Ch. 5 and the Preface).

In museums today there is a great interest in the making of meaning (Roberts 1997; Silverman 1995). The shift is to the deep levels of signification that visitors construct. Some fascinating studies show how idiosyncratic some of these meanings can be (Worts 1995). However, in order to study these meaning-making processes, the approach to research has to be radically altered. A move is necessary from the laboratory model of research, such as that used for early visitor studies, to a more sociological or ethnographic mode, which uses naturalistic settings and a more open-ended research agenda (Hein 1998). The resulting in-depth results are vital, but do not remove the need to use the more traditional quantitative methods to obtain overall patterns of museum use. The most sophisticated museum research will employ the strengths and weaknesses of both approaches to develop reliable data (see Ch. 31 and other chapters in Part IV).

If we begin to analyse the educational role of museums from the perspective of the visitor, with the knowledge that visitors come to museums with their own agendas, learning skills and interests, then we begin to approach the museum experience from a very different point of view. One of the first tools of analysis is an understanding of the interpretive processes that visitors are likely to use within museums.

Visitors construct meaning within museums using a range of interpretive strategies. The meaning made is personal, related to existing mental constructs, and to the pattern of ideas on which the individual bases his or her other interpretations of their experience of the world; but it is also social in that it is influenced by the individual's 'significant others' (family, peer group, friends, colleagues), which comprise the community of meaning-makers to which the individual belongs. The meaning that an individual constructs is also political, in the sense that both personal and social meanings come about as a result of life-chances, social experience, knowledge and ideas, attitudes and values. Running through the personal, the social and the political are the effects of class, gender and ethnicity. From this perspective it is easy to understand how deeply museums are embedded in the politics of culture.

ANALYSING THE PROCESSES OF INTERPRETATION

If we want to develop a focus on the strategies and processes of meaning-making that visitors use, where do we begin? The process of meaning-making is the process of making sense of experience, of explaining or interpreting the world to ourselves and others. In museums, meaning is constructed from objects,[4] and from the sites themselves. This involves an encounter between the past and the present, and an interpretation of the material matter. The processes of interpretation that visitors follow can be helpfully explained through the philosophical movement known as hermeneutics.

The word 'interpretation' is used in this philosophical movement to mean how individuals make sense of things. The process of interpretation focuses on the mental activity of the looker. In museums, the word 'interpretation' is used in a different way. Interpretation is a very loosely defined word in the museum context, but it usually means 'doing interpretation' for others. 'Exhibition interpretation' is the way the exhibition is designed to allow people to understand the ideas it wants to put across. 'Object interpretation' is the attempt to interpret objects for others, by making links between the object and the viewer that they might be expected to recognize. An interpretation officer might be an education officer, a designer, an exhibitions officer.

There is a major difference in emphasis between the way the words are used in hermeneutics and in the museum. In the museum, interpretation is done for you, or to you. In hermeneutics, however, *you* are the interpreter for yourself. Interpretation is the process of *constructing* meaning.

The making of meaning, the construction of understanding, is reached through the process of interpretation. Hermeneutics, and specifically the approach taken by Dilthey (1976) and Gadamer (1976), describes the process in some detail. The general process of interpretation is based on that of making meaning from a text. Dilthey suggests that understanding arises through a dialogical[5] relationship between the detail and the whole: 'the whole of a work must be understood from the individual words and their combinations, and yet the full comprehension of the detail presupposes the understanding of the whole' (Dilthey 1976: 115).

Gadamer uses this approach, discussing it in relation to texts and 'works of art': 'we must understand the whole in terms of the detail and the detail in terms of the whole'. Gadamer relates the process of understanding a text to the process of interpreting experience in general. This more general argument enables the broad application of his ideas to objects (Gadamer 1976: 117; and see Ch. 3 this volume).

We approach experiences and/or material matter with certain prejudices, or fore-knowledge, given by our own position in history, and with a certain openness. This receptiveness to our 'object', allowing it to 'speak for itself', creates a balance or dialectic between prejudice and openness (prejudice here means 'selective' rather than 'biased'). This dialectic permits revision of our prejudices towards a greater 'truth', but this truth is still relative, historical and social.

'Object' here is used with a double meaning. It means, on the one hand, the material evidence that comes to us from the past. At the same time 'object' also refers to what might be called 'object of study'; that is, the area under consideration. The basic principle, that selective focus and variable pertinence change what is perceived to be significant and meaningful, is the same with both contexts of use.

Any interpretation can never be fully completed. 'The discovery of the true meaning of a text or a work of art is never finished: it is in fact an infinite process' (Gadamer 1976: 124). As errors in understanding are eliminated and as new sources of knowledge emerge, so meaning is a continuing process of modification, adaptation and extension. The hermeneutic circle is never fully closed, but remains open to the possibilities of change.

Hermeneutics tells us that the construction of meaning depends on prior knowledge, and on beliefs and values. We see according to what we know, and we make sense of meaning according to what we see. In this way we construct our meanings, and do not find them 'ready-made'. The construction of meaning partly depends on how we relate the past to the present. All interpretation is, therefore, necessarily historically situated. Our own position in history, our own culture, affects meaning, as meaning is constructed in and through culture. Perception (what we see), memory (what we choose to remember) and logical thinking (the sense we choose to attribute to things) differ culturally because they are cultural constructs.

THE LIMITS TO PERSONAL MEANINGS: THE AUTHORITY OF INTERPRETIVE COMMUNITIES

However, there are limits to the range of meanings that can be accepted in any one place at any one time. Given that the process of interpretation involves prior knowledge, and that knowledge is socially and culturally based, our interpretation will be that which fits our particular place in the world. What we know is what we need to know to enable us to take our place in a particular society or group.

Only certain meanings appear to 'make sense', but the 'sense' that is made will depend on which 'interpretive community' is making it. 'Interpretive communities' is an expression that is drawn from literary theory, but one which I think finds an echo in contemporary museum thought (and see also Appadurai and Breckenridge 1992).

To the extent that we can identify a community of people who share interpretive strategies, we can identify 'interpretive communities'. Stanley Fish proposes that it is interpretive communities that produce meaning by using common interpretive strategies (Fish 1980: 14–15). Interpretive strategies include the priority given to certain forms of analysis, the language used to describe the object, and the background or specialist knowledge that enables certain elements of the object to be perceived. Thus an art historian will talk about a painting she or he has studied in a very different way from someone with no knowledge of either the painting or of art history.

These interpretive strategies exist prior to the act of reading and therefore determine the shape of what is read. That is, museum visitors encounter objects with certain 'reading strategies' already in place, and thus they know what to look for. According to what you look for, you will see certain things in certain ways. Thus it is the interpretive strategy that determines the meaning of the object, and in many ways determines how the object is seen and what counts as the object in the first place. 'Systems of intelligibility' (e.g. literary or aesthetic systems) constrain and shape us, 'furnishing us with categories of understanding with which we fashion the entities to which we then point' (Fish 1980: 332). In other words, in making meaning within museums, members of different interpretive communities will use their specialist knowledge, their categories of understanding, their modes of classification, their familiar concepts, in order to render intelligible what they see. And people are likely to see only that which they can go some way towards making intelligible. Without appropriate strategies of intelligibility, the collections appear (and indeed are) meaningless.

In Bourdieu's classic study of the 1960s,[6] *L'amour de l'art* (Bourdieu and Darbel 1991), he found that museum visitors who did not possess relevant interpretive strategies could not make much sense of what they saw. 'How can a perception so lacking in organising principles apprehend the organised meanings comprising a body of cumulative knowledge?' He quotes a shopkeeper from Lens: 'Trying to remember is something else. I didn't understand Picasso; I can never remember the names.' And a manual worker from Lille: 'It's hard for someone who wants to take an interest. You only see paintings and dates. To be able to see the difference between things, you need a guide-book. Otherwise, everything looks the same' (Bourdieu and Darbel 1991: 48–9).

Fish makes reference to specialist academic knowledge, which has considerable relevance within the museum context. One of the reasons that many people give for finding museums difficult is exactly that mismatch between the level of academic knowledge used to write texts and the level of knowledge that visitors themselves bring with them. A greater knowledge of the interpretive strategies employed by different communities of visitors would be helpful. This, of course, means in-depth research work.

The concept of interpretive communities can be expanded within the museum field to extend to those who have different cultural backgrounds and positions in history. Gadamer discusses how interpretation is influenced by historical and cultural position, and, as we saw at the beginning of this chapter, we are beginning to accumulate evidence of how different cultural communities react, and how different positions in history affect meaning-making (Hooper-Greenhill 1998).

Interpretive communities are not stable, but may change as people move from one to another. They may grow and decline as other things change. It is within interpretive communities that the meaning-making of an individual is tested, revised, supported and developed. The interpretive community both sets limits for and constrains meaning, and at the same time enables meaning.

Thus our individual meaning-making is supported or refuted by social meaning. We find our place, our interpretive position, according to our social, intellectual and cultural opportunities. These opportunities are life-chances; they position us within social structures that are placed within relations of advantage or disadvantage. Fish does not discuss the power of interpretive communities to impose or silence meaning. His 'authority of interpretive communities' is restricted to the level of signification and the construction of representation. These cultural fields are of enormous importance in societies that operate largely through hegemony; that is, through picturing social relations and their implications, rather than through brute force. But Fish does not acknowledge sufficiently the effect of the social positioning of individuals in class, ethnicity and gender relations that relate to the power to construct meaning and also to the characteristics of the meanings constructed.

The focus on interpretation and interpretive communities enables us to begin to analyse the meaning-making strategies of museum audiences. We can see that individuals and groups work from their own skills, knowledge and agendas (their systems of intelligibility, their interpretive strategies) to construe relevant meaning from the learning opportunities presented by the museum. A shorthand way of describing this is to say that the museum audience is 'active'. The 'active audience' has been a useful one in communication theory for some twenty years, and it is to ways of conceptualizing the processes of communication that we now turn.

COMMUNICATION THEORIES

Hermeneutics focuses on the interpretive strategies employed by people to make sense of their experience, including their experience in museums. In museums, the meanings of objects are modulated according to the other objects they are associated with, and according to the interpretive framework created by the accompanying words (labels and other texts). Although visitors will make sense of objects in their own ways according to their interests, skills, prior knowledge and interpretive strategies, the museum has the responsibility for producing an exhibition which has identified and researched its intended audiences, and which is designed with the results of this research in mind.

It is still the case in many museums that exhibitions are produced without much thought at all for who is going to visit them, or how they will be used. The model for exhibition development which is used depends on how audiences are conceptualized and how the processes of communication are understood. Although these concepts are discussed all too rarely, assumptions about audiences, and about communication as a process, are always implicit in the way in which museums operate, in their audience relationships, in the composition of their exhibition teams, and in the activities considered necessary to develop exhibitions.

We can begin to understand this by using communication theory. Two broad approaches to understanding processes of communication can be identified. These two approaches can be usefully related to the models for exhibition development that are used in museums. This next section discusses each of the two approaches and then relates them both to different ways of producing exhibitions.

The two approaches to communication are the transmission approach and the cultural approach (Carey 1989: 13–36). Both have long histories, but their relevance as ways of explaining social processes has shifted as societies have altered.

The transmission approach is perhaps the most familiar to museum people. It has been discussed over the years since the 1970s in the museum literature. An interesting debate between Cameron (1968) and Knez and Wright (1970) about how to understand communication in museums coincided with the discussion of communication as information-processing in relation to computer technology. Roger Miles (1985) pointed out some of the problems of applying the model within museums, and it has recently been reused and critiqued by Bicknell (1995) and McManus (1991).

The transmission approach is concerned with the sending of information from one party to another. Growing out of a wish to improve effectiveness in mass communication, it is based on a stimulus-response view of education that understands knowledge as external to the learner and sees the task of teaching as that of imparting information efficiently (see Hein 1998; and Ch. 6). This process can be described in a simple model (Figure 1.1).

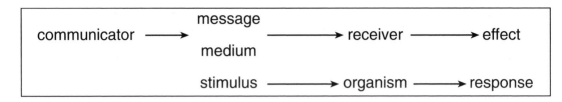

Figure 1.1 The transmission approach to understanding communication: based on the scientific paradigm, and the behaviourist view of learning, communication is understood as the functional linear transmission of a body of external objective knowledge from a knowledgeable communicator to a receiver/student

This approach to communication is American in origin and has been until very recently the dominant model within communication research, which saw itself as a 'practical art in a practical context' (Hardt 1992: 3). This stress on the empirical, which is ahistoricist and unreflexive, is partly explained by the mainstream reliance of American sociology on funtionalist, behaviourist and technological explanations of society. In this way of understanding society, individuals are atomistic (self-contained) functional cogs within the social machine.

The transmission model sees communication as a process of imparting information and sending messages, transmitting ideas across space from a knowledgeable information source to a passive receiver. A geographical metaphor is used – that of sending information across space, from one point to another. This is a metaphor of transportation – the sending of signals and messages over a distance for the purposes of control. Semaphore is a good example, or, of course, the telephone message (see Ch. 2). The focus of this approach is on the communication as a technology, how it works and what different agencies of techniques are involved. The social and cultural implications are much less considered.

The second approach is much broader than the first. The cultural approach understands communication as a society-wide series of processes and symbols through which reality is produced, maintained, repaired and transformed. As we represent our beliefs and values through cultural symbols, so reality is constructed. This is a dominant paradigm in present-day British cultural studies, and this approach also sits comfortably with the ideas we have been discussing from hermeneutics and literary theory about process of individual and group interpretation. The educational model used is close to that of constructivism, a model of learning that is of great interest to museum educators today (see Chs. 5 and 6).

From the perspective of the cultural approach, reality is not found intact, it is shaped through a process of continuous negotiation, which involves individuals in calling on their prior experiences to actively make their own meanings, within the framework of interpretive communities. This whole interpretive process is within the purview of 'communication'. Communication is cultural to the core, and culture is impossible without communication. It is difficult to encapsulate such multi-layered and complex processes in a model, but as figures are sometimes helpful in summarizing ideas, Figure 1.2 is one way of representing the cultural approach to communication.

Communication in this approach is understood as a process of sharing, participation and association. The root of the word 'communication' is found also in 'commonality', 'commonness', 'communion' and 'community'. Communication is understood as a process that binds groups and societies together within a specific time-frame;

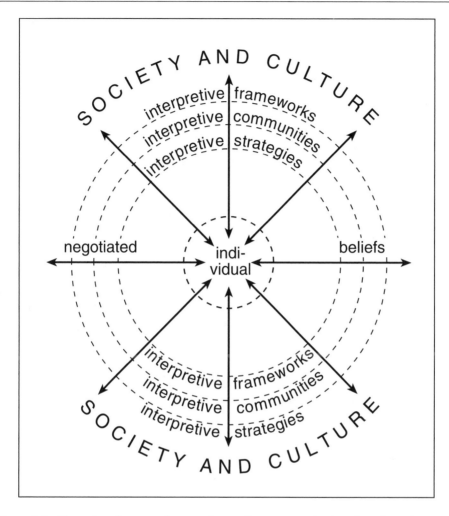

Figure 1.2 The cultural approach to understanding communication: based on the constructivist paradigm, communication is understood as a cultural process of negotiating meaning, which produces 'reality' through symbolic systems such as texts, objects, artworks, maps, models and museums

sociality and mutuality are important concepts. Beliefs and values are shared and explored together through communicative acts. Communication is a cultural process that creates an ordered and meaningful world of active meaning-makers.

The process of meaning-making is understood differently in each of these models. In the cultural approach, meaning is achieved by mutual active processes. All parties work together to produce a shared interpretation; beliefs and values are shared. The strength of this is the acknowledgement of the active participation in the construction of meaning by all parties. The weakness is the failure to recognize that social processes are not equal; in other words, there is no power analysis in the model.

In the transmission approach, the power relations are all too obvious. The source of the meaning in the message is the source of the information, the communicator or transmitter in Figure 1.1. The receiver of the message is assumed to be cognitively passive, a mere receptacle for the information being transmitted. Meaning-making is limited to the originator of the message. There is no sense of the receiver having its own way of understanding the message. Where the understandings of the communicator and receiver are at variance, it is assumed that the message has been incorrectly received.

How can we relate this to museums? The transmission model of communication has been applied to the process of exhibition production on a number of occasions. Duncan Cameron showed how one model of exhibition production relates (see Ch. 2). The exhibition development process is linear, it remains internal to the museum, and audience research, consultation with audiences, or evaluation are no part of the process (see Ch. 5).

In 1985 Roger Miles described this process as 'disabling' and proposed a more iterative process which involved introducing feedback into the exhibition development process at a number of key moments (see Ch. 2). In the UK this was the first time that evaluation had been introduced to the exhibition development process.[7]

The gradual development of exhibition evaluation in many countries, combined with visitor studies such as visitor surveys and market research, has led to the present-day interest in developing concepts for understanding how audiences construct meaning for themselves, and what the implications of this are for museums and their planning.[8]

It is at this point that the second approach to communication becomes relevant. What would an exhibition process look like if the cultural approach were the way that communication was understood? In this approach, it is acknowledged that all participants in communication processes play their part in negotiating meaning, and that communication as culture is central to the construction of personal and group identities. How can museums negotiate in the use of symbols, in the development of narratives, and in the representation of beliefs and values? The exhibition development process would not be limited to the producers within the museum, but members of the audience and others would work jointly to come up with ideas, to decide what objects to display, and how to display them, decisions being shared through mutual participation, and through the strong links with the community.

In fact, this is exactly what we see in some museums, especially those with social history collections, or those whose character closely links them to their communities (e.g. Selwood *et al.* 1996: Ch. 30). Where museum communicators work (however implicitly) within a cultural understanding of communication, the museum is responsive and self-reflexive. Processes of consultation and collaboration with audiences and stakeholders will be in place, and museum 'products' such as exhibitions and events will be subject to evaluation.

Where museums are not asking questions about the experience of the audience, are not self-reflexive, do not use evaluation and do not consult and collaborate with external stakeholders, it is likely that a transmission view of communication is held. Exhibitions are likely to be seen as 'for the general public' (an undifferentiated mass audience), and the task of exhibition developer (the curator) as limited to producing an efficiently laid-out display. The viewpoint will be that of the curator, who will be unaware that other points of view, based on other life-worlds, might also be possible. Even though many of the exhibitions produced in this way might be apparently very successful, it is likely that success will be limited to those sections of the potential audience who are familiar with museums and their techniques, and who uphold their traditional values. A close study of the two research reports discussed at the beginning of this chapter will illustrate how exhibitions produced within the long-standing model underpinned by the transmission approach to communication will fail to meet the needs of large parts of the potential audience, and may, with some interpretive communities, alienate them very successfully.

The use of communication theory has enabled us to understand how the transmission model positions 'receivers' as passive, and how the cultural model acknowledges that participants are active. These concepts of 'the passive audience' and 'the active audience' are useful in analysing how museums approach their actual and potential audiences, and in reviewing their exhibitions and other provision for visitors. However, these two concepts do not present us with a choice. The audience is always 'active', whether or not museums recognize this. Where potentially 'active' visitors find themselves unable to use their skills and knowledge and unable to become involved within a museum, where they are forced into a 'passive' mode, mental discomfort, a feeling of personal inadequacy, or feelings of being out of place are likely to result. The museum becomes a place to be avoided.

What then can be done in a practical way to enable people to become interested and engaged in museum displays, and to find points of interest and opportunities to use personal skills and knowledge? The next section considers the developing of effective exhibitions.

DEVELOPING AND DESIGNING EFFECTIVE EXHIBITIONS

Exhibitions are not always thought of as learning materials, but they are the environment where learning takes place, and they provide the framework for the meaning-making processes of visitors through the way they structure objects and ideas. Just as learning materials are designed according to the needs of who is to learn, so exhibitions must consider who is going to use them, and be designed accordingly. Research on the interpretive strategies used in exhibitions by visitors with different knowledges, skills and interests, with different cultural backgrounds and of different genders is urgently needed, but there is little detailed material as yet.

However, a range of strategies are now beginning to be used in the development of exhibitions that effectively increase the likelihood that more visitors will find them of relevance and interest. The development of exhibitions needs to take account of both *what* people want to know, would be interested in, and *how* they can come to know it – how they learn. The development process needs to be based on the cultural model of communication, with consultation and collaboration with audiences built into it (see Chs 17, 19, 26).

An exhibition develops in stages, which can be clearly defined. Each stage has a specific set of activities associated with it (see Ch. 19). However, although each of these activities may involve different kinds of expertise, some of the most successful exhibitions involve a team approach, where expertise and approach are shared and negotiated (see Ch. 17). As initial ideas develop, it is appropriate to test them against target audiences and other stakeholders. As the actual exhibits are built, it is useful to test them out. This is particularly important with interactive exhibits, and with written material. Studies of the effectiveness of the exhibition after it is up and running can provide information which may lead to modification at the time, or will be useful in the development and design of future exhibitions (see Chs 29 and 31). These exhibition-based studies are best developed as part of a strategic management approach to communication development (see Ch. 35).

Museums and galleries may be visited by an enormously diverse group of people, who may vary in age, life-style and cultural background, and in level of skills, ability and knowledge. One way to cope with this and to try to offer something that each individual will find relevant to him or herself, is to audit the exhibition plans; to review them from the different perspectives of audiences of different ages (Ch. 11), different life-styles and learning styles (Ch. 12), different cultural backgrounds (Chs 10 and 29), different interests and intelligences, using Howard Gardner's concept of multiple intelligences (Ch. 9), and possible disabilities (Ch. 28).

Although using each of these approaches very prescriptively might result in a rather mechanistic approach to thinking about complex human beings, as a combined set of issues for reviewing exhibition plans these ideas are useful. Any exhibition that has considered (and provided for) the range of needs of its audiences using such a wide analytical grid will offer a menu of opportunities that will enable a very diverse use. Although the different audiences seem sometimes to have rather contradictory needs, and indeed sometimes compromises have to be agreed, frequently providing a more relevant experience for one group will result in a better experience for many, if not all (see Ch. 24).

In developing and writing the texts for an exhibition, specific issues arise. An exhibition is not a book, and the conditions for reading are very different. There is a great deal of information available about how to write effective texts (see Chs 20, 21, 22), and Helen Coxall has shown how the words that are used have effects which go beyond those of readability (see Ch. 23).

One of the most exciting issues to emerge in museums in recent years has been the acknowledgement of the relevance of learning theory to exhibition design and development. For many years, the application of education theory and the development of educational practice were limited to the activities of the education department (or the work of the museum educators, whether in a department or not). Within the museum as an organization, this was held apart from the other aspects of the communicative role of the museum. As a result, in many institutions, a cultural model of communication and a constructivist approach to learning were in operation in the museum education work, but a transmission approach to communication and a behavioural approach to learning operated within the gallery display spaces.

This dislocation was not helpful. It disadvantaged visitors and, given the power relations operating in many museums, it undervalued the insights that the constructivist approach to education and communication offered.

These days are passing (rather too slowly in some places). In forward-looking and professionally managed museums, the museum educator is a valued member of the team; the lessons of constructivism, of audience studies and of community consultation are eagerly learned, and new applications of these lessons are being developed to suit the museum environment and purpose.

LEARNING IN MUSEUMS

Most visitors appreciate museums and galleries as places in which to extend their experience and also to enjoy a social occasion. Most visitors, therefore, have rather unspecific learning goals, and where people come in families[9] these may in fact relate more to the children in the group than to the adults. The learning experience for these visitors is likely to be informal, based on the public provision available at the time when they visit (exhibitions, events, handling tables, films), and could be described as leisure-learning.

Some other visitors will want a more educationally focused experience, perhaps provided by the museum educators or curators, or by visiting freelance experts, or artists, or volunteer docents.[10] Most museums of any significance make provision to respond to these needs and a range of modes of provision can be found.[11] The literature on learning and teaching in museums is now very extensive, although most work has been done in Britain and North America.[12]

It is significant that today much of the discussion focuses on 'learning' in museums, rather than on 'museum education'. This is a measure of the acceptance of the basic premise of constructivism: that learners construct their own meanings and make sense in their own way of the learning opportunities they experience; and that, accordingly, the role of the teacher is that of providing appropriate learning experiences where the knowledge of the student may be explored, increased and tested.

Learning involves a great many processes (Falk and Dierking 1995). The most basic are perception and memory. Perception is strongly influenced by prior experience – we see what we know, what we recognize. Learning is influenced by motivation and attitudes, by prior experience, by culture and background, and – especially in museums – by design and presentation and the physical setting. When we talk about learning, and particularly learning in museums, we are not talking about learning facts only. Learning includes facts, but also experiences and the emotions. It requires individual effort, but is also a social experience. In museums, it is the social experience that frequently is best remembered.

Museum learning is frequently focused on objects. Objects can be particularly stimulating in relation to learning processes when handled and studied closely. Objects can act to ground abstract experiences, can enable recall of knowledge, and can arouse curiosity. They can be relevant to all age- and ability-ranges and can be studied from a range of disciplinary perspectives. Children appreciate the opportunity to work directly with objects from a surprisingly young age (Hooper-Greenhill 1996: 21).

The 'conversation' between viewer and object can take a number of forms and range across a spectrum of intellectual and everyday fields. The initiation and facilitation of this conversation is frequently the role of the museum education officer (or curator). According to the needs of the individual, or more frequently the small group, concerned, the conversation can be introduced and structured in order to stimulate interest, to demonstrate relevance and to use existing information and experience (see Ch. 7). The techniques for teaching with objects are not frequently taught to teachers, and this continues to be a major task for museums.

Methods for using museums in teaching and learning are well established. Story-telling in galleries using paintings, drama using characters related to the collections, art-making and scientific experimental workshops, writing poetry as a response to objects and reviewing classification systems, developing fashion shows based on costume collections, measuring and recording buildings inside and outside, mapping sites and grounds, talking and listening to museum staff, visiting the museum stores or laboratories – there is much good practice to draw upon. Successful educational programmes are underpinned by an understanding of the needs of learners of different ages (see Chs 11 and 12), different perceptions and ways of representing the world (see Ch. 10) and different learning styles (see Chs. 9 and 12). They are based on active experience, followed by review and assessment of this experience, and then use of the skills, knowledge and values experienced. Successful museum education enables learners to feel valued as individuals, and both encouraged and stretched as learners.

CRITICAL PEDAGOGY IN THE MUSEUM

The educational role of the museum is complex; thinking about learning within a cultural institution means being aware of the link between culture and pedagogy (Jameson 1991: 50–1). It is not enough to focus only on the learning strategies of individuals, and the educational potential of museums and their collections, it is also necessary to place this within a knowledge of the social and cultural roles that museums play. The concept of critical pedagogy as used by Henry Giroux (1992) is helpful in articulating the relationship between museums as cultural organizations and museums as sites for learning.

Critical pedagogy is concerned with the way that students actually construct meaning, what the categories of meaning are, and what beliefs and values students bring to their encounters. Critical pedagogy recognizes that people 'write' meaning rather than just encounter or receive it (Giroux 1992: 153). In this sense, Giroux's critical pedagogy works from the same constructivist premise that informs both hermeneutics and the literary theory that underpins the concept of 'interpretive communities'. However, Giroux's critical pedagogy has not been developed with museums in mind. It is based on 'a need to name the contradiction between what schools claim to do and what they actually do' (Giroux 1992: 151). Schools claim to offer an equality of educational opportunity to all, but children from different social and cultural backgrounds have manifestly different school experiences. Museums, too, claim to be for everyone, but both the visitor statistics and the research studies reviewed earlier insist that museums are not experienced equally by all.

Critical pedagogy, working between cultural studies and educational theory, reminds us that knowledge is always concerned with relationships between power, language, imagery, social relations and ethics. Insofar as knowledge and culture construct individual identities, identities are also structured through these relationships (Giroux 1992: 156). Education is centrally concerned with the construction of identity through knowledge and experience, and it is perhaps here that museums can begin to fulfil some of their potential for individual and group empowerment. One of the tasks of a critical pedagogy is to provide students with a range of identities and human possibilities that emerge among, within and between different zones of culture, and this museums are well able to achieve.

Museums are not unified places. At any one time, any museum will represent the co-existence of a range of different convictions and beliefs, from the past and the present, between different epochs of the past and between different value-systems in the present. From this perspective, museums are not understood as monolithic and unchanging, but as sites of multiple and heterogeneous contact zones where different histories, languages, experiences and voices intermingle amidst diverse relations of power and privilege. Within these cultural borderlands, a range of practices are possible, a language of possibilities can be used, different sub-groups can be involved and different sub-cultures can push against and permeate the apparently homogeneous borders of dominant cultural practices.

Critical pedagogy can make a difference by making marginal cultures visible, and by legitimating difference (Giroux 1992: 170). Rather than asserting that objects have one unified meaning, and using museum displays to present an authoritative meta-narrative, museums can negotiate the meanings and significance of collections, and view their displays as provisional statements only. This opening-up to richer and deeper possibilities both brings museums closer to an expanded range of communities and offers enormous scope for the use of collections.

By using collections in new ways, opening up a range of legitimated cultural options, critical pedagogy in the museum can enable those from minority cultures to recognize and validate their own cultures, can honour the achievements of a greater range of individuals and can suggest that many ways of thinking are possible. Some museums are already finding ways to democratize their working practices, and to relate in a more sustained and long-term way to different communities. They are breaking down the long-established monolithic singular narratives that privilege dominant perspectives, and are introducing multiple perspectives that give sub-groups and difference a voice (see Ch. 17, and see also Hooper-Greenhill 1997).

This chapter has ranged widely, in an attempt to pull together the various elements that are involved in a discussion of the educational role of the museum. We began by considering what we know about museum use, reviewed the complexity of statistics, and turned to examine two research studies that probed the attitudes towards museums of two clearly defined audience groups. These studies showed, first, how museum audience research is changing from an approach based on quantitative work to more naturalistic studies which collect qualitative data; and, second, how much can be learned from this kind of in-depth study.

Both studies showed how people view museums from their own perspectives, and are active in making choices about whether to visit or not, through examining the value of a visit in relation to their own desires, and those with whom they might visit. The meaning of a museum visit is related to interpretations of history, culture and society as a whole, and these interpretations are structured to some degree in patterns that relate to gender, ethnicity, level of education and class position.

We moved on to examine meaning-making processes, using hermeneutic theory, and saw how the past and the present work together as an object of analysis is related to a social whole. Hermeneutics, and the processes of interpretation, confirm that people actively construct their own interpretations of what they experience, and the meaning that is constructed grows from an individual's previous knowledge and experience, but also from the interpretive communities to which the individual is affiliated. The strategies of intelligibility that are available for use in any interpretive community partly structure the meaning-making strategies of its members. Thus the construction of meaning is both individual and social.

We related these meaning-making strategies that groups and individuals use to the ways in which, in museums, we think about our publics. We examined the different meanings of the word 'interpretation' in hermeneutics, and in museums (two different interpretive communities, philosophers and museum professionals, use the same word in very different ways). In some museums and galleries, the audience is still implicitly treated as both unified (the 'general public') and passive, and a transmission model of communication is used. Where it is acknowledged that audiences are active and work from their own agendas, and where this is negotiated by the museum, a cultural model of communication is likely to be in place.

Both philosophy (hermeneutics) and learning theory (constructivism) insist that people construct their own worlds, through their interpretation of their experience. A concrete material world exists external to the knower, but it makes sense and becomes 'real' only through interpretation. There is no moment prior to interpretation, and no knowledge that is not social. Our 'real worlds' are our own complex and fluid constructions, shaped through our psychologies, biographies and histories, and our significant communities. This shaping of experience, this construction of the 'real world', continues as long as we live.

In museums, the meanings made are shaped by the experience of the museum and the interpretation of this experience according to the complex influences outlined above. As museum workers, we can change the experience that visitors have, and some ideas for the development and design of exhibitions that acknowledge the learning preferences of a differentiated audience were suggested. Exhibitions are the basis of the museum experience for the vast majority of museum visitors. Accessible exhibitions can lead to greater enjoyment and more effective learning, even though the nature of the learning is probably rather unfocused; leisure-learning, a stirring of interest, an extension of something already known. However, people have different learning needs and, if the exhibition permits, will learn as suits them best.

Following the discussion of the development of effective exhibitions, we briefly reviewed some elements of a more structured approach to the provision of museum education. More focused educational sessions generally prioritize learning from the analysis of objects, although sometimes the collections are a stimulus to drama, art, or other expressive outcomes. Both analytical and emotive relationships with objects are possible, and frequently both of these cross subject boundaries, and motivate further work that can extend over many weeks.

Finally, we considered the educational role of the museum from the perspective of education within a cultural organization. The concept of a critical museum pedagogy was introduced to highlight the complex interrelationships of educational and cultural issues.

To perceive the educational role of the museum as a form of critical pedagogy entails understanding the museum within a context of cultural politics; it means acknowledging the constructivist approach to knowledge and to learning; and it means recognizing the fact that museums have the potential to negotiate cultural borderlands, and to create new contact zones where identities and collections, people and objects can discover new possibilities for personal and social life and, through this, for democracy.

If, through a critical pedagogy, museums can work together with their audiences to achieve a cultural re-mapping, to rewrite cultural borders and thus to empower their learners, then the educational role of the museum will be justifiably celebrated.

NOTES

1 I use the word 'audience' because I want to talk about more than visitors. 'Visitors' signifies those who actually come to the museum, whereas museums also work with other people outside museums in the community. Those people who take part in a handling session in a community centre are part of the museum 'audience', although they are not strictly speaking 'visitors'. I use 'audience' to include actual and remote users, and also physical and virtual users, those who might 'visit' the museum electronically. The traditional 'visitor survey' is not able to count these users. I also use 'audience' to cover all those people who are not visitors, but who could be. Potential as well

as actual visitors are covered by the concept of 'audience'. Museums and galleries need to have regard to their entire audience when planning their public face. Planning just for existing visitors runs the risk of perpetuating unacknowledged discriminatory practices.

2 For a discussion of the pattern of visits to American museums see Falk (1998) and for Australia see Ch. 25 of this volume.

3 For a discussion of some of the reasons, see Chapter 29, in conjunction with the MGC report discussed here.

4 'Object' is a very ambiguous word. I use it to mean all those bits of material culture that comprise museum collections. I would call a picture or a photograph an object, and I would also include natural history or geological specimens (which are also bits of material culture, but I do not intend to argue why here).

5 Dialogical – meaning like a dialogue, or a conversation. Keep reading, it gets clearer as you go on.

6 This crucial study has been little used, probably because there was no English translation until 1991. It is worth looking back at, as the methodological and theoretical depth is rare in museum-related work.

7 It is interesting to study the background to the events at the Natural History Museum in relation to educational theory and exhibition development. One of the key elements in developing educational materials within the teaching and learning models used by educational technology is evaluation of these materials as they are produced. The application of ideas from educational technology to the museum field, and specifically to the design of exhibitions, led to the introduction of evaluation into the exhibition development process. This has been immensely valuable. However, educational technology is based on a behaviourist view of learning, which, working from a stimulus-response approach to teaching, understood the learner as 'the empty vessel to be filled'. The focus of the educational method was on the most appropriate preparation of teaching materials (in the museum, exhibitions), on the assumption that once this had been got right, students (visitors) would learn. This educational model ignored the key contribution to the learning process of the learner, who comes, as we have seen, with his or her own interests, skills and prior knowledge. After twenty years of careful work, the Natural History Museum staff came to the conclusion that the approach they had been using had not paid enough attention to the visitor's agenda (see Miles and Tout 1994).

8 *Museum International* XLV(2) (1993) devotes a complete issue to a discussion of these developments in visitor studies in many different countries across the world.

9 The concept of 'families' needs to be made clear. In museum visitor studies, especially those based on observation, a 'family' is generally interpreted as any group of adults with accompanying children, with the relationship of the adults to the children not probed. Adults may be parents, step-parents, grandparents, carers, friends and so on. This is the use I make of the concept here too.

10 A 'docent' is a familiar concept in North America, and means a volunteer teacher. This concept is less familiar in Europe.

11 For further details on the history, organization and management of museum education please see Hooper-Greenhill (1991).

12 See the Bibliography produced by the Group for Education in Museums (Stannett 1997) and also Falk and Dierking (1992).

REFERENCES

Appadurai, A. and Breckenridge, C. A. (1992) 'Museums are good to think: heritage on view in India', in I. Karp, C. M. Kreamer and S. D. Lavine, *Museums and Communities: the Politics of Public Culture*, Washington, DC: Smithsonian Institution, 34–55.

Bicknell, S. (1995) 'Here to help: evaluation and effectiveness', in E. Hooper-Greenhill (ed.) *Museum, Media, Message*, London: Routledge, 281–93.

Bourdieu, P. and Darbel, A. (1991) *The Love of Art: European Museums and their Public*, English edn trans. Caroline Beattie and Nick Merriman, Cambridge: Polity Press.

Cameron, D. (1968) 'A viewpoint: the museum as a communication system and implications for museum education', *Curator* 11(1): 33–40.

Carey, J. W. (1989) *Communication as Culture*, Boston, MA: Unwin Hyman.

Casey, B., Dunlop, S. and Selwood, S. (1996) *Culture as Commodity? The Economics of the Arts and Built Heritage in the UK*, London: Policy Studies Institute.

Davies, S. (1994) *By Popular Demand: a Strategic Analysis of the Market Potential for Museums and Galleries in the UK*, London: Museums and Galleries Commission.

Desai, P. and Thomas, A. (1998) *Cultural Diversity: Attitudes of Ethnic Minority Populations towards Museums and Galleries*, London: Qualitative Workshop for the Museums and Galleries Commission.

Dilthey, W. (1976) 'The rise of hermeneutics', in P. Connerton (ed.) *Critical Sociology – Selected Readings*, Harmondsworth, Mx: Penguin Books, 104–16.

Falk, J. (1998) 'Visitors: who does, who doesn't and why', *Museum News* (March/April): 38–43.

Falk, J. and Dierking, L. (1992) *The Museum Experience*, Washington, DC: Whalesback Books.

Falk, J. and Dierking, L. (eds) (1995) *Public Institutions for Personal Learning: Establishing a Research Agenda*, Washington, DC: American Association of Museums.

Fay, B. (1996) *Contemporary Philosophy of Social Science: a Multicultural Approach*, Oxford: Blackwell Publishers.

Fish, S. (1980) *Is there a Text in this Class? The Authority of Interpretive Communities*, Cambridge, MA and London: Harvard University Press.

Gadamer, H.-G. (1976) 'The historicity of understanding', in P. Connerton (ed.) *Critical Sociology – Selected Readings*, Harmondsworth, Mx: Penguin Books, 117–33.

Giroux, H. (1992) *Border Crossings: Cultural Workers and the Politics of Education*, New York and London: Routledge.

Glesne, C. and Peshkin, A. (1992) *Becoming Qualitative Researchers*, London: Longman.

Hall, S. (1997) *Representation: Cultural Representations and Signifying Practices*, London: Sage Publications.

Hardt, H. (1992) *Critical Communication Studies: Communication, History and Theory in America*, London: Routledge.

Harris Qualitative (1997) *Children as an Audience for Museums and Galleries*, Richmond, Sy: Harris Qualitative for the Museums and Galleries Commission and the Arts Council of England.

Hein, G. (1998) *Learning in the Museum*, London: Routledge.

Hooper-Greenhill, E. (1991) *Museum and Gallery Education*, Leicester: Leicester University Press.

Hooper-Greenhill, E. (1992) *Museums and the Shaping of Knowledge*, London: Routledge.

Hooper-Greenhill, E. (1994) *Museums and their Visitors*, London: Routledge.

Hooper-Greenhill, E. (ed.) (1996) *Improving Museum Learning*, Nottingham: East Midlands Museum Service.

Hooper-Greenhill, E. (ed.) (1997) *Cultural Diversity: Developing Museum Audiences in Britain*, Leicester: Leicester University Press.

Hooper-Greenhill, E. (1998) 'Perspectives on Hinemihi: a Maori meeting house', in T. Barringer and T. Flynn, *Colonialism and the Object: Empire, Material, Culture and the Museum*, London and New York: Routledge, 129–43.

Jameson, F. (1991) *Postmodernism, or, The Cultural Logic of Late Capitalism*, New York: Vergo.

Jensen, K. B. (1991) 'Humanistic scholarship as qualitative science: contributions to mass communication research', in K. B. Jensen and N. W. Jankowski, *A Handbook of Qualitative Methodologies for Mass Communication Research*, London and New York: Routledge, 17–43.

Jordan, G. and Weedon, C. (1995) *Cultural Politics: Class, Gender, Race and the Postmodern World*, Oxford: Blackwell.

Karp, I., Kreamer, C. M. and Lavine, S. D. (1992) *Museums and Communities: the Politics of Public Culture*, Washington, DC: Smithsonian Institution.

Knez, E. I. and Wright, G. (1970) 'The museum as a communication system: an assessment of Cameron's viewpoint', *Curator* 13(3): 204–12.

Loomis, R. J. (1987) *Museum Visitor Evaluation: New Tool for Management*, Nashville, TN: American Association for State and Local History.

McManus, P. (1991) 'Making sense of exhibits', in G. Kavanagh (ed.) *Museum Languages: Objects and Texts*, Leicester: Leicester University Press, 33–46.

Merriman, N. (1991) *Beyond the Glass Case: the Past, the Heritage and the Public in Britain*, Leicester: Leicester University Press.

Miles, R. (1985) 'Exhibitions: management, for a change', in N. Cossons (ed.) *The Management of Change in Museums*, London: National Maritime Museum, 31–3.

Miles, R. S. and Tout, A. F. (1994) 'Impact of research on the approach to the visiting public', in E. Hooper-Greenhill (ed.) *The Educational Role of the Museum*, 1st edn, London: Routledge, 101–6.

Peterman, F. (1997) 'Becoming constructivist museum educators', *Journal of Education in Museums* 18: 4–7.

Research Surveys of Great Britain (1991) *RSGB Omnibus Arts Survey: Report on a Survey on Arts and Cultural Activities in G.B.*, London: Arts Council of Great Britain.

Roberts, L. C. (1997) *From Knowledge to Narrative: Educators and the Changing Museum*, Washington, DC and London: Smithsonian Institution Press.

Schuster, J. (1995) 'The public interest in the art museum's public', in S. Pearce (ed.) *Art in Museums*, New Research in Museum Studies: an international series, Vol. 5, London: Athlone Press, 109–42.

Selwood, S., Schwarz, B. and Merriman, N. (1996) *The Peopling of London: Fifteen Thousand Years of Settlement from Overseas. An Evaluation of the Exhibition*, London: Museum of London.

Silverman, L. H. (1995) 'Visitor meaning-making in museums for a new age', *Curator* 38(3): 161–70.

Stannett, A. (ed.) (1997) *GEM Museum Education Bibliography, 1988–1996*, London: Group for Education in Museums.

Susie Fisher Group (1990) *Bringing History and the Arts to a New Audience: Qualitative Research for the London Borough of Croydon*, London: Susie Fisher Group.

Trevelyan, V. (1991) *'Dingy Places with Different Kinds of Bits': an Attitudes Survey of London Museums amongst Non-visitors*, London: Area Museum Service for South-Eastern England.

Walsh, A. (1991) *Insights: Museums, Visitors, Attitudes, Expectations – a Focus Group Experiment*, Los Angeles: J. Paul Getty Trust and the Getty Center for Education.

Worts, D. (1995) 'Extending the frame: forging a new partnership with the public', in S. Pearce (ed.) *Art in Museums*, New Research in Museum Studies: an international series, Vol. 5, London: Athlone Press, 164–91.

2

Communication in theory and practice

Eilean Hooper-Greenhill

This chapter examines the process of communication from the point of view of the transmission model of communication. It discusses the use of this model during the late 1960s and the 1970s, in trying to understand how museums communicate. The model explains some long-established ways of developing exhibitions rather well.

However, the model is flawed. It does not explain how communication actually works. The problems of the model are addressed and a more holistic approach to museum communication is proposed.

MUSEUMS AND MASS COMMUNICATION

In recent years many writers have emphasized the communicative nature of museums. Robert Lumley argues that 'the notion of the museum as a collection for scholarly use has been largely replaced by the idea of the museum as a means of communication' (Lumley 1988: 15). Hodge and D'Souza see the two roles as complementary:

> Museums are not only protectors but also communicators. . . . A museum display is an exercise in one branch of the mass media, requiring a special kind of understanding of the processes of communication, namely the nature of mass communication systems.

> (Hodge and D'Souza 1979: 146)

Mass communication systems are unnatural forms of communication, in that they operate at a distance and often in the absence of one of the two parties necessary before communication can take place. It is difficult, therefore, to be sure that the process has worked. Has the message really been understood? In 'natural' communication, which we can visualize as a face-to-face conversation between two people from a common background, the main message of the communication is interpreted through this common background. Shared experience enables the message to be decoded. The words that might be used are supported by many other channels of communication, such as gesture, facial expression, emphasis. Any point of misunderstanding can be verified by asking a question and by repetition or restatement. In a face-to face conversation, there is a possibility of the message's being modified by either party and being reshaped as ideas are exchanged. In natural communication, and particularly in a domestic situation where two people know each other very well, ideas are often exchanged in fits and starts, with frequent repetitions and clarifications. Often two conversations are carried on at once, or ideas are conveyed through a series of grunts and gestures, with perhaps a drink acting as mediation. The shared domestic environment makes this erratic and unelaborated transfer of ideas comprehensible to the two people concerned. In natural communication, then, we find the following features: interpretation through shared experience, modification or development of the message in the light of response, and many supporting methods of communicating. Natural communication has the potential to be direct, responsive and equal.

With mass communication situations, things are very different. Let us take television as an example. Here, at the moment of communication, one party to the communicative act is present (perhaps sitting at home in the evening), while the other (the team who prepared the programme) is absent. The transmitter (the team) must rely on their skill to produce a message that the receiver (sitting at home) will be interested in hearing. The message is one-way, with no chance of immediate feedback. If the message is not clear, there can be no clarification. There are few supporting channels, although the comment in newspaper listings might be seen as one source of extra information. If the message is boring, unenjoyable, or unpleasant, the remedy is simple; the television is turned off. Mass communication is one-way (indirect), is impossible to modify (unresponsive) and takes place in the absence of one of the partners (unequal).

In order to succeed in communicating through television, considerable research is undertaken, both into ways of putting the message across and into audience response (Alvarado *et al.* 1987). This research includes preliminary (front-end) research into what is likely to succeed, and summative research into the effects of the programmes on the audience. Those programmes that are not successful are quickly identified through audience ratings, and are axed. Successful programmes are repeated or developed. Market research is seen as a vital tool, and as an integral part of the communication process.

In museums, there are many of the features common to most forms of mass communication, but in addition there are opportunities for face-to-face communication. The museum is fortunate in that it has a variety of methods of communication at its disposal, and in museums this modifies the starkness of the mass communication situation. Traditional museum methods are now being modified to take account of visitor needs, and practices are changing, but in the past the experience of displays and exhibitions has shared the characteristic features of the experience of mass communications. One of the parties involved (the visitor/viewer) has been present, while the other (the exhibition team) has been absent. There have been few opportunities to modify the message of the display according to the response of the visitor. There has been no certainty that visitors would share the background of the museum communicator, although visitor surveys, in demonstrating the middle and upper-middle social class groupings of most visitors, probably illustrate that visitors are self-selected on this basis.

Those displays that demonstrated the features of mass communication were prone to a range of problems. These included a failure to transmit the intended messages, a distortion of communication and an inability to involve the visitor. These problems of communication, understood and explored at an empirical level in a range of forward-looking museums, have led to the shifts we can now observe, where methods of mounting displays are changing to take account of the needs of visitors and to provide opportunities for sharing and involvement through handling, activity sessions and collaborative exhibitions.

In addition to display methods which are close to the methods of mass communication, museums also have the opportunity to exploit natural communication, through talks, guided tours, meet-the-curator sessions, demonstrations, handling sessions, enquiries, discussion groups and social events. It is also true that the mass media themselves provide other opportunities for museums to make connections with people: by using television itself, either in advertising or as a part of an exhibition or event; through the use of videos, as an aspect of the interpretation of displays, as souvenirs to take home, or as outreach into the community; through newspaper and magazine advertising or articles; through posters, leaflets and flyers; and through publishing at all levels. The communicative methods for museums are extremely varied and this is surely one of the great advantages that museums have over many of the other institutions of the mass media. The 'communication mix' will become a vital concept in the next decade as museums and galleries develop policies and strategies for museum communication.

Mass communication, as we have seen, is likely to be prone to miscommunication, and this is as common in museums as elsewhere (Hodge and D'Souza 1979). The two most common problems with museum displays concern saying things that were not intended, and not saying what was intended. For museum workers, it is important to try to understand as well as possible the communication process itself, both in general and in museums. There is room for considerable theoretical development in museum communication methods. Most branches of the mass media now have extensive texts of methods, but in museums this is only just beginning. There is a need for new methods of communication to be tried out, evaluated and published.

In addition to developing knowledge and expertise in the techniques of museum communication, it is at least as important to try to understand people and how they react to museums. Again, work has begun in this area, and we will consider some of it later, but more is needed. Visitor surveys have been fairly common since the 1960s in Britain, but have tended to remain at the level of counting who comes, and how. Information has remained at the demographic level, and it is only very recently that more qualitative research has begun. Research into visitors is as important as research into communication methods. Indeed, the one cannot exist without the other. As we need to know more about how people respond to particular displays or events in order to evaluate and develop new techniques, so we will need to research attitudes to museums, opinions on a range of methods, feelings about a variety of different experiences and so on. In the same way as the mass media research their audiences to evaluate reaction to their products, so we will need to research the audiences of the museum to discover whether an exhibition, a poster, a café, or an event has been successful.

THE COMMUNICATION PROCESS

An act of communication is one that aims to produce an effect on another person or persons. If this intention is absent, the act tends to be expressive rather than communicative (Morgan and Welton 1986). Any study of communication, therefore, can logically assume a desire to influence, and can assess the strength and nature of this.

In museum exhibitions there is frequently a subjective element – the exhibition can be, and has been, seen as an act of expression on the part of the curator. Expressive acts, such as works of art, or exhibitions that are very largely the subjective work of a curator, can, and sometimes do, communicate effectively. They will communicate with those people who share the same subjectivity, the same interests, the same modes of expression. If, however, a broader audience for communication is looked for, an awareness of the mechanics and psychology of communication can help.

The understanding of the process of communication has evolved from the development of a simple model to something more complex (McQuail 1975). The initial simple description of the process of communication was based on the idea of one person sending a message to another, perhaps over the telephone, or through the post. The process involved a communicator, a receiver and a relationship between them. Several elements were required: an intention on the part of the communicator; the subject of the message; a common language; some shared experience; and, to demonstrate that something had in fact been communicated, some activity or change as a result of the process. Described like this, it seems very unproblematic. A simple diagram expresses this process well (see Figure 2.1).

Figure 2.1 A simple communications model

This simple model was elaborated slightly by Shannon and Weaver (see Figure 2.2) (McQuail and Windahl 1993: 17). Distinctions were made at the beginning of the process between the source and the transmitter, and at the end of the process between the receiver and the destination. Also introduced was the idea of 'noise', which is anything external (or sometimes internal) to the process that might interrupt the transfer of information.

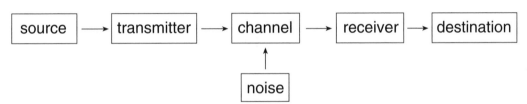

Figure 2.2 The Shannon and Weaver communications model

The Shannon and Weaver model has been applied to various forms of communication (McQuail 1975) (see Figure 2.3).

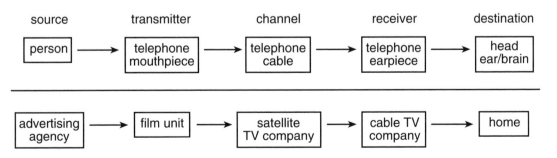

Figure 2.3 The application of the Shannon and Weaver model to a mechanical process and to a process involving agencies working together

The application of the Shannon and Weaver model works both with mechanical process (that of a telephonic message) and in the case of agencies working together. In the first instance the source is the person making the call, the transmitter is the telephone mouthpiece, the channel is the telephone cable, the receiver is the telephone earpiece, and the final destination is the head or the brain of the person receiving the call. In the case of agencies working together, the source is the advertising agency, which hires the transmitter (the film unit) to make an advertisement broadcast through the channel (the satellite TV company) to the receiver (the cable TV company) into the destination (the home).

The model can be applied to a museum exhibition. It is possible to describe the exhibition team as the source, the exhibition as the transmitter, with objects, texts and events as the channel of communication, the visitors' heads as the receivers, with the visitors' understanding as the final destination (see Figure 2.4). In this instance the 'noise' which interferes with the message might include anything from crowds to visitor fatigue, or workmen in the gallery next door. Internal sources of noise might include confusing signals, such as poor graphics or inappropriate use of colour (Duffy 1989).

The value of models such as the Shannon and Weaver model is the preliminary separation of a complex process into a series of elements. Each of these elements can be analysed as a unit, which is sometimes a useful way of beginning to penetrate a difficult and multi-layered event, such as the development of an exhibition or an event.

However, there are problems with simple models of communication, such as the Shannon and Weaver model. One very basic problem is that this model suggests that communication is the simple transfer of a message from one part to another. Communication is, of course, far more than this.

Two other ways of thinking about communication are as 'networks of contacts', or as 'hierarchized chains' (see Figures 2.5 and 2.6).

The idea of communication as a network of contacts works well in relation to the forms of communication that are sometimes to be found in families, or in informal

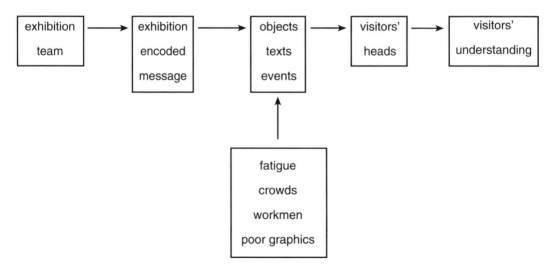

Figure 2.4 The Shannon and Weaver model applied to exhibitions

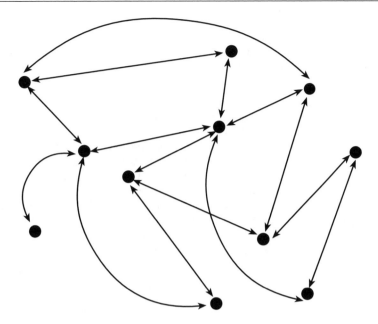

Figure 2.5 Alternative models of communication: a network of contacts

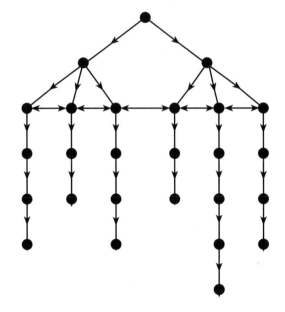

Figure 2.6 Alternative models of communication: hierarchized chains

33

groups. Messages are passed by word of mouth, letter, phone-call – non-hierarchically, in a free-flowing and mobile way. Any part of the network might contact any other part as required, and communication is relatively open and equal between parties. Power relations emerge from this network according to a multitude of factors, but are not enshrined within the structure itself.

'Hierarchized chains' describes a form of communication that is often to be found in formal institutions, including traditional large museums. It is premised on power and authority, with communication flowing from the top down, but not from the bottom up. The communication links are very closely delineated, and in fact *prevent* a great deal of communication taking place. In museums with a staff structure based on a director, two deputies and a number of departments, probably mostly based on divisions of the collections, such as archaeology, natural history, fine art, social history, with possibly an education and/or design department tacked on the end, this form of communication structure is all too familiar. In such museums, there is little communication between departments at the lower levels, and that communication which takes place between department heads generally operates as a form of defence of territory.

This rigid and authoritarian power structure is seen by modern management theorists as wasteful and lacking in cost-effectiveness. Industry is now moving towards flatter structures that are more flexible and democratic, that assign more power to branches, that are organized as units each with its own autonomy and network, and where a range of relationships to the work task is possible (Handy 1990).

The simple communications model, therefore, can be seen as only one way in which communication can be conceived. There are many other ways in which the process can be understood.

The simple communications model has been criticized because it makes a number of assumptions that are not always appropriate. The model proposes a wholly linear view of communication, one that begins with a source that also defines the meaning of the communicative act. The receiver is conceived as cognitively passive, and contributing nothing to the process. The role of the receiver is simply to receive. If this reception does not occur, the communicative process must be deemed to have failed.

Here, the concept of feedback enters the process. In order to test the system, we must see whether the message has been understood. If it has not been understood, then the message must be modified to make understanding more likely (see Figure 2.7).

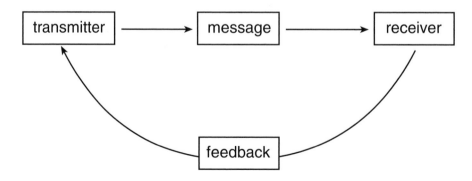

Figure 2.7 The simple communications model with feedback loop

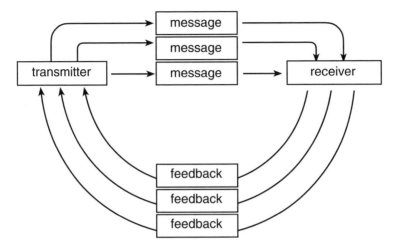

Figure 2.8 Successive feedback loops progressively alter the original message and eventually change the process from linear to circular

If (as it will) feedback indicates difficulties with the reception of the message, so the message is successively modified until it may well become fragmented out of all recognition (see Figure 2.8).

Once a feedback loop is introduced into the process, the message is likely to change. It is likely to change because any linear process of communication cannot be certain of speaking the language of the receiver, or even of having anything to say that is of interest to the receiver. In the absence of coercive power, the message may simply be ignored. Once the receiver is brought into the process to play a more active role, the whole process changes and begins to break up. The linearity of the process is altered. The meaning of the message is no longer defined only by the sender, but also by the receiver. The work of meaning-making begins to be shared between the two parties. The greater this sharing process, the more likely effective communication is to take place. The logical outcome of this process is to consult the receiver before any messages are sent, to try out a variety of messages to see which are appropriate and interesting.

This preliminary research can be carried out in relation to the content of the message, but might also usefully be carried out in relation to the medium through which the message is to be carried. Which is the most appropriate channel for which audience? What channels are the audiences used to? Which to they find difficult? Which do they enjoy? When a match can be made between the audience (the receiver) and both the content of the message and the nature of the medium, then a communicative process may be begun.

What is interesting in the above discussion is the amount of work that is required *before* the communicative process can start. It is now recognized that it is not enough to make a decision to communicate a message and to put the receivers on stand-by to receive it. If the receivers are not predisposed to appreciate the message, to find it relevant and to make it their own, then it is likely that no initial contact will be made at all. This explains the preliminary or piloting work that is carried out by television and advertising companies in the very early stages of a product, and it is clear that there are lessons here for museums and galleries.

COMMUNICATIONS MODELS IN MUSEUMS

The simple communications model was introduced to the museum world in North America by Cameron in the late 1960s, and this stimulated a debate (Cameron 1968; Knez and Wright 1970; Miles 1989). The focus of the debate was whether objects were the most important aspect of a museum's communication system, or were merely one form of communication. The debate seems a little sterile today, but it is instructive to note the uses and adaptations of the simple model of communication and to notice the concentration on the medium, and on how messages are transmitted.

Cameron used the model virtually intact, but suggested that, in a museum, there are many transmitters, many media and many receivers. The prime medium used is that of objects ('real things') (see Figure 2.9).

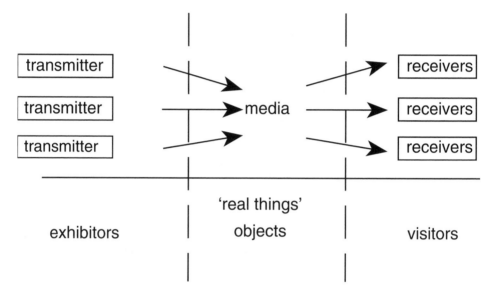

Figure 2.9 The use of a simple communications model by Cameron (1968)

Knez and Wright agreed with Cameron that the museum was, among other things, a communication system, and also agreed that a professional museum officer (whether curator, exhibit designer, or educationalist) was the 'transmitter', and that the 'receivers' were the visitors. However, Cameron's emphasis on objects as the medium of museum communication was challenged by Knez and Wright (1970), who proposed that a distinction could be drawn between those museums, such as science museums, that relied on verbal symbols (written or spoken words) as of primary importance in exhibitions, and those, such as art museums, where objects were more important.

Knez and Wright proposed that putting across ideas (intellectual cognition) was the primary function of museum communication, at least in science museums, and their suggestions led to the following modifications in the basic communications model (see Figure 2.10).

However the media for exhibitions is understood, and however this might vary with different types of museum, the basic linear 'hypodermic' model, able to 'inject' the

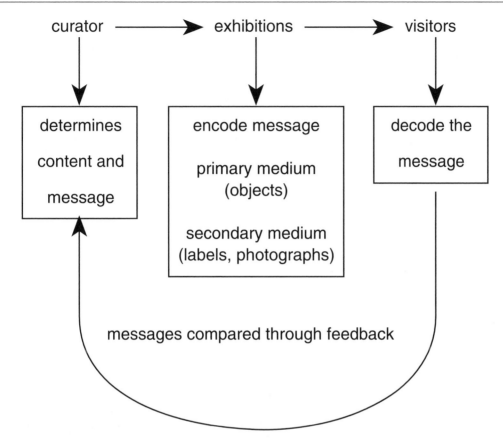

Figure 2.10 The communications model (particularly applicable to science museums) as suggested by Knez and Wright (1970)

receivers with ideas, remains (Morley 1980: 1). The model (and the writers) assumed that the audience was passive and merely reactive, and there was no acknowledgement of the fact that audiences actively interpret their experiences of museums in the light of many individual and social factors, including their backgrounds, cultural assumptions, levels of knowledge and personal agenda for the museum visit.

The influence of this model of communication on approaches to exhibition production is discussed by Miles (1985) who points out how this linear understanding of the communication process is mirrored in the linear process of making exhibitions (see Figure 2.11).

Miles has described museums as 'disabling institutions' when they produce exhibitions using this model. The model is based on people working independently in separate departments (curatorial, design, education), with no team-work and little co-ordination. The work of one department is finished before the work of another begins. Change is difficult and painful and leads to interdepartmental or interpersonal friction.

In this model the curators, as exhibition-generators, play the role of power-broker. They define the content and the message according to their own point of view, without taking into account the views of the other departments or of the audience. Designers

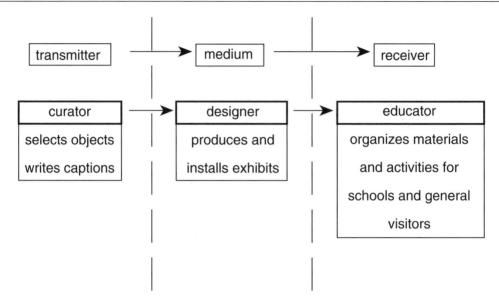

Figure 2.11 The simple communications model adapted as a way of understanding the exhibition process. The move from curator to designer to educator takes place in time

are expected to attend to packaging the ideas of the curator and are treated as functionaries and technicians rather than as communications professionals. The educator is brought into the process at far too late a stage to contribute to planning, and is forced into a remedial role, making the best of a bad job once the exhibition has opened, (re)interpreting it for those people who take part in events or activities. The absence of feedback from the audience means that any improvement is based on intuition or trial and error, and evaluation is impossible. The absence of preliminary audience-related research makes a communicative act unlikely.

Miles proposes a very different approach to exhibition production which is much more flexible and makes use of extensive research at all stages of the process, including market research before the process begins, trying-out of exhibits during production and summative evaluation after the exhibition opens (Miles 1985). Miles also includes reference to the concurrent development of the literature that is written to accompany the exhibition (which might include catalogues, handlists and teachers' packs), and the design of educational activities related to the exhibition (see Figure 2.12).

The simple communications model is here superseded by a vastly more complex and reflexive system, one which begins to reflect the various activities and their interrelationships in the production of exhibitions. The incorporation of research and evaluation into the processes of development and production enables the design of exhibitions, and their related literature and educational activities, so that it has some relationship to the proposed audiences.

The simple communications model has been discussed in relation to the production of exhibitions, and, on the whole, this is how it has been deployed in the literature. And although rarely overtly articulated in internal museum debates, the linearity of the information flow, the definition of the message, the attitude to visitors and the position of power for the curator/transmitter, can still be recognized in the exhibition

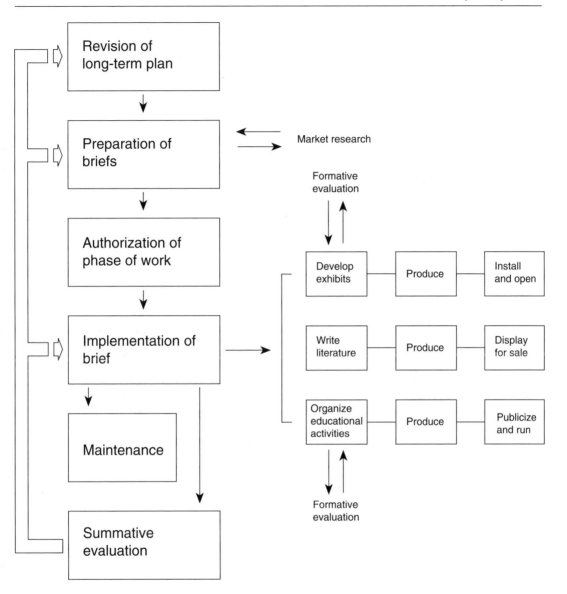

Figure 2.12 Activities involved in planning, designing and producing exhibitions, from Miles (1985)

process in many museums. Indeed it can be recognized in much more than this. Many of the attitudes to museum audiences that can still be found in museums can be traced back to the idea that visitors are passive receivers of those worthwhile experiences that are prepared for them by the museum transmitters.

In many museums there is still no understanding of the nature of the communication process, of the fact that it is a shared process, and that if two parties are not involved, the process may not occur at all. Very many exhibitions are still mounted and demounted at great cost, with visitors having little or nothing to do with them, to the extent in some museums of not even bothering to visit. All too few museums are involved in dialogue with their audiences, at whatever level, and all too few directors understand more than the rhetoric of the importance of effective museum communication for survival, let alone development, in the next decade.

A HOLISTIC APPROACH TO MUSEUM COMMUNICATION

The simple communications model has already been given much to answer for, but there is still one more aspect that we must address. One of the effects of the use of the simple communications model as it has been employed in the literature is to reduce

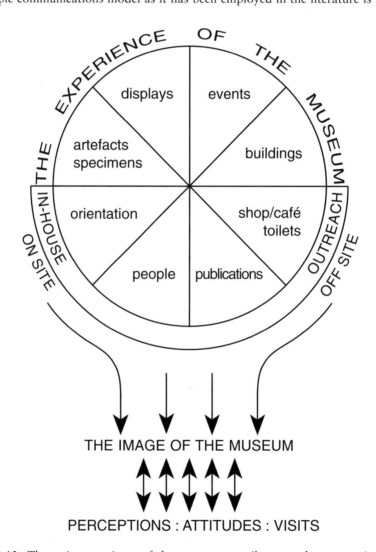

Figure 2.13 The entire experience of the museum contributes to the museum's image. The image of the museum affects the perceptions and attitudes of people, and will affect whether or not they decide to visit the museum

discussion of museum communication to discussion of exhibitions. It is all too easy for the notion of museum communication to become subsumed into the production of exhibitions. This is of course an important method of making connections with people, but museums are fortunate enough to have a whole battery of other methods. In addition to formal methods of communication, many other aspects of the museum need to be considered (see Figure 2.13).

In considering a holistic approach to museum communication we should be aware of museum-wide elements, those aspects of the operation of the institution that impinge either on the museum's image or on the general experience of the visit. These include the museum's buildings, both internal and external features; the attitudes and activities of the museum staff, including the director and the whole range of staff; the general atmosphere in the institution, which will owe much to management styles and staff morale; and the attention given to comfort, orientation and the general guiding of visitors through the experience of the museum.

Museums communicate on-site through a range of methods which includes exhibitions of many different types, functions, sizes and approaches to interpretation. The balance between, for example, a costly, short-term, popular blockbuster appealing to tourists and expected to raise money, and a small-scale exhibition of perhaps the work of a local adult education group, needs to be carefully considered. Different audiences need different provisions, and thought should be given as to how different types of exhibition or display can be used to attract different sections of the public.

Activities, events and educational programmes are generally designed to match the needs of particular audiences, and a vast range of approaches can be found in museums and galleries, including the use of actors or demonstrators; talks, lectures and tours; films or concerts; opportunities for handling or involvement with the collections; chances to try out practical skills such as dancing, drawing, or weaving; invitations to view the stores or the conservation laboratories; and so on.

Many museums have extremely well-organized shops where a range of goods are sold, the main criteria being one of relationship to collections. Many museums have taken the opportunity to develop specialist shops in tune with their missions; the Science Museum, London, for example, has an excellent specialist science bookshop. The shop is an opportunity to make the museum's scholarly work available through catalogues of the permanent collections, temporary exhibition catalogues, books and monographs. Postcards, information packs, calendars, notebooks, pencils and other small items can often be found alongside replicas of some of the collections. Some museums, and Ironbridge Gorge Museum is an example, have developed sophisticated and very successful mail-order systems.

In addition to communicating with visitors to the museum on-site, museums use a variety of means to communicate with people outside the building. These include the establishment of connections with the local and national media; the building-up of secure supporting networks among the local, and sometimes national, business, educational and cultural communities; and the use of a variety of marketing techniques, such as research, mailing and advertising. In addition, some museums have very lively and comprehensive outreach programmes, where activities and events are organized by the museum but take place in a community venue such as a shopping centre, a school, a day centre for the elderly, or a hospital (Beevers *et al.* 1988; O'Neill 1990, 1991; Hemmings 1992; Plant 1992). Some museums have established mobile units that carry collections and events to housing estates, school playgrounds, fairs, or pop

41

concerts. Some museums have collections of loan objects that are available to schools and other institutions.

The role of the museum as a communicator is enormously varied. It can include communicating information in a clear and effective way, perhaps through a leaflet or telephone answer service; enabling a learning experience related to the demands of school curricula, with a role-playing session for a small group of schoolchildren; promoting enjoyment and fun, possibly through manipulating interactive technology; and facilitating reminiscence and mental activity in the old and frail through the provision of suitable objects as stimulus.

Communication is one of the primary functions of museums and galleries. As such, it relates closely to the other main functions of the museum: the collection, conservation and management of artefacts and specimens, and the management of the whole institution. The priorities and policies for communication should be considered when decisions are taken in the other two main areas of museum work, just as communicators must consider management directives and conservation constraints when developing communicative approaches. For example, the use of objects should be considered before a decision to acquire is finalized. What is the object's value for teaching, for exhibiting, for handling, or for promotional purposes? If it has no use in any of these areas, how will it contribute to the knowledge-base of the museum, and can research work carried out on it realistically be disseminated to a broad audience? If the object can satisfy none of these requirements, is the collecting of it really justifiable?

When museum managers are making decisions over budgets, funds should be set aside to carry out research into visitors, their needs and their responses. There is little point in approving exhibition budgets without including ways of measuring the relevance and success of the exhibition. A little market research, some preliminary front-end analysis and attention to the lessons of earlier summative evaluation are likely to prevent expensive mistakes.

Communication can be considered from a number of different points of view. It impinges on all the activities of the museum, and for a good proportion of them its success is of vital importance. Up until now, in many museums, communication has been left to chance. Communicative activities have certainly happened, but often in isolation from each other, even when in the same museum. Education for schools and adults, exhibitions for whoever cares to come, and advertising through leaflets and posters have all been organized in a communication policy vacuum. A framework of institutional commitment has not often supported and inspired these activities. Many happen because of the enthusiasm of one individual, and without the help and co-operation required across the institution. This is clearly wasteful and frustrating.

Very few museums have coherent and well-managed communication policies. Some have exhibition policies and some are now producing education policies. A few marketing strategies are emerging. A few audience development plans are being introduced. But how do these relate to each other? Are they informed by the objectives of the museum? And once the plans or policies are written, what are their chances of being implemented? If strong links to a variety of publics including the governing body, visitors, new audiences, schools, the media and industry are required to sustain the museum in its work, then the communicative functions of the museum will need to be better understood, and better managed.

This chapter first appeared in Eilean Hooper-Greenhill (1994), Museums and their Visitors, *London: Routledge, 35–53.*

REFERENCES

Alvarado, M., Gutch, R. and Wollen, T. (1987) *Learning the Media: an Introduction to Media Teaching*, Basingstoke and London: Macmillan Education.

Beevers, L., Moffat, S., Clark, H. and Griffiths, S. (1988) *Memories and Things: Linking Museums and Libraries with Older People*, Edinburgh: WEA South East Scottish District.

Cameron, D. (1968) 'A viewpoint: the museum as a communication system and implications for museum education', *Curator* 11(1): 33–40.

Duffy, C. (1989) 'Museum visitors: a suitable case for treatment', paper for the 1989 Museum Association of Australia conference.

Handy, C. (1990) *The Age of Unreason*, London: Arrow Books.

Hemmings, S. (1992) 'Chinese homes', *Journal of Education in Museums* 13: 33–4.

Hodge, R. and D'Souza, W. (1979) 'The museum as a communicator: a semiotic analysis of the Western Australian Museum Aboriginal Gallery, Perth', *Museum* 31(4): 251–67; see Chapter 4, this volume.

Knez, E. I. and Wright, G. (1970) 'The museum as a communication system: an assessment of Cameron's viewpoint', *Curator* 13(3): 204–12.

Lumley, R. (1988) *The Museum Time Machine*, London: Comedia/Routledge.

McQuail, D. (1975) *Communication*, London and New York: Longman

McQuail, D. (1987) *Mass Communication Theory, an Introduction*, London: Sage Publications.

McQuail, D. and Windahl, S. (1993) *Communication Models*, London and New York: Longman.

Miles, R. S. (1985) 'Exhibitions: management, for a change', in N. Cossons (ed.) *The Management of Change in Museums*, London: National Maritime Museum, 31–3.

Miles, R. S. (1989) *Evaluation in its Communications Context*, technical report 89–10, Jacksonville, AL: Center for Social Design.

Morgan, J. and Welton, P. (1986) *See What I Mean*, London and New York: Edward Arnold.

Morley, D. (1980) *The 'Nationwide' Audience: Structure and Decoding*, London: British Film Institute.

O'Neill, M. (1990) 'Springburn: a community and its museums', in F. Baker and J. Thomas (eds) *Writing the Past in the Present*, Lampeter: St David's College, 114–26.

O'Neill, M. (1991) 'The open museum', *Scottish Museums News* (Winter): 6–7.

Plant, A. (1992) 'Expression and engagement', *Journal of Education in Museums* 13: 12–15.

3

Learning in art museums: strategies of interpretation

Eilean Hooper-Greenhill

The museum audience is active. Museum visitors work to understand the objects that attract their attention. What do they do? What processes of interpretation do they use? And are their conclusions personal or social?

The processes of interpretation are discussed, using a painting as an example. The processes are explained through hermeneutic theory. These processes are further elaborated through the concept of 'interpretive communities'.

The implications of these ideas for museums are explored. This way of understanding how meaning is made is related to the transmission model of communication, and the disparities are pointed out.

THE PROCESSES OF INTERPRETATION

What happens when we encounter a painting and want to try to understand it? What is the process of trying to make meaning? In order to unpick this process, I want to draw on two areas of study: first, that involved in teaching in an art museum, and in working with many different groups of visitors to explore art objects; and second, the insights offered through some aspects of hermeneutics. In teaching at the National Portrait Gallery in London, I frequently found myself working with groups with the portrait of Elizabeth I known as the Ditchley portrait (see Plate 3.1). Using this as an example, I want first to consider the process of exploring the painting, and then second to reflect on how some of Gadamer's ideas, which are drawn from the philosophical approach known as hermeneutics (which, broadly speaking, means 'interpretation'), relate to and explain this process. Understanding processes of interpretation lies at the heart of education in art museums.

A first glance at the Ditchley painting presents an overall impression of a woman in a white dress who looks as though she lived in the past. As human beings, we tend at a basic level of species recognition to be attracted to faces, and it is the face that we focus on next. This is followed by a scan of the image as a whole, looking at both the figure and the background.

At this stage, we try to recognize some aspect of the painting in more detail, to try to make a connection with something that we already know and feel confident about. This might relate to any aspect of the work. It might include elements of the image in the painting, such as the woman herself, the historical style or period, or parts of

Plate 3.1 The Ditchley portrait of Elizabeth I, queen of England (courtesy of the National Portrait Gallery, London)

45

the background of the painting. Or it might be that we recognize this kind of image as a general class of objects (portraits).

We try to find something that we can either recognize or remember, or grasp through analogy. If we can make this preliminary connection, the meaning-making process continues. If there is nothing to connect with, we are likely to give up and stop trying. This failure to continue the meaning-making process can result in a shallow and rather negative experience, and one which might well reduce our self-confidence.

However, assuming that a basic link is made (we recognize that this is a Tudor costume, for example, or we are intrigued by the jewels on the dress) we begin to look further at the details of the painting to see if we can continue the process of recognition and meaning-construction. We might observe any detail of the painting (hairstyle, make-up, dress, jewellery, hands, feet, map, sky). We begin to attribute meaning to these details according to what we already know.

Children, for example, frequently observe that the woman is wearing a great many jewels, are intrigued, and deduce that she must be rich; they see that she is wearing an elaborate dress of a fine material, and has something like a crown on her head, and think that she may be a queen. It is clear that the style of the clothes is not contemporary, but historical. The woman is standing on a map. We may recognize some of the place-names as from the south of England. From all of this, most people conclude quite rapidly that the image is probably of an English queen, from a previous historical period.

The sky behind the figure in the painting is different on one side of the picture from the other, with clouds and a suggestion of lightning to the right and the sun attempting to shine through the clouds to the left. If we do not recognize the queenly figure as Elizabeth I (and many British people do, as the image of the Tudor queen is relatively familiar through having been seen in history books, in films and on television), we may be moved to ask ourselves what the sky might mean. Sometimes, in discussing the painting, a prompt is helpful at this point. A little historical knowledge is needed to link the image of Elizabeth to war with Spain, and a little art-historical knowledge is needed to know both that and how symbols can be used in paintings. However, it is a relatively simple step from this to understand that the sky is used in the painting to symbolize Elizabeth leading England through the storms of war to the sunny days of peace. The metaphors are still the same in late twentieth-century England. If it is known that at the end of Elizabeth's reign there was a continuous question as to who would succeed her, it is not difficult to conclude that the painting is a propagandist image, demonstrating her wealth, standing and military power. The painting asserts her continued fitness to rule.

This process of attributing meaning depends on prior knowledge; how far it goes depends on how much is known, and how well we are able to interrogate and use what is known. Information from a range of fields of knowledge might contribute to the construction of meaning in relation to this painting. These might include: English history, English myth, English painting, portraiture in general, clothing and costume, literature (especially Shakespeare), queens and their images, and children's stories.

Attitudes and beliefs also affect the interpretation of what is seen and known. Ardent republicans may interpret the image differently from passionate royalists; feelings about the importance of the incident in the English Channel during the invasion by the Spanish Armada are linked to nationalism and patriotism. Ideological convictions are deeply embedded in individual psyches and influence how meaning is made, and how interpretations are developed.

As constructivist learning theory confirms,[1] the construction of meaning depends on prior knowledge, and on beliefs and values. We see according to what we know, and we make sense or meaning according to what we perceive. In contrast to those who hold that knowledge is a body of objective facts, external to the knower, constructivism asserts that knowledge exists only through the process of knowing, and that meanings are constructed by individuals, and not found 'ready-made'. Thus in coming to know the Ditchley portrait, an individual response to the painting emerges, related to the resources and skills the viewer can bring to the process of looking.[2]

The process of making sense of a painting is a process of looking from the whole to the detail and back again. It is a process of oscillation between observation and deduction, a dialogue. The process is dialogic.[3] In the Ditchley portrait, for example, if we look closely at the feet, we notice that they don't really look as though they support the body. The feet protrude from underneath the skirt of the queen in a very unrealistic manner. Have they a function other than that of supporting the body? The feet do, in fact, serve to draw attention to the origins of the painting. Marked between them is the name of Ditchley, the country house belonging to Sir Henry Lee who commissioned the painting as a courtly gift for the queen as part of her visit to the house. The feet and the way in which they are painted raise questions. Once the answers to these questions are found, aspects of the historical context of the painting of Elizabethan portraiture, and of the life of a Tudor courtier emerge. Thus a focus on the detail contributes to our understanding of the whole, both of the object and of society. The portrait begins to be placed within its social context.

As the portrait becomes more familiar, we are able to consider it as part of the whole of society both now (today) and in the past. We relate the painting to what we know now. We recognize it as an image of a queen and as a portrait. We place the portrait within a suite of images (photographs and paintings) of queens. Both the concept (queen) and this idea of representing it through an image are familiar to us in the West in the late twentieth century.

At the same time, we relate the painting to what we know of the past. The image of the queen is placed within our ideas about and knowledge of Tudor royalty. If we have a developed and sophisticated knowledge of the way in which the cosmos was imagined during the Tudor period, we can see evidence in the painting for the Great Chain of Being and the place of the queen within this. If our image of Tudor England is less well informed, we will still relate the portrait to what we do know, calling on our impressions of the past. At the same time, the painting will itself influence our imagining of the past. Unless a rigorous process of interrogating these imagined impressions of the past is undergone, assessing this image in comparison with others, and relating the information gathered from the image to information gathered from other sources, then our views may be and remain incorrect. For example, we may assume that the jewels sewn on to the dress are paste, because we cannot imagine that anyone would really do this with genuine precious stones. It would take either a friendly expert, or some historical research, to correct this impression.

The process of making meaning moves both between the whole and the part of the object and between the present and the past, simultaneously. A dialogue is established between the whole and the part, the past and the present, which enables continual checking and rechecking, revision of ideas, trying-out of new ones and rejection of those that do not work.

The process of constructing meaning from the painting[4] is circular and dialogic. We are in a question-and-answer mode, a continuous process as the answers build on those questions that have already been asked and answered. This circular movement involves both the whole and the part, but also the present and the past. Meaning is constructed through this circular action, with modifications to the sense we construct being made constantly.

THE HERMENEUTIC CIRCLE

The process of meaning-making is explored in hermeneutic theory. Philosophical interpretation, or 'hermeneutics', is the name of the movement in philosophy that is concerned with how meaning is made.[5] Some of the major figures are Gadamer, Dilthey and Ricoeur.

The word 'interpretation' is used in this philosophical movement to mean the process by which individuals make sense of their experience. In discussing how we relate to objects (as above with the Ditchley Elizabeth), we were talking about what we saw and what sense we made of what we saw. The process of interpretation focused on the mental activity of the viewer.

In hermeneutics, then, meaning is constituted through a circular action, the hermeneutic circle, where understanding develops through the continuous movement between the whole and the parts of a work, and where meaning is constantly modified as further relationships are encountered (see Figure 3.1). The process of constructing meaning

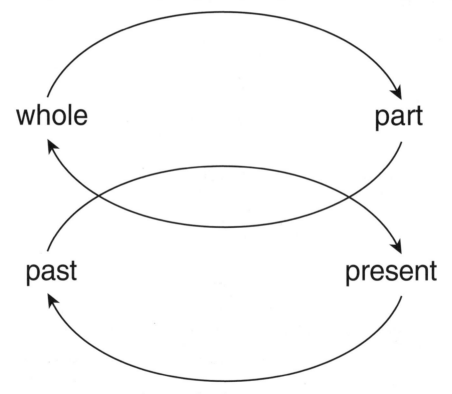

Figure 3.1 Hermeneutic circles, or circles of interpretation: interpretation, the construction of meaning, involves circular and dialogic processes that integrate the whole and the part, and the present and the past

is like holding a conversation. Any interpretation is never fully completed.[6] There is always more to say, and what is said may always be changed. The hermeneutic circle remains open to these possibilities and, in this sense, meaning is never static.

All interpretation is necessarily historically situated. Our own position in history, our own culture, affects meaning. Meaning is constructed through and in culture. Perception (what we see), memory (what we choose to remember), and logical thinking (the sense we choose to attribute to things) differ culturally because they are cultural constructs.[7]

For hermeneutic philosophers, meaning-making is shaped by the inevitability of prior knowledge; the effect of tradition, the past as it works in the present; the prejudices and biases that are part of being human; and the capacity to interrogate the past and to distinguish between productive and non-productive preconceptions (which are based on our prior knowledge).[8] This approach to knowledge and understanding is very close to that of constructivist learning theorists. Both propose that knowledge emerges through the interpretation of experience made by the knower, and is not an objective body of facts that can be transmitted. Both assert that knowers, or learners, or inter-preters, are active in the process of making sense of experience (including the formal or informal experience of learning). Both suggest that knowing is culturally inflected, and that in this sense knowledge is relative. Both stand against a transmission view of teaching or communicating. This transmission model works on the basis of know-ledge as external to the knower, as a discrete body of objective facts that may be transmitted through a linear process to the knower or receiver, who passively accepts the information. Both hermeneutics and constructivism wish to move away from this behaviourist model of learning, which is developed from a stimulus-response view of teaching and learning processes.[9]

INTERPRETIVE COMMUNITIES

To say that each individual makes sense of the world in his or her own way is to become open to the charge of extreme relativism. So far we have been talking about meaning-making as though it were an individual process; but although it often feels as though that is so, it is in fact a social process. Our individual strategies for making sense of experience are enabled, limited and mediated through our place in the social world.

We are all creatures of our particular time and place; we think and feel what appears to be natural to us, but this 'common sense' is 'natural' only to our particular time-period, geographical location, background and history.[10] Given that the process of interpretation involves prior knowledge, and that the world is known through culture, our interpretation will be that which fits our particular time and place in the world. What we know is what we need to know to enable us to take our place in a partic-ular society or group.

Different societies or groups require different knowledge bases and skills in order to exist. For example, on a recent visit to New Zealand, I felt 'out of it' because I didn't know about the musket wars, or the Treaty of Waitangi. If I went to a football match I wouldn't know how to evaluate the game, nor would I know the histories of the individual players. All communities, however defined, have their own ways of knowing, their own knowledge base and their own strategies for interpretation.

Literary theory tells us that, to the extent that we can identify a community of people who share interpretive strategies, we can identify 'interpretive communities'.

Interpretive communities are made up of those who share similar ways of reading objects, of identifying their significance and of pointing out their salient (relevant and important) features.[11] These strategies exist prior to the act of reading and therefore determine the shape of what is read. That is, you come to a painting (a book, an experience) with a set of 'reading strategies', and thus you know what to look for. According to what you look for, you will see certain things in certain ways.

Thus it is the interpretive strategy that determines the meaning of the object, and in many ways determines how the object is seen and what counts as the object in the first place.

For example, Hinemihi is a Maori meeting house now standing in the grounds of Clandon Park, a National Trust property near Guildford. To the National Trust, the house is seen as 'this work of art in our care', a collection of carved posts for which they have responsibility and a duty of custodianship. To the Maori community in England, Hinemihi is someone whom you should come and see when you are sick and unhappy and who will restore a sense of Maori identity. She is an important and well-remembered woman of the Ngati Hinemihi tribe, a place to bring visiting Maori relatives or friends.[12]

These two very different interpretations of Hinemihi stem from different attitudes to and definitions of art, different positions in and knowledge of history, and different attitudes towards the role of the past in the present. These knowledges, positions and attitudes result in different interpretive strategies, and we can immediately identify two very different 'interpretive communities'. Each knows the object in different ways, and those ways are both personal and social. The 'object' that is seen, which is the one and the same painted wooden structure, is not the same, but is both perceived, remembered and logically considered in completely different ways, and yet to each of these groups of interpreters, their way is 'common sense'.

The concept of 'interpretive communities' begins to explain this quite well. It is within interpretive communities that the meaning-making of an individual is tested, revised, supported and developed. The interpretive community both sets limits for and constrains meaning, and enables meaning.[13] Interpretive communities are not stable, but may change as people move from one to another. They may grow and decline as other things change.

INTERPRETATION IN THE ART MUSEUM

What are the implications of all that we have discussed for interpretation in the art museum? There are three main ideas to be considered: the relevance of hermeneutic approaches to understanding of the process of meaning-making; the importance of conceptualizing the audience as active in this dialogic process; and the concept of interpretive communities. One way of bringing this all together is to consider how interpretation is understood at the present time in the art museum.

There is a major difference of emphasis between the way the word 'interpretation' is used in theory (in hermeneutics and constructivism) and the way in which it is used in the museum. 'Interpretation', as understood by hermeneutics, is the mental process an individual uses to construct meaning from experience; *you* are the interpreter for yourself. Interpretation is the process of *constructing* meaning.[14] Interpretation is part of the process of understanding.

In the museum, 'interpretation' is a process that is undertaken on behalf of someone else. Museum staff undertake 'interpretation' for museum visitors. In other words, 'interpretation' is something that is done for you, or to you. A museum's interpretation officer could be one of many things – an education officer, a designer, or an exhibition officer. The emphasis is on the mediation between the collections and the visitors, but with, mostly, little understanding of the varying interpretive strategies that visitors might use.

Traditionally, in museums, the implicit model of communicating with the public is that of the transmission of objective bodies of authoritative facts to passive receivers. A more cultural and constructivist model may well be in place in the education department, but does not always influence thinking about visitors in curatorial circles.

If the ideas discussed in this chapter are accepted, then new ways of establishing and maintaining dialogues with visitors will be needed, and new ideas about how to link to the interpretive strategies employed by different communities will need to be developed. Some of the methods employed in the Young Tate project, which enable active meaning-makers to use their prior knowledge and their cultural experience to develop their own interpretive strategies that are validated by their specific interpretive communities, offer examples of some ways forward.

This chapter first appeared in Toby Jackson et al. (forthcoming) Young Tate, *Liverpool: Liverpool University Press and the Tate Gallery, Liverpool.*

NOTES

1 Hein 1995; Priest and Gilbert 1994; Russell 1994; Steffe and Gale 1995.
2 Csikszentmihalyi and Robinson 1990.
3 Dialogic – a dialogue between viewer and object (Jensen 1991: 41–3).
4 Here I am discussing the interpretation of a painting in relation to the image in the painting. It is, of course, also possible to interpret the painting as an object, in terms of its materials, provenance, etc., as it is for any object. The basic processes of interpretation are the same.
5 See Gadamer 1976a, 1976b, 1981; Gallagher 1992 (I am grateful to Viv Golding for this reference).
6 Any interpretation can never be fully completed. 'The discovery of the true meaning of a text or a work of art is never finished: it is in fact an infinite process' (Gadamer 1976b: 124). As errors in understanding are eliminated and as new sources of knowledge emerge, so meaning is a continuing process of modification, adaptation and extension. The hermeneutic circle is never fully closed, but remains open to the possibilities of change.
7 Ogbu 1995.
8 Gallagher 1992.
9 McQuail and Windahl 1993.
10 Belsey 1980.
11 Interpretive communities are made up of those who share interpretive strategies for writing texts, for constituting their properties and assigning their intentions (Fish 1980: 171).
12 Hooper-Greenhill (1998).
13 Fish (1980: 332): 'systems of intelligibility (e.g. literary system) constrain and fashion us and furnish us with categories of understanding with which we fashion the entities to which we then point' and (336) 'readers make meanings, but meaning makes readers' and (337) meaning is 'the ongoing accomplishment of those who agree to make it'.
14 Understanding is reached through the process of interpretation. Interpretation aims to uncover the meaning of a work through a dialogic relationship between the detail and the whole: 'the whole of a work must be understood from the individual words and their combinations, and yet the full comprehension of the detail presupposes the understanding of the whole' (Dilthey 1976: 115). Gadamer describes it thus: 'we must understand the whole in terms of the detail and the detail in terms of the whole. This principle [is applied] to the art of understanding' (Gadamer 1976b: 117).

BIBLIOGRAPHY

Belsey, C. (1980) *Critical Practice*, London and New York: Methuen.

Csikszentmihalyi, M. and Robinson, R. (1990) *The Art of Seeing*, California: J. Paul Getty Museum and Getty Center for Education in the Arts.

Dilthey, W. (1976) 'The rise and fall of hermeneutics', in *Critical Sociology: Selected Readings*, ed. Paul Connerton, Harmondsworth, Mx: Penguin Books, 104–16.

Falk, J. and Dierking, L. (eds) (1995) *Public Institutions for Personal Learning: Establishing a Research Agenda*, Washington, DC: American Association of Museums.

Fish, S. (1980) *Is there a Text in this Class? The Authority of Interpretive Communities*, Cambridge, MA and London: Harvard University Press.

Gadamer, H.-G. (1976a) *Philosophical Hermeneutics*, Berkeley: University of California Press.

Gadamer, H.-G. (1976b) 'The historicity of understanding', in *Critical Sociology: Selected Readings*, ed. Paul Connerton, Harmondsworth, Mx: Penguin Books, 117–33.

Gadamer, H.-G. (1981) *Reason in the Age of Science*, Cambridge, MA and London: MIT Press.

Gallagher, S. (1992) *Hermeneutics and Education*, New York: State University of New York Press.

Hein, G. (1995) 'The constructivist museum', *Journal of Education in Museums* 16 (1995): 21–3.

Hooper-Greenhill, E. (1997) 'Museum learners: active post-modernists', *Journal of Education in Museums* 18: 1–4.

Hooper-Greenhill, E. (1998) 'Perspectives on Hinemihi – a Maori meeting house', in *Colonialism and the Object*, ed. Tim Barringer and Tom Flynn, London and New York: Routledge, 129–43.

Husbands, C. (1992) 'Objects, evidence and learning: some thoughts on meaning and interpretation in museum education', *Journal of Education in Museums* 13: 1–3.

Husbands, C. (1994) 'Learning theories and museums: using and addressing pupils' minitheories', *Journal of Education in Museums* 15: 5–7.

Jensen, K. B. (1991) 'Humanistic scholarship as qualitative science: contributions to mass communication research', in *A Handbook of Qualitative Methodologies for Mass Communication Research*, ed. K. B. Jensen and N. W. Jankowski, London and New York: Routledge, 17–43.

McQuail, D. and Windahl, S. (1993) *Communication Models for the Study of Mass Communication*, London and New York: Longman.

Ogbu, J. U. (1995) 'The influence of culture on learning and behavior', in *Public Institutions for Personal Learning*, ed. J. H. Falk and L. D. Dierking, Washington, DC: American Association of Museums, 79–96.

Priest, M. and Gilbert, J. (1994) 'Learning in museums – situated cognition in practice', *Journal of Education in Museums* 15: 16–18.

Russell, T. (1994) 'The enquiring visitor – usable learning theory for museum contexts', *Journal of Education in Museums* 15: 19–21.

Steffe, L. P. and Gale, J. (eds) (1995) *Constructivism in Education*, Hove, Sussex: Lawrence Erlbaum Associates.

4

The museum as a communicator: a semiotic analysis of the Western Australian Museum Aboriginal Gallery, Perth

Robert Hodge and Wilfred D'Souza

Written by two lecturers in communication studies, the article forming this chapter examines the sign systems of an exhibition such as space, language, photographs and objects. The potentials and problems of the various signifying elements are discussed in detail and the capacity for deeply held attitudes to be revealed through the choices made by the writers and designers producing the exhibition is described.

The problems discovered in the case-study are identified as inherent in any act of communication. The communicative process is positioned within social, cultural and political contexts, and cannot therefore be considered outside of these contexts which shape our daily lives in very specific ways.

Museums exist for a variety of purposes. Mohammed Aziz Lahbabi, in his article 'The museum and the protection of the cultural heritage of the Maghreb', says: 'It is the function of museums . . . to be the living memory of the people and for the people.' Museums are not only protectors but also communicators of this living memory. A museum display is an exercise in one branch of the mass media, requiring a special kind of understanding of the processes of communication, namely the nature of mass communication systems. The essential thing to understand here is that mass communication is in some important ways an unnatural form of communication. We are all experts in natural communication, more expert than we are aware. We perform complex acts of communication with the confidence and unconsciousness born of long habit. So everyone is likely to adjust insufficiently to the major differences involved in a mass communication situation.

In a natural communication, typified by face-to-face conversation between two people of similar background, the main message of any one speaker is interpreted through this common background. It is backed up by innumerable supporting channels of communication (intonation patterns, gestures, expressions, etc.). It can be repeated, or parts of it emphasized, in the light of the hearer's response. The exposure-time of the message is controlled by the speaker, and is the same for speaker and hearer. Mass communication systems generally depart from all these conditions, and a museum display is no exception. This divergence from natural communication gives rise to characteristic kinds of communication failure or inappropriate communication in mass communications systems, which will be the main focus of attention in the present study.

Inappropriate communication here includes two basic kinds of breakdown: saying things you did not mean to say, as well as not quite getting across whatever it was you wanted to say. The first of these is very common and more insidious than the second, since for obvious reasons the communicator is less likely to be aware of its happening. Most of us realize that not all of our message is likely to reach target so we are inclined to react by raising the volume – like the well-known tourist strategy of speaking loudly to uncomprehending foreigners. But what if a 10 per-cent increase in message A (the intended meaning) can be achieved only at the cost of a 40 per-cent increase in message B, the meaning of which the speaker was not conscious?

In a traditional kind of museum, where exhibits are carefully organized into galleries and individual displays, there are certain features of the communication situation that make inappropriate communication more likely. One is the potential difference between communicator and communicatees. Visitors to a museum gallery may be different in age, class, sex, language and cultural background from the communicator and from each other. All these differences can be regarded as differences of language, and their effect is to stratify the whole display, so that the communicator's single message is received as a large number of different messages, some of them contrary to the original intended message.

This tendency of the single message to fragment is likely to be intensified by the existence of multiple channels of communication used in a display, which are required to substitute for the multiple channels of communication available in everyday conversation. The task for the communicator is a massive piece of translation, from a language he or she knows without realizing the knowledge of it into an artificial language system that neither he or she nor anyone else is thoroughly familiar with. Between conception and communication, then, there is likely to be many a slip. Communicators and public may seem at times as though they had seen entirely different exhibitions. Some diversity of response, of course, is natural and desirable, but it is well for the planner of a display to have some notion of the likely responses, and some responsibility for what the display is doing.

IDEOLOGY AND AIMS

As an example of a museum as communicator, we have taken one gallery, the Aboriginal Gallery of the Western Australian Museum, Perth which is administered by the local Western Australian state government. We are grateful for the generous assistance of the museum in compiling this study. Serving a population of 1,197,000, the museum is situated in Perth, the capital city, which has a population of 820,100. The Western Australian population is predominantly of European stock, with the Aborigines, the original inhabitants, now a dwindling minority.

In the past there has been open hostility between Aborigines and the newcomers, and there is continuing conflict over the role of Aboriginal culture in the Eurocentric dominant culture. An exhibition of this kind, therefore, necessarily has an ideological problem that interacts with the aims and effect of any possible display. The result is that the planners of the display show a characteristic kind of uncertainty about aims and unawareness of effects. This is only a particular instance of the general problem faced by museums that attempt to do justice to a minority culture or the culture of an oppressed or expropriated group within the society. However, any analysis of communication success has to know the answer to the question: Successful at communicating what? And it often happens that such a question asked very precisely brings out uncertainties or even contradictions in the general aims that affect the overall structure of a display.

Headings and introductory statements are clearly one place to start in determining the overall intention of a display, since this is where the member of the public will start. The title of this exhibition is 'Patterns of Life in a Vast Land'. This suggests a concern with the relation between humankind and the environment. 'Patterns' suggests a harmonious, aesthetically pleasing object of study, the plural indicating a diversity that adds to the aesthetic pleasure. The explanatory subheading narrows down the scope of this title. The 'Vast Land' becomes 'Western Australia', which is only one part of the 'Vast Land' covered. 'Patterns of Life' becomes 'The Story of The Aboriginal People'. Where 'patterns' suggests an arrangement of elements perceived at one time, 'story' suggests a narrative taking place through time, a kind of history. The explanatory description of the exhibition runs as follows:

> Europeans have inhabited Western Australia for a century and a half. But for tens of thousands of years this land has been the home of the aboriginal people and their ancestors. This exhibition is planned as a tribute to them, and as a record of the ways of life that served them so well, for so long.

The first two sentences discreetly mention the two races that have competed for possession of this country, and hint at claims of the Aborigines. 'Tens of thousands' is longer than a century and a half and 'home' is stronger than 'inhabited'. The tense 'has been the home' implies that it still is their 'home', which makes the Europeans who also 'inhabit' it seem like squatters. The impression that the exhibition has sympathy for the Aboriginal cause comes over clearly in the word 'tribute', which connotes a celebration or commemoration of the Aborigines by those conscious of a debt.

However, the display is both 'tribute' and 'record'. This dual function contains a potential contradiction. A record is a factual historical document, whereas a tribute is concerned to create an attitude that is favourable. What if the historical record is unflattering? What if facts are not enough to create the desired attitude? We have in fact four different though overlapping descriptions of the form of the exhibition: patterns, story, tribute, record. Two of these are concerned with pleasing, harmonious effects, two with factual, historical materials. The potential conflict here corresponds to the problematic dual function of the museum as educator: to correct prejudices, which are firmly rooted attitudes, and to overcome ignorance.

This preliminary analysis brings out the problems facing this display. The major messages we expect will concern key relationships, between humankind and the environment, European and Aboriginal, present and past, each of these relationships being blurred: and the thrust of the exhibition will be divided between scientific and educative, concerned with history and facts or with attitudes and values, as it presents Aboriginal life for a European and Eurocentred public.

SIGNS OF IMPORTANCE

One very general but very important message the display is designed to communicate is that an understanding of Aboriginal life is important. There are a number of resources, or sign-systems, that can be drawn on to indicate this meaning, for a display as a whole and for components of a display.

The location of notices and the size of the lettering on them comprise the two dimensions of one system of signs. The rule with size is, of course, that the larger the notice the more important the exhibit, 'larger' being relative to the norms for such notices. Other general signals of status include forms of conspicuous expenditure, lavish use of space being one important indicator of this. The Aboriginal gallery has a whole floor assigned to it, a sign of high status. Within the gallery there is free floor space, and room to move about the individual exhibits. This principle also indicates the relative importance of particular exhibits. In general, the more space there is, and the fewer the items in a given space, the more important the item or exhibit. In this gallery, top status is accorded to one component entitled 'The Aboriginal Way of Life', which is what the visitor sees first on entering the gallery (a sign of status), and which has the largest area in front of it, in absolute terms (a visitor can stand up to 40 feet [12 m] back from it); the opposite side has no competing exhibits for that large space.

Two other indicators of expense, and therefore status, in a museum display are the presumed cost of an exhibit and the deployment of technology. The difficulty of obtaining an exhibit is not usually made evident, though it could be. All that the members of the public have to go on is the distinction between artefacts, simulations and photographs. Of these, photographs are likely to be the low-prestige form, especially recent photographs, however much enlarged. Simulations if well done are high-prestige forms. Artefacts will tend to be intermediate in prestige, on their own. Technology will tend to add prestige. So a series of slides on a screen activated by a button will add prestige to the contents of the slides. Even simple technology, like lighting effects or machines that make things move, add to the status of the item, and cumulatively to the status of the gallery itself.

Indicators of status usually have the effect of drawing the attention of visitors to the item or exhibit concerned, and making it more likely to be remembered. However, there are two potential dangers with signs of status. One is that they make a kind of claim on the members of the public that has to be justified. That is, the public must feel that the items which the museum is signalling as important are important. Otherwise, they will at a subconscious level feel alienated from the museum's values, and the museum will have failed badly in its aim of changing the attitudes of the general public. The gallery section 'The Aboriginal Way of Life' illustrates the difficulties here. It has signals of importance due to position and space, as noted above, but it contains no rare objects, no recondite knowledge, nothing that seems special or difficult to obtain or worthy of close attention. This is because it is precisely the ordinariness and typicality of it that are important. However, the planner of an exhibition has to take care, with a potentially self-contradictory meaning like this, that he or she does not produce a display whose message cancels itself out: an important kind of unimportance.

A second danger inherent in the use of status signals is that they represent an intrusion by their user. They claim importance, but they are generally indeterminate as to the further questions: important to whom, and for what? Important to the museum, of course, but to the museum as representing the public, responding to demand, or the museum as teacher, educating the public, imposing more or less subtly its values on the public? Hugues de Varine-Bohan, in his article 'The modern museum: requirements and problems of a new approach', says:

> We would further plead that the museum should be selective and 'client-centred'. All too often present-day museums are regarded by their curators as providing 'lessons' for a homogeneous but perhaps non-existent public, a public which exists mainly in the curator's mind: a group of well-bred, culture-hungry, beauty-loving,

logically minded people with plenty of time to spare, inexhaustible physical stamina and, above all, at least an arts degree.

(de Varine-Bohan 1976: 139)

With such a gallery, which is designed as a 'tribute' to people who are themselves citizens of Western Australia, it is proper to ask the questions: important to whom, and for what? Against this pervasive evaluation by others of their culture, the value-judgements of the indigenous culture, which are so important a part of that culture, need to be prominent. The absence of Aboriginal signs of importance in this exhibition is a general though unconscious sign of the unimportance of Aboriginal values for the exhibitors. This kind of unintentional slight is probably widespread. Mohammed Aziz Lahbabi observes something similar in his article when he says:

Out of an alleged respect for tradition, the tendency was to see the indigenous culture in terms of fixed tastes and structures. Forms devoid of living substance. The structures of a vanished past cannot, however, help to overcome underde-velopment. Colonial domination took objectivity away from science and dispos-sessed the people of its authenticity.

(Lahbabi 1976: 148–9)

Some indications of status, such as the amount of space assigned to an item, are neutral between Aboriginal and European values, but others are not. In particular the use of technology and the products of white technology carries an ambivalent evaluation. It magnifies by association, but disparages by comparison. The signal transmitted can be 'We, the museum staff, are very skilful' rather than 'the Aboriginals are very interest-ing'. One example would be the display of spears, carefully arranged and labelled, superimposed on a picture of Aborigines holding spears. The photograph competes with the artefacts as though they were not interesting enough. The spears themselves form a set of parallel lines, losing their individuality and function in this rigid non-Aboriginal patterning. Similarly, the pattern of boomerangs is created by museum staff, which distracts attention from the patterns created by Aborigines on the boomerangs themselves.

CODES AND THEIR CAPACITY

The messages transmitted by a museum display come via many channels or media, each of which has a different communication potential. Kinds of message are often tied to a particular medium. For instance, messages about large numbers, or events over dif-ferent times or places, cannot easily be communicated through pictures, and conversely messages about qualities cannot easily be communicated by numbers.

The Aboriginal display uses the following main media: (1) objects and artefacts; (2) simulated environments; (3) photographs and slides; (4) diagrams; (5) labels and (6) writing. These media differ along a continuum with respect to their closeness to reality or their closeness to language. Artefacts are selected examples of reality, while language refers to reality but at some remove. We can generalize about this list of media, and say that the greater the predominance of earlier media the stronger will be the sense of reality being directly experienced. The distinctive mode of communi-cation for museums is through objects. Hugues de Varine-Bohan in his article expands on this emphasis and its value as follows:

The obtrusive image, the all powerful influence of words, bureaucracy, etc., must be counterbalanced. It is objects, real things, which will provide this antidote: the growing success, in every country, of nature reserves, the well-known popularity of zoos and botanical gardens and even the universal taste for tourism and for escaping to countries which are still 'authentic' show that such things meet a genuine need. What we said earlier also applies here: the man in the street is inundated with second-hand information which has been processed, arranged and commercialized: he wants not to be given but to be left free to choose for himself the first-hand information that he wants for its knowledge content.

(de Varine-Bohan 1976: 134)

Communication through objects and artefacts is generally less well understood than more developed forms. An artefact communicates by being what it is. It therefore communicates or signifies that perfectly. Potentially it is accessible to every sense. It can be seen, tapped, touched, handled, smelt and even tasted. This multisensual experience could communicate a complex and open set of messages with an incomparable vividness and immediacy. For instance, someone handling a *woomera* perceives directly what could be put in a large number of sentences: 'A *woomera* is made of wood, a hard wood with a distinctive resonance, hollowed out in the middle, between 1 and 2 feet [0.3 and 0.6 m] long, the point of balance near the middle' etc. The strength of artefactual communication is this immediacy and openness. The weakness is that these meanings are only potential, and are liable to disappear unless they are coded and retained in language. If a museum displayed only artefacts, without explanatory labels, neither museum nor public would know what had been communicated, which of course is bad communication. However, the strength of communication by objects and artefacts should not be underestimated. Precisely because it is pre-linguistic it is a kind of universal language, which can mediate between Aborigines and Europeans and communicate to all ages and classes of the public.

In a traditional kind of museum display, items tend to be kept behind glass cases. In Lahbabi's words:

> Museums seem to set a barrier between life and culture, appearing as places of contemplative silence. In North African museums, as things stand at present, a culture which enjoys official approval and prestige (because it is hermetic and above the general level) tends to co-exist with a culture which belongs more or less to the people. The co-existence is peaceful and neutral and there is neither complementarity nor interaction between the cultures.

(Lahbabi 1976: 146)

The glass barrier severely restricts the communication potential of objects and artefacts. They communicate only through one sense, the visual, that sense itself operating under certain restrictions, limited to a specific distance, angle of vision, etc. The eye with its high powers of resolution is the master sense, and visual cues can convey information to the other senses. However, this works abstractly, by inference, drawing on previous experience, and is inferior to direct experience by other senses. With rare or fragile items it would obviously be impracticable to allow items out of the display cases, but with some items that are common and robust, it ought to be possible to allow visitors to handle them, with suitable safeguards against theft or damage. A child who has picked up and handled a boomerang, for instance, tested its point of balance and felt its edge, will know more about boomerangs than a child who has gazed at one pinned down behind a glass plate. An exhibition intended to be accessible to the blind has to adapt in this way (Favière *et al.* 1976), and museums for the sighted should strive to incorporate such strategies. Simulated environments or reproduced objects have similar advantages over photographs. They are three-dimensional, which allows spatial information to be more fully coded. They have an advantage over reality in that scale can be controlled. This means, however, that scale is not communicated unequivocally in this medium. A *wiltja* shelter's size could not be deduced from the model shown.

Photographs have similar disadvantages, as a result of their greater flexibility. Their great strength as a communicating medium is that they can represent people and landscapes with something of the immediacy of artefactual communication. In a display concerned with the relations of humankind and the environment this is a crucial kind of message. Like an artefact, though, a photograph on its own cannot communicate abstract meanings. If we see a photograph of five Aborigines, for instance, we do not know what is meant to be interesting or important about them, or whether all Aborigines have the qualities claimed, or whether it is only particular individuals at a particular time.

Diagrams differ from photographs in that they contain only what is coded in them. Their strength is that they can contain in a visual form elements and relationships that are not simultaneous in space and time within a single perceptual frame. They can, therefore, communicate abstract meanings that are language-like, with something of the directness and immediacy of artefactual communication.

There are two kinds of use of language attached to museum displays: labels and full sentences. Full sentences have only the limitations of human language; which with all its imperfections is the best system of communication known to man. Labels, however, are very restricted in the kinds of meaning that they can communicate. Essentially they can communicate only two kinds of message: this is an X, or these are kinds of/parts of a Y. Labels are frequent in museum displays, including the one under review. It should be pointed out that labels give only a vocabulary, not a message. Labels on their own, therefore, cannot communicate any message about our relation to the environment, the major theme of the display.

Language itself can be categorized in a number of ways. Relevant here are two distinctions: between written and spoken language and between indigenous languages and the dominant language (in this case English). Spoken language (not written language read aloud, but language produced by and for oral communication) tends to have a different structure, and the majority of people even in a literate culture find it easier to process fully oral language. The language of the indigenous culture is another matter. One problem with using any single Aborigine language for such an exhibition is that there are so many distinct forms. However, if the aim of the exhibition is to convey an understanding of Aboriginal ways of life and attitudes to life, and their ways of thinking, some thought must be given to a way of conveying the qualities of their language: the sound of it and, more important, some of its syntactic and semantic resources, and the ways language functions in such a society; for example, how do Aborigines of the Bardi tribe say 'I am/he is stalking a kangaroo'? Such material could be presented attractively and it would help to correct the Eurocentric impression given by the display at present.

Lahbabi's description of the North African situation applies to all such cultures:

> A major part of the North African cultural heritage has come down to us by way of oral tradition. Music, song and poetry, for instance, are to a great extent anonymous and are passed in oral form during family or seasonal celebrations. It would be desirable for university research to be set up which, with the help of the regional museums, would be responsible for all oral arts and oral literature.

A healthy and militant North African culture cannot be envisaged unless the ground work is laid in this way.

(Lahbabi 1976: 146)

Given this aspect of museum communication, there are obvious advantages in the concept of the ecomuseum over more traditionally organized forms of display, if the concern is for total communication to a universal public.

COMBINING CODES AND MESSAGES

Language is the only medium that can communicate self-sufficient messages about the themes of the display; the patterns of life of the Aborigine people, their history and the relation between their way of life and the environment. The other media only communicate such messages in combination with language and each other. However, a museum must use more than language and photographs. Otherwise it will be no more than a walk-through book.

Objects and artefacts typically form the basis of a museum display, but on their own they contain none of the desired meanings. The aim of the display is to give the public access to a way of life through a collection of objects. The meanings that must be communicated concern relationships, involving one or more of the following: (1) origins, (2) manufacture, (3) use and (4) place in a system of values or meanings. Photographs plus artefacts and objects or texts can be used very effectively for (2) and (3). For instance, one photograph shows two women making a hair girdle, and wearing one, above a case that contains examples of them.

Photographs are used extensively in the display; one reason no doubt is that they are so cheap. Another justification is that they can represent many things that cannot be presented directly, and in particular they can show relationships between people and things, people and people, and people and the landscape. However, to communicate, photographs must be carefully chosen, and they must be supplemented by an appropriate text.

In general, photographs are an effective way of showing people making and using things. The relations between people and people present more problems for photographic communication. People in photographs can relate either to each other or to the viewer. In the latter case, the result is a posed photograph, which primarily communicates messages about the relation between photographer and photographee. This can be an interesting and significant message. Such a photograph also communicates messages about the social relations of the people concerned, but this is likely to be only the official version of these relationships. Unposed photographs can represent far more complex relationships.

The limitations of a photograph are that it shows only the disposition of bodies in space, whereas social relations are coded in many other ways, and even the language of spatial relations (who stands in front of whom, what distance expresses regret, or intimacy, etc.) is a code, relying on conventions that need to be translated for a viewer from a different culture. This difficult kind of meaning requires focusing sharply enough to pick up expressions and gestures, plus explanations of what these mean, as a key to interpretation.

Similar observations apply to the attempts to convey the relation between humankind and the environment. A photograph of a bare terrain is not enough, since this terrain constitutes both a set of problems and a resource for the Aboriginal people, having both positive and negative aspects. Careful selection and focusing plus verbal explanation are necessary to help visitors to see the meaning of this landscape for Aborigines, and its relation to their own lives.

Labels are always used in conjunction with something else, usually artefacts. Labels characteristically assign names and organize perception. These two functions can work together, or in opposition. The main heading of a showcase or sequence can help the viewer to grasp the separate items as part of a larger whole. However, a label attached to an item gives two things to attend to, and loads the memory, adding the name of the object as something to remember. This diverts attention from the rest of the display. The adverse effects are intensified if the label is a long way from the item, especially if it is attached via a number, through a numerical key. The only justification for this latter method occurs when the items make up a strong visual whole whose unity would be disturbed by prominence being given to labels. Otherwise, from a communication point of view it is unsatisfactory. In general, labels make exhibits easier to talk about, if they are learnt, but interfere with the strength and immediacy of response. But the messages conveyed by labels are only taxonomic; a label cannot convey a message about the theme of the display, which is concerned with relationships, functions and living.

Label size also affects the possibilities for coherence of a display. In general, if label and item are to be perceived as a single perceptual whole, then both must be decipherable from the same point in space. If the writing on the label is so small that a viewer cannot see the relevant item or exhibit even in peripheral vision, then the possibilities of meaning connecting with perception are reduced. Where letter size is so different that two adjacent messages cannot be read at the same time, the effect is again to fragment the whole. To illustrate with the opening words of the exhibition: the huge writing of 'Patterns of Life in a Vast Land' can be read at the same time as the smaller but still large writing of 'The Story of The Aboriginal People of Western Australia', and the large theme-picture of a group of Aborigines can also be seen within the same frame. However, the text beginning 'Europeans have inhabited . . .' is in smaller lettering that requires the viewers to stand so close to it that they cannot read the larger writing or take in the picture: so this is related only in an abstract way to these other components. The letter-size is influenced by the amount of text felt to be necessary, which is, of course, a decision to be made by the communicator, but the cost of a decision in favour of more text leads to fragmentation of the perceptual unity of a display.

STRATIFICATION OF THE MUSEUM PUBLIC

Visitors to the museum clearly have differences of age, class, educational background, sex and nationality, as well as differences of interest and intelligence. This creates problems for a mass communicator, since these differences all affect communication. They have an effect equivalent to differences in language. This stratificational effect is liable to interact with the differences in the media used in a display. In particular there is likely to be a polarization between communication through objects and communication through extended written prose. Communication that is strongly concrete and particular is known to be correlated with the young, and with the working class. It is reasonable to assume that communication through objects will be much more accessible to Aborigines than written elaborated language. So messages, and kinds of message, communicated through objects, or what could be called more generally the restricted codes, will be the main content of the display for at least three important groups of museum users. Such users will hardly be aware of the messages transmitted by what could be called the more elaborated codes or channels. Since, as we have seen, the majority of the messages concerned with the theme of the display are communicated mainly through elaborated-code media, this raises the worrying possibility that these messages are not reaching large numbers who would most need to receive them. A substantial proportion of visitors to this display are students, some very young, who would come into the category of restricted-code media users.

This suggests two areas for attention. One is to strengthen artefactual communication so that it can communicate the more abstract meaning and relationships desired. The other is to be more careful about the clarity and level of the explanatory material. Written language too can be a relatively more restricted form of elaborated code. The following text illustrates the difficulties of some of the language used:

> Life's Sacred Meaning
>
> In a time called the Dreaming, creative beings shaped the plants, animals, and landscapes; and established rules for Aboriginals to follow. The Dreaming is eternal, explaining the Aboriginal past, directing their present, and shaping their future.

Elaborated-code words here include 'creative beings', 'established', 'eternal' and 'directing', but the difficulty is not simply one of vocabulary. The syntax is difficult, more difficult than it appears on the surface because of a number of elisions. For instance, 'called' – who 'called' or 'calls' it this? Who is the subject of 'established'? We have to go right back to the mysterious 'creative beings'. And how can 'the Dreaming', which in the previous sentence was a time in the past, become 'eternal'? Even if it does, how can a time rather than a person 'explain' anything or direct or shape a present or future?

The result is a very difficult utterance, which would strain the capacity even of a university-trained elite to understand. The concept being conveyed is itself difficult, but this difficulty is concealed by the translation, which replaces interesting and important difficulties with extrinsic puzzles. Aboriginal ways of representing the concept might need supplementary explanations, they might need effort and imagination on the part of a European public even to be partially understood, but that effort and imagination are what a museum exists to foster. The language the museum has used is not deliberately difficult, and not untypical of the language used in this and other museums. It is natural that descriptions giving ideas or information from academic sources will be communicated in language that retains traces of that origin. The modern museum relies on a dedicated community of scholars to provide it with its intellectual basis. Inevitably exhibitions will make most sense in terms of the language and modes of thought of that community.

Leaving aside particular successes and failures of the exhibition we have looked at, the analysis brings out a number of points of fundamental importance in any museum display. The communication process is so pervasive and so unconscious that communication breakdown will be the rule, not the exception, and this breakdown will typically be invisible to communicators and public alike. The problems stem from the essential nature and functions of a museum, as an institution that must mediate between different communities and different cultures, offering its own physical and temporal unity as a guarantee that resolution of differences has occurred. A museum cannot suppress differences and antagonisms in the society it serves, however persuasive and sincere the image of reconciliation it offers may be. If it refuses to acknowledge these social realities in what it shows, they will silently determine what is seen. What is at issue is in some respects a failure to understand the complexities of the communication process, but this should not be regarded simply as ignorance of a set of communication techniques. Communication is inseparably bound up with habitual ways of thinking, feeling and seeing, which give definition to a culture and a community. Communication breakdown, then, is a consequence of the failure to mediate between the communities involved at the level of cultural differences. But total communication is an unattainable ideal for the modern museum, until all social differences have been eliminated and made all communication redundant.

This chapter first appeared as a paper in Museum *31(4) (1979), © UNESCO, 1979.*

REFERENCES

de Varine-Bohan, H. (1976) 'The modern museum: requirements and problems of a new approach', *Museum* 28(3).

Favière, J., Duczmal-Pacowska, H. and Delevoy-Otlet, S. (1976) 'The museum and the blind', *Museum* 28(3): 176–80.

Lahbabi, M. A. (1976) 'The museum and the protection of the cultural heritage of the Maghreb', *Museum* 28(3).

Part II
Learning in museums

This section contains papers which relate broadly across the area of learning in museums. The section begins by considering museum learners in the context of post-modernism and constructivist theories of learning. George Hein's chapter usefully examines a matrix of educational theories and looks at their assumptions and the results of these assumptions within museums.

This leads to a review of some of the philosophical and pedagogical issues involved in the interpretation of objects, with Hennigar Shuh describing some useful practical strategies for teaching through objects. The writing of worksheets offers further practical strategies, with a more generally applicable section on the range of questions that might be asked as part of a museum teaching strategy.

Specific audiences are considered, including children and adults, schools and communities, with multi-culturalism, multiple intelligences and differentiated learning styles described. These general learning characteristics can be usefully considered both in the planning and delivery of face-to-face teaching sessions, and in the development of exhibitions.

5

Museum learners as active postmodernists: contextualizing constructivism

Eilean Hooper-Greenhill

Constructivism has been enthusiastically taken up by museum educators in Britain, who use it as a contemporary theory that justifies the progressive teaching methods that have long been established in museums, although they are not always viewed favourably by governments.

Theories of education and theories of communication are compared and related, with the transmission and cultural approaches to understanding communication explained. The implications of the various theories are related to museum practices, both in the past and today.

ACTIVE AUDIENCES

In recent years the museum world has begun to accept that visitors are not a passive, homogeneous mass of people, 'the general public', but can be seen as individuals with their own particular needs, preferred learning styles and social and cultural agendas. The main characteristic of these individual museum visitors is that they make sense of things their own ways.[1]

The old passive 'general public' has become the new 'active audience'.[2] One of the ways that museum educationalists have begun to conceptualize this 'active audience' is through learning theory and, specifically, constructivism. Several papers in the *Journal of Education in Museums* in recent years have addressed this. The aim of this article is to link learning theory to communication and cultural theory. This will demonstrate that the move to conceptualizing museum visitors as active in the construction of their own knowledge is part of a much larger general paradigm shift represented by the move into the postmodern period. The active postmodern museum visitor can be explained in part through learning theory, but also through theories of communication and through literacy or cultural theory. Although only a brief introduction to some ideas, it is fascinating to see how fashionable museums and galleries have become recently as sites for research, much of which locates its approach in postmodernism and poststructuralism.

However, trying to understand local changes in museum education in the context of larger social change is important not only to discover new theories and research topics. There are also practical outcomes. A better understanding of how what we do on a daily basis relates to what others are doing and thinking in other fields helps to inform decision-making, set a framework for improving practice, and offer broad-based arguments for policy shifts. Museums are poised to play a large and exciting role in the postmodern world, if they are able to move successfully from their modernist roots, and this is the area where museum educators can make a substantial contribution.

EDUCATION THEORIES

George Hein has pointed out[3] how theories of education are composed of theories of knowledge (epistemologies) and theories of learning. A positivist, or realist, epistemology understands knowledge as external to the learner, as a body of knowledge absolute in itself. Knowledge is defined as that which can be observed, measured and objectified. A constructivist epistemology, on the other hand, understands knowledge as constructed by the learner in interaction with the social environment. Subjective interpretation cannot be avoided; it is part of what knowing is about.[4] Behaviourist learning theory understands learning as the acquisition of facts and information in an incremental way, while constructivism sees learning as the selection and organization of relevant data from cultural experience.[5]

These two broad approaches to epistemology and to learning processes underpin the interpretation of the role of the teacher. If we think of knowledge as being a body of knowledge external to the learner, and the learning process as being the acquisition of this body of knowledge, the task of teaching is to transmit the knowledge to the learner. The learner is seen as 'the empty vessel to be filled', as cognitively passive, as the receiver of knowledge transmitted by the teacher. However, if we think of knowledge as being actively produced by the knower, and we see the process of coming to know as an activity of mind within a social and cultural framework (as suggested by Piaget, Bruner and Vygotsky[6]), the role of the teacher is then recast as that of a facilitator or an enabler.

There are few people working in museum education who would not adopt some version of the constructivist view. The role of the museum educator is indeed in the facilitation of active learning through the handling and questioning of objects, and through discussions linked to concrete experiences. Social and cultural contexts for learning are well exemplified in museums, and although more research studies are needed to demonstrate the wealth of interpretations visitors make, some evidence does exist to show how unpredictable and idiosyncratic these can sometimes be.[7] The museum, in the person of the educator, may act as facilitator within a constructivist paradigm in a museum education context. However, in other aspects of the museum's relationship with its publics, the museum may take a more didactic stance, informed by a more positivistic epistemology.

Theories of active learning, including constructivism, are relatively recent. Histories of approaches to learning and teaching show how schooling has not been designed to facilitate individual learners, but at times to process a mass of students, viewed as a fixed structural unit, all at once.[8] During the eighteenth and nineteenth centuries, a positivist view of knowledge as objective, external and transmissable, with the teacher as the knower and the learner as passive and uninformed, prevailed. Learning consisted of the accumulation of facts and information, such that an 'educated man'[9] was one who was able to talk from a wide-ranging set of references, which were generally drawn from a narrow view of what counted as 'culture'. Today, we are increasingly valuing people who are able to think effectively and act appropriately across a variety of cross-cultural environments. Depth of high cultural information is less valued than breadth of cross-cultural experience. The shift from positivism and behaviourism to constructivism can be seen as a process which has happened across time, and it is still ongoing.

COMMUNICATION THEORIES

Shifts in ways of thinking about the processes of communication in the nineteenth and earlier twentieth centuries and today can also be seen. We can identify two broad approaches to conceptualizing communication: the transmission model and the cultural model.[10]

The transmission model sees communication as a process of imparting information and sending messages, transmitting ideas across space from a knowledgeable information source to a passive receiver. A geographical metaphor is used, that of sending information across space from one point to another. This is a metaphor of transportation, the sending of signals and messages over a distance for the purposes of control. Semaphore is a good example, or, of course, the telephone message. It is no coincidence that the transmission view of communication becomes more powerful during the age of exploration and discovery. Social processes made possible by this centre-margin paradigm include colonialism and imperialism.

As communication studies began in the early years of the twentieth century, the analytical focus emphasized the technology of communication, the agencies and techniques involved. The social and cultural implications were not considered. By the 1940s a model for communication as transmission had been developed, where the process of communication was conceived as linear, the definer of the content of the message was the transmitter or communicator, and the receiver of the message was expected to receive passively the information as it was sent (see Figure 5.1).

Referring back to education theory, it is clear that a realist and positivist epistemology and a behaviourist learning theory underpin this model. This transmission model can be applied to the process of exhibition production in museums[11] where the exhibition originator, frequently a curator, working on his or her own, defines the message, selects the objects and writes the text, and then passes all this as a fixed unity to the designer; later the educator is expected to find ways of making the exhibition relevant to visitors (see Figure 5.2). At no stage is the target audience considered or planned for: it is an exhibition 'for the general public'. This method of exhibition development, where the internal processes of the museum are carried out with no external reference, and with no concrete or focused consideration as to how the exhibition is to be used, is long-established and is still to be found in many museums and galleries.[12] The link back to communication and educational theory begins to explain why many of them fail.

The second view of communication is the ritual or cultural view. Communication is understood as a process of sharing, participation and association. This view can be

Figure 5.1 Simple model of communication as transmission

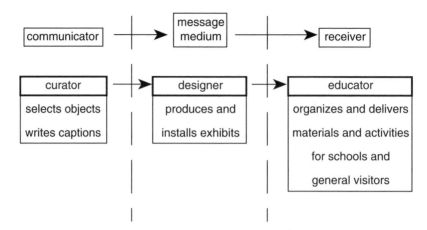

Figure 5.2 The simple communication model applied to exhibition development

traced back so far that dictionaries frequently list it as 'archaic'. It is related to sacred ceremonies as ritual, and to the mutual communicative ritual.

Communication is understood as a series of processes and symbols whereby reality is produced, maintained, repaired and transformed.[13] This view proposes that 'reality' has no finite identity, but is brought into existence, *is produced*, through communication. As we represent our beliefs and values through cultural symbols (words, maps, models), so we shape reality itself. Symbolic systems (art, journalism, common sense, mythology, science) construct, express and convey our attitudes and interpretations of our experience. Reality is therefore continually defined and redefined within negotiated frameworks or 'interpretive communities'.[14] The concept of 'interpretive communities' makes it possible both to achieve and to explain social change.

'What we know' is produced through our interpretation of our individual experience, but also through the testing and refining of our interpretation within significant communities. Where exhibitions such as 'The Peopling of London'[15] and 'Art on Tyneside'[16] have been produced in conjunction with audiences and in collaboration with interested individuals and groups, an 'interpretive community' comes into being, and through negotiation, a shared experience presents one or more impressions of 'reality'.[17]

This view of communication is not concerned with transmitting messages across space for the purposes of power and control; communication is understood as a cultural process that binds people together within particular space-frames, and as part of specific 'ritual'[18] procedures. It is concerned with the negotiated production, rather than the imposition, of meaning. Meanings are accepted as plural, rather than singular, open to negotiation, diverse rather than unified, and are seen as legitimately subjective.

Although this view of communication has ancient roots, it has not been dominant in Western thinking during the modern period. During the last 200 years, commonality and negotiated meanings have been superseded by the move to impose single unified world-views, defined by those who hold power in the communication process.

Putting learning theories and communication theories together, and considering their historical shifts, we can tentatively begin to see that during the last 200 years or so, a positivistic epistemology, a didactic learning theory and a transmission view of communication have prevailed. The learners, or receivers, of the transmitted knowledge were considered to be cognitively passive, and were regarded as an undifferent mass.[19]

Gradually during the last half-century, and gathering pace in the last 20 years can identify a move in education and communication theory towards acknowledging people as active in making sense of their social environments, towards acknowledging both that plural views exist and that they are all legitimate. Similar shifts are evident across a range of academic fields: literary theory,[20] archaeology,[21] art history[22] and science.[23] We are in fact in the middle of a paradigm shift, from the modern to the postmodern period.

THE MODERN AND THE POSTMODERN[24]

Museums as we know them today, are the creations of the Enlightenment, institutions that came into being in what we now characterize as the modern period. During the modern period, reason was invoked to supplant the superstitions and subjective knowledges of earlier times.[25] Attempts were made to construct knowledge that could be relied upon at all times and in all places; grand narratives (metanarratives[26]) were developed that stood as valid outside the context of the site from which they were spoken; institutions such as museums were established to spread out, as though upon a table, those things that could be observed, measured, classified, named and that presented a universally valid and reliable picture of the world.[27]

Now, of course, we understand knowledge as historically contingent; we accept that the site from which knowledge is produced relates to what counts as rational. Feminist critique has exposed the modernist metanarratives, one of which is the primacy of the male, as unsustainable;[28] postcolonial approaches have demonstrated the Eurocentric core of much of the history and culture that we take for granted in the West.[29] The certainties of modernism have been replaced by the fluidity of postmodernism, and we are still trying to understand what this means, in terms of how society should be organized. For museums, some relevant questions are the following. How should we organize, or reorganize, the past? What stories can be told about the past and the present, and who can legitimately tell them? How do we deal with artefacts collected at a time when the language used about them was considered to be unproblematic, when now we see that what we say influences how they are seen? How do we enable people to use museums for self-development and self-empowerment and self-directed learning? And what are the social uses of museums at the present time?

All these questions can be tied back to the implications of contemporary learning theory. If we take constructivism seriously, it is vital to explore its explanatory power, to probe its relationship to museum learning and experience. It is through the disseminated results of carefully carried-out research that we can begin to develop the 'interpretive community' that will be able to affect change.

This chapter first appeared as a paper in Journal of Education in Museums *18 (1997): 1–4.*

NOTES AND REFERENCES

1 Silverman, L., 'Visitor meaning-making in museums for a new age', *Curator* 38(3) (1995): 161–70.
2 The 'active audience' is a concept from communication/media studies; see Marris, P. and Thornham, S., *Media Studies: a Reader* (Edinburgh: Edinburgh University Press, 1996). I find the concept quite a useful shorthand, although it is premised on the transmission view of the communication process, discussed later in this chapter.

3 Hein, G., 'The constructivist museum', *Journal of Education in Museums* 16 (1995): 21–3. See Chapter 6, this volume.

4 There is a great deal to be said here about how individual knowledge is validated as social knowledge. I am currently playing with Fish's notion of 'interpretive communities', which is based in literary theory; see Fish, S., *Is there a Text in this Class? The Authority of Interpretive Communities* (Cambridge, MA: Harvard University Press, 1980). Foucault's 'interpretive analytics', which relates to discourse theory, is also of great relevance; see Dreyfus, H. and Rabinow, P., *Michel Foucault: beyond Structuralism and Hermeneutics* (Chicago: University of Chicago Press, 1982).

5 Hein, G., *Learning in the Museum* (London: Routledge, 1999), Ch. 2.

6 Russell, T., 'The enquiring visitor: usable learning theory for museum contexts', *Journal of Education in Museums* 15 (1994): 19–21; Hinton, M., 'Handling collections: a whole museum issue', *Journal of Education in Museums* 14 (1993): 16–19.

7 Worts, D., 'Extending the frame: forging a new partnership with the public', in Pearce, S. (ed.) *New Research in Museum Studies*, Vol. 5 (London: Athlone Press, 1995), 164–91.

8 Bernstein, B., 'Open schools, open society?', in *Schooling and Society: a Sociological Reader* (Milton Keynes: Open University, 1971), 166–9.

9 This is, of course, a concept that carries a freight of gender, class and racialized assumptions.

10 Carey, J., *Communication as Culture: Essays on Media and Society* (Boston, MA: Unwin Hyman, 1989), 13–36.

11 See, for example, Cameron, D., 'A viewpoint: the museum as a communications system and implications for museum education', *Curator* 11 (1968): 33–40, and Miles, R., 'Exhibitions: management, for a change', in Cossons, N. (ed.) *The Management of Change in Museums* (London: National Maritime Museum, 1985).

12 See Hodge, R. and D'Souza, W., 'The museum as a communicator: a semiotic analysis of the Western Australian Gallery, Perth', in this volume, pp. 53–63, for an example of an exhibition that treats the social groups and the cultural histories with which it is concerned as the property of the museum.

13 Carey, *Communication as Culture*, 23.

14 Fish, *Is there a Text?*

15 Merriman, N., 'The "Peopling of London" project', in Hooper-Greenhill, E. (ed.) *Cultural Diversity: Developing Museum Audiences in Britain* (London and Washington: Leicester University Press, 1997), 119–48.

16 Millard, J., 'Art history for all the family', in Hooper-Greenhill, E. (ed.) *The Educational Role of the Museum*, 1st edn (London: Routledge, 1994), 152–6.

17 This is not to deny that it is possible and indeed likely that interpretive communities will disagree with each other. As long as any community is large enough and vociferous enough to sustain its own point of view, this interpretation will remain one among the many options of socially possible ways of knowing. There is an interesting and important dialogic relationship between the individual subject and the group in the construction of knowledge.

18 This is used metaphorically; see Carey, *Communication as Culture*.

19 Although this might have been the dominant mode of social control through education and communication (and museums played their part in this), this does not mean to say that resistance was impossible, nor that more liberal intentions were not to be found in social actions, as, for example, in establishing a museum.

20 Fish, *Is there a Text?*

21 Tilley, C. (ed.) *Reading Material Culture: Structuralism, Hermeneutics and Post-structuralism* (Oxford: Blackwell, 1990).

22 Frascina, F. and Harris, J., *Art in Modern Culture: an Anthology of Critical Texts* (London: Phaidon, in association with the Open University, 1992).

23 The science as culture debate is relevant; and of course, constructivist learning theory is largely based in science education; see Steffe, L. and Gale, J. (eds) *Constructivism in Education* (Hillsdale, NJ: Lawrence Erlbaum Associates, 1995).

24 Whole libraries have been written on what these two words mean! I refer below to some work I have found useful.

25 Best, S. and Kellner, D., *Postmodern Theory: Critical Interrogations* (London: Macmillan, 1991); Wheeler, W., 'The Enlightenment effect', a Signs of the Times discussion paper, April 1997 (Signs of the Times, PO Box 10684, London N15 6XA); also available in Leicester University Library.

26 Lyotard, J. F., 'Answering the question: what is post-modernism?', in Jencks, C. *The Post-modern Reader* (London: Academy Editions, 1992), 138–50.

27 Hooper-Greenhill, E., *Museums and the Shaping of Knowledge* (London: Routledge, 1992).

28 Nicholson, L., *Feminism/postmodernism* (London: Routledge, 1990).

29 Williams, P. and Chrisman, L., *Colonial Discourse and Post-colonial Theory: a Reader* (New York and London: Harvester/Wheatsheaf, 1994); Ashcroft, B. *et al.*, *The Post-colonial Studies Reader* (London: Routledge, 1995).

6

The constructivist museum

George E. Hein

This is a second chapter on constructivism and how to contextualize it. Constructivism has become influential in America and elsewhere as well as in Britain.

This paper discusses this particular theory of education in the context of other approaches. Theories of education are shown to comprise both theories of knowledge and theories of learning. Placing these on a matrix, the writer explains how different ways of understanding knowledge and learning underpin different kinds of museum.

The constructivist museum is shown to be the most appropriate approach today.

INTRODUCTION

Current education literature is dominated by discussions of constructivism.[1] This new name for a set of old ideas has major implications for how museums address learning. Constructivism is particularly appropriate as a basis for museum education if we consider the wide age-range of museum visitors. How can we accommodate this diverse audience and facilitate their learning from our objects on their voluntary, short visits?

THE ELEMENTS OF ANY THEORY OF EDUCATION

In order to understand constructivism, it is useful to consider the nature of any theory of education. As two 1994 articles in the *Journal of Education in Museums* pointed out,[2] an educational theory consists of two major components: a theory of knowledge and a theory of learning. In order to consider how a museum is organized to facilitate learning, we need to address both *what* is to be learned and *how* it is to be learned.

Our beliefs about the nature of knowledge, our *epistemology*, profoundly influence our approach to education. It makes a difference whether we believe that knowledge exists independently of the learner, as an absolute, or whether we subscribe to the view that knowledge consists only of ideas constructed in the mind. Plato believed in the existence of ideal forms, independent of the learner. Thus, for him, learning consisted of arriving at knowledge through an intellectual process. Conversely, Berkeley believed that knowledge existed only in the mind of the knower. Thus, he answered in the negative the hypothetical question about the sound of a tree falling in the forest when no one is there to hear it. We can represent this epistemological dichotomy as a continuum, with the extreme positions at each end, as illustrated in the diagram.

Knowledge		Knowledge
independent		in the mind
	Theory of knowledge	
of learner		constructed
(realism)		by learner

The second component of an educational theory encompasses our beliefs about how people learn, our *psychology of learning*. As was the case for the epistemological domain, two extreme positions are possible. One assumes that learning consists of the incremental assimilation of information, facts and experiences, until knowledge results. This view leads to a behaviourist position; to the conclusion that learning consists of the addition of a myriad number of simple associations (responses to stimuli) and that the resultant 'knowing' is simply the aggregate of these small steps. Usually associated with this view is the belief that the original condition of the mind is a *tabula rasa*, and that all that is known has been acquired through experience. Locke is the best-known proponent of this view. A diametrically opposed view of learning postulates that the mind constructs schemata and that learning consists of selecting and organizing from the wealth of sensations that surround us. This synthetic view of learning is exemplified by Piaget's work. Proponents of this view also usually take the position that certain structures, such as learning language, are part of the anatomy with which we are born.[3]

This second dimension of educational theory can also be represented by a continuum along the dimension of the process of learning, as shown in the diagram.

Learning is		Learning is
incremental		constructing
	Theory of learning	
adding to a		meaning
tabula rasa		

These two dimensions of any educational theory can be combined to produce a diagram that describes four possible combinations of learning theory and epistemology. Figure 6.1 illustrates this combination. Each of the quadrants represents a different approach to education. One familiar position is represented by the top left quadrant, which I have labelled traditional lecture and text. Within this traditional view of education, the teacher has two responsibilities. First, he or she must understand the structure of the subject, the knowledge that is to be taught. This structure, the logical organization of the material, is dictated by the context that is to be learned. Much of the intellectual work of the Western world since the Renaissance has been devoted to elaborating systematic domains of knowledge with the assumption that the resulting schemata referred to something that existed independently of the minds that organized it. This intellectual work attempted to develop laws governing the movement of the solar system, classifications of plants and animals, or rules for the organization of societies that would be true under all conditions, independent of the humans that developed them.

The second responsibility of the traditional teacher is to present appropriately the domain of knowledge to be taught, so that the student can learn. Thus, there is a logical order of teaching dictated by the subject to be taught that would make it easiest to learn. The concept of a linear textbook, a great nineteenth-century invention, is predicated on this view of learning. The author presents material in a logical

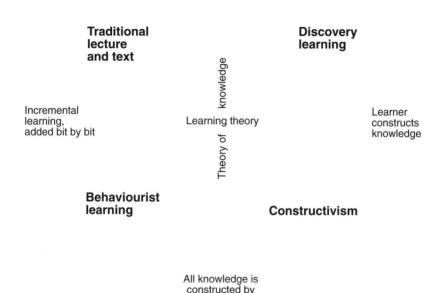

Figure 6.1 Four possible combinations of learning theory and epistemology

sequence, starting with the simplest[4] elements of the subject and moving on to more complex, until the entire field is covered. This approach to education can lead to 'The plain, monotonous vault of a school room', containing 'the little vessels then and there arranged in order, ready to have imperial gallons of facts poured into them until they were full to the brim'.[5]

A second educational position, represented on the top right quadrant of Figure 6.1, is discovery learning. It subscribes to the same positivist belief about knowledge as the previous one, but it takes a dramatically different view about how this knowledge is acquired. Proponents of this position argue that people construct knowledge themselves, they come to realize concepts and ideas as they build them up using personal, mental constructions. Thus, they also can acquire misconceptions. Proponents of discovery learning believe that in order to learn, students need to have experience; they need to do and see rather than to be told. Rather than organize the subject-matter based on its logical structure, from the simplest to the more complex, the teacher organizes it so that it can be experienced. Pedagogic simplicity takes on a practical aspect rather than an intellectual one. But the purpose of this hands-on approach is still for the student to comprehend ideas and concepts that are independent of the learner. Through experience, misconceptions will be replaced by correct conceptions.

Constructivism, the bottom righthand corner, represents still another quadrant of the diagram. Constructivism argues that both knowledge and the way it is obtained are dependent on the mind of the learner. This view, based on idealist epistemology as well as developmental psychology, and in recent years supported by research in cognitive psychology, comes as a shock to those who wish to preserve the idea of knowledge independent of individual learners or communities of learners. It has been called *radical* constructivism.[6] Proponents of constructivism argue that learners construct knowledge as they learn; they do not simply add new facts to what is known, but constantly reorganize and create both understanding and the ability to learn as they interact with the world. Further, the knowledge that is constructed through this process is individual or social, but has no ontological status outside the mind of the knower.

There is, of course, a fourth position illustrated in Figure 6.1, a position based on the belief that knowledge is gained incrementally but need not have existence outside the learner. Simple behaviourism fits into this quadrant, since behaviourism was originally a psychological learning theory and made no claims about the status of the knowledge gained from responses to stimuli.

THE CONSTRUCTIVIST MUSEUM

The educational positions outlined above can be applied to museums. For any consideration of learning in museums, we can ask an epistemological question: What is the theory of knowledge applied to the content of the exhibitions? We also need to ask a question about learning theory: How do we believe that people learn? These two components of our museum educational theory will lead to a set of four positions, similar to the ones described above, each of which represents a different kind of museum. These are illustrated in Figure 6.2.

The Systematic museum, represented in the upper left quadrant, is one based on the belief that

1 the content of the museum should be exhibited so that it reflects the 'true' structure of the subject-matter, and
2 the content should be presented to the visitor in the manner that makes it easiest to comprehend.

Examples of museums organized around systematic principles are common. The Deutsches Museum in Munich was intended to illustrate the structure of the sciences. Similarly, the Harvard Museum of Comparative Zoology was designed by Louis Agassiz to refute Darwin by illustrating the 'true' classification of animals. The National Portrait Gallery, for the most part, hangs its paintings chronologically on the assumption that this order will make most sense to its visitors. Similarly, it is common for exhibits to present material in a single, orderly manner deemed by the exhibit designers to be best suited for visitors to learn the message of the exhibit.

In contrast, proponents of the Constructivist museum would argue that:

1 the viewer constructs personal knowledge from the exhibit, and
2 the process of gaining knowledge is itself a constructive act.[7]

Examples of constructivist museums are harder to find, but exhibits that allow visitors to draw their own conclusions about the meaning of the exhibition are based on this constructivist principle. There is also an increasing number of exhibitions that are designed so that multiple paths are possible through the exhibit and the learner (visitor) is provided with a range of modalities to acquire information.[8]

Within this alternative and diametrically opposed educational view, the logical structure for any subject-matter and the way it is presented to the viewer depend not on the

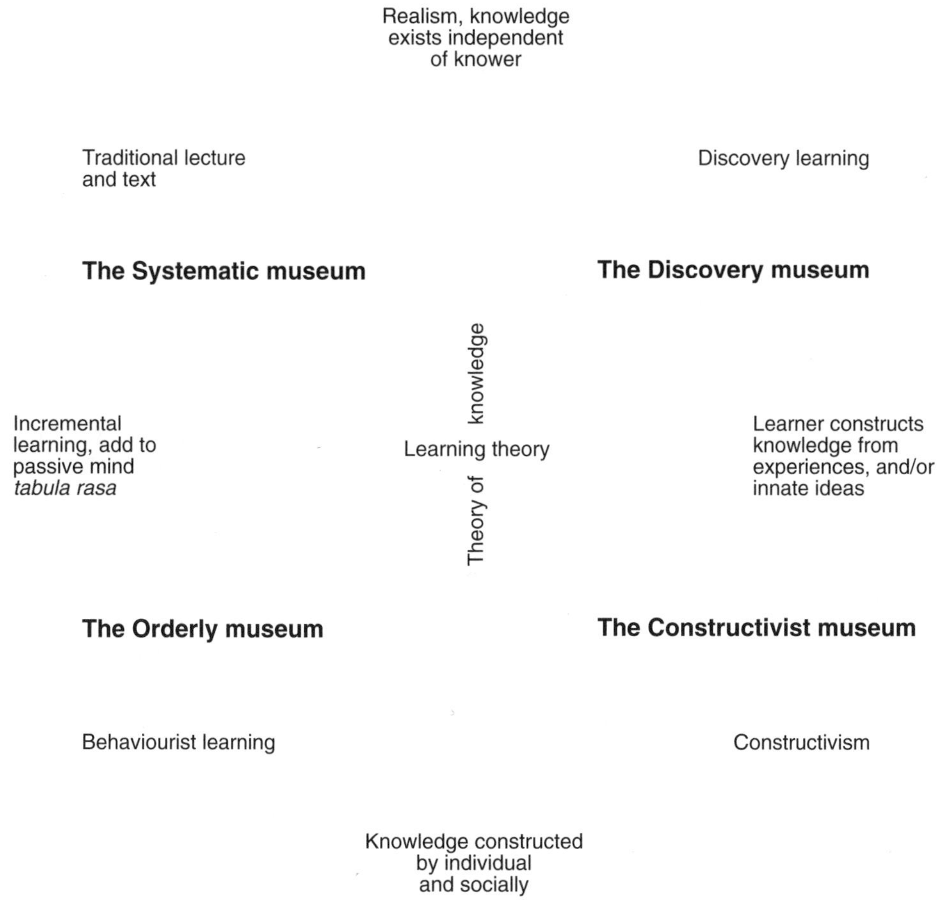

Realism, knowledge
exists independent
of knower

Traditional lecture
and text

Discovery learning

The Systematic museum

The Discovery museum

Theory of knowledge

Incremental
learning, add to
passive mind
tabula rasa

Learning theory

Learner constructs
knowledge from
experiences, and/or
innate ideas

The Orderly museum

The Constructivist museum

Behaviourist learning

Constructivism

Knowledge constructed
by individual
and socially

Figure 6.2 Four different kinds of museum

characteristics of the subject or on the properties of the objects on display, but on the educational needs of the visitor. In such a museum, it is not assumed that the subject-matter has an intrinsic order independent of the visitor, or that there is a single way for the visitor best to learn the material. Constructivist museum exhibits have no fixed entry and exit points, allow the visitor to make his or her own connections with the material and encourage diverse ways to learn.[9]

THE CHARACTERISTICS OF THE CONSTRUCTIVIST MUSEUM

What does a Constructivist museum look like? The lack of predetermined sequence has already been mentioned, as has the use of multiple learning modalities. Howard Gardner had the Constructivist museum in mind when he used the museum as a model for education.[10] Another component of the Constructivist museum would be the opportunity for the visitor to make connections with familiar concepts and objects. In order to make meaning of our experience, we need to be able to connect it with what we already know. Constructivist exhibits would encourage comparisons between the unfamiliar and the new. Inviting South Asian immigrant women into the V&A to design and make their own embroidered tent hangings[11] can achieve the aim of making the museum more accessible to the community. Inviting hundreds of youngsters from diverse countries to make exhibits about their local rivers and to share them in a grand festival[12] can help them all learn about each other's cultures.

CONCLUSION

Constructivist educational theory argues that in any discussion of teaching and learning the focus needs to be on the learner, not on the subject to be learned. For museums, this translates into the dictum that we need to focus on the visitor, not the content of the museum.

Museums are remarkable sites for learning. Their power for and influence on people are attested by the amazing learning associated with them. Individuals can recount instances of epiphany-like experiences in all types of museums.[13] Yet, the museum experience, on the whole, is fleeting and elusive.

By considering both the epistemological basis for our organization of exhibitions and the psychological basis for our theory of learning, we can develop museums that can respond to the dispositions of our visitors and maximize the potential for learning. The Constructivist museum acknowledges that knowledge is created in the mind of the learner using personal learning methods. It allows us to accommodate all ages of learning.

This chapter first appeared as an article in Journal of Education in Museums *16 (1995): 21–3.*

NOTES AND REFERENCES

1 Brooks, J. G. and Brooks, M. G., *The Case for Constructivist Classrooms* (Alexandria, VA: Association for Supervision and Curriculum Development, 1993); Steffe, L. P. and Gale, J. (eds) *Constructivism in Education* (Hillsdale, NJ: Lawrence Erlbaum Associates, 1994).
2 Jackson, R. and Hann, K., 'Learning through the science museum', *Journal of Education in Museums* 15 (1994): 11–13; and Russell, T., 'The enquiring visitor: usable learning theory for museum contexts', *Journal of Education in Museums* 15 (1994): 19–21.
3 In this brief discussion I am leaving out the social component of learning. Although crucial for understanding education it is beyond the scope of this classification scheme (see Vigotsky, L. S., *Thought and Language* (Cambridge, MA: MIT Press, 1962)).
4 'Simplest' may refer to either the nature of the subject, or the nature of learning. Some textbook writers (in some subjects) start with the fundamental aspects of what they wish to teach, others start with what is considered easiest to learn. But in either case, the reference point is the perceived logical structure of the material to be learned.
5 Dickens, C., *Hard Times*.
6 von Glaserfeld, E., 'An exposition of constructivism: why some like it radical', in Davis, R. B., Maher, C. A. and Noddings, N., *Constructivist Views of the Teaching and Learning of Mathematics* (Washington, DC: National Council of Teachers of Mathematics, 1991).
7 Hein, G. E., 'The significance of constructivism for museum education', in *Museums and the Needs of the People* (Jerusalem: Israel ICOM Committee, 1993).
8 Davidson, B. *et al.*, 'Increased exhibit accessibility through multisensory interaction', *Curator* 34(4) (1991): 273–90.
9 The two additional educational views also have their parallel in museums, leading to the Orderly museum and the Discovery museum. Examples exist, but are beyond the scope of this discussion.
10 Gardner, H., *The Unschooled Mind* (New York: Basic Books, 1991).
11 Akbar, S., 'The Nehru Gallery national textile project', in *Museums for Integration in a Multi-cultural Society, Proceedings of the Annual CECA Conference* (ICOM-Asia-Pacific Organization, 1993), 88.

12 Rozé, S., 'L'Europe des fleuves', in Gesché, N. (ed.) *European Museum Communication*, ICOM-CECA regional meeting, Brussels (Brussels: ICOM-CECA, 1993).

13 Falk, J. and Dierking, L. (eds), *Public Institutions for Personal Learning: Establishing a Research Agenda* (Washington, DC: American Association of Museums, 1995).

7

Teaching yourself to teach with objects

John Hennigar Shuh

Written in an easy-to-read style, this chapter explores some of the reasons why and how to teach with museum (and other) objects. Writing from practical experience, the author describes some of his own experiences working with objects in Nova Scotia, Canada.

Although this paper is written from a particular perspective in a particular environment, both the teaching methods and the conclusions about the value of using objects in learning are valid in a more general sense.

Trying out some of the ideas suggested in the paper is an excellent way to begin to practise teaching (and learning) with objects. New ideas and new methods emerge all the time.

> At the centre of all our programs at the Nova Scotia Museum is a belief in the tremendous power of objects to educate. In fact, we think it is as important for people to learn to use objects as a means of discovering things about themselves and their world as it is for them to learn to use words and numbers.[1]

I have worked at the Nova Scotia Museum now for four years and I am still fascinated by what I'm learning about the power of objects to educate. Furthermore, the longer I'm at it, the more I'm convinced that a museum approach to education has a great deal to offer classroom teachers. Unfortunately, learning how to use objects effectively in your teaching is not quite as easy as falling off a log. As is the case with acquiring other important teaching skills, it takes both some time and some effort. To get right down to it, what this means is that you have to learn to read objects as skilfully as you have already learned to read our printed language. And as in all skill development, there is no room for fudging the basics. The foundation of your being able to use objects as a teacher is your learning how to use them yourself for your own continuing self-education.

Since you probably were not trained as a child to read objects, it may be even harder for you to begin to learn this skill than it will be for your students. But don't worry; you don't have to become an expert in order to begin to use objects with your students, and as soon as you do begin you can start to reap some of the benefits.

So perhaps as a first step in helping you learn how to teach with objects, we should look at some of the advantages of this approach.

OBJECTS ARE FASCINATING

One of the major advantages is that most people are capable of being fascinated by 'things'. It seems to me that if you can focus your work with students on something that fascinates them, you are at least starting the race on the right foot.

Of course, to say that most people are *capable* of being fascinated by most objects is not to maintain that most of us actually go through our lives sparkling with enthusiasm for the multitude of objects we encounter daily. As a matter of fact, we simply are not equipped by our training even to see many of the things in our world, much less be fascinated by them; and often our schooling predisposes us to ignore even those things which surround us most closely every day. (We'll return to this later.) In spite of this, however, most people are capable of being fascinated by a tremendous variety of things which they might otherwise ignore – if their attention is drawn to those things. The simplest way of focusing someone's attention on an object, of course, is to point to it or hold it out to them, in effect saying, 'Here! Look at this!' It's also sometimes helpful to ask a simple focusing question or two such as 'Isn't this beautiful?', or 'What do you think this is?', or 'Have you ever seen anything like that before?', or 'What do you think is significant about this?' Museums have evolved quite elaborate devices called exhibits for drawing people's attention to objects – but usually in the classroom the simpler approach is all that is necessary to get the ball rolling.

It is perhaps worth noting that I have held up lots of different objects in front of an amazing variety of people, asked questions about them and never yet have I had someone shrug and say 'Who cares!', 'So what!', or 'Don't bother me with such trivia!' Indeed, my experience has been that when you encourage people to focus their attention on an object, especially the kind of objects we tend to have lying around museums, they generally respond with enthusiasm and begin to generate a whole series of interesting questions themselves.

On one occasion I even found myself involved in a quite exciting session of 'object-based discovery education' with a group of men who were hanging around a Halifax garage. I had been to an in-service in Truro and discovered on my way home that one of my tyres was soft. I pulled into a service station and backed up to the air pump. As I was attending to the tyre, I noticed that a couple of men who had been standing near the pump had caught sight of an open box of mammal skulls that I had carted along to my in-service, and which was now sitting on top of a pile of boxes in my back seat.

'Well, look at that!' one said to the other. 'I bet he was a mean critter,' the other replied. They motioned to some other men who were talking inside the garage, who sauntered over to join them. By the time I was finished with my tyre there was quite a group gathered around the back of my car and they had a lot of questions. 'What's that one?' 'Where did you get them?' 'Is that a dog?' 'No, it's a wolf, isn't it?' 'How can you tell what animal it came from?'

I could hardly ignore these questions. I brought out my box of skulls, set it up on the lid of the trunk and we talked for twenty minutes or so about animal skulls and teeth, and, among other things, about how you can look at the teeth and tell whether a skull came from a plant-eater, a meat-eater, or an animal who eats a bit of everything.

As I drove away, I felt strangely like a street-corner evangelist who had just delivered his first soap-box sermon. I wasn't quite sure I was comfortable with that. But I was also pleased; because I had been talking with a group of teachers earlier that afternoon about how fascinating such objects were and how useful this made them to teachers; and here my contention had been unexpectedly confirmed, albeit privately, but confirmed none the less.

OBJECTS ARE NOT AGE-SPECIFIC

A second major advantage of using objects in teaching is that, unlike print materials, objects are neither age-specific nor tied to a particular grade level. In other words, students do not have to have attained a specific reading level or stage of conceptual development in order for them to be able to see an object and engage in an educationally worthwhile discussion about it. This is not to say that every object will hold equal interest for students at all levels. But many objects – for example, a stone tool or a queen grab – could be used with equal success in a primary class and with a group of university students. I am, of course, not maintaining that students at various levels will see these objects in the same way. Students at each level will see a specific object through the eyes of their own experience and they will bring to it their own questions and make their own observations. Those of the Grade 1 student will likely be different from those of the Grade 11 student. But beware! This doesn't necessarily mean that the former will be less acute or less valid than the latter.

This point was driven home to me by an incident that occurred a few years ago. In those days, as I wandered around the province talking to teachers about using museum resources in their teaching, I took along a clutch of native Nova Scotia turtles. I used them to illustrate that one of the benefits of using objects was that even young children can often be helped to understand quite complex concepts when they can discover them concretely manifested in objects.

So, as an example, I suggested that the wood turtle, painted turtle and snapping turtle which I had with me could help students understand the quite abstract biological principle that in all creatures there is a symbiotic interrelationship between body structure and behaviour. And then I would demonstrate by taking the wood turtle out of the box and setting it on the floor among the teachers. The wood turtle has a heavy shell both on its back and its belly, which affords it ample protection against predators. So when it looked up at the eager faces of the humans that surrounded it, and perceived them as a threat, it responded by doing the typically turtle thing; it withdrew completely into its shell and became like a rock.

The painted turtle, however, has a much lighter and somewhat less extensive shell, so although it is possible for this turtle to withdraw into it, the shell doesn't afford nearly as much protection as that of the wood turtle. When I took the painted turtle out of its box and it perceived the threatening crowd of humans, it responded by using its very uncharacteristic turtle-speed to try to escape, scrabbling away across the floor.

Now, when I took the snapping turtle out of its box and we examined it, we saw immediately that it had no shell covering its underside, only a small, hard, diamond-shaped patch in the centre of its belly. So it simply couldn't withdraw into its shell. But of course, what the snapping turtle has developed is a very aggressive pattern of defensive behaviour. It snaps. It has a very powerful set of jaws and an amazing long neck, which can extend virtually to the back of its shell. Thus it can defend itself effectively, front and back.

So by examining my turtles, it was fairly easy to discover that each species had developed its own complementary adaptations of body structure and behaviour.

Usually the strength of the example was sufficient to make the point, but one day I dropped in with my kits and turtles to Plymouth School, which is down the Wedgeport road, and talked to teachers during their recess. I had been showing off the turtles and talking about them when one of the teachers said, 'My Grade 1's would really like to see your turtles, do you think you could bring them down to my class?'

Of course I agreed, but with some trepidation because I knew that while on one level this teacher was saying to me, 'Oh, do bring them down, my students would be delighted!', on another level she was saying, 'Come on! Put your money where your mouth is! Let's see if your theorizing works out in practice!'

Well, I was pretty sure it would, but I had never tried it out with Grade 1 students before, and so I mentally crossed my fingers as I walked down the hall towards her classroom.

I needn't have worried. I sat with her students who were gathered in a circle on the carpeted floor, and we looked at the turtles and talked about them. They were fascinated and asked good penetrating questions and I was delighted because they really did seem to be getting the point about the relationship between the turtle's physical and behavioural adaptations.

Everything was going well until I noticed out of the corner of my eye that one little brat over at the edge of the group was turning the snapping turtle over on its back. The poor turtle would no sooner right itself, than this beastly kid would turn it on its back again. This same procedure happened three or four times while I was rising up in righteous indignation (all my instincts for the prevention of cruelty to reptiles rushing to the fore) until I towered above the offender.

He looked up at me with innocent excitement on his face, powerful enough to stop me in my tracks. 'Look!' he cried. 'The snapping turtle doesn't just use his neck to get at you to bite you; he uses it to turn himself over so you can't get at his stomach!'

I looked. What he had said was true. The instant that you turned the snapping turtle on his back, he used his neck as a pivot and turned himself over again. We tried the same thing with the wood turtle; it hardly reacted at all. Indeed, it was as much a rock on its back as it was on its belly. Oh, eventually it would have turned itself over, slowly and languorously (I have since seen it do that), but it was obviously in no great hurry on that day.

I was excited! Because not only had this child obviously understood what I had been suggesting about animal adaptation, he had extended the concept beyond the point to which I had taken it. He had discovered something that I hadn't seen. I had spent a lot of time playing with the turtles, looking at them carefully, and discussing them with a wide variety of people, but I had never noticed what that little boy had noticed.

'Well, that's not too extraordinary,' I said to myself, 'after all I'm fairly new to turtledom.' So when I got home, I reported what we had discovered to Debby Burleson, the science educator in our section of the museum and the person who had taught me all I knew about turtles. She had never noticed this either.

So I went to talk to John Gilhen in the Science Section, who is 'Mr Nova Scotian Turtle', and who knows more about these creatures and their habits than anyone else I know. He had never noticed this either.

But the little boy in Grade 1 at Plymouth School had noticed it. That's exciting; and says a lot about the power of objects to educate.

OBJECTS HELP US TO DOCUMENT THE HISTORY OF ORDINARY PEOPLE

A third major advantage of using objects in teaching is that they can help you and your students understand something about the lives of the ordinary people who were your ancestors.

Until fairly recently, this sort of thing wasn't a great priority in our society. The conventional wisdom had it that some people 'made history' while others did not. And history, or so this view went, was made by the few and not by the many, by the kings and generals and cabinet ministers and prominent citizens and not by the great mass of ordinary people. This is a view of history with which I now profoundly disagree.

However, the way in which history was taught when I went to school and university certainly reflected this bias; the great concern was with political and military history, with battles, treaties and Acts of Parliament. We were led to believe that this was the true stuff of history.

But even then it didn't seem to have very much connection with who we were, and where we had come from. And I was a middle-class kid from Truro, supposedly the kind of student for whom school curriculums were designed.

I didn't even to begin to understand what alienation from school history really was until I taught working-class black kids and white kids in the North End of Halifax, and found that there were virtually no curricular materials available that bore any relationship whatsoever to their lives and their peoples' history.

It was some time around that point in my life as a teacher that I began to realize that, as far as I could see, the major reason for studying history was to learn about our past and thus understand something of the dimensions of our present and the possibilities of our future. But in order for this to work for my students, they had to perceive the history that we studied as their history. For most of the students that I ever taught, and, when you get right down to it, for most of your students as well, their history is not 'history in the great tradition' but the history of ordinary people. This need not limit the scope of your whole course of study, but it certainly does determine the starting-point and the overall perspective.

One of the problems is that for the most part our ordinary ancestors didn't leave much documentary evidence about their lives. Certainly, some of them wrote letters that survive; a few kept diaries that have been preserved; they were included in censuses, and recorded at their births, marriages and deaths. They also sang songs and told tales. From all of these things we can learn something. But among the most important 'documents' that ordinary people leave behind them are the things that they made and used in their everyday lives. And if you learn how to understand what these 'artefacts' have to say, they can shed great light for both you and your students on who these people were and what their lives were like, what their limits and possibilities were, how they thought, what they valued, and how they shaped our world.

USING OBJECTS HELPS STUDENTS DEVELOP IMPORTANT INTELLECTUAL SKILLS

Another significant benefit of learning how to use objects with your students is that it gives them the chance to develop their capacity for careful, critical observation of their world.

Developing this skill requires practice and often we don't provide enough opportunity for this in the course of our students' education. Also, there can be blocks to learning this skill. Sometimes the process is short-circuited because our students already have a name for what we'd like them to look at. 'Oh yes,' they say, 'I know what that is, it's a butterfly.' Period! End of conversation!

In a sense this is not surprising because the ability to put a name on something is in itself a skill that we spend a lot of energy promoting in schools. There is a great deal of emphasis, particularly in the early years of schooling, on helping children learn how to name and number the various things they experience. You can usefully think of names and numbers as generally accepted conceptual and symbolic pigeon-holes into which we stuff the actual things we experience.

This process of naming and numbering is undeniably important. It certainly is vital to our communicating with each other. It helps us to organize our experience. It liberates us from having to treat each thing we encounter as something new and different. And, because we can name and number, we are freed to play with the abstractions without having to lug around the heavy baggage of countless individual things.

So this whole business gets legitimate emphasis in the early years of schooling. Indeed, naming and numbering are the foundation skills of language development and mathematics respectively and these are, of course, keys to the entire educational enterprise.

But often it is important to be able to see our world freshly and without the baggage of old names and numbers, for these can insulate us from clearly seeing the fullness of the world which lies behind our abstractions. We need to develop the ability to suspend our reliance on conventional abstractions so that we can look at things anew, and in a careful, critical way. Ironically, when we do this effectively, it often leads to the generating of new, subtler sets of names and numbers to express our new understanding about the world.

This power of critical observation, then, is ultimately as important an intellectual skill for your students as is the power of naming and numbering. The capacity for fresh, critical observation is the basis of good research, and as your students advance in school that skill becomes increasingly vital. But being able to see the world clearly and to ask good probing questions of it is important in a whole variety of non-academic life situations as well. So it is certainly worth spending time developing this facet of your students' intellects. Using objects in your teaching provides the opportunity.

GETTING STARTED

Enough of the advantages of incorporating objects in your teaching. How do you get started?

As I suggested above, the basic thing you need to do before you can use objects effectively with your students is to learn something yourselves about looking at things carefully and probingly and critically. You need to get enough experience working with objects yourselves that you begin to trust them as legitimate sources of information. That can be hard, especially for people who were trained in academic disciplines like history where written materials (books, newspapers, pamphlets, manuscripts, letters, grocery lists, etc.) tend to be treated as the only truly valid sources of information.

But how to get started? Well, just as in learning to read there is no substitute for reading, and in learning how to write there is nothing quite like writing, the best way to develop your capacity for looking at objects is to look at objects. It's not even necessary to use museum objects in order to get started. Museums are undeniably a good source of fascinating artefacts and specimens; after all, that's our business. But the world is filled with all sorts of things that will amply reward careful, probing observation, and there are certain advantages to starting with something that is part of your own world – advantages that, I hope, will become clear as we proceed. So choose something that you find lying around your home or school and begin.

AND NOW FOR A LITTLE PRACTICE . . .

A contemporary artefact that I often use in my discussions with groups of teachers is the styrofoam cup. There is no particular reason for choosing styrofoam cups over a whole host of other possible things, other than the fact that in most rooms where I find myself talking with teachers these cups seem to be amply distributed, in people's hands, on tables, on floors and even sometimes in trash cans. And for the most part, the cups don't seem to belong to anyone, so are easily appropriated for my purposes. I've also used ballpoint pens, paper diapers, tape recorders, electric irons, chairs, doorstoppers, hamburger containers and a whole variety of other contemporary objects with equal effect.

So pick up a styrofoam cup and join me in looking at it. How would you describe it? It's a white cup with a narrow base, and sides which flare gradually to a wider lip.

Is there anything significant about this colour and shape?

Yes. It's white because that's the colour of the foam that was used to make it. You can even see the individual beads of foam on the surface, so it's really quite unadorned. I guess there's been no attempt to decorate it because its purpose is simply utilitarian. There is a kind of beauty, though, in the cleanness and simplicity of the solid colour and the plain lines.

What about the cup's shape?

The flared sides make them easy to stack, and convenient to store. Also, styrofoam cups don't have a handle. They don't need one because styrofoam is a good insulator, so you won't burn your hand holding a hot cup of coffee. But this makes its shape more like that of a glass than that of a cup. I suppose we call it a cup because it would sound strange or contradictory to call it a styrofoam glass.

That's an interesting point. Is there anything else worth mentioning about its size and shape?

Yes. The lip is thicker than the rest of the side. I suppose that this strengthens it, although it may also be more comfortable to drink out of a cup with a thicker lip. It's hard to say. Oh, I also measured how much liquid this cup would hold: six ounces [170 ml], as compared to eight or ten ounces [225 or 285 ml] in an average mug.

I guess that means you get more cups out of the coffee-maker if you're serving a group.

Yes, and make a bigger profit if you're selling it.

Is there anything else worth mentioning about the physical characteristics of this cup?

Yes. The following words and symbols are embossed on the bottom: Fibracan/700S/ Montreal & Toronto.

What do they tell you?

That the company that made the cup was called Fibracan and that it has offices or factories or both in Montreal and Toronto. I suppose 700S is some sort of product code; I'm really not sure. There's also something about the sound of 'Fibracan' – it seems to fit with the current fashion for contracted names and corporate logos that has given us names like Domtar, Alcan, Devco and Canfor. Twenty-five years ago, if the company existed, it was probably called The Fibre Container Company of Canada or something like that. So either it's a new company, or an old company with a new name. Maybe the old company needed a new name when it started making containers out of styrofoam rather than wood fibres.

That would be something worth checking on. What else do you see?

In the centre of the bottom there's a somewhat raised circle about 7 mm in diameter, and the surface of this circle seems rougher than the surface of the rest of the cup.

What do you make of this?

I don't really know. It strikes me that it may have something to do with the way the cup was made.

How was the cup made?

I don't really know. But as I mentioned before, it seems to be made from thousands of tiny particles of foam. Maybe the cup was made in a mould, and the rough part on the bottom indicates the place where the particles were injected into the mould. But that's just speculation. It's obviously machine-made rather than hand-made. But I'd only be guessing at what the machine was like and precisely how the cup was made.

But even your not knowing is significant in a sense.

I don't follow you.

Well it seems to me that it's not unusual that you don't know these things. In some sense it's characteristic of our time in history that we tend not to understand how the things that we use every day are made, what they're made from, where they're made or by whom. This is true not only of styrofoam cups, but of all sorts of things that are probably even more important to us. Our grandparents knew much more than we do about where the things they used came from, how they were made, from what and by whom.

You mean, compare a styrofoam cup with a tin mug, for example?

Sure. The one is made from a strange material, in a mysterious way, in an anonymous factory hundreds of miles away . . .

. . . And the other was made from tin and solder, by Earle Lantz the local tinsmith, in a way that requires some skill, but which our grandparents knew about since they had watched him do it in his shop which was right behind his store, which was in the centre of their village.

Exactly. So maybe our styrofoam cup tells us that we're a bit more alienated from our world than our grandparents were from theirs.

At the very least, it says something about the complexity of our world, compared with the simplicity of theirs.

What else is significant about your cup?

It's cheap!

What does cheap mean?

It means that it didn't cost very much, of course; that you can buy these cups for only pennies apiece.

If you drank your coffee and tea out of styrofoam cups every day, how many would you use in the run of a year?

At least two a day – somewhere between seven and eight hundred in a year.

Is that cheap?

I suppose not. But at least styrofoam cups are sanitary and convenient.

What do you mean, 'convenient'?

You don't have to wash them. People don't like washing dishes; they'd rather spend their time doing other things.

What do you do in the time you save not washing coffee cups?

It's not that I do anything in particular. I guess it's more a general attitude than a specific exchange. People today always seem to be in a hurry; we're always looking for ways of saving time. And there's another aspect to this too.

What's that?

Well it always used to be the women teachers in our school who were commandeered into washing the cups and saucers. We just aren't willing to do that any more.

That makes sense. What do you do with your styrofoam cup rather than wash it?

I throw it away. It's disposable; it's made to be used only once and then tossed out.

What happens to it when you toss it out?

It becomes garbage.

And what then? Does it decompose easily?

No, like a lot of things that we throw away, it isn't bio-degradable and so it just sits there without rotting. So if it's thrown on the street it becomes part of a garbage problem.

Some people would maintain that we have so many disposable things in our society that even if people didn't throw them on the sidewalk, the sheer bulk of our disposables would mean we'd have a garbage problem.

That's true. Look at the difficulty we have trying to find landfill sites. I wonder if there's a way of re-cycling styrofoam?

Not that I know of. It would be a useful project for someone to work on. By the way, what's styrofoam made from?

I don't really know; but I think it's made from petroleum.

Oh! So we must have lots of oil, since we can afford to throw away things that are made from it so readily.

I'll ignore your sarcasm and answer your question anyway. No, of course, we don't have oil to throw away; but I'd be willing to bet that styrofoam cups were developed at a time when we thought we did. I wonder if our current consciousness about the energy crisis will have any effect on the use of styrofoam cups?

I'm sure it will. You know you can often learn a lot by looking at changes in the patterns of use and distribution of artefacts, and I've been in two schools lately where I've noticed changes that might turn out to be trends. In the first school, some teachers were washing their styrofoam cups and leaving them in their mail boxes. In the second school, they have stopped buying them altogether. They say that since the energy crisis they have become more expensive and that that, coupled with the budgetary crisis in education, has made them unaffordable.

Maybe the museum had better start collecting them before they all disappear.

Not a bad idea.

CONCLUSION

I hope that the foregoing exercise will begin to give you some sense that there is a lot that can be learned from a careful look at even apparently insignificant things like styrofoam cups. The styrofoam cup has quite a story to tell if we're able to listen. It is a story that is not only about styrofoam cups, but also about us, about some of our values and the choices we make, about some of our limits and possibilities, and about some of the crises that characterize our world.

As you're developing your skills with objects it is sometimes easier to see the connections between objects and their broader context if you start with things from our own world. So I think it is worth beginning with the familiar. But after you get the hang of it you'll discover that the same sorts of questions can be asked of historical artefacts, and that they too have exciting stories to tell about the context from which they come and about the lives of the people who made and used them.

As you develop your skills, you'll begin to see all sorts of ways of using objects profitably with your students.

Try it.

FIFTY WAYS TO LOOK AT A BIG MAC BOX

1 Smell it.
2 Taste it.
3 Feel it all over.
4 Does it make a noise?
5 What are its measurements? Height, weight, diameter?
6 Describe its shape, colour and any decoration.
7 Can you write a description of it that would give a clear picture to someone who has never seen a Big Mac box? (A sketch would help.)

8 Why is it the size it is?

9 Are all McDonald's boxes the same size?

10 Have the sizes of McDonald's boxes changed over the years; will they change with metrification?

11 How much has the box's shape been determined by the material used, the method of construction and the box's function?

12 Why isn't the box plain white (or black, or purple)?

13 What is the function of the decoration?

14 What does the lettering tell you?

15 Why are symbols, logos and trademarks so important in our society?

16 How much is the name 'Big Mac' a reflection of the fashions of our time?

17 What does the circled R signify?

18 What material was used to make the box?

19 What raw material was used to produce this material?

20 Is this a renewable resource?

21 What does this say about attitudes towards conservation in our society?

22 Why was this particular material chosen?

23 What are its advantages; its disadvantages?

24 How might the box have been different if a different material had been used: for example, wood, or ceramics, or metal, or paper?

25 What can you learn from looking at the box and the lettering about how the box was made?

26 At what stage of manufacture do you think the lettering was applied?

27 Have you ever seen anything like this being made? What does that suggest to you about our society?

28 Is the box well designed?

29 Does it work well for the purposes for which it was designed?

30 How might the design be improved?

31 If someone twenty, fifty, or one hundred years ago had set about to design a container for a hamburger, how might they have done it differently?

32 Did people eat hamburgers then?

33 What might the hamburger container of the future be like?

34 What does the number on the inside bottom of the box signify?

35 Is this a clue as to where the box was made?

36 Where was the box made?

37 What did these boxes replace?

38 Why not just serve a hamburger on a plate?

39 What does a Big Mac box tell us about the people who use it, the people who pass it out and our society in general?

40 Show the Big Mac box to as many people as you can within a ten-minute period. How many people failed to recognize the box? What does this tell you?

41 Would you get this response in Moose Jaw, Saskatchewan; Burbank, California; or Perth, Australia? What does this tell you?

42 Where is the headquarters of McDonalds? What does this tell you?

43 Do you deserve a break today?

44 How many of these boxes are used across North America every day?

45 For how long is each box actually used?

46 What is done with them after they have been used?

47 Why do you find Big Mac boxes on sidewalks and lawns and beaches?

48 Is there anything that could be done to recycle these boxes?

49 Is there anything that could replace them?

50 What do you think is the single most significant thing about a Big Mac box? Why?

And now, imagine that you are a Big Mac box and write the story of your life.

This chapter first appeared as a paper in Journal of Education *7(4) (1982): 8–15.*

NOTE

1   These words are a direct quotation from an internal Nova Scotia Museum document on museum education, but paraphrase part of a statement concerning the educative power of objects written by the editors of *Art to Zoo*, a publication of the Office of Elementary and Secondary Education of the Smithsonian Institution, Washington, DC 20560. Their statement appeared on page 4 of the September 1980 issue of *Art to Zoo*.

8

Improving worksheets
Gail Durbin

Many people dislike worksheets, arguing that they result in limited experiences which focus on filling in the sheet rather than anything more productive. However, if well-designed and carefully piloted, worksheets can structure a museum visit in terms of space used, time spent, knowledge gained and objects looked at, all of which are essential.

This chapter discusses how to plan and write good worksheets. It sets out the various issues involved including practicalities, questioning techniques, skills involved in completing the sheet, and relationship with the curriculum. A useful annotated bibliography is included.

It is very easy to pick holes in worksheets and it is a very skilled task to design good ones. The purpose of this article is not to rehearse the arguments for and against worksheets; this has been covered elsewhere (Fry 1987). I start from the premise that worksheets are one of many methods of interpreting museum collections. Large numbers of teachers use and feel comfortable with worksheets so it is worth spending time assessing them critically and looking for ways of making them more effective.

This article suggests five areas to consider when assessing a worksheet. These are:

practicalities
questioning techniques
variety
developing a sense of the whole
curriculum context

PRACTICALITIES

There are a host of minor things that can stop a worksheet being effective. These are obvious to those with experience but pitfalls for the unprepared. It would be wise to examine worksheets for the following points.

- Are a large number of children going to be focused on one small space or item at once? Can the sheet be designed so that children can be spread round the space more evenly to avoid the frustration of not being able to see?
- What else might stop the child seeing the object referred to? Are the cases too high? Is there a reflection on the glass at child height?

- Is it clear where the answer is to be found? Name the room, gallery, or case as appropriate. Give clear instructions when children have to move to another location.
- Is it clear what kind of answer is expected? Say if notes are wanted rather than continuous text. Children with little experience of the worksheet approach will find it easier if you provide a box for a drawing to be done in or dotted lines for a written answer. If you are expecting several answers then numbered spaces are a useful hint to children to keep looking.
- Look at the level of vocabulary and the length of the text. Does it suit the age- and ability-range aimed at? Keep sentences short and vocabulary simple. The difficulty of coping with a strange place, a clipboard and the general excitement may well depress a child's reading level.

QUESTIONING TECHNIQUES

The nature of the questions asked is at the heart of the success of a worksheet and it is worth spending time analysing them. Here are some questions on *Goldilocks and the Three Bears*:

1 How many bears are there in the story?
2 What is porridge?
3 How would you have felt if you were Baby Bear?
4 Should Goldilocks be punished for breaking the chair?
5 Who went into the house where the three bears lived?
6 What happened first in the story?
7 What happened first after Baby Bear's chair broke?
8 Do you think the three bears will lock their door the next time they leave their house?
9 Is this story like another bear story you've read?
10 Are all little girls like Goldilocks?

Some of these questions require simple recall of the story and low-level thinking (nos. 1, 5, 6, 7), some require opinion and higher-level thinking (nos. 3, 4, 8, 9, 10) and one (no. 2) requires previous knowledge, for no amount of careful listening to the story will provide any more information than the fact that porridge is edible and can be the wrong temperature!

An effective worksheet will probably require both low- and high-level thinking but it is generally easier to think of low-level questions. Devising more stretching ones take time and practice. However, you will find that small adjustments to the phrasing of a question can change its nature. 'How many bears are there in the story?' could become, for example, 'Is the number of bears in the story significant?'

Questions that require only a yes/no answer can generally be upgraded to become more interesting. Similarly questions that require counting are useful only if the information is needed to answer a further question. Avoid questions that require guessing. Make the activity more precise by asking for either an estimate or an opinion.

In *The Good Guide: A Sourcebook for Interpreters, Docents and Tour Guides* Alison Grinder and Sue McCoy outline a four-level question classification. The types they identify are:

memory questions
convergent questions

divergent questions
judgemental questions

Memory questions

These questions seek a single right answer. They are the narrowest type of question requiring the lowest level of thinking. They require facts, precise recall, recognition, descriptions of previously obtained factual knowledge or observation. The answer may often be supplied in one word. The question may begin with:

'How many ... '
'What is the ... '
'Name the ... '
'Which one ... '

Convergent questions

These questions seek the most appropriate answer or the best answer. They focus on specifics and on what is already known or perceived. They may require explanations, comparisons, or interrelationships. A higher level of thinking is required than for the memory questions. The questions may be phrased as:

'What does ... do?'
'How is this ... like that one?'
'How do ... and ... differ?'

Divergent questions

These questions allow for more than one possible right answer. They demand imaginative thinking, and require the formulation of a hypothesis and the ability to use knowledge to solve problems.

Prediction, inference and reconstruction may be needed. The questions may be phrased as:

'What if ... '
'How many ways ... '
'Imagine that ... '

Judgemental questions

These questions provide personal and possibly unique answers. They require choice and evaluation and demand the formulation of an opinion, a value, or a belief. A view may have to be justified and evidence be assembled to defend a position. Criteria may need to be applied or standards of judgement developed. This is the broadest type of question requiring the highest level of thinking. The questions may be phrased as:

'What do you think about ... '
'Do you agree that ... '
'What is your reaction to ... '
'Which do you think ... and why?'

Applied to an exhibit displaying a pair of hair-powdering bellows the classification might produce the following questions. A progressively more taxing worksheet could be designed by selecting questions from each level.

Memory

What is this?
What is it made from?

Convergent

What was the purpose of this object?
How did these bellows work?

Divergent

How could the design of these bellows be improved?
What does this object tell us about the society that produced it?

Judgemental

Do you think it is important to spend public money preserving items like these?

Do you think this would be more appropriately displayed as a work of art, as an example of craftsmanship, or as a social history object?

Good questions for worksheets are not just stimulating ones, they have to be appropriate too. The whole point of going to a site or museum is to learn from physical things and the questions should direct attention towards the object not the label. It is, of course, often easier to frame a question about the label because it is likely to provide specific facts and figures. Asking questions about the object requires an understanding of the potential of artefacts to reveal information about the societies that made, used and preserved them. The main emphasis of the work should be on observation not reading.

Consider how far previous knowledge is essential to completing the sheet. On one level the success and the sophistication of the task accomplished in the museum will depend on the child's previous knowledge and preparation. A child who has an understanding of historical sources and their range will be better placed to make an assessment of a specific object or display. But there are other types of question requiring previous knowledge that should be avoided. 'Who built Hampton Court?' cannot be answered by observation of the building. You either know the answer or you don't. 'What year was Hampton Court built?' presents similar problems. If a question can be better answered away from the site in the comfort of the school library then omit it. Examine your worksheets carefully for these kinds of question as they creep in almost unnoticed.

Questions need to be unambiguous and it is helpful to have only one question in a sentence. One technique for achieving greater clarity is to start with a verb in the imperative as this is an instant pointer to the action required; e.g. 'List the differences between X and Y' rather than 'What differences are there between X and Y?' Other suitable verbs might be 'draw', 'discuss', 'explain' or 'estimate'.

GCSE has made teachers more aware of the questions they ask. The desire to encourage children to show what they can do and the need to differentiate levels of attainment have sharpened practice and will have a beneficial effect on worksheet design.

VARIETY

A well-constructed worksheet will be varied in content and approach. Where appropriate you may want to provide variety through games or exercises such as word-searches, crosswords, joining matching pairs, annotating, completing sentences or drawings, underlining, sequencing, or spotting similarities or differences.

Call on as many different skills as possible, not just verbal ones. Drawing should play an important part at all ages. Since observation is at the root of work in museums an activity that slows a child up and keeps the eye engaged will be valuable. It is also important to learn that there are other ways of conveying information than through the written word and that drawing for recording is a different sort of activity from drawing as art. You might ask simply for an object to be recorded or you might set a task that required selection such as asking for a drawing of something the child found beautiful or for details of decorative style.

Mathematical skills can be brought into play. Measuring and estimating are useful ways of recording buildings and room layouts and give a good opportunity for reinforcing classroom skills. Dealing with scale and devising methods of working out weights and volumes all have a place. Children could, for example, work out how far a housemaid walked to provide hot washing water for all or what volume of water had to be carried to fill a slipper bath.

The design of a worksheet will also provide variety and should motivate. Good layout and interesting lettering set high standards of expectation. Illustrations may be appropriate where they are central to the activity but beware of using them simply as space fillers or of letting them discourage children's own efforts.

DEVELOPING A SENSE OF THE WHOLE

One of the great dangers with worksheets is that you learn to design practical and varied activities directed through well-framed questions and yet the children still only end up with a collection of disparate facts and ideas. The thought process behind the worksheet may be more obvious to the writer than to the student. Try writing down the answers to your own worksheet and see if they retain any sort of coherence.

This problem can be dealt with in a number of ways. First there needs to be a reason for collecting the information that is as clear to the children as it is to the teacher. It is important that the need to know has been created and that the children have to apply their new knowledge in some way.

The children may need to do research in order to make an accurate model or put on a play. They may be trying to find out what kind of person lived in that room or worked at that place. They might be trying to see whether a television play on medieval life was accurate. They could be looking for the strengths and weaknesses of archaeological evidence. This can be made clear at the outset and then the questions on the worksheet guide them to the displays to use and the information they need. They become a form of guided note-making and the ultimate aim will be for children to generate their own questions and recording method.

An alternative approach is problem-solving in role outlined by Barbara Roberts (1988). Giving children a problem to look at through a specific pair of eyes makes the questionnaire approach redundant. Instead the worksheet sets the problem and can be used for recording the solution. With care it is possible to allow the children to establish their own criteria through discussion so that much of the work of thinking is shifted from the teacher to the child. The article did not give many examples so here are a few designed for use at Osborne House on the Isle of Wight but easily transferable to other sites and circumstances.

> You are a stage designer working on a play based on a murder in a country house. You have decided to base your work on Osborne. You still need a scene for a party and a scene for a plot to be hatched. Choose the most appropriate spots and make some sketches of the architecture and the furniture to help you when you return to your studio.

> You are the curator and you have been told that the load on the floor is too great. Which pieces of furniture are you going to put into store? You are anxious not to spoil the atmosphere of the house for visitors.

> *Next*'s new household range has been enormously successful. They have asked you to design a range of frames and mirrors based on Victorian designs. You have decided to use Osborne for your inspiration. Make some sketches. Which three designs are you going to recommend?

> You are researching the pictures for a book on conservation. You still need examples of things that have and have not been protected from light, touch and general wear. Can Osborne provide you with any suitable illustration?

CURRICULUM CONTEXT

Although this section comes last in the chapter it should come first in the mind of the teacher who should have a very clear idea of why the visit is being made and how it fits in with the curriculum.

Some sites refuse to provide any written material at all, saying that the only effective material is that written by the teacher in the context of the topic and approach being followed. Ideally, written material should come from a discussion between the teacher and the museum education department where the teacher's knowledge of the class and the curriculum can be married to the museum educator's knowledge of the collection and specialization in wringing ideas and information from apparently mute objects. There may, however, be pressures of time and there is still a value in the experienced museum teacher creating some more general teaching material. This may be used as a stand-by by the hurried or unconfident teacher or adapted by the more experienced one. Worksheets will benefit from being tied to one or more specific National Curriculum attainment targets.

There is no such thing as the perfect worksheet. Fashions and educational ideas change but constant critical appraisal can improve practice.

This chapter first appeared as a paper in Journal of Education in Museums *10 (1989): 25–30.*

FURTHER READING

Davis, H. B. (1980) 'Kids have the answers: do you have the questions?', *Instructor* 90: 64–6, 68. Suggests ways of converting low-level thinking questions into higher-level thinking ones. The source of the questions on Goldilocks.

Fry, H. (1987) 'Worksheets as museum learning devices', *Museums Journal* 86(4): 219–25. A survey of changing attitudes to worksheets with a positive tone and a helpful bibliography.

Grinder, A. L. and McCoy, E. S. (1985) *The Good Guide: A Sourcebook for Interpreters, Docents and Tour Guides*, Arizona: Ironwood Press. The section on questioning strategies has been drawn on heavily for this article.

Hall, N. (ed.) (1984) *Writing and Designing Interpretive Material for Children*, Design for Learning and Centre for Environmental Interpretation, Manchester Polytechnic. Includes written material with AVs and audio-tours.

Jones, L. S. and Ott, R. W. (1983) 'Self-study guides for school-age students', *Museum Studies Journal* 1(1): 36–42. Survey with examples of practice both sides of the Atlantic.

Lauritzen, E. M. (1982) 'The preparation of worksheets', in T. H. Hansen, K. E. Anderson and P. Vestergaard (eds) *Museums and Education,* Copenhagen: Danish ICOM/CECA, 43–6. Suggested procedure.

McManus, P. (1985) 'Worksheet-induced behaviour in the British Museum (Natural History)', *Journal of Biological Education* 19(3): 23–42. Study of conversation between groups filling in worksheets. A warning.

O'Connell, P. S. (1984) 'Decentralizing interpretation: developing museum education with and for schools', *Roundtable Reports* 9(1): 17–22. Designing material in collaboration with teachers.

Roberts, B. (1988) 'How do you clean a chandelier?', *Journal of Education in Museums* 9: 9–11. Introduces problem-solving activities in role.

9

Open windows, open doors

Jessica Davis and Howard Gardner

The concept of multiple intelligences has been adopted enthusiastically in museums in recent years. Its most useful application is in carrying out an audit of exhibition plans, or in reviewing and evaluating existing exhibitions. If learners really do have a range of capacities and skills, how are these provided for?

Although the multiple intelligence theory has been attacked from various quarters, it works extremely well in this limited way within the museum context. It is an easy idea to grasp and to share with colleagues, and it makes a great deal of sense in planning exhibitions for varied audiences.

Davis and Gardner describe their project and discuss some ways in which the ideas can be applied in museums. These ideas are limited to the kinds of questions that might be asked of paintings.

I have also used the ideas rather more broadly, in Museums and their Visitors *(London: Routledge, 1994), 146–52.*

Though often linked in the public mind, museums and schools operate in distinct spheres. Museums are undeniably centres for learning, but they are certainly not schools. There are similarities between the out-of-school learning that goes on in museums and in-school learning, but important differences exist that make museums ideally suited for the individually centred learning many schools are currently trying to achieve.

For reasons ranging from mission to survival, there has been a recent surge of interest in the museum as an educational institution. The question naturally arises: In which ways can recent innovations in the areas of educational research and practice inform and enrich the stage and scene of museum education? We suggest that museums as educational institutions consider a shift in perspective and a change in emphasis: a shift from a focus on the information museums provide to a concentration on the audience of learners they serve. At a time of national reflection and reform, we invite museum educators to join the 'break the mould' mentality of modern school educators and consider ways to create individually centred museums that would be both similar to and different from individually centred schools.

As a historical backdrop, it was almost a century ago that Alfred Binet invented the IQ test, an instrument designed to determine which children would be most likely to succeed at school and which most likely to fail. Although IQ has come to be thought of as 'general intelligence', it is important to remember that the IQ test was really meant to measure 'school intelligence'. As most of us who are old enough to know have observed, this sampling of intelligence does not necessarily serve us well in the bulk of life and experience spent outside the school walls.

It would be interesting to try to imagine a test that determines which children would be most likely to succeed at 'museum', and which most likely to fail. Would the museum achievers be the same children as the school success stories, or might there be some telling discrepancies? In a school culture where facility with maths is held in high esteem, the child who makes meaning out of visual images might not be a likely success story. In art museums, where much of the curriculum is on the walls, that visual meaning-maker might go to the head of the class.

The reader may protest that an ability to make meaning out of images is not as truly an 'intelligence' as the ability to solve maths problems or logical syllogisms. However, recent research has suggested the contrary – that the making of meaning out of images is as much a form of intelligence as the making of meaning out of mathematical symbols. Responsively, our views of intelligence and learning need to be expanded.

At Project Zero, part of the Harvard Graduate School of Education, researchers have studied meaning-making in various cognitive domains or symbol systems for more than twenty-five years. Project Zero's early research was founded on the belief that arts learning was serious intellectual or cognitive activity and that studying how children develop aesthetic production and perception in visual arts, music, and language constituted serious cognitive research. The rarity of these views justified our choice of name – zero was known about the cognitive approach to the arts.

Out of this work came a view of different symbol systems as different problem spaces through which the individual meaning-maker negotiates his or her way, finding and solving problems *en route*. From this perspective, different sets of 'know-how' allow individuals to find and make meaning in gesture, language, visual art and music. Redefining intelligence as the ability to solve problems and fashion products, these sets of 'know-how' emerge as intelligences that congregate in different mixes in each individual.

Our theory of multiple intelligences proposes that there are at least seven (and no doubt more) different intelligences that manifest themselves in various configurations of differing degree. They are: (1) linguistic (out of which writers and poets are made); (2) logical-mathematical, which traditionally leads to success in school, and of which scientists are made; (3) musical; (4) spatial (pilots, architects, chess players, and surgeons exhibit these skills); (5) bodily kinaesthetic (in which the body serves as the agent for solving problems or fashioning products – dancers or mechanics exhibit this intelligence); (6) interpersonal (understanding other people, exhibited by salespeople and therapists); and (7) intrapersonal (understanding self).

Schools have traditionally valued and catered to students exhibiting strong evidence of linguistic and logical-mathematical intelligences. Museums, however, may naturally engage and value more varied configurations. Indeed, if we contemplate the domain of the art museum as a subject to be learned, we see it consisting of such different elements as curatorship, art perception and exhibit planning. In this light, linguistic and logical-mathematical intelligences would not necessarily be the ticket to success in 'museum'.

Certainly curatorship also draws heavily on spatial intelligence; art perception calls for both personal intelligences; and exhibit planning entails the spatial, bodily kinaesthetic, and sometimes musical intelligences. The point here is that at a time when schools are rethinking their priorities and regrouping, museums are in a ready position to (or already do) value, employ and cater to all intelligences.

In those schools where children have traditionally been asked to parrot information spoon-fed them by teachers, an awareness of multiple intelligences mandates serious revision of the pedagogical scene. From our perspective, schools need to provide rich opportunities for students to achieve and demonstrate what they know in different ways. Different points of entry into knowledge need to be established to accommodate the different lenses through which learners see.

We propose five different windows on learning that have a natural appeal for learners whose learning profiles are determined by their different configurations of intelligences. Let us apply our example of these windows to learning in an art museum, where they might provide different entry points into a particular episode of learning: a dialogue with a painting on a gallery wall.

The first is the *narrational* window – the story approach to learning. Considering a painting in an art museum, the viewer might be asked (not told): What story seems to be depicted in this painting? What do you think happened in the scene portrayed just before the moment captured in this image? What happens just after? What is the life-story of the artist who chose to paint it?

The second window is the numerical or *quantitative* approach. From this perspective learners may, for example, have an interest in the relative monetary values of the various artworks in the museum, the number of paintings the painter created, the exact years of his or her life, the materials used, and even vital statistics of the donors. Much of the information traditionally provided on labels in art museums is presented through this window.

Next, the *foundational* approach provides a window on to the scene made up of such basic questions as: Why is this painting considered a work of art? How does it relate to other paintings in the museum? Why is it important?

The fourth window, the *aesthetic* approach, would seem the most appropriate window for an art museum. Questions about the painting – How does it make you feel? or How are the forms organized or balanced? – would fuel an aesthetic approach.

The last window is the *experiential*, or hands-on, approach. In responding to a work of art from this approach, observers might be asked to draw the shapes they see or to design a dance capturing the movement of forms in the painting. In terms of the experiential approach, the typical prohibition on touching a work of art is particularly frustrating.

The five windows invite and admit a range of representations of meaning and call on the learner to construct his or her own understanding of an artwork. They encourage the viewer to search out the relevant information needed to inform that perspective. This is in contrast to the situation in which a museum decides what the viewer needs to know and thereby dictates a preference for one way to make meaning over another.

Individually centred schools try to provide multiple windows into learning in order to grant access to many more learning styles and strengths. The provision of many windows in itself conveys an important lesson: knowledge can be validly represented in more ways than one. Indeed, a sign of expertise may be the ability to understand in multiple ways, to be able to consider various understandings and diverse solutions to the same problem.

101

While some schools may need major overhauling to install the multiple-window approach to learning, museums are intrinsically natural settings for this type of individually centred pedagogy. First of all, in many schools the configuration of rows of desks of seated children facing one standing teacher contradicts the notion of a group of individual learners claiming their own points of entry to knowledge and crafting their own performances based on that understanding. The traditional schoolroom is set up for the empty-vessel approach to education, teachers filling empty students with knowledge poured from one particular pitcher.

School students are captive audiences to whatever theatre of learning teachers and administrators prepare for them. Museums, on the other hand, are naturally designed to be exploratoriums, in which individual museum-goers are free (though not always encouraged) to map their own course through the expanse of diverse learning stimuli. In museums learners are clients and their repeated attendance is of key importance to the museum. Attendance is a measure of success for a given exhibit, not a pass or fail on a test of a requisite amount of information. Indeed, the fact that no one can 'flunk museum' should allow learners the freedom to take the sort of risks that underlie most worthwhile adventures into learning – into the forbidding and/or enticing territory of the unknown.

Certainly different sorts of museums offer different experiences. Children's museums and science museums, for example, are more naturally hands-on than art of history museums. It might then be argued that in certain classes of museum some of the five windows are more open than others. Yet all types of museums will at one point or another encounter the full spectrum of learning style and hence need to provide entry points for them all.

In order to grant wide and genuine access, several museums have collaborated with psychologists and educational researchers, a process that puts into practice an institution's commitment to provide service to more than one individual learning profile. Such collaborations are never easy: the cultures of social science research institutions are quite different from the culture of museums. To work out these differences takes time and high degrees of motivation, a willingness to listen and to adjust. Yet when pursued seriously over a significant period of time they can be quite rewarding, enlarging the perspective of all concerned.

Harvard Project Zero's first experience of working with a museum was in 1975 with the Minneapolis Institute of Arts. At the institute, researchers and museologists investigated museum-goers' knowledge bases and their preferred ways of learning in a museum. The findings indicated that a real desire exists on the part of visitors for the museum to supply them with information. Their preference, however, was for handouts with generalizable information about visual analysis rather than biographical information about the artists or art-historical facts.

More than a decade later, Project Spectrum – a Project Zero study of learning profiles among pre-school children – collaborated with the Boston Children's Museum to create within the museum learning activities that extended the boundaries of the pre-school classroom by making thematic connections on topics such as 'day and night' and 'all about me'. These topics were explored within the comfortable and familiar structure of the classroom while being enriched beyond the classroom's capacities by the vast resources of the museum. Drawing on the museum's interactive technology, the collaboration designed experiences that called for the range of multiple intelligences and provided young children with a rich context in which to demonstrate their varied performances of understanding. Parents and teachers saw student strengths that might have remained invisible at home or at school.

With the Cleveland Museum of Art, Project Zero studied the differences in museum experiences between novice and expert museum-goers and considered the effect of different label texts that appeal to multiple learning styles. The study also revealed that expert visitors return to the museum over and over again to re-encounter themselves through repeated experiences with select works of art. Transcending all the factual data novice museum-goers suspected they were meant to know, the experts valued direct personal encounters with favourite works of art.

Thanks to a grant from the Bauman Foundation, we currently have undertaken a research initiative with the Isabella Stewart Gardner Museum in Boston in which Project Zero researchers are working with the director, education curator and other staff members to develop an innovative curriculum that will encourage and empower local schoolchildren and community members to claim ownership of that intriguing museum and hopefully also be of use to museum educators in other settings. We have produced a game that facilitates individualized optimal points of contact with works of art.

Our work with museums has generated a new perspective on education. Traditionally museums have supplemented school learning – the trip to the museum of natural history lending substance to the class unit on dinosaurs, the visit to the art gallery adding colour and background to a Renaissance history project. In most cases, this supplementation has been subject-based. We, however, recommend that the educational focus be turned away from the subject-matter to the learner, from information to opportunities for individually centred learning. We maintain the uniqueness of museums as centres of learning naturally suited for the sort of individualized learning schools need to provide. Yet we also recognize that a conscious effort to provide access to all sorts of learners is not necessarily problem-free.

Open windows, like open doors, may make room for new faces in museums, places that traditionally have been reserved for an elite minority of patrons and learners. Will traditional audiences and their support be threatened or bolstered by the appearance of new, diverse groups of museum-goers? If learners are empowered to construct their own understandings in museums, to navigate their own course of learning, to decide for themselves what they will and will not look at and what information best facilitates the unique understandings they are constructing, what will become of the museum educator? If an educator is accustomed to standing in front of a group of visitors – like the teacher before the class – pouring facts into the ready but empty vessels attending (the educator hopes) to every word, that educator will have to rewrite the part. But then, nothing worthwhile is easily gained; no change is without risk.

Many museum-goers, novice or not, feel like outsiders in museums. Even when they are given free passes, they sense a subtle lack of welcome. Yet the question 'Who are the insiders in museums?' is likely to get as many different answers as individuals questioned. In schools, on the other hand, we have learned that the real insiders, the children Binet assured us would do well in school, are few and far between. Instead of dismissing the varied and vast array of performances of understanding of which different children are capable, educators have been encouraged to rise to the challenge of individually centred schools.

Many out-of-school youth museums already provide individually centred learning experiences that educators can complement in school. At the same time, other museums seriously dedicated to the mission of education are adding elements that are uniquely and ideally suited for individualized learning. In this way they are opening both windows and doors to many otherwise disenfranchised learners. The individually centred museum is an exciting work in progress: a plot and a set in ready position, a script that is being rewritten, and a whole new cast of characters ready to step on stage.

This chapter first appeared as an article in Museum News *(January/February 1993): 34–7, 57–8.*

10

Museum multicultural education for young learners

Joseph H. Suina

Multicultural education underpins all education work, including museum education. Symbolic, iconic and enactive learning modes are described, with museums being identified as rich with iconic and enactive learning opportunities. Through their objects museums can provide the knowledge and stimulate the thinking skills, social and academic skills, and values and attitudes that can help achieve society's goal for multicultural living.

Multicultural education has been defined in numerous ways by various groups and individuals for the past twenty years.[1] Some definitions reflect the perspectives of specific disciplines such as psychology, anthropology and sociology. Others represent the views of professional organizations and accrediting agencies that are concerned with what teachers need to teach and what students need to learn for effective participation in the multiple realities of life. An example of this is the statement on multicultural education issued by the American Association of Colleges for Teacher Education.[2] Still other definitions have been developed and adopted by educators within schools and school districts across the country.

Most teachers recognize the multiple realities that exist within the population of each school and, in many cases, within each classroom. They are also very aware of the demands that society places on them for preparing students for the world in immediate and long-range terms. These demands mean students must learn to communicate and interact with people from a wide range of cultural backgrounds. Thus multicultural education is first of all a process through which individuals develop ways of perceiving, evaluating and behaving within cultural systems unlike their own.[3] Second, multicultural education requires a consideration of the forces that exert powerful influences within local, national and global settings. These forces will affect priorities and direction in education at all dimensions.

In the final analysis multicultural education is education for all students in what is reality today – a multicultural society. What classroom teachers and museum educators ultimately do depends upon their point of view and their knowledge and ability to provide positive cross-cultural experiences and attitudes for their students.

Museums possess a tremendous potential for the development and encouragement of the goals of multicultural education. By their nature and function, museums confront the multiple dimensions of human cultures across time and space. For schools, museums serve as places where people collect, display and share fragments of the world in which we live. Many focus on non-human topics, such as desert ecology, and many more focus on people from different cultures or at least on a part of their life. This slice of culture may be the world of work, or inventions over the years, or a famous artist. Museums are filled with a wealth of real things and replicas of people, places, processes and events. Most important, museums are places for teaching and learning.

G. W. Maxim describes learning experiences for young students through three modes of contact with the material to be learned.[4] One is through the symbolic mode. The symbolic mode is by far the most prevalent in elementary schools, and it almost always takes the written form. Yet, while literacy is much valued in our society, experts tell us that the symbolic mode is highly abstract and too advanced for many elementary school-age pupils. Their concrete stage of cognitive development may not permit sufficient comprehension of the material even if the word symbols are recognized. The limited experience of most young children further limits the use of the symbolic mode.

The second type of contact is what Maxim refers to as the iconic mode. This mode involves 'imagery' or the use of representations of the actual through physical models, films and other means. Student-made dioramas or scenes from a unit of study are examples that can be found in classrooms. Pioneer life might be presented by means of a small-scale but lifelike model of a frontier town. Iconic material need not, however, be to scale; the important thing is that it illustrates in realistic form what is being taught. Students may have an opportunity to interact with iconic material through some kind of hands-on experience, but most often they experience it through the medium of film.

The enactive mode is the third form of learning experience. It is learning through the use of authentic items, events, ideas and people. This form is only rarely used in classrooms, but it does occur when, for example, a community resource person is brought in to do a demonstration or students are taken on a field trip to observe a process. Because the enactive form requires planning, co-ordination and possible fees, learners are not often exposed to the 'real thing'.

Yet the iconic and enactive modes are the most successful because younger learners learn best by doing and 'just messing around' with materials and ideas, by experiencing through touching, hearing, seeing, smelling and tasting. Firsthand interaction with learning materials tantalizes senses not usually exercised in symbolic school experiences. At best, textbooks provide facts and information about names, dates, places and events, but models and authentic experiences 'breathe life' into the print on the page.

At the same time, museums are incredibly rich with iconic and enactive learning opportunities. They furnish firsthand experiences and allow for learning by discovery. One museum, for example, offers a 'Try-out Tools Kit' of materials from a prehistoric culture. Through their objects museums can provide the knowledge and stimulate the thinking skills, social and academic skills, and values and attitudes that can help achieve society's goals for multicultural living.

While all the kinds of learning that museums foster are important, their promotion of knowledge, values and attitudes are most essential in the achievement of positive multiculturalism. Since museums frequently present different cultures at various points in time, their contribution to greater understanding and appreciation of different lifeways can be invaluable. Many museums state that their goal is to enhance the visitors' ability to understand, appreciate, and respect the cultures they feature. This goal can be accomplished through responsible and sensitive teaching practices in collecting, exhibiting and explaining artefacts and ideas.

In museum education, as in any education, the educators are the critical variable. It is they who make the goals of acceptance, appreciation and respect attainable. As teachers, they provide the inspiration for others to adopt pluralism as a positive goal to strive for.

The critical variable that begins with the teacher requires constant self-scrutiny.[5] Museum educators, like everyone else, have developed their share of biases and prejudices. Educators are often reluctant to admit that they harbour feelings and attitudes that relegate certain groups to lesser status. Like most people, they tend to think of prejudice and racism as blatant expressions of hatred toward those who are different. Since most educators do not perceive themselves as blatant discriminators, they might see themselves as free of prejudice. Yet their 'colour-blind' approach may be nothing more than a veneer of acceptance over true feelings, just below the surface, that remain unexamined and so ready to come into play. Dealing with these biases begins with individual awareness. Once the biases have been recognized, action can be taken to correct prejudices and to develop more suitable attitudes and behaviours.

It is important to recognize that the perception of the culturally different almost always involves some degree of ethnocentrism. The perceiver's own culture naturally tends to be the standard against which others are measured and quite unconsciously is accorded superior status.[6] The danger is that such measurement tends to obstruct understanding. Museum educators come into contact with schoolchildren who hold varying degrees of ethnocentrism, and the educators cannot be held responsible for that. They do have to assume responsibility, however, for the impression they leave with the schoolchildren.

It is extremely important that museum educators do not encourage the natural tendency toward ethnocentrism through insensitive dissemination of information. Instead, they should provide a context for the cultures they present, explaining the circumstances of time, place and situation the people of the culture faced.

For many visitors both young and old, the museum may be the only 'educational' contact they have had with another culture. The impression they get from the museum will persist in future encounters, be they casual conversation about the culture or face-to-face associations with the people and their descendants.

Proper presentation of a culture begins with a sound preparation for working with young people and a thorough knowledge about the culture to be shared. The knowledge should be accurate, up-to-date, and deep enough to cover what is significant for young learners. The presentation should allow the learners to understand people in terms of universal concerns as well as differing responses. Detailed information helps educators present individual artefacts in broad context. Projectile points, for example, can be presented as important food-gathering tools as well as viable weapons for use against the enemy. Recognizing similar needs and cross-cultural concerns provides a framework within which young learners can achieve understanding and empathy.[7] It is also an effective means for combating stereotypes, which develop by identifying those who are different through only a few isolated, salient features.

Knowledge also provides a basis with which to model respect for the culture. It is very important, for example, to know and respect a culture's prescribed practice for disposal of the dead. Some cultures believe that the spirit of the dead resides in the remains and will never be at rest until they are properly placed in the final resting site. Violating mores like these denigrates museums and those who run them. And insensitivity propagates insensitivity. On this issue of human remains, one Asian-American woman remarked, 'Anglos have no sense of right and wrong, and that's just the way they are!' The victim culture will not be the only one to react with disdain on such matters. Many informed groups outside a culture have protested insensitive treatment of one group by another.

In situations where it is permissible to share skeletal remains, the sharing should always be with the utmost respect and dignity. An example of a serious breach of respect occurred in a display of the remains of a prehistoric woman at a much-visited museum. The museum staff renamed her Esther. No doubt the idea was that the name would affectionately personalize the woman, but in reality the name encouraged her to become the brunt of modern-day humour among the museum employees. This humour, thought to be clever, was shared, to the delight of museum visitors. One day Esther was adorned with a tourist hat and sunglasses and a cute notation at her side. After a while she became just a joke.

Callous, inhumane treatment of people and cultures should not be condoned, especially by those charged with the task of developing respect and appreciation for world cultures. Consider that none of us would want to have our remains or those of our loved ones on public display, much less be the brunt of jokes no matter how innocent the intent. Second, such treatment not only violates common decency across cultures but repulses many people. But most tragically, it sends a clear message to schoolchildren that it is perfectly acceptable to treat other human beings in this manner as long as they are not a member of one's immediate concern.

Religion is an area that is highly susceptible to misinterpretation and ridicule, particularly religions that are not Judeo-Christian. A religion that is not fully understood may appear to be 'odd' or superstitious. That does not mean, however, that it cannot serve its people or that those who practise it are simple-minded pagans. When shamans are discussed, for example, they are often confused with witch doctors, magicians and medicine men. Even when the term 'medicine man' is correctly applied, it is often thought to suggest primitivism that closes off understanding. Yet the unexplained cannot be explained through scientific reasoning or modern-day religion. The truth of the matter is that many modern-day religions do not fare much better in their explanations of the metaphysical, resorting to faith as the catch-all justification through which the unexplained becomes acceptable.

Some cultures have artefacts that are regarded as highly sensitive and even forbidden because of their deep religious significance. That is, the artefact and the meaning it holds are not to be shared with non-members of the culture. In some cases they are not to be shared with members who are not yet privileged: children who have not reached a predetermined stage of maturity or adults who have not been initiated.

While this meaning may seem like nothing more than information and so legitimate for sharing by the general public, museum educators need to take care that non-privileged members of the culture are not exposed to the meaning. It is not always possible to honour a specific taboo, yet museum educators, particularly when they take a travelling display to a classroom, need to be alert to the composition of the student audience. One example of a forbidden artefact is the kachina doll or model of the Pueblo Indian spirit in the American south-west. Kachinas are considered highly sacred and should be respected accordingly. To the people of the Pueblo culture, museum displays or programmes using kachinas violate the taboo that the dolls should not be seen in any form outside the ceremonial context. To them such a display or sharing is as sacrilegious as permitting children to play with a holy communion host would be to Roman Catholics. In both instances the artefacts were intended to be shared only under well-defined conditions. Some cultures represented in museums no longer exist, but there are others whose members maintain traditions, and issues regarding the display and treatment of their artefacts are increasingly sensitive.

There are other taboos of a less severe nature that still need to be acknowledged if not adhered to, especially if it is known that the cultural group will be affected in a personal way. Telling and reading stories designated for seasonal use are examples. One culture may have stories for winter use only. If possible, those should be read in winter only, and the seasonal associations should be explained. Such action is a lesson in respect for all cultures. In this way, children develop the caring and sensitivity that are essential to the values and attitudes of positive multicultural education.

In summary, museums offer young learners experiences that are highly desirable for their developmental level and have the potential to involve multiple senses in a discovery learning format. The content of this museum learning is often the culture of a people. Thus museum educators are in an excellent position to develop ideas and attitudes critical to the success of young learners in understanding and ultimately participating in our multicultural world.

This chapter first appeared as a paper in Journal of Museum Education *15(1) (1990): 12–15.*

NOTES

1 Sleeter, C. E. and Grant, C. A., 'An analysis of multicultural education in the United States', *Harvard Educational Review* 57(4) (1987): 421–40; Hernandez, Hilda, *Multicultural Education: A Teacher's Guide to Content and Process* (Columbus, OH: Merrill, 1989).
2 American Association of Colleges for Teacher Education, *AACTA Statement on Multicultural Education* (Washington, DC: AACTA, 1972–3).
3 Ramsey, P. G., 'Multicultural education in early childhood', *Young Children* 37(2) (1982): 13–24.
4 Maxim, G. W., *Social Studies and the Elementary School Child* (Columbus, OH: Merrill, 1987), 267–8.
5 Gold, M. J., Grant, C. A. and Rivlin, H. N., *In Praise of Diversity: A Resource Book for Multicultural Education* (Washington, DC: Teacher Corps, Association of Teacher Educators, 1977).
6 Ramsey, P. G., *Teaching and Learning in a Diverse World: Multicultural Education for Young Children* (New York: Teachers College Press, 1987).
7 Moyer, J. E. and Engelbrecht, G., 'Multicultural education: where do we begin?', *Childhood Education* 53 (March, 1977): 241–4.

11

Children, teenagers and adults in museums: a developmental perspective

Nina Jensen

A developmental perspective based on the work of Jean Piaget and Erik Erikson is used to describe the different needs of children, teenagers and adults in museum learning. Common to all is the tenet that our perceptions are based on our individual and unique histories and experiences. None the less, there are broad similarities in the ways in which people of different life-stages view the world. Knowledge of these can help with programme planning.

This chapter is based on the panel 'Museum audiences: the educator's perspective', presented at the 1981 American Association of Museums (AAM) Annual Meeting. The panellists, museum educators who have applied developmental theory to their work with museum audiences, were Peggy Cole, director of the Fieldston Lower School, Riverdale, NY, and formerly on the faculty of the Bank Street College of Education, New York, NY, who spoke on elementary-school children; Kathryne Andrews, manager of School and Youth Services at the Brooklyn Museum, Brooklyn, NY, who spoke on teenagers; Adrienne Horn, museum consultant in adult education and programme co-ordinator for the Center for Museum Studies, John F. Kennedy University, San Francisco, CA, who spoke on adults; and Theodore Katz, chief of the Division of Education at the Philadelphia Museum of Art, Philadelphia, PA, who spoke on creativity and motivation. The panel was co-chaired by Nina Jensen, acting director of the Museum Education Program at the Bank Street College of Education, and Susan Reichman, former director of the programme. This chapter has been a collaborative effort of the panellists and was edited by Nina Jensen.

Museum programmes must relate to the life-experiences of the audiences they seek to motivate and engage. As museum staff members come to understand their audiences in greater depth, they can create programmes more directly relevant to them.

Traditionally, museum audiences have been considered demographically – by age, ethnicity, occupation, and so forth. There is, however, another perspective – that of developmental theory. The term 'development' refers to the sequential changes in circumstance and perspective that all people experience over time. Loosely linked to chronological age, developmental growth is organized in distinct stages or eras through which all people pass, pushed by a combination of physiological maturation and increased understandings, abilities and knowledge. Developmental theorists whose work has important implications for museum programming include Jean Piaget and Erik Erikson. While their ideas have played a crucial role in shaping current educational theories in schools, their impact has been much less widely felt in museums.

An important tenet of developmental psychology is that all experiences are a unique function of our individual past. Since everyone has a different history and a different way of looking at the world, no two individuals, even of the same age, family, or socio-economic background, have identical perceptions. On the other hand, our experiences also have some important elements of commonality. There are broad descriptors of how infants are different from 5-year-olds, 5-year-olds from 20-year-olds and 20-year-olds from 50-year-olds. These descriptors are useful to educators.

This article will examine the characteristics of three major age-groups – elementary-school children, teenagers and adults – and their implications for museum programming. Issues of creativity and motivation that cut across developmental lines will also be considered.

ELEMENTARY-SCHOOL CHILDREN

Because the experiences of adults in museums are qualitatively different from those of children, it is often difficult for adults to understand the museum visit from the perspective of the child. An important idea from developmental psychology, with implications for children's programming in museums, is that children bring their own experiences and conceptions of the world with them. These conceptions determine how they receive what is presented to them and what they will learn from it. For example, Michael, an 8-year-old intensely interested in the Middle Ages, was taken to see the armour at the Metropolitan Museum of Art. A week later he asked if people had metal in the Middle Ages. When reminded about the armour he had seen in the museum, he replied, 'Yes, but what does that have to do with the Middle Ages?'

This question suggests that children have only the vaguest ideas about how an object gets into a museum and why it is there and even what a museum is. It illustrates how our life-experiences limit our ability to understand objects in the context of a museum. It also suggests the errors in adults' assumptions about what children experience. Despite his interest and background Michael did not understand that the objects in a museum come from another historical period. He has been in the world only eight years, and the armour has been there a lot longer. His experience tells him that something old is dirty, whereas the armour at the Metropolitan is polished and shiny – attributes he associates with new things. Michael's confusion illustrates a phenomenon described by Jean Piaget – that perception is shaped and limited by experience.

Another important idea from developmental psychology is that interaction is the most powerful mode of learning. Interaction is the opposite of passivity. We do not simply bring experiences to the world, nor do we perceive what is there in pure form. We impose our experiences on the world, be it an object or another person. In terms of Kantian epistemology, the basis of Piagetian theory, 'The mind gives the law to nature'. Knowledge is acquired in a continuous process of accommodating prior expectations and beliefs to new realities learned through interactive experiences.

Learning involves conflict between a person's conception of reality and new encounters with the real. This conflict or dissonance leads to what Piaget calls 'accommodation'. Children (and adults also) are constantly restructuring their ideas about the world as new information is received. This dynamic process between the learner and his or her experiences is basic to what happens in museums.

Words are confusing to children who do not have experiences to back them up. Piagetian theory suggests that ideas are formed first, words second – not the other way around. But words have a special seduction for children because their language acquisition is at an all-time high. Most children who have heard Peter Rabbit stories have chamomile tea in their vocabulary, but their ideas of what it is are often confused, even humorous, because they have no experience with it. One can find out about chamomile tea only by drinking it; it has a particular colour, smell and taste. Because children can recite words by rote without understanding their meanings, they may seem to know more than they do. Learning moves from the concrete to the abstract more slowly than many educators care to admit. Because their thinking is so concrete, children often are confused about what is real and what is representational. They can become frightened by images of things; the distinction between reality and fantasy is not always clear. A costumed mannequin in the Brooklyn Museum's eighteenth-century period rooms magically came to life for a fourth grader as he exclaimed, 'Look! I saw her move!'

Elementary-school children have trouble dealing with the past because their understanding of time-periods is incomplete. Since many museum programmes and collections require an understanding of the context of historical periods, and since most children have not got this understanding worked out yet, they make the most amazing connections between things that have no relationship. For example, a group of 10-year-olds had just completed a detailed study of how Christopher Columbus had preserved food during his voyage to the New World. They had learned that the food was hung over the side of the ship to dry in the air. When the teacher asked the children what the sailors used for containers, some children thought they used baggies.

Children experience a sense of powerlessness in museums, as they do in many aspects of their lives. Unlike other age-groups, they are rarely in museums by free choice. For the most part adults tell children what to do; adults have control, while children wish that *they* did. By offering children choices during museum visits, such as allowing them to choose a work of art on which to focus, educators can give them some feeling of power and command over their museum experience.

In addition, museum programmes for children should focus on only a few objects of interest to them and present ideas about those objects that are graspable and relevant. Otherwise the artefacts in museums will be for children like so many other things in their lives – simply there, without explanation and outside their control. A selective and limited focus will foster in children a sense of mastery and command in a potentially strange and overwhelming setting and will increase the chances of their really understanding the ideas behind the words and objects to which they are introduced.

TEENAGERS

Developmental theory plays an important role in understanding the museum experiences of teenagers as well as children. These experiences are necessarily modified by the cultural setting in which US teenagers find themselves, a setting shaped by their families, their peers and the larger aspects of American society in the late twentieth century. The reasons teenagers visit museums less often than younger children or adults are suggested by a study of teenagers and museums done at the Brooklyn Museum.[1] The teen years are a volatile point in emotional development. Teenagers are especially sensitive to condescension, and museum staff who act in patronizing ways merely confirm their opinion that museums are 'not for them'. Preoccupied with their own independence and coming separation from their families, they often reject museum visits because of their close association with family values.

Teenagers are, physically speaking, adults. Capable of giving birth or carrying a gun to war, they are, at the same time, financially and intellectually dependent on their families. They live with the continual contradiction that while they have the capacity to be on their own, apart from their families, most in fact do live at home. Required to comply with family viewpoints and roles in exchange for financial support, teenagers often feel conflicts of allegiance.

It is in their groups that teenagers develop a sense of themselves as individuals. Thus, for most teenagers a vital aspect of their school life is social as well as academic. Museums are also viewed as places in which to socialize with friends. In fact, visiting museums without friends holds little interest for them. Over two-thirds of the teenagers interviewed in the Brooklyn Museum study were significantly more interested in museum visits when they could attend with friends.

Because non-academic clubs and interest groups are voluntary, they serve important social needs for teenagers. Groups play a very large role in teenagers' lives, and teenagers devote enormous amounts of time to them. In seeking teenage audiences, museums might productively turn to these groups, both within and beyond the school setting. Teenagers for the Brooklyn Museum study, for instance, came from voluntarily attended youth and community groups. Interest groups can be formed by the museum itself. In conjunction with an exhibition of documentary photographs, the Brooklyn Museum invited photography students from several high schools to create their own exhibition. One of the most important aspects of the programme was simply the opportunity for these teenagers to meet and talk shop with peers from other schools.

Today's teenagers have a practical outlook on life. School is often perceived as a means to an end – getting into college and getting a good job in the face of high unemployment and economic instability. The Brooklyn Museum study found teenagers to be singularly lacking in curiosity and without access to an aesthetic, humanistic, or historical framework to help them appreciate the objects in a museum. Their life-experience is necessarily narrow. Museum educators are thus challenged to present programmes that focus on universal human experiences and that teach the tools or frames with which to think and perceive. We need to help teenagers understand, for instance, that art and history can connect them to the thoughts and feelings of others. As they learn how artists have expressed feelings about power, conflict, war, justice and love, they may be helped to understand these and other issues in relationship to their own lives.

Despite their lack of curiosity, teenagers have the capacity to be imaginative and thoughtful and to extend themselves into the lives of others. They need opportunities for self-expression and creative learning. When asked what they did like about museums, teenagers in the study stated that museums gave them opportunities to 'have conversations about important issues' and to 'absorb ideas about other cultures into our own thoughts'. One 16-year-old girl commented that 'seeing a painting is like reading a poem'.

Perhaps most of all, teenagers want and need opportunities to learn in ways that support their self-esteem and growing independence. Having developed the ability to think at least somewhat analytically and abstractly, they need to know that their ideas will be listened to and respected in the museum setting.

ADULTS

Over the years attention to human growth, learning and development has focused on childhood and adolescence. Recent changes in our society and its values, however, together with an ageing population, have created a greater awareness of learning and development in adult life.

Adult learning is different from that of children. Malcolm Knowles, a scholar widely respected in the field of adult education, has explained the characteristics of adult learners that make them different.[2] To children experience is external, something that happens to them; to adults personal experience has defined their individual identity. Because adults have a richer foundation of experience than children, new material they learn takes on heightened meaning as it relates to past experiences. For example, because middle-aged and older people have a personal sense of history – they have lived through events – they relate to history in a way that few youngsters can. Adults see how various social problems have recurred during their lifetime; they see vital movements and issues with an insight that children cannot have.

For children, learning tends to be teacher-directed; children learn what is taught by parents and teachers. Adults, on the other hand, are independent learners and search for education programmes that answer their own questions instead of those of someone else. They seek learning experiences related to their changing roles as workers, parents, spouses and leisure-time users. Adults enrol in classes or participate in programmes related to their personal interests or to acquire skills and understandings that will help them answer immediate questions. Children, by contrast, view education as something to be used in the future. For adults education is an independent and personal choice. Since they take responsibility for their own learning, they expect excellence in education programmes.

While adult learning ability may remain relatively stable throughout adult life, there is still substantial growth and development. The popular conception of adulthood as a time of little change over the course of many years has been challenged by the findings of developmental psychology. Knowles points out that adults have a 'readiness to learn' which, at its peak, presents a 'teachable moment'. Just as a child cannot walk until it has crawled and its leg muscles are strong enough, so adults, too, have their phases of growth and development, their teachable moments. The development of adults, however, is not primarily physiological; it is related to their changing social roles.

Adults experience developing patterns of interest as they move through the life-cycle. Generally speaking, vocational life and family life are the primary concerns of young adults (ages 18–35) as they seek to establish themselves in work and at home. In middle adulthood (ages 35–55) these concerns decrease in favour of interests in health and civic and social activities. As they near retirement adults become occupied with interpreting culture and life, with the health problems of advancing age.

The unique perspectives of adulthood have implications for museum programme themes and topics. Themes from the humanities can be of particular interest to adults who, because of their own experiences, may identify personally with the subjects presented. The Toledo Museum of Art's programme 'The new American scene' examined various aspects of the life-styles and art of contemporary American society. Some natural history museums have used the humanities to link their collections with life-related issues. The Carnegie Museum of Natural History in Pittsburgh has used the theme 'Becoming human' to explain the influence of biological and cultural forces on the processes of human development.[3] Relating museum programmes and collections to the broad threads of human experience is one means of bringing objects to life in a way that is emotionally stimulating and meaningful to a broad spectrum of adult audiences.

In considering the stages of adult development, it is important to recognize that the adult population is not homogeneous. Obviously many variables, such as occupation, sex, social class, income level, educational background and ethnicity, further define adult groups. In programming for its exhibition 'Manifestations of Shiva', the Seattle Art Museum appealed to adults with various interests and at different stages of their lives. Elements of the programme, which dealt with the culture of India – its music, literature, history, religions, art and daily life – were adapted to different segments of the public, such as families, senior citizens and scholars. Museums can conduct 'needs assessments' in order to determine what programmes are of interest to their potential adult audiences.

Regardless of the motivation – the particular reason for the 'teachable moment' – it is important for museums to capitalize on the readiness of adults to learn. Adults bring their own expectations, goals and experiences to museums, and museum programmes should recognize and accommodate them.

PROGRAMMING FOR CHILDREN, TEENAGERS AND ADULTS

Accepting the implications of developmental theory as it pertains to potential participants in museum programmes, we face the challenge of providing rich encounters for diverse audiences from our equally diverse collections. Is the ultimate implication of developmental theory that there should be separate exhibitions or programmes for separate audiences? Can a single programme reach all three groups?

This is what the Division of Education of the Philadelphia Museum of Art set out to discover through a programme entitled 'Art as a reflection of human concerns'.[4] As the basic goal was to produce a programme that would make possible significant and interesting experiences for visitors of all ages, the subject had to be broad. Seven themes were selected – family, humour, religion, ageing, death, birth and love – each to be considered for a period of one month. Topics focused on the vital importance of these themes, not only in subject-matter but as inspiration for human creativity. Consideration of developmental theory helped staff members to design specific activities introducing the monthly theme to various age-groups. Gallery talks, films, workshops, concerts, plays and lectures were planned and presented specifically for children, teenagers, adults and family groups. These related the monthly theme to selected objects from the museum's collections. Information sheets as guides to independent study were available as well as other handout material that visitors could pick up around the museum each month. Staff members developed these 'pick-me-ups', each of which presented a brief, humanistic interpretation of a work of art selected from the collection.

For elementary-school children, programmes combined education with entertainment so children would want to participate instead of feeling their visit was one more activity forced upon them by adults. During the Family month children viewed such films as *The Red Balloon* and *The Golden Fish*; during Humour, they participated in a live mime presentation. Peter Pan came to life in a performance during the month on Ageing. Even the programme concerning Death – a theme that might be expected only to frighten youngsters – became an enjoyable learning experience through an afternoon of story-telling and folk songs.

For teenagers, pre-eminently concerned with asserting their own identities and independence, programmes were designed to consider what the world looks like when coloured by the strong private visions of artists. Teen activities were not structured around group sessions with their atmosphere of authority. Instead young people were given printed programme material and directed to the galleries on their own. One programme appealed to their interest in personal identity by asking them to match self-portraits in the galleries with written passages either by or about the portrait subjects. The 'detective work' aspect of the activity further appealed to their sense of challenge and gamesmanship.

For adults, programmes aimed to cut across divisions of social class, cultural interests and race. Lectures by visiting scholars on topics such as 'Are pictures to be smashed or worshipped?', 'Ageing: East and West' and 'Family: fragmented or whole?' further reinforced programme themes, as did gallery talks like 'Humour in oriental art' and 'Ageing and agelessness in the painting of Thomas Eakins'. *Beauty and the Beast, The Clowns* and *Ulysses* were among the films shown during the course of the programme. A visitor survey administered at these programmes confirmed that most people attended because of their interest in the topics rather than in specific speakers or works of art. Because topics such as birth, family, ageing and death speak directly to the developmental concerns of all adults, the programme successfully attracted a large and diverse new audience. Over half those attending the programmes were not museum members, and significant numbers were not regular museum-goers. Variations in age, sex, race and level of education were much greater in those attending these programmes than in more traditional museum offerings.

William James said:

> Every new experience must be disposed of under some old head. The great point is to find the head which has to be least altered to take it in. . . . The great maxim in pedagogy is to knit every new piece of knowledge on to a preexisting curiosity – i.e., to assimilate its matter in some way to what is already known![5]

An important implication of developmental theory as it pertains to museum programmes is that the museum environment must reward the individual's attention. The enjoyment of, and learning from, museum collections will vary according to the individual's perception and learning abilities. We must know our audiences, their interests and their abilities, in order to offer programmes and exhibitions with which they will identify. We must respect the value of initial 'engaging' activities; from the immediately attractive and easily accessible, visitors can proceed to consideration of the content of collections in more sophisticated and subtle forms. With attention to developmental theories, exhibitions and programmes can be designed to reveal the richness of museum collections not only as ends and objects of study, but also as beginnings, subjects for wonder and exploration, insights into one's own identity and potential.

This chapter first appeared as a paper in Museum News *(May/June 1982).*

NOTES

1 Andrews, Kathryne and Asia, Carolyn, 'Teenagers' attitudes about art museums', *Curator* 23 (1979): 229. This article is a report on a study, funded by the National Endowment for the Humanities, on the interests and needs of Brooklyn's teenagers and the development of museum programmes.
2 Knowles, Malcolm S., *The Modern Practice of Adult Education*, 8th edn (New York: Association Press, 1977).
3 The programmes developed by the Toledo Museum of Art and the Carnegie Museum of Natural History are described in detail in Collins, Zipporah W. (ed.) *Museums, Adults and the Humanities:*

A Guide for Educational Programming (Washington, DC: American Association of Museums, 1981), 177–97, 211–18.
4 'Art as a reflection of human concerns' is described in detail in ibid.: 236–56.
5 Quoted in James, William, *Psychology: Briefer Course* (New York: Collier Books, 1966), 332–3.

12

Museum-goers: life-styles and learning characteristics
Charles F. Gunther

What research is available to help understand why adults come to museums and what they learn there? This article describes psychographic and market research, and discusses the learning style of adults according to life-stage and individual preferences.

The needs of adult learners within the museum are identified and suggestions made as to what provision would be appropriate.

> This museum is a lot more than pretty pictures on the wall.
> This is a hall of ideas!
>
> (Michael Morgenstern,
> sculptor and former factory worker)

The author of the epigraph tells us as much about his needs as an adult as he does about the museum. In attempting to analyse these needs, researchers have acquired a great deal of general information about adults, their leisure-time activities, and their values, life-styles and learning characteristics. Moreover, visitor studies in museums have shown us who our adult visitors are and how they behave. Community studies have also revealed who the *potential* visitors are and how to bring them into the museum.

While this research assists us in meeting the learning expectations of adults, the really creative opportunities and choices about the museum experience and its programmes fall to adult educators, either within the museum or in university continuing education programmes. This chapter examines some of the available data explaining how and why people use museums, and it explores the role that learning plays in attracting people to museums and in enhancing the museum experience. The final section deals with applying this information, not only to the museum environment and programmes but to co-operative efforts with continuing education programmes.

ADULTS: LEISURE TIME, VALUES AND LIFE-STYLES

Adults who come to the museum will of course vary, but the ideal visitor comes initially because the museum offers a new experience and a chance to be around other people. If this visitor has a good time, he or she will most likely return. Thus, the crux of the issue is determining what 'having a good time' means for different segments of the population and ways in which that knowledge can be applied to enhance the museum experience.

In researching her doctoral dissertation 'Adult attitudes toward leisure choices in relation to museum participation', Marilyn G. Hood found five attributes of pleasurable or satisfying leisure experiences, based on literature in the fields of leisure science, sociology and marketing:

- the opportunity to learn
- social interaction
- the challenge of new experiences
- participating actively
- feeling comfortable in one's surroundings[1]

In conducting community research in the Toledo metropolitan area, Hood identified a sixth condition that had received minor attention in the literature; doing something worthwhile, or performing some service for other people while engaging in leisure activities. This last attribute emerged from focus groups in a community where over 1,000 volunteers were contributing some 8,300 hours of their time annually to the museum.

This research indicates that a leisure experience must be seen as a package of good and bad moments, with total worth to the individual balanced against the total cost (travel, time, mental saturation fatigue, cost, etc.). Studies of theatre and symphony attendance show that the decision to participate is based on the likelihood of liking the particular programme, understanding what is going on, enjoyment of the event by one's companions, and attending a stimulating event.[2] A recent University of Chicago study talks about 'the problem of providing fertile enough conditions so that viewers might encounter works of art with interest, confidence, and the anticipation of a positive and enjoyable experience'.[3]

Both family and friendship groups list social interaction as a prime reason for participation in cultural events. In the Toledo community study, the most important leisure factors for occasional visitors were found to be opportunities for social interaction with family and friends, feeling comfortable in one's surroundings, and active participation. Beaches, parks and zoos are recreation places not only because of the activities that occur there or because of their physical environments, but because of the social meanings attributed to them by the people who go there.[4] The socialization process, or transmission from parents and reference groups of values, attitudes, skills, social norms, tastes and expectations that may predispose a person toward certain future actions or life-styles, also proved to be a major motivating factor for participation in leisure activities.[5]

The Values and Lifestyles programme (VALS), begun in 1978 by the marketing research firm SRI International, has focused on behavioural analysis, with an emphasis on the individual as consumer. With attention to theories of human motivation, such as Abraham Maslow's needs hierarchy, SRI has developed a typology for American consumer behaviour that identifies nine different market segments; see Table 12.1.[6]

In 1983, the Association of College, University and Community Arts Administrators (ACUCAA) contracted with SRI to study the most affluent and generally sophisticated 40 per cent of Americans in relation to attendance at performing arts events. This research, which focused on only four of the VALS market segments, provides very useful information about those adults most likely to visit museums and participate in museum-continuing education programmes:

> **Achievers** Strongly outer-directed, middle-aged, prosperous, self-assured leaders and builders of the traditional American dream, the least well educated of these four VALS groups. 'Arts and music are important in my life' – 11 per cent strongly agree; 15.44 per cent mostly agree.

Table 12.1 Typology of US consumer behaviour

	% of population
Need-Driven	11
Survivors	4
Sustainers	7
Outer-Directed	67
Belongers	38
Emulators	21
Achievers	8
Inner-Directed	20
I-Am-Me's	3
Experientials	5
Societally Conscious	12
Integrated	2

Experientials Youthful, tend to be single females seeking direct experience, artistic, intensely oriented toward people and inner growth. Many are employed part-time. 'Arts and music are important in my life' – 31.1 per cent agree; 17.0 per cent mostly agree.

Societally Conscious Mission-oriented, mostly married, excellently educated, self-aware, liberal, having wide-ranging interests, reasonably affluent, inner-directed. See themselves as middle- or upper-class. 'Art and music are important in my life' – 24.6 per cent strongly agree; 24.6 per cent mostly agree.

Integrated Psychologically mature, balanced, flexible, having an excellent education; often concerned with 'the big picture'. 'Art and music are important in my life' – 11.4 per cent agree; 18.2 per cent mostly agree.[7]

In general, adults attend concerts and performances to be entertained, or to see a particular show, performer, or group. More specifically, *achievers* are motivated by external reasons, such as sociability and business, while *societally conscious* persons are largely inner-oriented. They attend in order to be moved or to fulfil themselves. *Experientials* value these events as social celebrations. SRI concluded that persons in the categories of *integrated* and *achievers* appear to be users of the performing arts, rather than enjoyers. They detected a hint that these adults attend out of obligation rather than pleasure.

The upscale consumers who form the core of performing arts patrons had extensive exposure to the arts as children. An early background in the arts seemed more important for music than for theatre or dance. To be active as an artist, however, seemed unrelated to attendance. In general, those surveyed by SRI had positive feelings about the arts, which they generally regarded as pleasurable, creative, fun, inspiring and educational. These adults were most likely to be involved in the arts and were potential future marketing targets.

In the SRI study for ACUCAA, Arnold Mitchell observes that individuals are not fixed at one level but may move to another level that brings with it a whole new set of values rearranging, redefining and extending those of the previous stage.[8] So an individual's totality consists of layers of spheres of values 'like the layers of an onion'. The more developed a person is, and the more levels she or he has moved through, the more complex her or his value-based reactions.

More recently, the National Association for Senior Living Industries commissioned SRI International to conduct studies similar to the VALS programme, but focused on older Americans. Pre-testing of the Lifestyles and Values of Older Adults Survey questionnaire revealed that older adults are uncomfortable with such age-based terms as 'senior citizen', 'retiree', and 'golden years'.[9] Rather, products and services intended for the older market are best sold as gateways to personal growth and development. To older people, the value of a discretionary product or service is determined by its potential for consequential experiences or its capacity to serve as a gateway to other pleasurable experiences.

ADULTS AS LEARNERS

Museum visitors represent a full range of educational levels and learning styles. However, most are well educated: they have high-level occupations and high incomes. Many are young professionals who also enjoy being outdoors and active. They tend to be involved in the community and participate in various cultural events.

In the museum, some of these adults appear to wander aimlessly but want to be left alone; others seek out information. Their enjoyment of any given gallery or object will be more intense if past experience has given them some relevant knowledge or insight. In fact, they will seek out those areas that reinforce current preferences and knowledge, and will avoid areas foreign to them. If you tried to reach all these adults through a lecture tour, the majority would not learn as well as the 25 per cent who thrive on this format.

Over the past twenty-five years, theories about adult education (often called 'andragogy', as opposed to 'pedagogy', the teaching of children) have blossomed and now provide a rich resource for educators who are developing museum programmes. Perhaps the most widely known and accepted theories have been developed by Malcolm S. Knowles, who identified these major characteristics of learners:

1 They are highly independent and self-directed in their choices of learning opportunities. Further, they teach themselves much of what they learn.
2 Their backgrounds and experiences provide rich resources for learning.
3 Phases of social development often motivate their choices of learning activities (young parent, upward-moving professional, retiree, etc.).
4 They choose learning opportunities that address a specific problem or that permit the information or skill to be used immediately.[10]

To recognize and capitalize on the characteristics of adult learners, Knowles and others recommend designing learning experiences in a climate of openness and respect, with mutual collaboration to identify what adults want and need to learn. Adults enjoy planning and carrying out their own learning exercises, and they need to be involved in evaluating their progress toward self-chosen goals. Adults, says Knowles, define who they are in terms of past experience. Failure to recognize the experiences of an adult learner is equivalent to rejecting the adult as a person.

Adults choose development tasks that increasingly move them toward social and occupational role competence. Readiness to learn and teachable moments peak when a learning opportunity is co-ordinated with a recognition of the need to know. A young father enrols himself and his child in a museum family workshop because he wants to transmit his own cultural values. A mother with grown children signs up for a photography class because she finds herself with more time to develop her own interests. A retired couple attends a weekly series on Japan because they have more opportunity to travel, while the business executive comes because of new contacts with Japanese counterparts.

Addressing the need for immediate application of knowledge and skills requires a strong emphasis on the concept of students learning rather than teachers teaching. Practical, hands-on experiences that result in an end-product and gallery activities that require using new information to make additional discoveries, have proven to be highly successful with adults. In an article called 'Why adults learn in different ways', Mary Jane Even notes that learning is private while teaching is public, and she stresses the need to use many examples, techniques and approaches. She observes that each individual learns in a unique manner due to 'personal life experiences, neurological brain responses, style preferences, personality dimensions, resultant interests, predispositions to select topics and approaches to work to life, and to processes which generate individual interest and need'.[11]

Individual learning styles have been the focus of research by Bernice McCarthy, who has combined her teaching experience with analysis of twentieth-century learning theory to identify four basic types of learners. Variations in learning styles describe those educational conditions under which adults are most likely to learn and where their comfort level will be high. To some degree, these learning styles explain what sorts of experiences adults are looking for in a museum. A brief summary of McCarthy's descriptors follows.

The 4Mat system of teaching–learning styles

Type One Learners
Perceive information concretely and process it reflectively. Learn by listening and sharing ideas. Like discussions. Excel in viewing direct experience from many perspectives. Value insight thinking. When visiting museum, they are seeking personal meaning. Favorite question: 'Why?'

Type Two Learners
Perceive information abstractly and process it reflectively. Like facts and details. Need to know what the experts think. Critique information and collect data. Are uncomfortable with the subjective. When visiting a museum, they will read all the labels looking for facts. Favorite question: 'What?'

Type Three Learners
Perceive information abstractly and process it actively. Are pragmatists who apply common sense. Are skills-oriented. Need to know how things are put together. Seek information which is useful. When visiting a museum, they want to know how artists create and how objects evolve. Favorite question: 'How does it work?'

Type Four Learners
Perceive information concretely and process it actively. Learn by trial and error. Believe in self-discovery. Like variety and are enthusiastic about new experiences. Like to get involved. They would tend to take museum classes where they can experiment with new material and different ideas. Favorite question: 'If?'[12]

McCarthy observes that all four learning styles are equally valid and are usually found equally present in the typical group of adult learners. Museums must recognize that visitors are approaching the experience of viewing their collections from different points of view. If learning is directed toward only one type of learner, the others are not receiving the message.

ADULTS AS MUSEUM VISITORS

Some adults visit museums frequently, while others come only for a special reason, such as an exhibition opening or social event. Frequent visitors may comprise as much as 50 per cent of a museum's annual attendance.

One segment of adult visitors, often seen in family groups, seem to be truly uncomfortable in museums. If children are with them, the adults tend to act as disciplinarians. In observations of parents at several New York City museums, Deborah P. Benton noted they were often unprepared for the role of teacher, and frequently misinterpreted the museum and its meanings. Few of these people allowed their children to set the pace or to interact with exhibits. Rather, the majority of parents directed both their children's behaviour and their attention, eliminating much of the magic of encounter possible in a museum.[13] For such a group, visiting the museum is not a pleasant, rewarding experience. They feel obliged to bring their children to the museum, but it is a foreign environment that is difficult to decode.

By contrast with this group, some older visitors will visit the museum in pairs and find it immensely enjoyable now that life's other cares and responsibilities are behind them. While some older visitors feel animosity toward museums, many are fascinated by ideas, and the museum satisfies this craving. This need for ideas and challenges is not exclusive to older adults; young professionals seek similar experiences, often to balance their highly technical weekday world.

Childhood experiences in museums were found by Hood to be a factor in enjoyment of museums later in life. She cites several sources, including Paul DiMaggio, Michael Useem and Paula Brown, who pointed out that arts appreciation is primarily developed through training. Understanding most works of art requires familiarity and some background information. This kind of orientation usually takes place through family and school socialization and is most likely to be available to upper-education, upper-income, upper-occupation families.[14]

Hood observed that adults are likely to choose leisure activities that are valued by those people important to them. Several researchers noted that the same leisure activity may be an outlet for different interests as one moves through the life-cycle. Hood's research in Toledo showed that influence of family life-cycle stage on leisure decisions was less important than the age of the adult decision-maker.[15]

The six attributes of leisure participation described earlier correlate with Hood's identification of three types of museum visitors: frequent participants, occasional participants, and non-participants. Each audience perceives benefits of a museum visit in a distinctive way.[16]

Frequent participants are the minority of the present museum audience, but they account for a large proportion of the annual attendance. While representing only about 14 per cent of the Toledo metropolitan area population, they made up 40 to 50 per cent of the annual attendance at the museum. Frequent visitors believe that art museums embody all six of the important attributes for pleasurable and satisfying leisure experiences cited by Hood. Three of these attributes are of utmost importance to them: the

123

opportunity to learn, the challenge of new experiences, and the achievement of something worthwhile during leisure time. They are empathetic with museum values, understand the language of art and the museum code, and are familiar with the social norms of participation in museums.

Their adult involvement with museums usually was a conscious choice made from a wide exposure to cultural organizations and activities from childhood. These people do not mind visiting a museum alone and may even relish the chance to explore at their own pace. Because they visit museums so frequently that they feel at home, the comfort factor is no longer a consideration for them. Making the best use of leisure time is important. They believe that visiting a museum is a worthwhile activity, which provides feelings of accomplishment and expanding horizons. These feelings are closely linked to volunteer involvement. Volunteers know the staff, know all the inside news about what is happening and will happen. At a museum, volunteers enjoy leisure activity that is of service to others and yet personally stimulating.

Frequent participants are less likely to have parental responsibilities than are the other two groups. Since they are less involved with family responsibilities, they are freer to make individual plans. If they are new to the community, they may not yet have established a circle of friends. If they have had pleasurable experiences in museums elsewhere, newcomers to a city are likely to seek a local museum as a focus for their intellectual and cultural life. For frequent visitors, the benefits of museum participation consistently outweigh the price of a visit.[17]

Occasional participants in art museums go once or twice a year. Though they do visit museums, they more closely resemble the non-participants than they do frequent visitors in their values, attitudes and expectations. Because occasional visitors often do not feel comfortable in a museum – or are even intimidated by the building and by exhibitions they do not quite understand – they do not return frequently.

Young adults and parents of young children are interested in social interaction and entertainment activities, but are usually least interested in learning opportunities and doing something worthwhile in leisure time. The social interaction provided by a support group, such as family, friends, or organized clubs, is important because it offers a transition into the less-familiar environment of the museum and validates their being in this setting.

Occasional participants are more likely to be high-school educated and strongly family-oriented. The very recognition by occasional visitors that a museum offers learning opportunities may be a negative element, for their leisure is equated with relaxation, which is associated with interacting socially and informally with a close family or friendship group. Occasional participants are most likely to find a museum visit worthwhile when a special event or exhibition occurs at the museum or when they are entertaining out-of-town guests.[18]

Non-participants in art museums are nearly the opposite of frequent visitors in their values, attitudes and life-styles. Of the three groups, they least value the six leisure attributes identified by Hood. Minimally interested in learning and the challenge of new experiences, they are most interested in social interaction and entertainment activities.

Most are high-school educated individuals whose socialization from childhood has not emphasized cultural experiences. Since they may have had negative experiences with formal education and no socialization to prepare them to read the museum code, museum visits are studious, exacting experiences rather than the casual, relaxed diversion they seek in leisure time. Non-participants feel that museums are useful for teaching children, but they find no reason for adults to visit a museum. The attributes they value are minimally present in museums. Consequently, they seek and find rewarding experiences elsewhere.

It is important, however, *not* to dismiss non-participants as apathetic or unintelligent. These adults are active persons who find great satisfaction outside of museums. Home and family responsibilities restrict leisure time, in many cases because both parents have to work. At middle age, they not only have responsibilities for their children but often for ageing parents. As devoted do-it-yourselfers, they gain great satisfaction from making home improvements and from other activities that permit them to use their hands. When leisure time is available, they seek family-centred experiences.[19]

Additional insights into the reasons why adults come to museums and also into the ways museums can meet their expectations are provided in Ross J. Loomis's book *Museum Visitor Evaluation: New Tool for Management.* In one of the most useful surveys summarized in the book, participants in a nationwide Canadian survey were interviewed at home and completed a follow-up mail-in questionnaire in the 1970s. The study suggested that the decision not to visit a museum was influenced less by negative images than by problems of accessibility and lack of communication. Admission fees were less of a barrier than lack of information about the museum and problems in gaining access. Three of the researchers of this study concluded that efforts to increase museum attendance should be concentrated on those who already attend.[20] Hood confirmed this point in her Toledo research, emphasizing that occasional visitors offer the greatest opportunity for museums to develop new audiences.

The Canadian National Survey went on to say that museums can and should improve communication, be more accessible and inform people about the kinds of experiences provided. A lack of public information about the museum results in no expectations at all. Moreover, hindrances in travelling to and from the museum or problems in gaining access increase visitors' fatigue and colour their final recollection of the visit.

TOLEDO SURVEYS

Surveying audience perceptions can be done on a modest scale using small discussion groups. In 1986, I questioned a group of adults who had taken studio or art-history classes at the Toledo Museum of Art. They agreed that the most appealing aspects of attending classes at the museum were the non-threatening atmosphere, the quality of instruction and the personal attention they received. The museum environment was considered very important, and anything that detracted from that environment lessened the total experience.

Such detractions could occur before or after the actual experience in the museum, such as an impolite entrance guard or a parking problem. It could even be a diminished sense of ownership because children and university students were using the same instructional space. However, the atmosphere was positively reinforced by the socializing that took place in the classroom and the 'halo' effect of having access to great works of art. Basically, these adults felt that they were improving themselves through worthwhile activities in a pleasant and important setting.

As a follow-up, a questionnaire was sent in 1987 to 250 adults who had taken studio or art-history classes or workshops at the Toledo Museum. Four questions were asked, in hopes of learning more about adult attitudes and expectations regarding the museum. Seventy-eight questionnaires, or 31 per cent, were returned.

The first question, asking why the student had taken a course at the museum, established that nearly every respondent listed one of Hood's conditions for a satisfying use of leisure time. Seventy-four per cent, however, also mentioned reasons such as the opportunity to learn, self-fulfilment, a chance to produce artworks, the reputation of instructors, or personal growth. Seventy per cent had participated in other activities at the museum.

When asked what they considered unique about visiting the museum, 31 per cent mentioned the quality of the collection, while another 25 per cent described the environment, using such words as 'escape' or 'entering another world'. The widest range of answers came in response to the question 'What is the most meaningful experience you have had at the Toledo Museum of Art?' Taking classes was the most common answer, given by 41 per cent of those responding. We obtained similar responses from surveys of an Elderhostel group in 1987.

The results of these informal Toledo surveys are not particularly surprising. Generally, they confirm the findings of the more professional researchers cited in this essay. Perhaps of greater importance, surveys have helped us establish a stronger rapport with a segment of our audience, showing these patrons that the museum cares about their interests and needs.

Moreover, the responses on these surveys describing what is unique about visiting a museum and what are the most meaningful experiences in museums relate to research conducted by University of Chicago behavioural scientist Mihaly Csikszentmihalyi. He has studied activities and the enjoyment of objects that 'give a sense of transcendent harmony'.[21] He describes enjoyment as 'the flow condition in which one acts with total involvement and excludes the pressing concerns of everyday life'.[22] Clearly it is this flow condition that many who enjoy museums have come to anticipate and expect.

In their unpublished report submitted to the J. Paul Getty Trust, 'The art of seeing: toward an interpretive psychology of the aesthetic experience', Csikszentmihalyi and Rick E. Robinson elaborate:

> When philosophers describe the aesthetic experience, and psychologists describe the flow, they are talking about essentially the same state of mind. What this in turn means is that human beings enjoy experience that is more clear and focused than ordinary experience is. When this state of consciousness occurs within an aesthetic context – in response to music, painting, and so on – we call it an aesthetic experience. In other contexts – in sports, in hobbies, in challenging work and social interactions – we call it a flow experience.[23]

Many of my recommendations for meeting the learning expectations of adults in museums and of adults in continuing education who would use museums as a resource are based on that specific expectation. A myriad of other adult needs have been raised throughout this essay; none of them should be ignored. Indeed, in satisfying those more practical needs, museums may greatly enhance the act of perception and potential for flow.

MEETING THE LEARNING EXPECTATIONS OF ADULTS

'The primary skill one needs to unlock the magic of things is that of seeing them objectively and subjectively at the same time, thus joining the nature of the perceiving subject with the nature of the object.'[24] All this research on leisure needs, values, life-styles, and learning characteristics has provided insight into 'the nature of the perceiving subject'. Based on those insights, the recommendations below are logical. Some are directed at museums themselves; others are for those continuing educators who might like to use museums as a resource.

Everyone on the museum staff is an educator

Because the totality of the museum visit is what visitors remember, every person they encounter teaches them what a museum is. For occasional or non-participant visitors, initial encounters are crucial. Car park attendants, cloakroom assistants, information desk volunteers, security officers, and a host of others must be sensitive to their potential for winning over adults as frequent visitors. Even municipal and state governments can have an impact if the museum is difficult to find because of inadequate signs or if public parking is not available. (How lucky we were in Toledo when state and city officials agreed to post highway and street signs directing visitors to the 'El Greco of Toledo' exhibition in 1982!)

Help adults to decode the museum environment

Be sure that signs and floor plans are easy for occasional visitors to understand. Try mock-ups with visitors before permanent signs are printed. Continuing education programmes might offer a workshop on decoding the museum for those upwardly mobile VALS groups who want to begin visiting museums. It could be a course on language, symbols and objects. We take for granted that everyone understands that museums require umbrellas or large parcels to be deposited, that many museums are closed on Mondays but open at weekends, that touching is not permitted, and that gallery arrangements have a certain logic. Museum staff are mistaken if they assume that adult visitors will know exactly what everything on an object label refers to. (Many of us have overheard visitors wondering if the accession number is the price.)

Such seemingly obvious museum information as the difference between an original print and a photographic reproduction could save first-time visitors from asking embarrassing questions. I am not suggesting that such information is the real meat of a museum visit; but understanding these things raises one's comfort level and clears the way for the optimum museum experience.

Learning and fun are not mutually exclusive

Combining a traditional learning activity (tour, lecture, film) with a social activity (refreshment) is an obvious way to satisfy people. If you can enlist volunteers or frequent visitors to act as hosts and make sure people meet one another, you could win a whole new crowd of frequent visitors for future educational offerings. Offer more opportunities and programmes that incorporate the three attributes that occasional visitors value, so there will be more incentive for them to come (social interaction, active participation, and comfort in area surroundings).

Less is more, if you can do it

Blockbuster exhibitions and attendance figures notwithstanding, our programme participants tell us often how much they appreciate personal attention and opportunities for interaction with speakers, instructors and other participants. One solution to the numbers game is to offer popular events more than once. We always invite audience members to come up and meet speakers after lectures, and many do so, if only to thank them. Even during the 'El Greco' exhibition, visitors commented that they felt they received personal attention from our volunteers and staff. Amenities such as frequent resting places, easy-to-locate lavatories and drinking fountains, food service, gift shops, and comfortable lecture rooms all indicate personal concern. The frequent visitor who has experienced all of this constitutes a high percentage of our attendance figures. Blockbuster visitors seldom return.

Museums should consider the distinct advantage of the 'un-blockbuster' exhibition. In 1987, the Toledo Museum of Art participated in an exchange with the State Hermitage in Leningrad, which presented one painting by Rembrandt from Leningrad and twenty-two Rembrandt etchings. Visitors described an optimum aesthetic experience that focused their attention in an atmosphere that encouraged contemplation. They seemed to be challenged to *look* rather than press on to another painting.

Avoid canned presentations

All of the information on adult learning characteristics underscores the need to be flexible. The speaker or docent who acknowledges that audience members may have some background or experience related to the subject, may have learning goals slightly different from the presenter, may choose other learning opportunities quickly if this one proves unfulfilling, has won over the audience at the outset. Beyond acknowledging these factors in theory, the speaker must be able to respond flexibly to circumstances that may develop during the presentation.

Overall, the museum and its continuing education staff must demand this kind of sensitivity to audiences. It is not satisfactory to bring in reputed scholars who put people to sleep. For several years, the museum education staff at Toledo has sought recommendations from people who have heard a scholar speak before inviting that speaker to lecture at the museum. Our success rate with our audiences has been much higher as a result.

Use new technologies to win new audiences

In Toledo, we are sadly behind many museums that have begun to incorporate new technologies into their educational offerings. The possibilities are broad and are expanding almost daily. Hood has noted the potential for museum education through techniques such as 'the linking of TV sets with computers or telephones for information delivery, video cassette recorders and players, high quality home satellite reception, culture-only channels on pay TV, low-power TV to serve specific audiences, and greater targeting of audiences by network TV as its percentage of viewing time declines'.[25] Museums must not fail to exploit these opportunities.

Offer a balanced curriculum for different types of learning

I have already made suggestions to help non-visitors take their first steps into a museum. For occasional and frequent visitors, educators must be sensitive to those who are self-directed and need only an opportunity to visit a museum, as well as to those who are looking for formal instruction to fill in the gaps in their background.

The different learning styles identified by Bernice McCarthy emphasize the need for a variety of programmes to attract adults. For example, art museums can use a range of techniques, including lectures, demonstrations, films, videos, discussion groups and studio experiences. Other possibilities include more humanities presentations, such as discussions of social history, performance events, or experiences with food, costume, or theatre. Universities provide rich resources for these types of programmes in museums.

Go with the flow

Finally, I would like to return to the opening quotation of this chapter: 'This is a hall of ideas!'[26] This statement reflects what Csikszentmihalyi finds in his research, namely, that the optimum museum experience is one of transcendence, of flow, that many call an aesthetic experience. After we have helped visitors become comfortable in the museum, after we have socialized with them, given them personal attention, and then given them an outstanding educational presentation in a controlled, distraction-free environment, what we really hope will happen is that they have a flow experience. We hope their focused attention will provide an experience in which their intelligence and feelings will become one, and this challenge will be their joy.

As educators, we might begin by sharing these factors with our clients. In our courses and workshops, we must give them not only information about our collections but also clues on how to evaluate those objects. Authors such as Rudolph Arnheim, Harry Broudy and E. B. Feldman have given us plenty of ideas for teaching visual analysis. We need to use those ideas, and then go one step further and ask people simply to look at the objects. And then look a little longer. And then just a few seconds more to be sure nothing was missed.

The challenge for educators is that once this is done, new skills will be needed on an even higher level. Then we as educators will realize that the learning expectations of adults in our museums will never end. Our challenge is to know our audience, to raise their expectations continually, and to make their excitement our flow.

This chapter first appeared in J. W. Solinger (ed.) (1989) Museums and Universities: New Paths for Continuing Education, *Phoenix, AZ: American Council on Education.*

NOTES

1 Hood, Marilyn G., 'Adult attitudes toward leisure choices in relation to museum participation', PhD diss. (Ohio State University, 1981); Ann Arbor, MI: University Microfilms International, cat. no. 8121802, 3. I am very grateful to Dr Hood, who has not only shaped our staff's understanding of what we know and what we ought to know about our audiences, but has also offered valuable advice about the contents of this article.
2 ibid., 24.
3 Csikszentmihalyi, Mihaly and Robinson, Rick E., 'The art of seeing: toward an interpretive psychology of the aesthetic experience' (University of Chicago, 1987), report submitted to J. Paul Getty Trust, 108.
4 ibid., 26.
5 ibid., 356.
6 Mitchell, Arnold, *The Professional Performing Arts: Attendance Patterns, Preferences, and Motives* (Madison, WI: Association of College University and Community Arts Administrators, 1984), 8.
7 ibid., 13–16.
8 ibid., 18.
9 Wolfe, David B., 'The ageless market', *American Demographics* 9 (July 1987): 29.
10 Knowles, Malcolm S., *The Adult Learner: A Neglected Species* (Houston, TX: Gulf, 1978), 184–5.
11 Even, Mary Jane, 'Why adults learn in different ways', *Lifelong Learning* (10 June 1987): 25.
12 McCarthy, Bernice, *The 4Mat System: Teaching Learning Styles Using Right/Left Mode Techniques* (Barrington, IL: Excel, 1986), 3–6.
13 Hood, 31.

14 ibid., 28.

15 ibid., 284.

16 ibid., 282.

17 ibid., 296–8.

18 ibid., 298–300.

19 ibid., 300–4.

20 Loomis, Ross J., *Museum Visitor Evaluation: New Tool for Management* (Nashville, TN: American Association for State and Local History, 1987), 125.

21 Csikszentmihalyi, Mihaly and Rochberg-Halton, Eugene, *The Meaning of Things: Domestic Symbols and the Self* (Cambridge: Cambridge University Press, 1981), 244.

22 ibid.

23 Czikszentmihalyi and Robinson, 10.

24 Czikszentmihalyi and Rochberg-Halton, 246.

25 Hood, Marilyn G., 'Adult attitudes', report of a study done at the Toledo Museum of Art (1981), based on the author's dissertation, 33.

26 Morgenstern, Michael, 'Artists Talk About Art', public lecture at the Toledo Museum of Art (22 February 1987).

13

Whose museum is it anyway? Museum education and the community

Jocelyn Dodd

Museums are slowly changing to meet the needs of their communities, and along with this change goes a shift in the skills used and roles played by museum education staff. As museums become more consumer-oriented, so collecting, display and education policies must evolve to meet new challenges.

Like many museum education professionals, my invaluable pre-museum experience was teaching. But is museum education about teaching any more? In the past, museum education has concentrated primarily on formal education, structured curriculum-led school parties, student teachers, teachers' planning sessions, In Service Education for Teachers (INSET) courses and museum loans. How many of us have done endless sessions on 'the Victorians', for an albeit enthusiastic junior school audience? Perhaps we have the government to thank for a few more decades of that, now it is laid down in the History National Curriculum. But we do so much more as well – family fun days, holiday playscheme events, reminiscence sessions, though these tend to be extras, in addition to formal education. We live in a time of change and challenge: increased accountability, local management of schools, poll tax capping and the recession have decimated some services. It has forced many to rethink, reorganize, refund, question and justify their positions. It has necessitated a radical rethink of the role, function, practices and outcomes of museum education.

What, I think, lies at the heart of the matter is the question 'Whose museum is it anyway?' How can we begin to define what we do in terms of education unless we know whom we are educating? Some, perhaps still too many, curators would have us think that museums were for that select little gathering of highly motivated, highly informed, white, middle-class intellectuals with a passion for eighteenth-century ceramics. There are signs that those days of intellectual elitism at last are beginning to wither.

Why then have we, as educators, concentrated on an often equally small section of our museums' clientele? In the case of Nottingham museums only about 10 per cent of our visitors are in formal educational groups. Perhaps a different agenda was set for me from that of many colleagues. Nottingham museums are city council funded, with no grant or financial support from the LEA. Actually being called an education officer can stir wrath in councillors. Why should they be funding something which is the function of the LEA? (Before long, we may all be wondering what LEAs were anyway!) But education is not just about schools; it is about lifelong learning. Of course it is about children, but equally about adolescents and about adults. Do they suddenly stop learning when they leave formal educational establishments? What then of the community whose members, as tax-payers, are the financial providers of the service? How much are they considered? Or are they just another neglected user group or potential group? Do museums actually serve the needs of the community at all?

How do we even begin to define 'the community' – as a society it defies the confines of a restricted definition. It is, in an all-encompassing sense, people between 'the cradle and the grave', mother and toddler groups, the elderly, youth groups, partially sighted people, groups from specific cultural communities, groups from women's refuges. Many are disadvantaged, lack confidence, and lack any sense of feeling that museums have anything to do with their lives. Perhaps what we are defining is the 'rights of the public'. We certainly live in a rapidly changing society, with more active old people than ever before. Only one in five households is a traditional nuclear family. More people live alone than ever before and are looking for interactive social opportunities. Rising un-employment has left huge numbers of people with seemingly endless spare time. Many communities are now multicultural, multilingual, multiethnic and multifaith. As communities change, so do our museums' potential audiences. Are our thinking and our provision evolving to keep pace with these new challenges?

The process of first meeting the community, and then working with it, requires many skills different from those traditionally used in formal museum education. Such skills are less concerned with systematic learning, but much more about negotiating, net-working and confidence-building. To meet these new needs, we need staff with different skills and knowledge, and experience of working with community groups is essential. The vocabulary and networks are different from formal education, and teaching ability may in future become just one of several skills we will be looking for.

Our curatorial colleagues have sometimes led the way with good practice of community collaborations. For example, a project at Springburn Museum influenced and shaped the whole museum from its instigation. From collecting to exhibitions, the creation and ownership of the museum lay within the community. In Glasgow, the community at large made a huge impact in a major city project with the People's Palace. Does this sense of ownership by community lie only with local authority museums? I think not; Springburn is a trust museum. The Bass Museum in Burton on Trent is a company museum, yet strongly reflects the ethos and involvement of its local Burton community. What these projects all have in common is a social history basis, perhaps the most comfortable and most obvious bedfellows of museum collections and community involvement. The challenge for us, as educators, lies in making all collections accessible to the community at large, from fine art to natural history, decorative art to archaeology.

The process of introducing community groups to museums is not about high levels of educational achievement. Rather it is concerned with negotiating, confidence-building and providing opportunities. It is about empowering community groups to realize that museums are as much for them as for the social elite, and that they too can have access to them culturally, physically and intellectually. It can be a political process, with repercussions for the status quo within museums. As new groups gain confidence, they will begin to question the institutions – why they collect what they do, what their displays are like, how 'relevant' they are, what facilities and provision they make for the community at large, even the fundamental role of the museum. How often do museums really address the question, 'Why are we here?'

The impetus for change may come from a small encounter, like a Sikh community group in Nottingham, previously non-museum-goers, who were outraged to see cere-monial Sikh swords displayed alongside those used in battle. This incident resulted in a whole Sikh project being undertaken and the investigation of a community showcase and huge curatorial involvement. It brought into question why the only Sikh collections the museum had were 'ethnographic', and may culminate in a change in collecting policies to reflect the cultural diversity of Nottingham's population as a whole. A more customer-led museum service is slowly evolving in place of the traditional object-led, curatorially biased service of the past. Objects are still of prime importance – museums wouldn't exist without them – but which objects are displayed, how they are inter-preted, and for whom, is of the essence.

A fundamental change is taking place in the relationship between the public and museums; a change towards a collaboration of joint interest, joint views, feelings and sensitivities. This calls for new skills on the part of museum educators, but it means a fundamental redefining of research, too. No longer will exhibition and display research be just about the museum content, but about the social content of user groups as well. It will question whether we can continue to produce general museum displays aimed at 'the public'. How often do we, as educationalists, make remedial use of exhi-bitions and displays aimed at some undefined audience, quite inappropriate for our specified groups? How often are exhibitions selective in their audience, actually aimed at children or specific groups of adults? We need to be bold in defining exhibition objectives with specific audiences in mind, aiming to create inspirational museums rather than didactic exhibitions. Perhaps now, as educationalists, we are forced to address the questions we should have faced long ago. When most museum education services were set up, it was to meet demands from schools. We have developed very effective strategies for dealing with these. We have increased the popularity of museums, with excellent handling sessions and terrific loan materials, but meanwhile museum displays have remained static and traditional. Often, as museum educators, we were put in a ghetto separate and remote from the fundamental planning of the museum. We did not insist that curators developed a new skill base in order to create displays which met the needs of the users. Now we need to take up a joint challenge of meeting the needs of the community, while redefining the nature of curatorship. Building up their collections is as much a product of the museums' relationship with their communities as any outreach work.

Museum educators' involvement with the community began with educators diversifying and working with groups outside the formal education sector. Some museums have appointed community outreach officers, but provision is still patchy and the area is as yet largely unformed. The process of enabling and empowering the community forces a radical rethink of the role and purpose of museums and their relationship with the community. This may lead to a redefining of curatorship and the role of museum edu-cation. But if we are committed to 'lifelong education' for the community, we must commit ourselves to a central role in the creation of those newly shaped museums.

This chapter first appeared as a paper in Journal of Education in Museums *13 (1992): 31–2.*

Part III
Developing effective exhibitions

Exhibitions are one of the core educational methods of museums. The first three chapters consider a range of issues that relate to learning from museum exhibitions. The following three chapters analyse some aspects of the process of exhibition development. We begin with a discussion of the whole process, looking at the value of internal team-working, and external consultation and testing of ideas and design solutions. The issue of how to think about the space of the exhibition follows, and then the various practical activities that ensue at different moments in the development process are outlined.

A further group of chapters considers a range of issues in relation to text, with two examples of carefully developed and tested exhibition texts. We conclude the section with an example of good practice in reviewing and increasing the access of an exhibition.

14

Learning from learning theory in museums

Eilean Hooper-Greenhill

Learning in museums has a long history. But how has learning theory been used in museums? This chapter discusses the poverty of use, and the failure to think of museum audiences as real people.

The use of educational theory at the Natural History Museum, London, is discussed and the path taken from a base in educational technology through to the realization of the active nature of the visitor is briefly described. This is placed within the context of the development of visitor studies as a whole.

The importance of the role of the museum educator in today's approach to exhibition development is emphasized. Many museum educators, at least in Britain, have a background in teaching either in schools or elsewhere. The experience of planning for real people in the classroom is a valuable one to apply within the museum, but it needs to be thought through carefully to be of the most use.

INTRODUCTION

Museums have long been thought of as educational institutions. A mid-nineteenth-century comment from the First Report of the Department of Practical Art, the government institution that originally ran the Victoria and Albert Museum, demonstrates this well:

> a Museum presents probably the only effectual means of educating the adult, who cannot be expected to go to school like the youth.
>
> (Hooper-Greenhill 1991: 18)

Lawrence Haward, curator of the Manchester City Art Galleries, speaking in 1917 at a Museums Association conference in Sheffield, drew attention to the educational possibilities of museums in teaching children. He said that visits to the galleries

> have the result of increasing the children's critical faculties and their capacity for self-expression. The children are . . . being made to think and feel for themselves.
>
> (Hooper-Greenhill 1991: 32)

So the idea of learning in museums is not new. However, it is my feeling that until fairly recently learning theory has been significantly used only in the education department of museums. Here, museum teachers have learnt how to adapt classroom teaching and adult education practices for the museum environment. At its best, this has been

137

an outstanding success. There are a range of approaches to learning and teaching that have been developed in the delivery of face-to-face teaching and learning sessions, including workshops, drama, role-play, problem-solving and so on. Without perhaps any rationalizing or thinking in grandly theoretical terms, practical methods of direct teaching have evolved.

What has been more problematic has been the use of learning theory in museum exhibitions. With the notable exception of the work at the Natural History Museum in London there appears to have been little thought given, in Britain, to how learning theory might improve exhibitions. Indeed, it is only recently that museums and galleries have begun to consider audience responses at all. Up until now, the process of exhibition production has not included a concrete picture of the users. The complex processes of object research, conservation, design and construction have taken on their own momentum, and although visitors have always theoretically been part of this process, the part played has been rhetorical and abstract, and the visitors themselves have remained mythical.

In terms of effective communication, this is very unreliable. There will be some success, mainly for those who understand and are interested in the story being told; or those who have prior knowledge of the content; or those who already know a little about the objects. It will be very unlikely that exhibitions planned in this way will excite those new to the subject; or those who want a sociable leisure experience in the museum; and it is even more unlikely that new audiences will be attracted. Ineffective communication leads to lack of interest, lack of attention, lack of excitement and no learning.

However, for a number of reasons, we now see a great deal of interest both in making museums more attractive to existing visitors and in developing new audiences.

So, how can learning theory help us to do this? What has been done so far?

THE ANTECEDENTS

The only museum to work systematically with educational theory in Britain has been the Natural History Museum in London. Here, a very interesting experiment was begun in the 1970s.

You will have noticed that I have stopped using the expression 'learning theory' and have used the broader term 'educational theory'. The work that was carried out at the Natural History Museum was more concerned with 'teaching theory' than with 'learning theory'.

Recognizing that most museum and gallery exhibitions had an educational component, and that exhibitions in science museums were concerned in a very large part with teaching, Miles and his team looked to current educational theory to help them develop more effective exhibitions, exhibitions that would teach better.

Miles argued that exhibitions should have justifiable and worthwhile objectives (Miles *et al.* 1988: 2), and that the uninformed visitor needed help (Miles *et al.* 1988: 3). Teaching, he argued, was about introducing the learner to higher-level relational thinking, showing the learner how facts were related and thereby explained causal links (Miles *et al.* 1988: 29). The model of teaching was essentially didactic and concerned with developing cognitive abilities. Intuition and affective education are not acknowledged. In this sense, the model was perhaps a creature of its time. Science teaching was possibly one of the last areas to be moved by the progressive educational theories of the 1960s.

Although learners were acknowledged to be curious, and it was recognized that they needed to feel that the exhibition's teaching points were attainable, learning was less an adventure of self-discovery, and more a journey along a previously defined path. These learners were still mythical, unreal players in the museum exhibition game. Equally, they were to a greater or lesser degree 'uninformed' and thereby brought few resources with them into the museum. As the research progressed, discussions and evaluations revealed the importance of understanding the audience as real people.

Miles and his team looked towards educational technology as an appropriate educational theory to apply within exhibitions. They developed the concepts of behavioural objectives for exhibitions, so that exhibition teams could better define and describe what they were trying to do. They introduced the notion of the content of the exhibition delivered as a 'teaching sequence that builds up smoothly' (Miles *et al.* 1988: 31). At first they assumed that learning must take place in educational exhibitions through looking, although this looking would be made more effective if it were accompanied by the chance to 'do' things (Miles *et al.* 1988: 32). As the work continued, the approach became more interactive, more flexible and more informed by the agendas brought into the museum by visitors. The emphasis shifted from theories of how to teach, to the construction of opportunities to learn.

The main site of the debate over the work done in the Natural History Museum has not, to our shame, been in Britain, where the work has been largely ignored, but in North America, and particularly the United States. Here, it plays an important role in the struggle to develop the new museum discipline of Visitor Studies.

A second major use of educational theory, again in a science museum, can be seen in the Exploratorium, which was founded by Frank and Jackie Oppenheimer in San Francisco in 1969. The theories developed in this museum were much closer to 'learning theory'. A basic emphasis was on the empowerment of the visitor, where the role of the museum was to 'make it possible for people to believe they can understand the world around them' (Hein 1990: xv). This was a broad philosophical aim, held together with a conviction that the museum should be a place in which people could directly experience and manipulate things, rather than be told about them. The educational goal was self-liberation.

Again, visitors were recognized as curious, but this in itself was to be celebrated rather than controlled, and play, both in the spirit of enquiry and in the roaming of the imagination, was to be a guiding principle of the exhibits. A non-hierarchical teaching ideal was aimed for, where visitors helped themselves and each other to learn (Hein 1990: xviii), and where staff and visitors could learn together.

The Exploratorium rejected the dualism of art and science, and worked from the principle that science has an aesthetic dimension and art a cognitive one. Both art and science offer insights than can help develop our concepts of reality (Hein 1990: xvi). Thus in the museum, where work by artists stood alongside exhibits from experimental science, both cognitive and affective elements within understanding could be mobilized.

A major method of the museum was, and is, interactivity. The exhibits are participatory and depend upon the physical engagement of the visitor. To understand the world it is necessary to act upon it. The democratic philosophy of access to knowledge and ideas led to the development of ways to achieve this, using the medium of a science museum.

Interactivity, as we all know, has been enormously successful. However, initially the methods and their underpinning philosophies at the Exploratorium were seen as controversial and, certainly for most museums, not very relevant. Science centres were not regarded as 'proper' museums. However, the runaway box-office effects of hands-on exhibits have forced a reappraisal of this rather pious attitude.

Although in education departments we have known for a long time how popular the handling of exhibits and objects has been, it is only recently that we have seen the principles of interactivity beginning to be applied in art galleries, archaeology displays and history museums.

THE DEVELOPMENT OF VISITOR STUDIES

A common thread that links the diverse approaches of the Natural History Museum and the Exploratorium is the notion of evaluation. Both educational technology and interactivity demand evaluation to ensure effective exhibitions, and evaluation was indeed built into the development processes in both institutions. At the same time as the evaluation of exhibitions was emerging, external constraints pushed museums towards visitor surveys and market research. Summative evaluation (carried out when the exhibition was open to the public), soon led to the need for formative evaluation (testing of exhibits during production) and front-end evaluation (preliminary research to see if the idea for the exhibition was feasible in the first place). Preliminary research was also carried out to see how much people knew about the subject-matter of the proposed exhibition.

Soon evaluation and market research began to overlap. Clearly visitor surveys also somehow related. At the present time, we are witnessing the birth and very rapid development of something I mentioned earlier – Museum Visitor Studies. A recent volume of *Museum International* (no. 178) is entirely concerned with Museum Visitor Studies and demonstrates through overviews from Europe and North America how this is happening. Work in Visitor Studies is also going on in Scandinavia, Russia, Greece, Australia, New Zealand and India.

Visitor Studies is a hybrid discipline, drawing on theory from sociology, psychology, education, marketing, management, communication and leisure studies. It covers a huge range of material – demographics and other data on attendance and non-attendance; psychological and personality profiles of visitors (learning styles, attitudes, language skills and time-frames); patterns of visitor behaviour (who goes where, with whom, fatigue, return visits, use of services, preferences for types of exhibit); ability to understand exhibition messages (and the impact of the exhibition on attitudes, behaviour, interests); how the design and presentation of elements within museums and exhibitions such as signage, layout, media and noise affect reading behaviour, way-finding, attention. Finally Visitor Studies is concerned with the development of evaluation methods to assess learning, the short-term and long-term impact of the exhibition, social behaviour patterns, attendance and post-visit interests (Screven 1993: 6).

As you might expect, Visitor Studies as an approach is unequivocal about the necessity for gathering and using this kind of information. However, it goes further in stating that what is really required is a major shift in the system of exhibition production from curators/subject specialists and exhibit designers, to educators, instructional designers and evaluators. In the article introducing the issue of *Museum International* just mentioned, C. G. Screven proposes separating the object-based scholarly work of curators, which elaborates the messages that objects can convey, from the work of delivering these messages to the public. The work of delivery – that is, of designing and producing exhibitions or programmes – should be left to people experienced in educational communications and evaluation (Screven 1993: 10).

This may seem either very daunting, or very unrealistic in relation to one's own personal situation. Nevertheless, I think Screven is right and also I think it is beginning to happen. Education staff are being drawn more into exhibition design and production, and I would use Norfolk and Leicestershire as two recent examples. At the same time, the knowledge that educators have is being increasingly recognized – even the Museums Association shows signs of this! And many young curators are very committed to the educational work of museums, either finding ways to increase their skills to become experienced educational communicators, or finding ways to acknowledge the expertise and support the methods of their educational colleagues.

I think, therefore, that education staff have a role that is growing in importance, and we need to grow in skills and confidence to meet it.

So, as educators faced with relating what we know to the production of exhibitions, what can we do? We know well how we design a range of learning experiences. If we see exhibitions as just one more of these learning experiences, what happens?

PLANNING FOR REAL PEOPLE

What do we do if we design a learning experience? (I am using the expression 'learning experience' as a generic one, as I think the basic approach is much the same whether we are teaching adults or children, and whether we are designing a workshop, a lecture or a classroom activity.)

First, we carry out research. If we want to teach something we make sure we know as much as needed about the subject-matter. Then we think about our audience, who they are and how they will respond to it. Sometimes it happens the other way round. We know who we are working with and we think they would enjoy and learn from a particular idea, experience or approach. There is a great deal of interaction, at the planning and research stage, between content and audience. The nature of the audience influences the choice of theme, the amount of material, the bias of the ideas, and of course the nature of the delivery, which in itself influences the subject-matter. The relationship between the content and the audience is dialogic. The reason why this is so important is that, as educators, we must plan for success, so we need to know what our audiences can achieve. We are able to plan effectively because of the realness of the audience. As educators, we plan for real people, or for an audience that has the characteristics of real people we have worked with previously.

If I were planning for an art lesson in school with 2P6, for example, I would think very carefully indeed about what I was going to do. In the second year of the comprehensive at which I taught for some years, 2P6 were the bottom stream of twelve streams. They were angry children, often inarticulate, who found concentration difficult, were sometimes physically violent, and were distrustful of all adults at first. If I were planning a specific activity, I would think very carefully about whether I could actually envisage Jimmy Coomber doing it, and if not what I *could* envisage. Many stunning ideas about what to do were rejected this way. Jimmy had to have something he could succeed at, within a fairly short period of time, which meant an activity that was easy to understand, and not too challenging, but would result in something to be admired and to feel proud of (Jimmy Coomber, chisel maniac and butcher's assistant).

Planning for 2H1 was very different. These were the top stream: very sophisticated children, experienced world travellers with large vocabularies and efficient thinking processes. These youngsters needed more complex activities, or at least they needed to think about them in a more detailed way. Could I imagine Melissa Wedgewood doing whatever I was planning? What would she do when she had finished?

Later, I taught sculpture to adult beginners. Many were complete beginners, but some had a great deal of experience as painters but were beginners in sculpture. Some were elderly, with arthritic hands and impaired vision. If I were planning a session, I had in mind how Mary, Colin and Ruth would respond to the particular stimulus I was considering.

In this way, planning a learning experience involves a predicted reaction and response from a known individual. After a while in teaching, these reactions and responses become more predictable, and the planning becomes faster, with perhaps less visualization. None the less, classroom teachers, who communicate face-to-face, work from the basis of knowing their learners, and plan something that they know that real individuals can do, enjoy, feel challenged by and learn from.

Museum exhibitions are rather different. There are many different audiences, and we know none of them as individuals. Nevertheless, each audience is made up of individuals, all with their own specific needs, interests and approaches to the world, and we need to consider this very seriously.

Audiences can be broken down into groups with definable characteristics – families, young children, teenagers; or beginning or experienced learners; or people who learn through looking, reading, or doing. The technique of visualization holds good here: can we imagine our parents, grandparents, children, or friends in this exhibition? But we need to go further than this. A first step is defining the audience. Target groups, once defined, can be approached and small groups or individuals can be walked through test exhibits, or comment on models, drawings or plans. Trends in response will quickly become apparent.

Screven suggests that the reason some curators and designers produce exhibitions that do not maximize their learning potential is because they have an idealized view of the public, formed through their own social circles – in other words, they think everyone is pretty much like themselves. In general, educators come into contact with and work with a very much broader social spread, and have, therefore, a much more cosmopolitan view of 'the public'. This is a great strength, and a great beginning. It needs to be built upon. We need to find ways of acting dialogically with the exhibition audience, in the same way as we would with our classroom audience. Just as we mentally scanned our class of individuals for reactions to our lesson plans, we need to be able mentally to scan our audience groups for reactions to our exhibition plans. The mental scanning can be done only on the basis of real knowledge and real experience of the groups concerned.

So, we should feel confident that our knowledge of people is a necessary component in exhibition planning. A wonderfully pompous expression I once heard a senior academic use might be helpful: 'My experience tells me . . .'

We should also feel confident to relate what we have learned about lesson planning to exhibition planning. Visualization was one thing we were taught, but other matters concerned defining and developing clear objectives, timing, variation in the mode and rate of delivery, assessment and modification. All of these have application in relation to exhibitions.

WHAT DO WE KNOW ABOUT HOW PEOPLE LEARN?

I have recently read a book that I have found helpful both in thinking about my own teaching and in considering how exhibitions might be made more effective. The book is called *When Teaching Becomes Learning*, by Eric Sotto (Cassell 1994). Sotto reminds us that learning theory proposes that when we listen to people talking, or read a book, or watch a TV programme, if we have a working model, a schema, in our heads that relates to what is being discussed, we can follow what is being said and relate to it. If we want to learn something completely new, however, where we have no working model, talking and reading are not enough. To learn something new, experience and action are necessary to build the model (Sotto 1994: 32–3). It is, in large part, through activity that models of the world become established in our heads (Sotto 1994: 24).

If we need schemata, or mental models, to understand abstract concepts outside the museum, it is the same inside the museum. In order to relate to the content of a given exhibition, we need a pre-existing schema. In planning an exhibition, therefore, it is important to discover what models the intended audiences have in relation to the exhibition content. In the presentation of the exhibition, these models can then be assumed and be built upon. If the models are not established, or need expanding, then ways need to be found to do this.

For example, if science exhibits depend on the concept of gravity, we need to be sure that visitors know what gravity is. If they don't, an introductory exhibit exploring the concept must be provided. In New Zealand, I found copious references in exhibits to 'pas'. Being at that stage totally ignorant of what a 'pa' was, I couldn't make sense of the exhibition. If New Zealand museums want foreign tourists to understand their displays, they need to explain that a 'pa' is a fortified and stockaded historic Maori village.

People construct meaning and sense about the world through the patterns they create. Individual fragments of information or reality mean little. It is common to find disconnected fragments of the world in museums. Meaning emerges through links and connections. The same object is something different in different contexts. A brick, for example, can be used to smash a window, build a wall, warm a bed, prevent a car from rolling. In each case it is a brick, but in each case it is also something else. The difference lies in the context, in how it is used. Meaning is drawn from the pattern of activities and material things within which the object is placed (Sotto 1994: 42–3). In museums, individual objects mean little, however beautiful. We need to find ways to enable people to perceive the objects in relation to a pattern, to make connections between the objects and their lives, their experiences and their existing knowledges.

Pattern recognition is one of the great joys of living. Finding sense in previously unrelated fragments is immensely satisfying. Learning theory tells us that most people learn through trying to work things out, where they perceive a problem (Sotto 1994: 52). Something intrigues us and we try to find an answer. It is very difficult to learn where there are no questions. In exhibitions therefore, we perhaps need to find ways to pose questions, to make things intriguing, to expose discontinuities, rather than to present a seamless and perfect narrative.

When given a set of instructions, perhaps for a new household appliance, for example, it is the rare learner who reads to the end. Most people read the first few lines and then try to learn the way the thing works by handling it.

Sotto describes the learning process, which begins when we discover there is something we need to know. It continues with an immersion in the problem, probably with initial puzzlement, and requires an active engagement, with the opportunity to obtain information and test hunches. Repeated exposure to the learning situation, with an expert who – acting as a model of competence – answers questions, together with the innate capacity of the mind to understand, leads to periodic insights (Sotto 1994: 54).

There are various levels of knowing. The strongest comes when we have had an appropriate experience. This kind of knowing is coded within us in a felt, compacted, living, tacit form and is part of our total mental structure (Sotto 1994: 99). With some effort we can make this kind of knowledge conscious and think about it verbally. This can help us to do such things as rehearse it, modify it, extend it, plan ahead, or communicate it. This is achieved through language, but the ability to work in this way, to link events, to consider experience, to plan and so on, depends on the extent of our experiential knowledge.

Sotto suggests, therefore, that there are two major forms of knowing – verbal and felt knowledge. The felt-meanings are essential to the overall growth of knowledge and understanding. Verbal experience only – words, reading and listening – is not enough to engender true learning. The feeling processes must also be engaged. The only way to do this is through action.

Feeling processes are mostly unconscious. Thinking processes are mostly conscious. Sometimes we can make our feeling processes conscious but not always (Sotto 1994: 85–7). Much of our experience is therefore encoded in a non-verbal form and is difficult to access consciously (Sotto 1994: 94). But this is where we truly feel we know things. This is the case even when we are wrong in our knowing. We may sometimes have to unlearn in order to learn. Our basic feeling processes enable us to apprehend things directly, enable us to respond to many things at the same time, enable us to take a global view, do not require the meaning of language, and work in an abstract way.

Our most powerful learning, therefore, takes place when we have had an appropriate experience and are able to reflect on what has happened (Sotto 1994: 98).

A recent book on effective science teaching (Woolnough 1994) endorses this. The author says very clearly that research into successful science learning shows that there are two factors involved: first, good teaching in the classroom, and second, effective use of extra-curricular activities. Extra-curricular activities are defined as student research projects and stimulus activities. Through stimulus activities, which of course include science centres, to which the writer gives a very warm endorsement, students gain knowledge, understanding and appreciation of the sciences, confidence in and competence at doing science, and enjoyment, enthusiasm, and commitment to the science appropriate for their own lives (Woolnough 1994: 44).

The important thing about the extra-curricular work, including the stimulus activities, is that they enable students to be active, to devise their own problems, to hypothesize, and to try things out. Science centres, with their mix of contemporary, striking exhibits, informal explainers, and the opportunity for enjoyment, enable tacit learning and affective gain, often, to quote the author, 'making a deep impression that will prove a permanent foundation for future learning and career aspirations' (Woolnough 1994: 90).

It is wonderful to see such an endorsement for the role of museums in science learning. I haven't yet found a comparable one for the use of museums in other parts of the curriculum. However, if Sotto is right about the need for felt-learning, or tacit-learning as the foundation for true knowing, and I don't doubt he is, then museums and galleries have as much to offer other areas of learning as they already offer to science. The real experiences that we offer, of objects, of buildings, of sites and of people, are essential to learning.

In conclusion, as educators we need to take Sotto's message to heart. We ourselves need to learn to verbalize from our own feeling-processes, our practical experiences of how individuals we know personally have learned. We need to excavate the unconscious knowledge of people that has grown through actual contact with real individuals and use it to help shape useful galleries and museums; and we need to demonstrate to our colleagues how vital real experience is in the construction of mental models and in acting as the foundation for true knowing. I can't think of a better justification for the existence of museums.

This chapter first appeared as a paper in GEM News 55 (1994): 7–11.

REFERENCES

Hein, H. (1990) *The Museum as Laboratory*, Washington, DC and London: Smithsonian Institution Press.

Hooper-Greenhill, E. (1991) *Museum and Gallery Education*, Leicester and London: Leicester University Press.

Miles, R., Alt, M. B., Gosling, D. C., Lewis, B. N. and Tout, A. F. (1988) *The Design of Educational Exhibits*, London: Unwin Hyman.

Screven, C. G. (1993) 'United States: a science in the making', *Museum International* 178: 6–12.

Sotto, E. (1994) *When Teaching Becomes Learning – a Theory and Practice of Teaching*, London and New York: Cassell.

Woolnough, B. E. (1994) *Effective Science Teaching*, Buckingham and Philadelphia, PA: Open University Press.

15

Intrinsic motivation in museums: why does one want to learn?

Mihaly Csikszentmihalyi and Kim Hermanson

The 'flow' experience has been of interest for some time to museum educators. Here, the writers explain what this means to them, describing this rather specialist use of the word 'flow'. They discuss in detail how the idea can be of use in planning exhibitions.

The concept is usefully conceptualized in relation to educational theory, including theories of motivation, and Vygotsky's theory of proximal development. The need for more research into museum learning is pointed out.

One often meets successful adults, professionals or scientists who recall that their life-long vocational interest was first sparked by a visit to a museum. In these accounts the encounter with a real, concrete object from a different world – an exotic animal, a strange dress, a beautiful artefact – is the kernel from which an entire career of learning grew. For others with an already developed curiosity about some field such as zoology, anthropology, or art, the museum provided an essential link in the cultivation of knowledge – a place where information lost its abstractness and became concrete. In either case, many people ascribe powerful motivation to a museum visit, claiming that their desire to learn more about some aspect of the world was directly caused by it.

Granted that these accounts of 'crystallizing experiences' (Walters and Gardner 1986) attributed to museums might often be embellished and exaggerated in retrospect, it would be rash to dismiss them entirely, for the fascination of museums seems to be a very real psychological phenomenon. The question rather becomes: How do museums motivate viewers to learn? Is there a unique, *sui generis* 'museum experience' that helps viewers start on the long journey of learning? How do museums present information in a meaningful way, a way that deepens a person's experience and promotes further learning? To begin answering these questions, it will be useful to review what we know about human motivation in relation to learning.

Children are born with a desire for knowledge, and some of the most stupendous feats of learning – to walk, talk, get along with others, to take care of oneself – are accomplished without seeming effort in the first few years of life. It would be difficult to see how a species as dependent on learning as we are could have survived if we did not find the process of making sense of our environment pleasurably rewarding. But this spontaneous propensity is often extinguished as children's desire to learn is rechannelled in new directions by societal goals and expectations. The abstract, externally imposed tasks children confront in school undermine the motivation to learn for many, often for the rest of life. Research indicates that the natural motivation to learn can be re-kindled by supportive environments (Deci *et al.* 1981; Deci 1992; McCombs 1991); by meaningful activities (Maehr 1984; McCombs 1991); by being freed of anxiety, fear and other negative mental states (Diener and Dweck 1980; McCombs 1991); and when the challenges of the task meet the person's skills (Csikszentmihalyi 1990a, 1990b).

The view of learning taken in this chapter is broader than mere knowledge acquisition, although that is certainly an important part of it. In our view, learning involves an open process of interaction with the environment. This experimental process develops and expands the self, allowing one to discover aspects of oneself that were previously unknown. Thus the learning experience involves the whole person, not only the intel-lectual but the sensory and emotional faculties as well. And when complex information is presented in a way that is enjoyable – intrinsically rewarding – the person will be motivated to pursue further learning.

EXTRINSIC AND INTRINSIC MOTIVATION

Human action is motivated by a combination of two kinds of rewards: extrinsic and intrinsic. Action is extrinsically motivated when the anticipated rewards come from outside the activity. In this case, performance is simply a means to some other end – to obtain praise or to avoid punishment, to get a degree, or to live up to societal expectations. A person acts for the sake of intrinsic rewards when the performance itself is worth doing for its own sake, even in the absence of external rewards. For example, most sports, games and artistic activities are intrinsically motivated, because except for a few professionals, one gets no rewards from performing them beyond the experience itself. Usually we are motivated by both extrinsic and intrinsic rewards at the same time. I might go to work every day primarily because, if I don't, I will get fired, and I need the job to pay my bills. But if in addition I also enjoy my job, the quality of my life will improve, and I am likely to get better at what I am doing.

This general principle holds for learning as well. Most learning in schools is extrin-sically motivated (Csikszentmihalyi and Larson 1984). The acquisition of knowledge is rarely enjoyed for its own sake, and relatively few young people would continue to learn in schools in the absence of parental and social pressures. Because of the stress on external incentives in formal education, intrinsic motivation in schools has been rarely studied. Classic examples are studies that seek to find ways to make the task of learning subject-matter and participating in classroom activities more intrinsi-cally motivating (e.g. Benware and Deci 1984; Lepper and Cordova 1992).

Learning is intrinsically motivated when it is spontaneous. The most clear examples of intrinsic motivation may be found watching children at play. When playing, chil-dren pay attention because they want to, because they find the information interesting and important in its own right. People are intrinsically motivated when they are freely expressing themselves by doing what interests them (deCharms 1968; Deci and Ryan 1985; White 1959). Dweck (1986) and others (Nicholls *et al.* 1985; Heyman and Dweck 1992) describe students who are intrinsically motivated as having 'learning goals', while students who are extrinsically motivated have 'performance goals'.

Students who are intrinsically motivated tend to have higher achievement scores (Hidi 1990; Lepper and Cordova 1992; Gottfried 1985), and they develop their aptitudes further over time (Csikszentmihalyi *et al.* 1993). Intrinsic enjoyment of learning appears to be associated with higher creativity as well (Amabile 1983, 1985). Under certain conditions, external rewards appear to undermine intrinsic motivation and to decrease performance (see, e.g., Deci 1971, 1972; Lepper and Greene 1978; McGraw 1978). When one's mind becomes focused on meeting an external goal or requirement, attention or 'psychic energy' is split and no longer fully focused on the task at hand.

Schools can afford to ignore intrinsic rewards to a certain extent, because they have strong external incentives – grades, truant officers – to enforce learning. Of course, such extrinsically motivated learning is very wasteful and inefficient. But museums, without external means to compel a visitor's attention, must rely almost exclusively on intrinsic rewards. How then, can intrinsic rewards be made a part of the museum experience?

THE ORIGINS OF INTRINSIC MOTIVATION

Psychologists began to write about intrinsic motivation in the late 1950s, when some researchers concluded that the basic physiological needs for food and security did not seem to explain why rats explored new territory, were willing to work just to see novel sights and experimented with challenging tasks (Csikszentmihalyi and Nakamura 1989). These findings suggested that the basic list of 'drives' had to be expanded by adding novelty, curiosity and competence drives (Butler 1957; Harlow 1953; Montgomery 1954; White 1959). More recently, Deci (1992) stated that the inherent psychological needs are competence, self-determination and relatedness (see also White 1959). In any case, the desire to learn for its own sake appears to be a natural motive built into the central nervous system. A species could not survive long if it did not find pleasure in processing information (Butler 1957; Hebb 1955; Miller 1983: 111; Montgomery 1954; Tiger 1992; Csikszentmihalyi 1993). As Miller wrote, 'The mind survives by ingesting information.'

Clearly, however, not all information is equally attractive. Because a person cannot process more than a limited amount of information at a time (Kahneman 1973; Hasher and Zacks 1979; Csikszentmihalyi 1978, 1993), environmental stimuli compete for attention with each other. Attention is a scarce resource – perhaps the most precious scarce resource there is (Simon 1969, 1978). Even though we are surrounded by exponentially increasing waves of information, the amount of it that any person actually notices and then retains in memory may be less than it was in the days of our cave-dwelling ancestors, and it certainly cannot be much more. Therefore what information we select to attend to, and how intently, is still the most important question about learning.

Curiosity and interest

In the first instance, we choose what information to attend to in terms of curiosity and interest. Curiosity refers to individual differences in the likelihood of investing psychic energy in novel stimuli. For instance, if we say that Mary is curious we mean that compared with other persons she will devote more effort to find out things she does not know (or is not supposed to know). Of course we are all curious to a certain degree, in that our attention is attracted by novel or unexplained stimuli – a loud noise, a sudden bustling activity, a strange animal, or a mysterious object. It is by appealing to this universal propensity that museums can attract the psychic energy of a visitor long enough so that a more extensive interaction, perhaps leading to learning, can later take place.

Interest refers to a differential likelihood of investing psychic energy in one set of stimuli rather than another. To say that Mary is interested in horses means that she is likely to talk about horses, to seek out information about them, to think about them and to wish that she could feed, groom and ride horses more than she does these things in relation to, say, dogs, cats, elephants, or gerbils. If we had no interests, the sensory world would be completely confusing, because we would literally not know where to turn. As William James (1950 [1890]: 402) remarked over a hundred years ago:

> The moment one thinks of the matter, one sees how false a notion of experience that is which would make it tantamount to the mere presence to the senses of an outward order. Millions of items in the outward order are present to my senses which never properly enter into my experience. Why? Because they have no *interest* for me. *My experience is what I agree to attend to.* Only those items which I *notice* shape my mind – without selective interest, experience is an utter chaos.
>
> (James 1950: 402)

Interests are partly universal, partly the result of individual experiences and one's idiosyncratic personal history. Most people are interested in food when hungry, in the opposite sex, in whatever gives them power or acclaim, in babies and pets. But beyond these few human targets, interest soon becomes unpredictable. Some people are attracted to car engines, others to ancient Mesopotamian toothpicks, some to maps, and others to baseball cards.

Most researchers regard interest as a phenomenon that emerges from an individual's interaction with the environment, and they distinguish between situational interest and individual interest (Krapp *et al.* 1992). Situational interest occurs when one encounters tasks or environments with a degree of uncertainty, challenge, or novelty. These environments nourish our built-in propensities for curiosity and exploration. According to Berlyne (1960, 1974), certain structural stimulus characteristics, such as novelty, surprisingness, complexity and ambiguity, lead to motivational states that result in curiosity and exploratory behaviour.

Contextual characteristics that evoke situational interest – or curiosity – tend to be similar between individuals. These contextual stimuli provide the 'hook' for museums to capture visitor attention. Without such situational interest, viewers may not attend to an exhibit at all. Hence unobtrusive observation of how visitors allocate attention is one of the most widely used techniques for assessing the effectiveness of museums (Loomis 1987; Serrell and Ralphling 1993).

But because situational interest 'tends to be evoked suddenly by something in the environment, it often has only a short-term effect and marginal influence on the subject's knowledge and reference system' (Krapp *et al.* 1992: 6). Thus situational interest may not affect one's motivation to learn more. In contrast, individual interest is defined as a relatively enduring preference for certain topics, subject areas, or activities (Hidi 1990). The pursuit of individual interests is usually associated with increased knowledge, positive emotions and the intrinsic desire to learn more (Krapp *et al.* 1992).

In *Interest and Effort in Education* (1913) John Dewey described the importance of individual interest. Students who are not genuinely interested in learning a particular subject do not identify with the material and put out only temporary, marginal effort. Dewey described this type of learning as forced and coercive. He believed it resulted in mechanical knowledge and did not effect a qualitative change in the individual (see also Schiefele 1991: 300). On the other hand, individual interests are intrinsically motivating, propelling an individual to pursue further learning opportunities. While interests tend to be individually unique, they are broadly characterized as having high personal meaning (Dewey 1913; Maehr 1984; Schiefele 1991). But an activity need not be already meaningful to a person in order for it to provide intrinsic rewards. For instance, John may reluctantly agree to join his friends in a game of bridge, expecting it to be a waste of time. Yet after a few hands the stimulation provided by the game turns out to be so enjoyable that John can hardly leave the table.

Museum visitors may at first attend an exhibit because of curiosity and interest. But unless the interaction with the exhibit becomes intrinsically rewarding, visitors' attention will not focus on it long enough for positive intellectual or emotional changes to occur. Therefore it is important to consider what makes an experience rewarding in and of itself, so as to understand what may motivate a person to look and think about an exhibit for 'no good reason' – that is, in the absence of external rewards.

The flow experience

Studies conducted in a great variety of settings by different investigators have shown that a common experiential state characterizes situations in which people are willing to invest psychic energy in tasks for which extrinsic rewards are absent. Chess players, rock climbers, dancers, painters and musicians describe the attraction of the activities they do in very similar terms, stressing the fact that what keeps them involved in these demanding activities is the quality of the experience that ensues. Many activities that are also well rewarded with money and prestige, such as surgery or computer programming, also seem to offer intrinsic rewards in addition to the extrinsic ones; and these are similar to the ones that artists and athletes mention. We have called this common experiential state the flow experience, because it is generally described as a state of mind that is spontaneous, almost automatic, like the flow of a strong current (Csikszentmihalyi 1975, 1990a). If a museum visit can produce this experience, it is likely that the initial curiosity and interest will grow into a more extensive learning interaction.

A general characteristic of activities that produce flow is that they have clear goals and appropriate rules. In a game of tennis, or of chess, one knows every second what one would like to accomplish. Playing a musical instrument, one knows what sounds one wishes to produce. A surgeon has clear intentions during an operation, and it is this clarity of purpose that allows people to become so thoroughly involved with what they are doing. Conflicting goals or unclear expectations divert our attention from the task at hand. In addition to clear goals, flow activities usually provide immediate and unambiguous feedback. One always knows whether one is doing well or not. Musicians find out immediately if they hit a wrong note, tennis players if they hit the ball badly, and surgeons know right away if they have made a mistake. This constant accountability for one's actions is another reason one gets so completely immersed in a flow activity.

Another universally mentioned characteristic of flow experiences is that they tend to occur when the opportunities for action in a situation are in balance with the person's abilities. In other words, the challenges of the activity must match the skills of the individual. If challenges are greater than skills, anxiety results; if skills are greater than challenges, the result is boredom. This equation holds for the broadest possible range of skills: for instance, it includes physical, mental, artistic and musical talents. I will be frustrated reading a book that is 'above my head' and bored when reading a book that is too easy and predictable. As skills increase, the challenges of the activity must also increase to continue the state of flow. The skills involved are those perceived by the individual, however, and not necessarily the actual ones. If one thinks of oneself as an incompetent football player, this perceived incompetence will affect performance regardless of its validity. Even if one is involved in an activity that typically induces flow, flow cannot be attained if one is worried about performance or if other negative mental states prevail.

Research has substantiated the importance of a positive state of mind for learning. McCombs (1991: 119–20) writes that 'in the absence of insecurity (e.g. feeling afraid, being self-conscious, feeling incompetent), individuals are natural learners and enjoy learning. . . . Insecurities and other forms of negative cognitive conditioning interfere with or block the emergence of individuals' natural motivation to continually learn, grow, and develop in positive and self-determining ways.' Negative mental states such as self-consciousness, depression, anxiety, loneliness, or anger also disrupt the flow experience (Csikszentmihalyi 1985). The research done by Dweck and her colleagues (Dweck 1975; Diener and Dweck 1980) on 'learned helplessness' highlights the serious effects of low self-esteem and anxiety on learning achievement. The intrinsically motivated learning state is characterized by unselfconsciousness, joy, serenity, involvement and happiness (Csikszentmihalyi 1985).

When goals are clear, feedback unambiguous, challenges and skills well matched, then all of one's mind and body becomes completely involved in the activity. Attention is focused and concentration is so intense that there is nothing left over to think about anything irrelevant or to worry about problems. In the flow state, a person is unaware of fatigue and the passing of time; hours pass by in what seems like minutes. This depth of involvement is enjoyable and intrinsically rewarding. In many cases, individuals describe the experience as becoming 'one' with the environment – the painting, the music, the team. People often mention a sense of self-transcendence, as when chess players feel their moves becoming part of a universal field of forces or when dancers feel the rhythm that moves them as part of the 'harmony of the spheres'.

Flow activities lead to personal growth because, in order to sustain the flow state, skills must increase along with the increased challenges. Flow involves the person's entire being and full capacity. Since flow is inherently enjoyable, one is constantly seeking to return to that state, and this need inevitably involves seeking greater challenges. In the process, flow activities provide a sense of discovery; we discover things about ourselves as well as about the environment. Flow activities, whether they involve competition, chance, or any other dimension of experience, provide a sense of discovery, a creative feeling of being transported into a new reality. They push us to higher levels of performance and lead to previously unexperienced states of consciousness. In short, they transform the self by making it more complex. In this growth of the self lies the key to flow activities. One cannot enjoy doing the same thing at the same level for long. We grow either bored or frustrated; and then the desire to enjoy ourselves again pushes us to stretch our skills or to discover new opportunities for using them.

If these conditions are present, it is possible for individuals to be in flow in any activity, be it conversation, solving differential equations, or driving a car. A participant in one of our studies was in flow while watching the Chicago Bulls play basketball on television. He knew in detail each of the players' strengths, weaknesses and definitive plays. 'I can totally shut away everything else. . . . I played basketball when I was in high school. I think it's the most talent-demanding of professional sports. . . . You get to know what people do, and you get sucked into their techniques because you can practically predict [their next move].' However, when the New York Knicks game came on, he became distracted and bored, as he was not as familiar with the play patterns of this team. A person who becomes interested in hockey will feel that it is the 'most talent-demanding of professional sports', and the same holds for soccer or baseball; in other words, what we invest a great deal of attention in is bound to become ever more interesting and salient.

It is often assumed that cognitive processes are more important than affective processes for learning. But as Schiefele (1991) points out, it is likely that affective processes are at least as important for evoking broader conceptual understanding rather than simple fact retention. Because emotional factors may influence learning only indirectly by stimulating cognitive processes, their importance is easily underestimated (Schiefele 1991: 316; Isen *et al.* 1987; Pekrun 1990).

From flow to enduring meaning

When a person is in flow, or fully enjoying an intrinsically motivated activity, he or she usually describes two dialectically related characteristics. On the one hand, when involved in the activity, the individual fully expresses the self. In the process, he or she discovers previously unknown and unrealized potentials and skills. Following Aristotle's views on the purpose of life, Dante wrote: 'In every action . . . the main intention of the agent is to express his own image. . . . In action the doer unfolds his being' (quoted in Csikszentmihalyi and Rochberg-Halton 1981: 48). The statement 'It is like designing, discovering something new' is the one most strongly endorsed by people as being similar to the phenomenology of the flow experience (Csikszentmihalyi 1975). One recent study participant told us that she finds 'learning often comes as a surprise'. This process of discovery and learning about who we are could be thought of as *differentiation* – the process of developing a unique self.

On the other hand, people in flow tend to feel connected with other entities, such as nature, a team, the family, or the broader community. Or in the case of many solitary pursuits, the activity connects one with a system of thoughts or beliefs. A rock climber may declare that climbing is for him a form of 'self-communication' (Csikszentmihalyi and Csikszentmihalyi 1988). Cameron (1992: 53) says that 'attention is an act of connection'. When we fully attend to something, we connect with life and thus fulfil the basic human need for relatedness. 'The flow experience . . . is symbolic because it brings together the psychic processes of the person and unites them with a set of objective stimuli in the environment. This is opposite from the state of alienation, in which one feels separated from oneself and from the elements of one's life' (Csikszentmihalyi and Rochberg-Halton 1981: 247). This process of connection could be referred to as *integration*. Moore (1992: 261) says that 'when we allow the great possibilities of life to enter into us, and when we embrace them, then we are most individual'. When this integration occurs, an activity becomes meaningful, and we become both more connected and more differentiated.

Meaningful experiences are those that are both differentiated and integrated. This dialectical process of integration and differentiation is necessary for psychological development and personal growth (Damon 1983; Fowler 1981; Kohlberg 1984; Loevinger 1976; Maslow 1968). For example, the psychiatrist H. F. Searles (1960: 30) states this dialectic as follows:

> The human being is engaged, throughout his life span, in an unceasing struggle to differentiate himself increasingly fully, not only from his human, but also from

his nonhuman environment, while developing, in proportion as he succeeds in these differentiations, an increasingly meaningful relatedness with the latter environment as well as with his fellow human beings.

This dialectic between integration and differentiation is the process by which we learn and grow. On the one hand, we must discover the limits of our being by expressing the purposes and potentials inherent in our biological organism. Only through self-control, through shaping events to our intentions, can we learn who we are and what we are capable of. On the other hand, we must find ways to expand our limited selves by forging ties with other human and non-human systems. Motivational research has highlighted the importance of both individual autonomy and connection for facilitating intrinsic learning.

IMPLICATIONS OF INTRINSIC MOTIVATION FOR MUSEUMS

How do these general principles apply to the kind of learning that can take place in museums? A schematic representation of the process of intrinsic motivation at work in museums is presented in Figure 15.1. Following the steps of this process, it will be easier to see the concrete implications of motivational theory. Of course, such a schematic approach cannot deal with all the practical problems museums face. One of the major obstacles to an easy movement from theory to practice is the fact that visitors come with such a broad range of interests and backgrounds that no single recipe for motivating them could possibly apply across the board. Nevertheless, these broad outlines can be quite helpful if one takes the trouble of adapting them to particular specific conditions.

The 'hook'

The first step in the process of intrinsically motivated learning suggests that the museum exhibit must capture the visitors' curiosity. Michael Spock, as experienced a professional as they come, says that dinosaurs and mummies are the surest exhibits to attract attention. Probably the reason for this attraction is overdetermined: both dinosaurs and mummies are ancient and therefore mysterious; both invoke awe and a thrill of fear without actual danger. These seem to be universal reasons for people to want to pay attention. Others are pleasing displays with bright colours, interactive exhibits, large size, and other stimuli that provide the situational interest necessary to attract attention.

Museum researchers have already demonstrated that visitors remember better displays to which they have paid more attention (Falk 1991; Koran *et al.* 1989). However, we still are far from knowing what the fundamental dimensions of situational interest are. Until we collect systematic knowledge on this topic, we shall have to proceed by trial and error, finding out which components of an exhibit are most attractive, for whom, under what conditions. In other words, museum work will continue to be an art rather than a science. Although this is not necessarily bad, a larger contribution of scientific knowledge would surely help.

After the individual's curiosity is aroused, the exhibit must engage sustained interest in order for learning to take place. While individuals vary in what they are interested in – astronomy, sports, mechanics, archaeology, biology and so on – some general guidelines could be proposed. Most important, the link between the museum and the visitor's life needs to be made clear. To inspire intrinsic motivation, the objects one finds and the experiences one enjoys, while possibly inspiring awe and a sense of

153

A. The 'Hook'

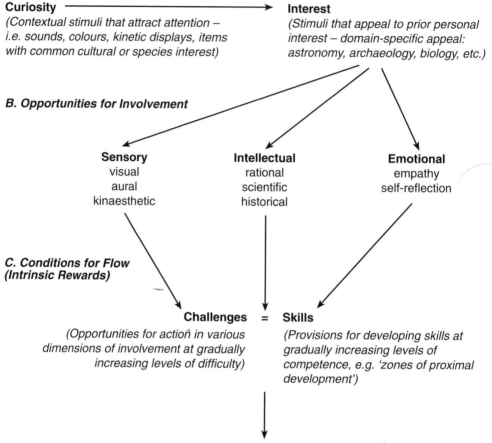

Curiosity ──────────────────────➤ **Interest**
(Contextual stimuli that attract attention –   *(Stimuli that appeal to prior personal*
i.e. sounds, colours, kinetic displays, items   *interest – domain-specific appeal:*
with common cultural or species interest)   *astronomy, archaeology, biology, etc.)*

B. Opportunities for Involvement

Sensory	**Intellectual**	**Emotional**
visual	rational	empathy
aural	scientific	self-reflection
kinaesthetic	historical	

C. Conditions for Flow
(Intrinsic Rewards)

Challenges = **Skills**
(Opportunities for action in various   *(Provisions for developing skills at*
dimensions of involvement at gradually   *gradually increasing levels of*
increasing levels of difficulty)   *competence, e.g. 'zones of proximal*
    development')

D. Growth of Complexity in Consciousness
(If involvement is intrinsically rewarding, visitors wish to maintain the flow experience. This requires increasing challenges to avoid boredom, and increasing skills to avoid frustration. The consequence of this dynamic involvement is a growth of sensory, intellectual and emotional complexity)

Figure 15.1 The development of learning through intrinsic motivation in museum settings

discovery, should not feel disconnected from one's own life. Moore (1992: 285) asserts that 'when art is removed as the province of professional artists, a dangerous gulf develops between the fine arts and the everyday arts. The fine arts are elevated and set apart from life, becoming too precious and therefore irrelevant. Having banished art to the museum, we fail to give it a place in ordinary life.' What Moore says about art could be said of museums in general. It is to be hoped that the museum experience will inspire visitors to see the relationship between the exhibits and their own concerns and perhaps be stimulated to create art, pursue science, and so on, after leaving the museum.

For example, an exhibit on rock formations may be informative and pleasantly arranged. In addition, the exhibit may have features that are challenging and allow one to explore and develop skills. But the features of the exhibit that will induce the motivation to learn more are the deeper sense of meaning it provides. How does this exhibit pertain to me? How does knowing about these rock formations link me to other people and times, the larger cosmos? Education should 'speak to the soul as well as the mind' (Moore 1992: 36). How does knowledge of rock formations provide a 'soulful' connection? Unless we make progress in answering such questions, the information provided in the display is likely to disappear from the visitor's consciousness without leaving any trace in memory.

Opportunities for involvement

Learning involves the use of sensory and emotional faculties, as well as intellectual ones, and this connection leads us to the third step in the process. To engage intellectual faculties, the exhibit should encourage what Langer (1993; see also 1989) has termed 'mindfulness'. Mindfulness is the 'state of mind that results from drawing novel distinctions, examining information from new perspectives, and being sensitive to context. It is an open, creative, probabilistic state of mind in which the individual might be led to finding differences among things thought similar and similarities among things thought different' (Langer 1993: 44). Exhibits that facilitate mindfulness display information in context and present various viewpoints. For example, Langer (1993: 47) contrasts the statement 'The three main reasons for the Civil War were . . .' with the statement 'From the perspective of the white male living in the twentieth century, the main reasons for the Civil War were . . .' (ibid.). The latter approach calls for thoughtful comparisons. For example: How did women feel during the Civil War? the old? the old from the North? the black male today? and so on.

Information that is presented as true without alternative perspectives discourages the motivation to explore and learn more. Langer (1993: 45) terms this situation a 'premature cognitive commitment', denoted by rigid beliefs mindlessly accepted as true (see also Langer and Imber 1979). In sum, intrinsically motivated learning is an open process involving uncertainty and the discovery of new possibilities. A fixed presentation of the material thwarts such further exploration. It is only through the conscious choice of various possibilities that one can learn who one is, what one's interests and beliefs are and where one's unique talents lie (Csikszentmihalyi and Rochberg-Halton 1981; Csikszentmihalyi and Robinson 1990).

But when we are intrinsically motivated to learn, emotions and feelings are involved as well as thoughts. For example, our wish to know about peoples in faraway places includes not only the desire for intellectual understanding but the desire to feel emotionally connected to them as well. We are often drawn to exhibits containing diaries and personal letters because they connect us with another's feelings. As Moore (1992: 208) states:

> We have spiritual longing for community and relatedness and for a cosmic vision, but we go after them with literal hardware instead of with sensitivity of heart. . . . Our many studies of world cultures are soulless, replacing the common bonding of humanity and its shared wisdom with bites of information that have no way of getting into us deeply, of nourishing and transforming our sense of ourselves. Soul, of course, has been extracted from the beginning because we conceive of education to be about skills and information, not about depth of feeling and imagination.

Museum researchers have become increasingly aware that it is not enough to attract the fleeting attention and interest of visitors; to be effective, museums must provide opportunities for the kind of deep absorption that leads to learning (Harvey *et al.* forthcoming; Thompson 1993). This is what Bitgood (1990: 1) calls 'simulated immersion' or 'the degree to which an exhibit effectively involves, absorbs, engrosses, or creates for visitors the experience of a particular time and place'.

Conditions for flow

When the visitor is interested in an exhibit and engaged through sensory, intellectual and emotional faculties, he or she should be ready to experience an intrinsically rewarding, optimal experience. But for this experience to occur, the conditions for flow must be present. In the previous section, we have seen that one of the main requirements for flow is to have clear goals. Unfortunately, one of the complaints visitors most often voice is that they do not know what to do when they enter a museum. Helping visitors set manageable goals, both for the entire visit and for each stop at an exhibit, is one way to make the experience more enjoyable. Without feedback, however, involvement is unlikely to be sustained. Successful displays tend to be those that ask visitors to commit themselves to making guesses, evaluating, responding – and then provide information by which the visitors can compare their responses with some other standard (Bitgood 1990).

Another feature of successful exhibits is that they offer opportunities for involvement that can be matched with a broad range of visitor skills. This notion was made familiar to the museum community through the 'social design movement', one of whose principal aims is to increase the fit between people and their environment (Sommer 1972) or between visitors and informal learning environments (Screven 1976).

In this regard, Vygotsky's (1978) zone of proximal development provides a framework for understanding how to moderate challenges so that they are at the right level. The zone of proximal development is 'the distance between the actual development level as determined by independent problem solving and the level of potential development as determined through problem solving under adult guidance or in collaboration with more capable peers' (Vygotsky 1978: 86). When individuals are assisted in particular tasks, they can learn at different levels. With assistance, one third-grade student may learn at a fifth-grade pace, while another learns at a fourth-grade pace. In developing exhibits, it is useful to ask: How much assistance is available for visitors with different levels of knowledge and ability? Do exhibits present gradually increasing levels of difficulty? And are there provisions for developing skills at gradually increasing levels of competence?

In addition to a balance of challenge and skill, the visitor must be able to concentrate and devote full attention to the given exhibit or activity. Well-known physical distractions include crowds, noise, intimidating guards, hunger, bladder pressure and fatigue. In addition, preconceived notions may provide internal distractions. Concentration can be hindered by rigid expectations – either one's own or someone else's. For example, as Falk and Dierking (1992: 54) point out, museum visitors often have the expectation that they 'should see the entire museum'. Such prior expectations decrease the openness necessary for a meaningful learning experience by causing fixation on an external goal and anxiety over the ability to meet that goal. Another example frequently occurs in art museums when patrons feel they 'should' be getting something out of the experience (Csikszentmihalyi and Robinson 1990: 144). When visitors feel intimidated or fearful, or when they try to sustain some rigid self-concept or achieve some predefined result, they also lose the openness necessary for an enjoyable learning experience. The physical sources of distraction can be remedied by physical means – reducing crowds, providing better facilities – while the psychological causes must be addressed through information and education.

In addition to the negative expectations that a person may bring to the museum, negative mental states can be caused by the social context (Deci *et al.* 1981; McCombs 1991). Thus, the museum environment can either facilitate or hinder flow. Anxiety, embarrassment, or self-consciousness usually vary depending on where we are and whom we are with. Social environments that facilitate intrinsically motivated learning support personal autonomy and responsibility rather than trying to control behaviour. These supportive environments provide people with choices (Zuckerman *et al.* 1978) and acknowledge their perspectives or feelings (Koestner *et al.* 1984). We express who we are through our conscious choice of actions. Thus it is important to allow individuals to choose whenever possible. People are more open to learning when they feel supported, when they are in a place where they can express themselves and explore their interests without fear of embarrassment or criticism, and when there are no predefined expectations constraining their behaviour. Support, security and trust are critical for allowing openness to discovery and intrinsically motivated learning. For personal growth and development, one must become less dependent on, or constrained by, outside guidance, so that spontaneous motivation will have a chance to awaken.

Growth of complexity in consciousness

If a museum exhibit induces the flow state, the experience will be intrinsically rewarding. The visitor will be motivated to explore, and as he or she learns more, skills will increase. The consequence of this dynamic involvement is a growth of sensory, intellectual and emotional complexity. This growth is especially important to realize now that we live in an information society, when multimedia technology and computers are rapidly changing how we learn and how we are entertained. By pressing a button, in the comfort of our own home, we can learn about the entire history of art, complete with detailed images on the screen; we do not need to enter a museum. But museums offer the opportunity to interact with a real environment, one in which the objects are still imbued with the blood, the tears, the sweat of their makers. Does this contact with the facticity of the historical object actually matter? Or will virtual reality experienced in the communications room of one's home give an even more vivid learning experience than museums now provide?

The jury is still out on these questions. In one respect, however, museums seem to have a distinct advantage over solitary media-induced experiences. They provide information in a public space, where there is a potential to develop the integrative dimension of personal growth. We learn about connectedness through rituals – such as ceremonies or rock concerts – and whenever we are exposed to an event that is shared with others that feeling of connectedness is reaffirmed and strengthened. In modern society, however, there are fewer and fewer venues to experience such shared events. Perhaps one of the major underdeveloped functions of museums is to provide opportunities for individually meaningful experiences that also connect with the experiences of others.

It is essential to realize, however, that current knowledge is insufficient to provide a basis for a thoroughly informed museum practice. While we are getting to understand general principles of motivation tolerably well, the necessary details are still largely lacking. For instance, we have no table where we could look up the elements that will attract the curiosity of different types of visitors; we cannot anticipate the interests of the audience; we have only a rudimentary understanding as to how to balance the challenges of the exhibit with the visitors' skills; we are not sure how to nurture the growth of complexity in the visitors' consciousness after the first sparks are struck. Many of these issues will take decades of basic research to resolve.

In the meantime, however, it seems that each museum could generate knowledge about these pressing questions by taking a more experimental approach, by becoming a more active learning institution. If even 10 per cent of museum space and staff efforts were devoted to collecting systematic information about how visitors are affected by the visit, we would soon have a much better idea of what learning takes place within the walls. Only by experimenting with one alternative after the other, in an iterative process, can we learn what works and what does not (Screven 1976). Trying out different displays, different signage, different ways of involving visitors – while making sure that only a single variable is changed at a time – and then measuring the results will yield useful results. It is important to remain flexible in one's policies, so that mistakes can be corrected swiftly and successes can be built on. These are the main features of the experimental method on which all of science is based. But then, as the philosopher Karl Popper said, science is but common sense writ large. There is no reason museums could not use more common sense and develop the habit of writing it large. We would all benefit from it, and museums could go on performing their educational function with a clearer purpose and a renewed sense of self-confidence.

This chapter first appeared in J. Falk and L. Dierking (eds) Public Institutions for Personal Learning, Washington, DC: American Association of Museums, pp. 67–77.

ACKNOWLEDGEMENTS

The authors wish to acknowledge the helpful suggestions of the participants at the Annapolis Conference, and especially Margie Marino and Mark Harvey for their assistance with the literature on museum visitors research.

REFERENCES

Amabile, R. M. (1983) *The Social Psychology of Creativity*, New York: Springer-Verlag.
Amabile, R. M. (1985) 'Motivation and creativity: effects of motivational orientation on creative writers', *Journal of Personality and Social Psychology* 48: 393–7.
Benware, C. and Deci, E. L. (1984) 'The quality of learning with an active versus passive motivational set', *American Educational Research Journal* 21: 755–65.
Berlyne, D. E. (1960) *Conflict, Arousal and Curiosity*, New York: Grove.
Berlyne, D. E. (1974) 'Novelty, complexity, and interestingness', in *Studies in New Experimental Aesthetics*, ed. D. E. Berlyne, New York: Wiley, 175–80.
Bitgood, S. (1990) 'The role of simulated immersion in exhibition', Report 90–20, Jacksonville, AL: Center for Social Design.
Butler, R. A. (1957) 'The effect of deprivation of visual incentives on visual exploration motivation', *Journal of Comparative and Physiological Psychology* 50: 177–9.
Cameron, J. (1992) *The Artist's Way: A Spiritual Path to Higher Creativity*, New York: Putnam.
Csikszentmihalyi, M. (1975) *Beyond Boredom and Anxiety*, San Francisco: Jossey-Bass.
Csikszentmihalyi, M. (1978) 'Attention and the wholistic approach to behavior', in *The Stream of Consciousness*, ed. K. S. Pope and J. L. Singer, New York: Plenum, 335–58.
Csikszentmihalyi, M. (1985) 'Emergent motivation and the evolution of the self', *Advances in Motivation and Achievement* 4: 93–119.
Csikszentmihalyi, M. (1990a) *Flow: The Psychology of Optimal Experience*, New York: HarperCollins.
Csikszentmihalyi, M. (1990b) 'Literacy and intrinsic motivation', *Daedalus* 119: 2, 115–40.
Csikszentmihalyi, M. (1993) *The Evolving Self*, New York: HarperCollins.
Csikszentmihalyi, M. and Csikszentmihalyi, I. (eds) (1988) *Optimal Experience*, New York: Cambridge University Press.

Csikszentmihalyi, M. and Larson, R. (1984) *Being Adolescent*, New York: Basic Books.

Csikszentmihalyi, M. and Nakamura, J. (1989) 'The dynamics of intrinsic motivation: a study of adolescents', in *Research on Motivation in Education*, Vol. 3, *Goals and Cognitions*, New York: Academic Press.

Csikszentmihalyi, M. and Rathunde, K. (1993) 'The measurement of flow in everyday life', *Nebraska Symposium on Motivation* 40: 58–97.

Csikszentmihalyi, M., Rathunde, K. and Whalen, S. (1993) *Talented Teenagers: The Roots of Success and Failure*, New York: Cambridge University Press.

Csikszentmihalyi, M. and Robinson, R. (1990) *The Art of Seeing*, Malibu, CA: J. P. Getty Press.

Csikszentmihalyi, M. and Rochberg-Halton, E. (1981) *The Meaning of Things: Domestic Symbols and the Self*, New York: Cambridge University Press.

Damon, W. (1983) *Social and Personality Development*, New York: Norton.

deCharms, R. (1968) *Personal Causation: The Internal Affective Determinants of Behavior*, New York: Academic Press.

Deci, E. L. (1971) 'Effects of external mediated rewards on intrinsic motivation', *Journal of Personality and Social Psychology* 18: 105–15.

Deci, E. L. (1972) 'Intrinsic motivation, extrinsic reinforcement, and inequity', *Journal of Personality and Social Psychology* 22: 113–20.

Deci, E. L. (1992) 'The relation of interest to the motivation of behavior: a self-determination theory perspective', in *The Role of Interest in Learning and Development*, ed. K. A. Renninger, S. Hidi and A. Krapp, Hillsdale, NJ: Lawrence Erlbaum Associates.

Deci, E. L. and Ryan, R. M. (1985) *Intrinsic Motivation and Self-Determination in Human Behavior*, New York: Plenum.

Deci, E. L. and Ryan, R. M. (1991) 'A motivational approach to self: integration in personality', in R. Dienstbier (ed.) *Nebraska Symposium on Motivation*, Vol. 38, *Perspectives on Motivation*, Lincoln, NB: University of Nebraska Press.

Deci, E. L., Schwartz, A. J., Sheinman, L. and Ryan, R. M. (1981) 'An instrument to assess adults' orientations toward control versus autonomy with children: reflections on intrinsic motivation and perceived competence', *Journal of Educational Psychology* 73: 642–50.

Dewey, J. (1913) *Interest and Effort in Education*, Boston, MA: Riverside Press.

Diener, C. I. and Dweck, C. S. (1980) 'An analysis of learned helplessness: the process of success', *Journal of Personality and Social Psychology* 39: 940–52.

Dweck, C. S. (1975) 'The role of expectations and attributions in the alleviation of learned helplessness', *Journal of Personality and Social Psychology* 31: 674–85.

Dweck, C. S. (1986) 'Motivational processes affecting learning', *American Psychologist* 41: 1040–8.

Falk, J. H. (1991) 'Analysis of the behavior of family visitors in natural history museums', *Curator* 34: 44–51.

Falk, J. H. and Dierking, L. D. (1992) *The Museum Experience*, Washington, DC: Whalesback.

Fowler, J. W. (1981) *Stages of Faith*, New York: Harper & Row.

Gottfried, A. (1985) 'Academic intrinsic motivation in elementary and junior high school students', *Journal of Educational Psychology* 77: 631–45.

Harlow, H. F. (1953) 'Motivation as a factor in the acquisition of new responses', in *Current Theory and Research on Motivation*, Lincoln: University of Nebraska Press, 24–9.

Harvey, M. L., Birjulin, A. A. and Loomis, R. J. (in press) 'A virtual reality and human factors analysis of a renovated diorama hall', in *Visitor Studies: Theory, Research, and Practice*, ed. D. R. Thompson, A. Benefield and S. Bitgood, Vol. 6, Jacksonville, AL: Center for Social Design.

Hasher, L. and Zacks, R. T. (1979) 'Automatic and effortful processing in memory', *Journal of Experimental Psychology* 108: 356–88.

Hebb, D. O. (1955) 'Drives and the C.N.S. (Conceptual Nervous System)', *Psychological Review* 62(4): 243–54.

Heyman, G. D. and Dweck, C. S. (1992) 'Achievement goals and intrinsic motivation: their relation and their role in adaptive motivation', *Motivation and Emotion* 16(3): 231–47.

Hidi, S. (1990) 'Interest and its contribution as a mental resource for learning', *Review of Educational Research* 60: 549–71.

Isen, A. M., Daubman, K. A. and Gorgoglione, J. M. (1987) 'The influence of positive affect on cognitive organization: Implications for education', in *Aptitude, Learning, and Instruction*, Vol. 3, *Conative and Affective Process Analyses*, ed. R. E. Snow and M. J. Farr, Hillsdale, NJ: Lawrence Erlbaum Associates, 143–64.

James, W. (1950 [1890]) *The Principles of Psychology*, 2 vols, New York: Dover.

Kahneman, D. (1973) *Attention and Effort*, Englewood Cliffs, NJ: Prentice-Hall.

Koestner, R., Ryan, R. M., Bernieri, F. and Holt, K. (1984) 'Setting limits in children's behavior: the differential effects of controlling versus informational styles on intrinsic motivation and creativity', *Journal of Personality* 52: 233–48.

Kohlberg, L. (1984) *Essays on Moral Development*, Vol. 2, *The Psychology of Moral Development*, San Francisco: Harper & Row.

Koran, J. J., Jr, Foster, J. S. and Koran, M. L. (1989) 'The relationship among interest, attention and learning in a natural history museum', in *Proceedings of the Annual Visitors Studies Conference*, ed. S. Bitgood, A. Benefield and D. Patterson, Jacksonville, AL: Center for Social Design, 239–44.

Krapp, A., Hidi, S. and Renninger, K. A. (1992) 'Interest, learning and development', in *The Role of Interest in Learning and Development*, ed. K. A. Renninger, S. Hidi and A. Krapp, Hillsdale, NJ: Lawrence Erlbaum Associates.

Langer, E. J. (1989) *Mindfulness*, Reading, MA: Addison-Wesley.

Langer, E. J. (1993) 'A mindful education', *Educational Psychologist* 28(1): 43–50.

Langer, E. J. and Imber, L. (1979) 'When practice makes imperfect: the debilitating efforts of over-learning', *Journal of Personality and Social Psychology* 37: 2014–25.

Lepper, M. R. and Cordova, D. I. (1992) 'A desire to be taught: instructional consequences of intrinsic motivation', *Motivation and Emotion* 16(3): 187–208.

Lepper, M. R. and Greene, D. (1978) *The Hidden Costs of Reward: New Perspectives on the Psychology of Human Motivation*, Hillsdale, NJ: Lawrence Erlbaum Associates.

Loevinger, J. (1976) *Ego Development*, San Francisco: Jossey-Bass.

Loomis, R. J. (1987) *Museum Visitor Evaluation: New Tool for Management*, Nashville, TN: American Association for State and Local History.

McCombs, B. L. (1991) 'Motivation and lifelong learning', *Educational Psychologist* 26(2): 117–27.

McGraw, K. O. (1978) 'The detrimental effects of reward on performance: a literature review and a prediction model', in *The Hidden Costs of Reward*, ed. M. R. Lepper and D. Greene, Hillsdale, NJ: Lawrence Erlbaum Associates, 33–60.

Maehr, M. L. (1984) 'Meaning and motivation: toward a theory of personal investment', in *Research on Motivation in Education*, Vol. 1, *Student Motivation*, New York: Academic Press.

Maslow, A. H. (1968) *Toward a Psychology of Being*, New York: Van Nostrand.

Miller, G. A. (1983) 'Infomavors', in *The Study of Information*, ed. F. Machlup and U. Mansfield, New York: Wiley.

Mills, R. C. (1991) 'A new understanding of self: the role of affect, state of mind, self-understanding, and intrinsic motivation', *Journal of Experimental Education* 60(1): 67–81.

Montgomery, K. C. (1954) 'The role of exploratory drive in learning', *Journal of Comparative and Physiological Psychology*, 47: 60–4.

Moore, T. (1992) *Care of the Soul*, New York: HarperCollins.

Nicholls, J. G., Patashnick, M. and Nolen, S. B. (1985) 'Adolescents' theories of education', *Journal of Educational Psychology* 77: 683–92.

Pekrun, R. (1990) 'Emotion and motivation in educational psychology: general and European perspectives', in *European Perspectives in Psychology*, ed. P. J. Drenth, J. A. Sergeant and R. J. Takens, Cambridge: Cambridge University Press, Vol. 1, 265–95.

Schiefele, U. (1991) 'Interest, learning, and motivation', *Educational Psychologist* 26(3–4): 299–323.

Screven, C. G. (1976) 'Exhibit evaluation: a goal-referenced approach', *Curator* 19: 271–91.

Searles, H. F. (1960) *The Nonhuman Environment*, New York: International Universities Press.

Serrell, B. and Ralphling, B. (1993) 'The momentary shrine: a new way of thinking about visitors, exhibits, and time', typescript.

Simon, H. A. (1969) *Sciences of the Artificial*, Boston, MA: MIT Press.

Simon, H. A. (1978) 'Rationality as process and as product of thought', *American Economic Review* 68: 1–16.

Sommer, R. (1972) *Design Awareness*, San Francisco: Rinehart Press.

Thompson, D. R. (1993) 'Considering the museum visitor: an interactional approach to environmental design', PhD diss., University of Wisconsin, Milwaukee.

Tiger, L. (1992) *The Pursuit of Pleasure*, Boston, MA: Little, Brown.

Vygotsky, L. S. (1978) *Mind in Society: The Development of Higher Psychological Processes*, Cambridge, MA: Harvard University Press.

Walters, J. and Gardner, H. (1986) 'The crystallizing experience: discovering an intellectual gift', in *Conceptions of Giftedness*, ed. R. J. Sternberg and J. E. Davidson, New York: Cambridge University Press, 306–31.

White, R. W. (1959) 'Motivation reconsidered: the concept of competence', *Psychological Review* 66: 297–333.

Zuckerman, M., Porac, J., Lathin, D., Smith, R. and Deci, E. L. (1978) 'On the importance of self-determination for intrinsically motivated behavior', *Personality and Social Psychology Bulletin* 4: 443–6.

16

Cognitive psychology and interpretation: synthesis and application

Sam H. Ham

Research into how we learn (cognitive psychology) offers some useful hints on how to structure and present communicative acts, whether they are exhibitions, talks, or texts.

Meaningfulness, relevance and conceptual organization are identified as key elements for information processing. The focus of the chapter is on the way in which people respond within a communicative situation. Ways to shape interpretation so as to enable people to respond are suggested. Although focusing on face-to-face communication the ideas discussed are of great relevance to exhibitions.

Although interpretive research has traditionally borrowed from other behavioural sciences (e.g. educational psychology, social psychology and sociology), little attention has been given to the existing vast body of research on human cognition. Dick *et al.* (1974) based an earlier paper on the contention that interpreters were often unaware of communication principles that could be derived from social psychology and persuasion research. Although otherwise impressive in its breadth, the Dick *et al.* paper was notably void of references to cognitive psychology.

The purpose of this paper is to show the application of cognitive psychology in interpretive research and practice. As such, the focus is both theoretical and applied. The first part of the paper examines past experiments on human cognition and suggests five propositions for future interpretive research and theory. The second part of the paper discusses potential applications of cognitive psychology in designing interpretive presentations.

COGNITIVE PSYCHOLOGY AND INTERPRETATION

Cognitive psychology examines how humans gain and store external information in memory, and how they utilize it to direct their attention and behaviour (Solso 1979). It includes such topics as sensory perception, pattern recognition, attention, memory, mental imagery, semantic organization, thinking and problem-solving. Although a discussion of each of these topics is beyond the scope of this paper, interpreters should intuitively find many of them relevant. Consequently, it has probably *not* been a lack of relevance that has prevented interpretive researchers from considering cognition research, but rather that cognitive psychology has not traditionally focused on human communication *per se*.

Nevertheless, knowledge of how humans gain, organize and store information can be useful in better understanding interpretation. Hammitt (1981), for example, borrowed heavily from cognition research to reformulate Tilden's seminal principles of interpretation, and Tai (1981) and Hammitt (1978) both adopted a cognitive psychology framework to evaluate the effectiveness of self-guided interpretive services. In this paper I attempt to apply cognitive psychology to the problem of designing personal interpretive presentations, with emphasis on the variables of audience attention, comprehension and recall.

For present purposes, 'interpretation' is viewed as an agency's communication with non-captive audiences in leisure settings. The distinction between captive and non-captive audiences is necessary since it is well accepted that people in leisure settings place special demands on interpreters and interpretation (Field and Wagar 1973). Perhaps the most important of these demands state: (1) interpretation must be entertaining and interesting since external incentives for audiences to pay attention (e.g. exams, grades, etc.) do not exist in leisure settings; and (2) interpretation must be understandable and therefore relatively easy for audiences to process mentally. Central to the interest and understandability of interpretation are factors of *meaningfulness*, *relevance* and *conceptual organization*. I will discuss these factors as they relate to the development of personal presentations for non-captive audiences. (See Witt (1983) for a discussion of psychology pertaining to audio-visual presentations.)

The meaningfulness of information presented to audiences (particularly non-captive audiences) is important to achieving the purposes of presentations – recall, conceptual understanding, and so forth. Considerable research in cognitive psychology focuses directly on this topic, and a number of studies have indirect bearing. Most of this research empirically substantiates what Freeman Tilden (1977: 9) said in his first principle of interpretation:

> Any interpretation that does not somehow relate what is being displayed or described to something within the personality or experience of the visitor will be sterile.

For instance, Glucksberg *et al.* (1966) found that when a child located on one side of an opaque screen was given verbal instructions for a recognition task by another child on the opposite side of the screen, performance was fair to poor. However, when the same child was later read *his/her own* instructions (the same ones he/she had earlier given to another child), performance improved dramatically. The authors suggested that people can more readily understand information if it is presented exactly as they themselves would say it.

Commenting on the Glucksberg *et al.* study, Dale (1972) attributed the results to egocentrism (the child's inability to see reality through another's eyes). A *meaningfulness* hypothesis, which holds that improved understanding is due to the similarity between the information presented and the recipient's own verbal style, would be even more pertinent.

Meaningfulness can be viewed as the number of semantic associations a person has for a particular word. The greater the number of associations, the more meaningful the word (Ellis 1978). This conceptualization is consistent with results of the Glucksberg *et al.* (1966) study, given that people describe their world in the most meaningful descriptors possible. Therefore, it might follow that the more similar the semantic structure of a message and the verbal style of an audience, the more meaningful the audience will find the message. Thus we see today's trend toward plain-language contracts and insurance policies, as well as Bibles written in twentieth-century style.

162

Meaningfulness, of course, is only one factor determining our interest in a message. Perhaps even more important is the relevance of the message (i.e. the degree to which we have prior ego-involvement with the topic). An interesting phenomenon illustrating the importance of ego-involvement has been repeatedly observed in laboratory experiments on selective attention. These studies have utilized an experimental method called 'shadowing' in which a subject is presented with simultaneous tape recordings of two messages, and is instructed to focus attention on one and ignore the other. In addition, the subject is asked to repeat (shadow) the attended spoken message as it is presented. To control for the discriminating effect of voice tonal qualities the same speaker records both messages. The subject usually wears stereo headphones to prevent overlap of messages in the same ear.

Cherry (1966) conducted such an experiment and found that his subjects were reasonably able to shadow under certain conditions, but that the content of the shadowed message was poorly remembered. The unattended message, of course, was even more vague. In fact, it was so poorly understood that a switch from English to German on the unattended channel went undetected. In an earlier study Moray (1959) obtained similar results and discovered that subjects could say little about the unattended message despite the fact that selected words were repeated up to thirty-five times. However, when he prefaced the unshadowed message with *the subject's name* the subject paid more attention to it and remembered more about it.

An experiment by Neisser (1969) demonstrated that the same striking phenomenon occurs when we read. Neisser had his subjects read the lines of one colour from a text consisting of sentences in alternating colours. As in the Cherry and Moray experiments, little was retained from the unattended message except when the subject's name appeared. Thus, people appear to listen to and look at the world selectively. Although individuals pay attention to only a small number of stimuli at one time, there is considerably more monitoring going on than is realized. And, it is evident people will readily switch their attention to those stimuli most important to them. Solso (1979: 122) summed up the universality of this phenomenon:

> And isn't this also true at the cocktail party? Someone on the other side of the room says: 'And I understand Bob and Lee . . . ' And, until then completely engrossed in other conversations, all the Bob's and Lee's turn a live ear to the speaker.

E. F. Hutton stock consultant advertisements on television present a similar example of selective attention. Also consider how well parents can distinguish between the shouting of countless children in a nursery or playground and that of their own.

Based on results of these studies, it can be hypothesized that audiences will be more interested in presentations that occasionally mention their names. This not being very likely (or practical) under most circumstances, one might speculate that presentations which (as Tilden suggested) rely on information important to the *common experiences* of the audience will command greater attention. Numerous investigations have shown the influence of self-reference on audience retention of information. In fact, there is evidence to indicate that simply *telling* audience members to use themselves and their experiences to judge the relevance of presented information can significantly improve learning and recall (Rogers 1977, Cartwright 1956). In other studies, Craik and Tulving (1975) and Rogers *et al.* (1977) reported that subjects' recall of words that remind them of themselves was superior to their recall of other words. Consistent with Craik and Lockhart's (1972) 'Levels of processing theory', these findings demonstrate that personally relevant information is more deeply encoded than other kinds of information, and hence more easily remembered.

Put another way, human perception capabilities are limited. There is a constant trade-off between what we attend to and what is ignored. People will consciously choose to focus on information which is most important to them for the moment. That is, temporarily at least, some information is more relevant than the other stimuli vying for attention. High relevance seems to make perception and processing of information easier. (Consider the sometimes extreme effort required to pay attention to boring presentations one is later expected to know something about.) Thus, people are more sensitive to relevant information than to stimuli of questionable relevance. Such information is sometimes termed *low threshold* since it easily enters the conscious experience despite the existence of considerable competing stimuli (Morton 1969, Tulving and Gold 1963).

In summary, the relevance of a message appears to be strongly influenced by the recipient's background. A person's name, members of his/her family, occupation, religion, values, semantic style and other factors which exist permanently in memory can significantly affect the perceived importance and meaningfulness of information to that individual. To be most relevant and most meaningful, presentations must be geared to audience characteristics that enhance ego-involvement and understanding of the topic.

A presentation that is relevant and meaningful at one point, however, may not necessarily be so at the next. If the topic becomes confusing or dull, or for any reason requires the audience to expend undue effort to maintain attention, the audience will likely tune it out by switching attention to a more gratifying stimulus.

Clearly, the presentation must remain relevant throughout, and it must be organized in a way that allows the audience to process incoming information as rapidly and as efficiently as possible. When the organization of the presentation becomes fuzzy to the audience, the audience must work harder to maintain the train of thought. This effort is then spent at the expense of processing subsequent information; it also (especially for non-captive audiences) increases the likelihood of attention-switching. Therefore, not only should presentations be geared toward common experiences of the audience, but they must also be couched in an organizational framework which helps audiences organize and understand the connections between separate bits of information.

THE EFFECT OF CONCEPTUAL FRAMEWORKS

Without a clear conceptual framework an audience will usually attempt to provide its own. This may be accomplished by asking questions of a speaker. Although few non-classroom settings are conducive to two-way interaction, at least one study (Ham and Shew 1979) suggested that opportunities to participate verbally significantly increased audience enjoyment of interpretive activities. If circumstances or inhibition prevent the individual from asking questions in order to clarify the conceptual framework, he/she may resort to an implicit (or assumed) organization. Thus, when people enter a movie or conversation late, the information they attempt to process is out of context. Normally, they wait until they think they have got the gist of the conversation before jumping into it. Undoubtedly, some are less patient and are willing to guess about conceptual frameworks earlier than others. Often such guesses result in 'off-the-wall' (out of context) statements and provide humour and embarrassment for the conversationalists and newcomer, respectively.

It seems individuals are continually checking what they *think* is the conceptual organization of a message against each new piece of information processed. As long as the pieces fit into the context perceived up to that point, the processing of information occurs efficiently (almost effortlessly). When a piece does not readily fit the conceptual framework, however, it is held out of context until the organizational 'error' has been discovered. If the error is discovered relatively soon, little interest or understanding is lost. If, on the other hand, a workable framework is not soon constructed, considerable extraneous information may build up out of context and the individual becomes hopelessly confused. At this point attention-switching is likely to occur, especially for non-captive audiences not willing to spend the extra effort to sort things out.

Studies on how humans recognize and utilize patterns help to demonstrate the effect of conceptual frameworks on learning and understanding. Many studies (e.g. Allen *et al.* 1978; Biederman *et al.* 1973; Lockhart 1968; Palmer 1975; and Tulving and Osler 1968) have collectively demonstrated that: (1) one pays more attention to information rich in association, while tending to ignore unassociative (out-of-context) information; (2) a conceptual framework will add meaning and relevance to new information only to the extent that the new information is consistent with the conceptual framework; (3) once established, the conceptual framework is used by the audience to judge the relevance of subsequent information; (4) information not readily processed into the conceptual framework is lost in a relatively short period of time; and (5) people can consciously control attention and often appear to do so on the basis of contextual clues and ease of processing. Thus, there is strong evidence that recall and learning are made easier by contextual information, and this is precisely what conceptual frameworks do for verbal presentations.

Of particular importance to interpreters are experiments by Thorndyke (1977) which illustrated the influence conceptual frameworks can have on audience comprehension and recall of information presented in story format. Thorndyke presented to his subjects four different versions of the same story. The versions were nearly identical in information content but varied in how the information was organized within the story. His findings revealed that story comprehensibility and audience recall were indeed determined by how much 'plot structure' a story contained.

A major finding was that presenting the theme (plot structure) at the outset of a story served as a major organizer which allowed subjects to see the context of subsequent information. In fact, in presentations containing no theme statement at all, even presenting sentences in *random order* made no difference in subjects' recall or comprehensibility ratings of the story (i.e. both were low). Thus, an athematic presentation can make as little sense to us as a random presentation of unrelated sentences. In addition, when subjects were later asked to summarize the story in their own words, they tended to remember information reflecting the conceptual organization of the story, and to forget details and other subordinate information. This indicates that not only do conceptual frameworks facilitate the processing of information, they also constitute most of what is retained in memory after a message is communicated.

Contextual clues also permit a phenomenon called *chunking* (or clustering). Chunking is the term given to our ability to consolidate diverse pieces of information into a lesser number of manageable conceptual *chunks* (i.e. putting similar pieces of information into categories or patterns).

The human mind is limited in the number of unrelated stimuli it can simultaneously process. Miller (1956) demonstrated a principle that still stands: human perceptual capacity is limited to about seven (actually seven ± two) discrete stimuli. Thus, processing four pieces of unrelated information would be relatively easy for most people, whereas processing eight or more pieces would provide insurmountable difficulty. Cognitive chunking considerably (perhaps indefinitely) increases the raw amount of information that can be simultaneously processed by humans. In short, if contextual clues are available, meaningful associations among diverse stimuli can be recognized and *categories* rather than individual pieces of information are held in memory. Thus seven ± two categories, each containing several associated elements, can be processed.

There is much support for the idea that chunking makes pattern recognition possible for humans. Biederman and his associates (Biederman 1972; Biederman *et al.* 1973) found that subjects could more accurately and more rapidly recognize test objects when the objects were located in the real world rather than jumbled scenes. Palmer (1975) obtained similar results and concluded that contextual clues provided by situational characteristics normally associated with an object (e.g. a college campus, or a line drawing of a face) provide a meaningful conceptual framework which makes possible recognition of the object (a particular dormitory or an isolated part of the drawing). In recognizing a face or a campus scene, of course, countless stimuli are simultaneously perceived and recognized as a pattern. Similarly, Chase and Simon (1973) found that although master chess players and beginners could think ahead the same number of moves, engaged in similar searches for strategies, and spent about the same amount of time scanning the board, the masters could reconstruct a chess pattern from memory much more rapidly and accurately than beginners. As Solso (1979: 67) pointed out:

> these data indicate that the ability to see 'chunks' or meaningful clusters of chess pieces made it possible for the better players to gather more information in the given time.

A series of experiments by Tulving (Tulving and Gold 1963; Tulving and Pearlstone 1966; Tulving and Osler 1968; Tulving and Psotka 1971; Tulving 1974) dramatically demonstrated the influence of chunking on learning and recall of information. In all cases, subjects who memorized contextually related words were better able to recall them at a later time than subjects who had memorized unrelated words. Furthermore, when the words to be remembered were explicitly asked for in terms of category names that helped organize the word list, recall was as efficient as the original learning itself, even after ten minutes. In no case, however, had subjects been given the category names ahead of time; nor had they been permitted to rehearse the lists of words (ranging from 24 to 120 total words) during the waiting period. Bower *et al.* (1969: 340) who conducted similar experiments, summarized the significance of such findings:

> If (a subject) can discover or learn a simple rule or principle which characterizes the items on a list and which relates them to one another, then he uses that rule as a retrieval plan in reconstructing the items from memory, with a consequent improvement in his performance.

In the Bower *et al.* study, recall was two to three times better for organized presentations than for randomized lists of words.

The implication of these studies for applied communication is that presentations must be carefully designed to direct audience members' natural tendency to chunk discrete information into meaningful generalizations. Since much information in interpretive activities may be new to audiences, it is important that contextual clues be readily discernible. If these clues already exist (or have associates) in a person's memory, they will be even more useful organizers of information. For instance, consider the difficulty one might have recalling the letter serial:

FB ... IPH ... DTW ... AIB ... M

If, however, the serial was changed so that the sequence of the letters elicited associations from long-term memory, the task might be remarkably easy. That is essentially what Bower and Springston (1970) found when they presented the same serial to subjects as:

FBI ... PHD ... TWA ... IBM

The results for this serial (and others) were that recall was more accurate when the discrete letters were presented in meaningful context (i.e. only four pieces of information had to be stored in order to recall the twelve-letter serial).

Clearly, the processing of incoming information is made easier when the information is presented in a way that encourages chunking. For instance, the complex natural history of a mammal might seem amazingly simple if presented in the context of just three or four key organizers (e.g. food, cover, space or niche, habitat and competition). Therefore, although perceptual capacity is only about seven units, the amount of raw information contained (chunked) in each unit can vary enormously, and according to one psychologist (Solso 1979), perhaps up to the limits of the central nervous system itself. Consequently, the *amount* of information presented in an interpretive activity may not be as important as the conceptual framework used to present it. As previously emphasized, the easier it is for audiences to receive a message, the more likely it is that they will pay attention and be able to recall it later.

RECOMMENDATIONS FOR DESIGNING PRESENTATIONS

An old cliché in speech communication goes: Tell them what you are going to say; then say it; and then tell them what you said. From the standpoint of providing a conceptual framework, this is undeniably good advice. But it may oversimplify a complex task by ignoring the issues of meaningfulness and relevance outlined earlier. The following discussion attempts to integrate the research described by suggesting a more theoretically grounded approach to planning and organizing interpretive presentations. Central to this discussion is the concept of *theme* which is presented in some detail.

Selecting the theme of a presentation is an important organizational step for interpreters. *Theme* and *topic*, although frequently used synonymously, are not equivalent. Whereas the topic delineates the *subject-matter* of a presentation (thereby restricting the range of possible themes), the *theme* is viewed as the underlying thought or major point the interpreter wants to make (Lewis 1980). Thorndyke (1977) describes it as 'the general focus to which the plot adheres'. In essence, the theme is the answer to the question, 'So what?' The theme of a presentation whose topic is desert animals might be: 'Desert animals have developed unique ways of adapting to hot environments.' An alternative theme might be: 'Many desert animals are nocturnal.' Although the themes are related in content, development of the alternatives might be substantially different.

Clearly, *how* a theme is developed is important to whether audiences will find it easy or difficult to follow (Thorndyke 1977). It is therefore recommended that the body of the presentation be produced first in a flow chart format showing the theme and cognitive pathways through which it is to be developed (Figure 16.1). People do this covertly in a variety of situations. Consider the mental processing one uses to recall

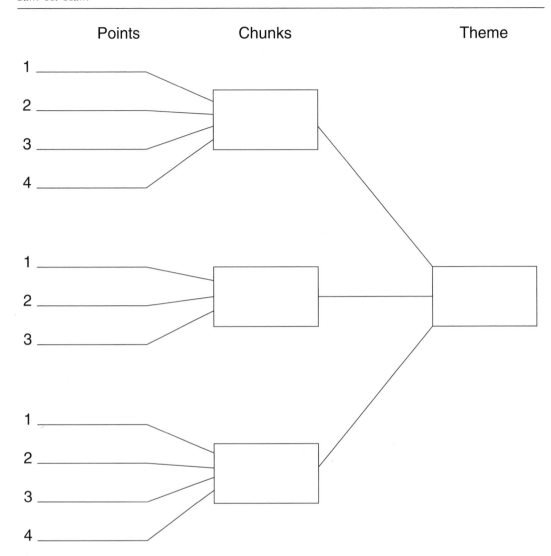

Figure 16.1 Conceptual relationship between individual pieces of information, cognitive 'chunks' and the theme of a hypothetical presentation

and retell a joke one has not told for some time. Normally one first thinks of the punchline, the 'so what' of the joke (theme). Then the attention turns to the pieces of information required and the sequence in which they must be mentioned to ensure that the intended humour will be realized (and hopefully appreciated) by the listener. After one has considered these things, one has implicitly developed a conceptual framework around a theme, and has designed the framework to accomplish predetermined ends.

Usually, the development of other types of presentations will require three distinct parts – an introduction, body and conclusion. In addition, careful thought should be given to the *vehicle* with which the theme is to be developed. Each of these considerations will now be discussed.

The way the theme is introduced and concluded depends entirely on the specific points to be mentioned in the body. For this reason, the body of the presentation should be developed first. This should be approached as in the 'joke' example above. Based on the theme, one should select the discrete points that need to be presented (Figure 16.1). Consider the sequence of these points required to provide contextual clues and to enhance the listener's processing of information. Changes in thought or direction will require transitions. Transitional phrases are often overlooked in interpretive presentations, yet if these crucial threads are lacking, an otherwise well-organized presentation may fall apart. Transitional phrases demonstrate the relationship of what *has* been said to what *will* be said. Thus they facilitate chunking and reduce required audience effort.

The discrete points selected, their sequence of presentation and the nature of transitional phrases depend on the *vehicle*. Even the most carefully designed conceptual frameworks can be dull. The vehicle is essentially a strategy adopted to enhance the audience interest in the topic.

If, as Craik and Tulving (1975) and Rogers *et al.* (1977) suggest, the *appeal* of information is a function of its personal relevance, one can readily see why the vehicle of a presentation can be so important. One could develop the theme 'Forests are important renewable resources and must be managed wisely' by presenting awesome quantities of statistics about wood production and use. Another vehicle might be used to relate a vivid fictional (but believable) account of a twenty-first-century community which differs strikingly from its twentieth-century counterpart because wood products are scarce. Further analogies might be drawn between the twenty-first-century 'wood shortage' and the all-too-familiar twentieth-century 'oil shortage'. The analogous vehicle might be more effective because it is more personal. Other story vehicles could include irony, humour, suspense, mystery, sadness, melodrama, or surprise.

The conclusion of the presentation follows logically from the body. Its tone and organization also depend in part on the introduction. It is necessary, therefore, that concurrent thought be given to the introduction at this point, but it is suggested that the introduction be developed last. The main purpose of the conclusion should be to wrap up the theme. It should offer an answer or answers to the 'so what' question. It should present the big picture or the moral to the story. In other words, the conclusion demonstrates the wisdom of the conceptual framework and vehicle adopted for the presentation.

Such wisdom is verified if the audience readily sees the logic between what was presented and what was concluded. The most profound conclusions often suggest (explicitly or otherwise) some new action or perspective on the part of the audience. If, as Tilden recommended, the answer to the 'so what' question is couched in experiences the audience is likely to have in the future, the likelihood of inspiring (or at least provoking) the audience is increased.

Developing the introduction after the body and conclusion often improves the presentation. This makes sense if one considers the two main purposes of the introduction: (1) to entice the audience to select the presentation instead of the countless other stimuli that vie for its attention, i.e. make the audience *want* to hear more; and (2) to establish the vehicle and conceptual framework upon which the rest of the presentation will hinge. Only *after* the rest of the presentation is designed can the interpreter really know *what* is to be introduced and *how* it should be done. Thus, the introductory remarks that later conjure up irony, humour, sorrow, etc., are developed with full knowledge of the direction of the theme and its conclusion.

169

It is during the introduction that audiences learn what the theme is and how it is going to be organized. Concurrently, they decide whether the conceptual framework is relevant enough to pay attention. They also receive important clues that suggest chunking strategies and help audiences to process the rest of the presentation. Because of the influence the introduction can have on listeners' attention and information-processing, it may well be the most important and most difficult part of the presentation.

Obviously, this '2–3–1 Rule' (body-conclusion-introduction) is flexible. While it makes intuitive sense to proceed in the order described above, it would be impractical to ignore other parts of the presentation while focusing on the design of one. In fact, it seems essential not only to plan each phase in light of the others previously designed, but also to rethink everything at each step of the process.

SUMMARY AND CONCLUSION

I have suggested possible applications of cognitive psychology to interpretation, focusing on verbal presentations for non-captive audiences such as those attending interpretive activities in parks and other leisure places. Although research in cognition is infrequently used to illuminate findings of interpretive research, at least five principles can be seen that have their grounding in cognitive psychology. These can be stated as general propositions:

1 matching the verbal style of a presentation with that of the audience increases the meaningfulness (and interest) of the presentation;
2 audiences will attend more faithfully to presentations which elicit associations from long-term memory as new information is presented. This is because such associations make the new information more meaningful and more relevant to the audience;
3 keeping the number of perceptual units to be processed by the audience at or below seven increases the likelihood that the audience will pay attention for the duration of the presentation;
4 providing a conceptual framework that enhances audience opportunities for chunking information will facilitate information-processing, and thereby increase the likelihood that the audience will attend for the duration of the presentation;
5 information rich in associative character and couched in meaningful context will be more accurately recognized, recalled and understood by audiences.

On the basis of the research reported, a strategy for planning interpretive presentations was discussed. It appears that cognition research may prove insightful in improving interpretive efforts. Thus, cognitive psychology should be examined for its potential contribution to theory and practice in interpretation and related fields.

This chapter first appeared as a paper in Journal of Interpretation 8(1) (1983): 11–27.

REFERENCES

Allen, G. L., Siegel, A. W. and Rosinski, R. R. (1978) 'The role of perceptual context in structuring spatial knowledge', *Journal of Experimental Psychology: Human Learning and Memory* 4(6): 617–30.

Biederman, I. (1972) 'Perceiving real world scenes', *Science* 177(1043): 77–80.

Biederman, I., Glass, A. L. and Stacy, E. W. (1973) 'Searching for objects in real world scenes', *Journal of Experimental Psychology* 97(1): 22–7.

Bower, G. H., Clark, M. C., Lesgold, A. M. and Winzenz, D. (1969) 'Hierarchical retrieval schemes in recall of categorized word lists', *Journal of Verbal Learning and Verbal Behavior* 8(3): 323–43.

Bower, G. H. and Springston, F. (1970) 'Pauses as recoding points in letter series', *Journal of Experimental Psychology* 83(3): 421–30.

Cartwright, D. (1956) 'Self-consistency as a factor affecting immediate recall', *Journal of Abnormal and Social Psychology* 52(3): 212–19.

Chase, W. G. and Simon, H. A. (1973) 'Perception in chess', *Cognitive Psychology* 4(1): 55–81.

Cherry, C. (1966) *On Human Communication*, 2nd edn, Cambridge, MA: Massachusetts Institute of Technology.

Craik, F. I. M. and Lockhart, R. S. (1972) 'Levels of processing: a framework for memory research', *Journal of Verbal Learning and Verbal Behavior* 11(6): 671–84.

Craik, F. I. M. and Tulving, E. (1975) 'Depth of processing and the retention of words in episodic memory', *Journal of Experimental Psychology: General* 104(3): 268–94.

Dale, P. S. (1972) *Language Development: Structure and Function*, Hinsdale, IL: Dryden Press.

Dick, R. E., McKee, D. T. and Wagar, J. A. (1974) 'A summary and annotated bibliography of communication principles', *Journal of Environmental Education* 5(4): 8–13.

Ellis, H. C. (1978) *Fundamentals of Human Learning, Memory and Cognition*, 2nd edn, Dubuque, IO: William C. Brown Publishers.

Field, D. R. and Wagar, J. A. (1973) 'Visitor groups and interpretation in parks and other outdoor leisure settings', *Journal of Environmental Education* 5(1): 12–17.

Glucksberg, S., Krauss, R. M. and Weisberg, R. (1966) 'Referential communication in nursery school children: method and some preliminary findings', *Journal of Experimental Child Psychology* 3(3): 333–42.

Ham, S. H. and Shew, D. L. (1979) 'A comparison of visitors' and interpreters' assessments of conducted interpretive activities', *Journal of Interpretation* 4(2): 39–44.

Hammitt, W. E. (1978) 'A visual preference approach to measuring interpretive effectiveness', *Journal of Interpretation* 3(2): 33–7.

Hammitt, W. E. (1981) 'A theoretical foundation for Tilden's interpretive principles', *Journal of Interpretation* 4(1): 9–12.

Lewis, W. J. (1980) *Interpreting for Park Visitors*, Philadelphia, PA: Eastern National Park and Monument Association (Acorn Press).

Lockhart, R. S. (1968) 'Stimulus selection and meaningfulness in paired-associate learning with stimulus items of high formal similarity', *Journal of Experimental Psychology* 78(2): 242–6.

Miller, G. A. (1956) 'The magical number seven, plus or minus two: some limits on our capacity for processing information', *Psychological Review* 63(2): 81–97.

Moray, N. (1959) 'Attention in dichotic listening: affective cues and the influence of instructions', *Quarterly Journal of Experimental Psychology* 11(1): 56–60.

Morton, J. (1969) 'Interaction of information in word recognition', *Psychological Review* 76(2): 165–78.

Neisser, V. (1969) 'Selective reading: a method for the study of visual attention', paper presented to the 19th International Congress of Psychology, London.

Palmer, S. E. (1975) 'The effects of contextual scenes on the identification of objects', *Memory and Cognition* 3(5): 519–26.

Rogers, T. B. (1977) 'Self-reference in memory: recognition of personality items', *Journal of Research in Personality* 11(3): 295–305.

Rogers, T. B., Kuiper, N. A. and Kirker, W. S. (1977) 'Self-reference and the encoding of personal information', *Journal of Personality and Social Psychology* 35(9): 677–88.

Solso, R. L. (1979) *Cognitive Psychology*, New York: Harcourt Brace Jovanovich.

Tai, D. B. (1981) 'An evaluation of the use and effectiveness of two types of interpretive trail media in Yellowstone National Park', unpublished MS thesis, University of Idaho, Moscow, Idaho.

Thorndyke, P. W. (1977) 'Cognitive structures in comprehension and memory of narrative discourse', *Cognitive Psychology* 9(1): 77–110.

Tilden, F. (1977) *Interpreting Our Heritage*, 2nd edn, Chapel Hill, NC: University of North Carolina Press.

Tulving, E. (1974) 'Cue-dependent forgetting', *American Scientist* 62(1): 74–82.

Tulving, E. and Gold, C. (1963) 'Stimulus information and contextual information as determinants and tachistoscopic recognition of words', *Journal of Experimental Psychology* 66(4): 319–27.

Tulving, E. and Osler, S. (1968) 'Effectiveness of retrieval cues in memory for words', *Journal of Experimental Psychology* 77(4): 593–601.

Tulving, E. and Pearlstone, Z. (1966) 'Availability versus accessibility of information in memory for words', *Journal of Verbal Learning and Verbal Behavior* 5(1): 381–91.

Tulving, E. and Psotka, J. (1971) 'Retroactive inhibition in free recall: inaccessibility of information available in the memory store', *Journal of Experimental Psychology* 87(1): 1–8.

Witt, G. A. (1983) 'Media psychology', *Technical Photography* 15(1): 38–40.

17

Collaboration: towards a more holistic design process

Hank Grasso and Howard Morrison

The production and design of exhibitions is most effectively achieved as a team effort. The team should include curatorial, design and education specialists. Scriptwriters and subject researchers are also of great value. This paper describes a holistic collaboration between members of an exhibition team, and discusses the processes that were followed in the various stages of the exhibition.

Visitors to 'American Encounters', a Columbian Quincentenary exhibition opening 24 June 1992, at the Smithsonian Institution's National Museum of American History, saw some of the ways American Indians and Hispanics have interacted with each other and with Anglo-Americans in New Mexico for nearly 500 years. Visitors to the exhibition *also* saw the result of a unique, collaborative exhibit development and design process.

Nearly three years before, the museum assembled a team of four curators, a scriptwriter, an education specialist, a designer, a New Mexico-based researcher, and a project manager; one of the curators served as project director. Such teams usually function as autonomous collectives in which individuals responsible for a particular domain meet merely to co-ordinate the execution of their separate tasks; but the 'American Encounters' team functioned as a collaborative body.

Collaboration does not preclude individual responsibility and accountability; team members were assigned specific duties and areas of concern. But, at each crucial decision-making point, they *shared* roles and responsibilities. Everyone participated in the decision-making that determined the content and design of each part of the exhibition. Collaboration is more difficult when some team members are contractors rather than staff employees; contracts link payments to specific tasks and must be written to accommodate some blurring of the lines of responsibility.

Many exhibits might benefit from this kind of holistic approach. When the entire team participates in all aspects of the development and design process, individual differences in perspective and interpretation as well as in personality and agenda become assets rather than liabilities. There are fewer surprises, fewer last-minute (a.k.a. costly) demands for changes by competing interests. There are also more opportunities for sharing potential solutions with colleagues outside the team, test audiences, and a wide variety of consultants – in this case, tribal and community representatives, artisans, photographers, collectors and scholars.

The challenge, as anyone who has ever tried to do anything by committee knows, was to establish a collaborative rhythm within a group of diverse individuals. What follows are brief descriptions of the series of group problem-solving exercises that allowed the 'American Encounters' team to arrive at collaboration in the development and design of the exhibit.

EXERCISE I: IDENTIFYING INTERPRETIVE GOALS

What is the most important message the exhibit should convey to the audience? What is the essential aspect of that message that the audience must understand for the exhibit to have meaning? The first step in answering these fundamental questions was to allow each member of the team to express what he or she believed to be the purpose of the exhibit. The free exchange of ideas was crucial; for there to be collaboration, everyone on the team must have a say, must have a stake in the exhibit.

The 'American Encounters' team retreated to West Virginia for three days of brainstorming with a professional meeting facilitator. The result was not consensus but a collection of wide-ranging, commonly acknowledged interpretive goals to show cultural continuity, cultural change, cultural diversity and cultural unity.

These and other goal statements provided the basis for in-depth audience studies using visitor surveys and interviews as well as focus groups. In addition, a broad-brush statement of purpose was presented in an illustrated brochure produced on a colour photocopier. The brochure was distributed to community and scholarly consultants as well as to potential financial backers.

EXERCISE II: ORIENTING CONCEPTS AND EXPERIENCES

What core ideas should the exhibit present? What kinds of visitor experiences should it provide? Even though members of the 'American Encounters' team had differing ideas on the exhibit's abstract goals, they were able to work collaboratively when answering these and other concrete questions.

For this exercise, everyone on the team literally had to put their suggestions on the table by means of a paper swatch floor plan. Each specific content idea or exhibit experience was written on a small, medium, or large square of paper and taped to a single oversized sheet of paper. Suggestions were assembled in relation to each other. Some needed more space; others less. Some needed to come before others; some after. Some were transitional; others were unrelated.

This exercise produced a seemingly helter-skelter wish list, but, in the process, core ideas and experiences began to emerge.

EXERCISE III: EXAMINING POSSIBLE SEQUENCES OF VISITOR EXPERIENCES

By translating the swatches of paper into large and small circles, it was possible to lay out the interrelationships of concepts and experiences in a bubble diagram. The result was a schematic representation of the sequence and relative importance of ideas and experiences.

EXERCISE IV: DEVELOPING A PRELIMINARY FLOOR PLAN

Spaces in the exhibit were allocated by superimposing the bubble diagram on a plan that showed the size and configuration of the actual space available. How must the space be entered? How may it be exited? How many different ways can visitors move through the space? Team members, with pencils in hand, joined in marking up floor plans to develop various possible layouts for the preliminary floor plan.

The transfer of elements from bubble diagram to floor plan provided a reality check on the sequence and scale of proposed concepts and experiences. Ideas that were vastly too large for the space available were dropped or shifted to video or other media that can compress many images into a compact experience.

Ideas over which the group disagreed often found a place in the exhibit simply by configuring a wall in a certain way or by changing the amount of space allotted to a certain element. Persistent disagreements were dealt with outside the group forum. A mediator shuttled between differing parties carrying proposals back and forth to work out agreements.

This exercise was the most difficult one in the series because the team had to define real visitor experiences in terms of actual sections of the exhibition.

EXERCISE V: CHOOSING OBJECTS AND IMAGES

What objects and images are available to tell the stories identified on the preliminary floor plan? The team began to assemble snapshots of objects and graphics (paintings, illustrations, and archival photographs) in a series of plastic sleeves housed according to exhibit section in loose-leaf binders. Objects and images were shuffled, added, deleted, or returned to various exhibit sections with ease. In this way, team members defined sets of two- and three-dimensional items for each section of the exhibit. These interpretive sets in turn helped the team refine specific stories that would be told in each part of the exhibit. For example, pottery suggested itself as a metaphor for continuity and change among Pueblo Indians; weaving did the same for Hispanics.

EXERCISE VI: VISUALIZING EXHIBIT CONTENT

How will the objects, images and stories selected for the exhibit actually work when they are brought together? The next step in the development and design process was to render the exhibit in a series of storyboards. Colour copies of graphic images and of photographs or drawings of objects were mounted to section-specific illustration boards along with a brief statement of teaching goals.

These storyboards provided an affordable way for team members to visualize the exhibit. The boards helped them to fine-tune preliminary organizational decisions. Storyboards also provided colleagues, museum management, outside consultants, and ordinary visitors with an opportunity to respond to plans for the exhibit. The boards produced for 'American Encounters' were used for presentations and meetings. They were then installed in the museum's exhibit preview area where visitors were invited to write their comments on forms provided. A more formal audience survey was not conducted but would have been useful.

EXERCISE VII: VISUALIZING THE EXHIBIT SPACE

The next step was to build a three-dimensional foam core model of the exhibit. The model enabled team members to see in scale how spaces and elements within the exhibit related to each other when viewed during a walk-through. The model was a working tool not a presentation piece. Foam core walls went up and came down, exhibit cases were moved, and vantage points were shifted. To reinforce larger interpretive messages, spatial patterns within the exhibit were derived from cultural forms: the Pueblo Indian section of the floor plan is circular, suggesting the cyclic patterns common in their culture, while the Hispanic community section is rectangular, like a village plaza.

After repeated trials and discussions, the model became the basis for detailed construction drawings. These drawings, which were prepared in consultation with an architect, included exhibit-specific information on wall placement and case openings as well as public space-specific information on acoustic attenuation and electrical, lighting, audio-visual and emergency systems.

EXERCISE VIII: SELECTING FORMS, COLOURS AND TEXTURES

Team members regrouped to decide on specific personalities for each section of the exhibit, using the model to test various solutions. They looked to objects in each section that suggested certain patterns and hues. They drew upon cultural or environmental elements related to exhibit content that could be abstracted in forms and textures. The team also decided to incorporate actual contextual elements from each community in New Mexico (being careful to avoid those elements that were clichéd or stereotypical): adobe and carved wooden architectural components, stone label substrates, coyote fencing, and signs.

Material palettes with samples of fabrics, paints, floor and wall coverings, and label panel were developed for each section of the exhibit. Only materials that met durability requirements for public spaces, fire codes and conservation mandates were considered.

EXERCISE IX: DEVELOPING A GRAPHIC IMAGE VOCABULARY

The goal was to devise a palette of type styles and symbol sets that could be employed to convey ideas. Because the abstract qualities of typefaces and symbols are hard to articulate, the designer prepared several sample solutions for the group to consider. He selected a wide range of typefaces; he created symbol sets using various combinations of elements derived from cultural icons to identify things such as exhibit sections and labelling hierarchy.

The group discussed these and chose those that seemed better or more appropriate. The group selected a single typeface for the entire exhibit but used distinctive symbol sets for each section. For example, the section of the exhibit that looks at twentieth-century tourism in New Mexico uses a chili pepper symbol and graphic organizational bars that fuse dollar signs with patterns derived from weavings. A graphics designer could be engaged to assist with this exercise.

EXERCISE X: ESTABLISHING HUMAN FACTOR OR ERGONOMIC PARAMETERS

A full-scale mock-up of a typical exhibit component made using foam core, colour photocopies of objects and photographs, and photocopies of sample labels and graphics was used to address various design solutions as well as federally mandated accessibility requirements. The team experimented with the arrangement of objects and the size and placement of labels. They tested vertical heights, viewing distances and angles of reading surfaces – exercises typical of industrial design services. They tried various ways to code maps, timelines and other information-dense graphics.

Once the team settled on a range of standards, the mock-up was moved to a public area. A visitor study was conducted using a mock-up of entrance panels and two exhibit cases, one from the Pueblo Indian section and one from the Hispanic section. Visitor observations and interviews conducted by an audience research firm suggested changes that were incorporated into the design control drawings.

EXERCISE XI: FINDING AN EXHIBIT VOICE

The preparation of the label script for 'American Encounters' began with three curators writing labels for specific content areas (the group as a whole had already established a four-level labelling hierarchy: main labels were written first, then section, group and object labels). To make three different voices one, the team's writer reworked each label, preparing a draft script for the entire exhibit.

The team regrouped at this point to review the draft. Reading aloud, they went through the script line by line, day after day, considering everything from conceptual intent to word choice. *Every* team member participated; everyone made contributions to all sections of the exhibit, resulting in the final script. The document was reviewed by colleagues, the museum's director, its management committee, consulting scholars and community members in New Mexico. Once revisions based on their comments were incorporated into the script, it was sent to copy editors.

EXERCISE XII: CONSIDERING CASE-SPECIFIC SOLUTIONS

Having begun this series of exercises with the broadest possible focus, the team made a series of decisions about increasingly specific design questions. As team members resolved each question, they moved on to the next one; they wasted no time retracing their steps. Now it was time for the last step.

The team used white models – renderings of each exhibit case with scale likenesses of objects, supports, pedestals, and graphic and label panels – to consider final designs for each exhibit case. The models enabled the team to decide not only on the placement of elements within the exhibit case but on other design questions as well. For example, should object supports in a given exhibit case be abstract or realistic?

In the course of their discussions, the team (joined in 1991 by a collections manager) worked closely with conservators to ensure that the overall design of each exhibit case as well as specific object supports and brackets met conservation guidelines.

The final designs for each case were rendered as case elevations or production drawings and turned over to exhibit fabricators.

These problem-solving exercises allowed the 'American Encounters' team to arrive at collaboration. Why? The exercises provided the structure that made it possible for team members to set aside job-title divisions; at crucial decision-making points they were able to share roles and responsibilities in a non-competitive environment. The exercises gave team members a common language and made it necessary for them to use it; when they spoke to each other of alternative solutions, they were spared the confusion that results from speaking in curatorese or designerese or educatorese. Finally, the exercises were solution specific; team members had to focus on the narrowly defined problem at hand, ensuring that their discussions were creatively motivated. The cumulative result was a kind of gestalt that influenced the development and design of the exhibit at every step.

The 'American Encounters' team included Richard E. Ahlborn, co-curator; Harold Closter, project manager; G. Benito Cordova, researcher; Richard Doty, co-curator; Lisa Falk, education specialist; Hank Grasso, designer; Rayna Green, co-curator; Howard Morrison, writer; Susan Ostroff, collections manager; and Lonn Taylor, co-curator and project director.

This chapter first appeared as a paper in History News *47(3) (1992): 12–15.*

18

Spatial considerations

Communications Design Team, Royal Ontario Museum

In planning an exhibition, we are working in a three-dimensional environment. This needs serious consideration.

There are basic matters to be thought about such as the positioning of the exits and entrances and the effect that these will have on the exhibition experience. Movement (or flow) within the internal spaces also needs thought.

More substantive matters are those concerned with the relationship of knowledge to space. How can knowledge, information and experience be mapped on to the space of the exhibition?

This chapter is from the influential book Communicating with the Museum Visitor, *published by the Royal Ontario Museum in 1976. Although research has moved on since then, much of the early work undertaken by this museum remains of interest.*

Once a basic approach to a gallery is defined, then the organization of the material within the gallery becomes a major concern. One of the means of accomplishing this is through the spatial organization.

Spatial considerations, while of great significance, are one of the least well-understood areas of gallery design. De Borhegyi provides a useful introduction to the subject through a summary of some of the available knowledge about human reactions to space and about behaviour in space. He indicates that 'space and design communicate in very much the same way as does the voice. . . . Unquestionably, people take cues from the space around them. Space can crowd or over-awe' (de Borhegyi 1963: 18). However, he points out that 'museum people are not sure whether spacious and formal, or small and intimate, lobby areas are better; whether lowered ceilings are better than high ceilings; or whether long vistas are better than winding exhibit corridors' (ibid.).

He refers to various categories of space that have become part of our vocabulary – territorial space, personal space, transactional space, sociopetal and sociofugal space – and notes that 'it is the job of museum exhibit hall planners to create the type of space best suited to their exhibit topic' (ibid.: 19). However, as he also comments, 'in the museum field . . . we do not even know the optimum distance between the visitor and the exhibits' (ibid.: 21). He emphasizes the imperfections of our current state of knowledge, and stresses the need for a 'thorough understanding of human reaction to space' (ibid.). He indicates some known cultural differences – Japanese visitors in a museum 'head straight to the center exhibit, while our North American visitors follow the walls to the right and exhibit confusion and indecision as to just when or how to approach the center exhibits' (ibid.: 22).

He concludes with an indication of the importance of spatial considerations by pointing out that 'when spatial concepts are confusing, the visitor invariably feels out of place, and his irritation with space may subconsciously be transferred against the museum and/or its management' (ibid.).

Lehmbruck has stressed the need for considering space as part of an integrated approach to gallery design. In his view:

> A museum is the very place in which perception and behaviour are almost identical, and this means that the exhibits and the space in which visitors move around must be planned together.
>
> (Lehmbruck 1974)

Stuart Silver has indicated that in his experience people respond differently to the same material in different spatial environments: 'There is such a thing as a calm space, a threatening space, a tense space and a transitory space' (Silver 1976).

The impact of spatial arrangement upon museum visitors is obviously great, and our knowledge is admittedly inadequate to provide specific solutions. However, there is some applicable knowledge which, together with an understanding of the specific opportunities and constraints of an existing space and collection, can result in responsive spatial concepts. The development of a spatial concept will therefore be discussed in terms of a physical context, the demands of subject-matter, and circulation requirements.

THE SPATIAL CONTEXT

The development of a spatial concept for a gallery must start with some awareness of the constraints and opportunities posed by the particular space that is to be made available for that gallery. The conditioning elements include the relationship to adjacent galleries and the architectural quality of the space.

These elements establish the context in which the spatial organization of the gallery can take place. Obviously, the extent of variation of such enclosing space is endless, and the specific constraints and opportunities are unique to each gallery.

The surrounding galleries and public spaces condition what can occur within a gallery. These include circulation patterns (where people will generally arrive from and where they are likely to go), and aesthetic factors (the brightness or darkness of the gallery, and its general atmosphere). Such factors obviously set some basic ground-rules which must be considered even before the individual space allocated to the gallery is explored.

The *architectural quality* of the building depends, or course, on when it was designed and built, and on whether it was intended to provide 'limitless flexibility and undifferentiated space' (Browne 1965: 10) for galleries or to form fixed and specific settings for displays. The extent to which a strong architectural 'container' is desirable is a matter of some debate. Peter Kimmel, in his study of twelve art museums and galleries, found that viewers seemed to object to any architecturally prominent feature which distracted attention from the paintings (Kimmel and Maves 1972). On the other hand, historical buildings have been effectively and dramatically adapted as museums. An excellent example is the Castello Sforzesco Museum in Milan in which 'the design . . . relates the exhibition to the historical building which houses it and which . . . [itself] has now considerably influenced subsequent museum design' (Browne 1965: 41).

In some instances, particular features – elaborately designed entranceways, clusters of columns, arches and domes – can present specific constraints or opportunities. At the Field Museum the current renovation programme carefully respects such historical features, resulting in enhancement of the building as a whole, but in some instances creating constraints within individual galleries.

In the case of the Arts and Industry Building of the Smithsonian Institution in Washington, restoration of the 100-year-old exhibition building to its original state was part of a major Bicentennial project. In that case the building becomes a major part of the exhibit, and not simply a container for it.

Beyond the architectural merit of the space the major constraint is its actual form and nature – the ceiling height, the shape of the gallery, the location of entrances and exits, and the sources of natural light. Older museums frequently have very tall ceilings (over 20 feet [6 m]). These present a number of design options: they allow designers to maintain the full height to display very large objects, to provide a mezzanine where this is felt to be useful, and to supply lower ceiling heights or special cases for the display of smaller artefacts.

The locations of entrances and exits of a building or gallery are fundamental determinants of both spatial and circulation patterns, which the overall design of the gallery must recognize from the beginning. Where the location of these elements is not fixed, greater flexibility is possible, with less constraint on the design. Where they are fixed, the implications of their location should be understood.

The configuration of a gallery plan sometimes forms natural spatial subdivisions. Where appropriate, these can become part of the spatial organization of an exhibit. According to Lehmbruck, basic shapes are important because various plan-forms elicit different responses from the viewer. His work indicates that round or square plan-forms are more restful than oval or rectangular ones; and that converging lines or variations in level imply movements, while parallel lines or flat planes suggest repose (Lehmbruck 1974). In some cases, the opportunities for creating various plan-forms are limited by the nature of the enclosure. In other instances, where the enclosure is less definitive, the spaces may be designed to utilize spatial effects.

Some galleries will have opportunities for natural light, while others will not. This can have implications both for lighting effects and for spatial effects, sometimes allowing long-distance views in contrast to the more limited ones within a gallery.

SPACE AND SUBJECT-MATTER

The fit between space and objects

One of the first considerations in the spatial organization of a gallery is the appropriateness of the space or set of spaces for the subject-matter being presented. The relationship between the objects and the space around them is of particular consequence. Lehmbruck states:

> Every object needs space if its qualities are to be brought out. Every visible form projects itself beyond its limits and to a certain extent invests the 'empty' surrounding area with its presence. ... Since the spatial characteristics of the environment determine the shape and the position of the visible object, space must be organized in a way which is in harmony with them.
>
> (Lehmbruck 1974)

He suggests that a major design consideration within a museum is the creation of clearly defined spaces, which are easily perceived by the visitor. 'As long as the space is not easily perceptible, the visitor will continue to search, albeit unconsciously. The resulting uneasiness renders contact with the object more difficult' (1974: 192).

The specifics of how spaces should be arranged to ensure a fit between object and space is clearly complex. One of the most obvious relationships is that of scale. In simple terms, small objects and large objects can look awkward if constrained by available space. A good illustration of an effective spatial arrangement is found at the British Museum where long, high-ceilinged halls housing the magnificent Greek and Roman collections have mezzanines inserted within them, creating small-scale areas for the presentation of small objects. This contrasts effectively with the large objects in high-ceilinged portions of the rooms. As a result, the viewer can be at ease in both kinds of spaces, viewing two scales of objects.

An illustration of a different type of space–object relationship is the recreation of historical settings for collections of objects. Period rooms, for example, can harmoniously combine the decorative artefacts of a particular age in their appropriate spatial setting, allowing the visitor to perceive the relationships between the internal spaces of an era and its furnishings.

Some objects, because of their intrinsic qualities, demand adequate space, or tensions will be communicated to the viewer. The space surrounding an object is further complicated because an object in a case relates to the scale of the case as well as to that of the surrounding area. The art of spatial fit is based upon the creative use of both sets of spatial relationships. A small but important artefact carefully placed in a small case can be made to look grand by the shape of the surrounding space.

Space and storyline

Where a storyline is employed, spatial organization should obviously be used to reinforce it. In simple terms, the spatial subdivisions should relate to the subdivision of subject-matter. The degree to which subdivision should be directive or random is constrained by the extent to which the storyline is sequential. In the view of Hans Zetterberg, a sequential layout is necessary since 'education is not achieved by random exposures, but in a planned sequence' (1968: 25). However, he also suggests that no sequence should be so rigid as to be inescapable; spatial arrangements should allow for choices amongst viewers – choices which can be based upon varying degrees of interest and involvement in the subject-matter. Shettel's study maintains that exhibits which place content in a rational sequence will be better instructional devices than those that do not (Shettel *et al.* 1968: 157).

On the other hand, a number of studies indicate that lineal sequencing does not necessarily make a difference to the effectiveness of the exhibit (Bernardo 1972: 100). In effect, there is evidence that both approaches are valid. However, in reacting against the traditional unstructured presentation of artefacts and in responding to the opportunity for thematic cohesion, there has been a temptation to create rigid sequences which are not necessarily suitable for accommodating the variations of interest amongst visitors.

One useful reminder by Hal Glicksman is that one should not forget the end of the exhibit (1972). Care should be taken to avoid the exhibit merely fading away; some spatial emphasis should be given to lend a sense of clarity to the end. This is particularly important as the visitor's natural tendency is to move more quickly through the latter part of an exhibit.

Space and comprehensibility

The spatial organization of a gallery should be evident without strain to the viewer. The visitor should be able to move along the gallery easily, making logical decisions as to which way to go. Albert Parr emphasizes the usefulness of spatial 'cues' in assisting the visitor to find the way. He points out the disadvantages of the traditional grid system of displaying artefacts in a series of neatly lined-up cases:

> it does not take much knowledge of psychology to realize the tiring effect of having to make an endless series of choices that are without real relevance to the main purpose or motivation. And the less there is to choose between at each decision point, the greater the strain of deciding.
>
> (Parr 1964)

He indicates that one of the main sources of museum fatigue is 'our failure to provide adequate spatial cues for the guidance of our visitors, and the consequent creation of meaningless decision points' (1964: 138).

The same point is made by Hannelore Kischkewitz, who proposes the creation of a focal point or a series of focal points to enable the visitor to move through a gallery easily and with absolute confidence (Kischkewitz 1975). This was noted in reference to a gallery which consisted of a series of rooms. A series of focal points set the theme for each room within the gallery, and, at the same time, provided a source of unity for the entire gallery. A strong element near the entrance can serve both as a cue and as an orientation device. In suggesting the need for a clear and comprehensible direction through a gallery, Parr indicates that this does not mean 'that we cannot expose our guest to unexpected sights and temptations en route' (1964: 138), but suggests simply that a comprehensible arrangement of space is less likely to produce irritation and fatigue in the visitor.

Subdivision of space

Whatever form or sequence an exhibit takes, there seems to be almost uniform agreement that the subdivision of space is both desirable and useful. There is some evidence that the scale of a gallery may attract or repel a visitor: in one study, a glance from the entranceway revealing a vast space was found to be a deterrent to entry (Lakota 1975: 63).

Many advantages can accrue from the subdivision of a large gallery into small areas, including the creation of small culs-de-sac. Small-scale areas create manageable perceptual environments, reduce movement, and isolate the visitors from remote distractions (ibid.: 90). In addition, a gallery concept which includes spatial subdivisions can 'make the audience encounter a variety of spaces, which in themselves, are conducive to sharpened awareness' (Parker 1967).

Arminta Neal comments on the spatial arrangement of display cases, suggesting that the visitor finds it less exhausting if cases are arranged not in tidy rows but in gently curved lines to take advantage of traffic flows, or are arranged so as to form alcoves to show different divisions within the subject area (Neal 1963). In another article which argues for such a spatial organization, the point is made that the division of space created by a grouping of artefacts or a subdivision of theme should, where possible, be directly related to the natural physical spaces created within the available space (e.g. between a corner and a door) (Glicksman 1972).

In practice, all of the preceding spatial considerations, as well as whatever practical constraints are involved, obviously form part of the decision about how space should be subdivided.

CIRCULATION

The other major determinant of spatial arrangement is the circulation pattern, which includes determining the best routes through a space or series of spaces, and recognizing appropriate resting-places. Movement patterns should include both primary and supplementary or secondary ones, and should make provision for quiet areas for more lengthy contemplation or detailed examination of artefacts, or simply for sitting and relaxing.

A series of basic principles that can be useful in evolving circulation systems are described below.

Entrance

It is useful to provide orientation information at the entrance to a gallery to inform the visitor about what is there (so that a decision can be made as to whether to enter or not) and to help the visitor to find the way around.

Need for clarity

An overriding requirement in the development of a circulation system is the need for clarity. Maze-like circulation has the potential for creating confusion and irritation. This is an important reminder in evolving gallery layout, as there has been an increasing tendency to create complex movement patterns in order to take visitors through a highly directive sequential pattern.

Exit gradient

There is a general tendency for visitors to move through a gallery slowly at first and then gradually more quickly; when the exit sign comes into view they tend to move even more quickly directly towards the sign and out.

Decision points

It is important to assist the visitor wherever a circulation system presents a number of alternatives within a gallery. At these decision points orientation information should be available to enable the visitor to decide whether to turn to the left or right or whether to go ahead.

Movement to the right

There is a general tendency for North American visitors to move to the right upon entering a gallery. The typical pattern is described by de Borhegyi: 'museum visitors almost invariably turn to the right when entering an exhibition hall. They follow the exhibit cases along the wall moving from right to left, reading the labels in each display from left to right' (1965). This can cause disruption in the traffic flow and confusion in the sequence of didactic material. However, the pattern is not uniform and is becoming less dominant as a larger proportion of North Americans are now permitted to be left-handed.

Tendency to stay at perimeter

There is a tendency for museum visitors to circulate around the periphery of a gallery. In large galleries, visitors will tend to stay at the periphery of the gallery unless attractions are provided in the centre to attract them. This again is not uniformly the case; Japanese visitors in particular tend to head to the centre exhibit (de Borhegyi 1963).

Rate of flow

Another aspect of the pattern of movement within a gallery is the rate of traffic flow. Some useful guidelines concerning the relationship of display presentation and traffic flow are noted by Stephan de Borhegyi:

> *Areas of constant crowd flow* should have terse, repetitive exhibits that can be quickly understood by the viewers. Such displays are most useful when they include limited introductory material desirable for all visitors.
>
> *Areas of crowd stoppage*, in addition to displays of a general nature, should have a few exhibits of a conceptual nature which can be absorbed and enjoyed unhurriedly while the visitor waits his turn to move on. Both types of exhibits need to be geared to the educational level of a general audience.
>
> *Areas of variable crowd flow* should allow the visitor to choose among simple and complex exhibits. Displays here need a single, easily read sentence covering the over-all theme of the display, a lead paragraph or image which communicates the main idea, intermixed with more complex exhibits with longer statements which can be studied at leisure by the more interested visitors.
>
> (de Borhegyi 1965)

These are illustrated in his design for the 'Hall of Life and Earth Processes' at the Milwaukee Public Museum (Figure 18.1).

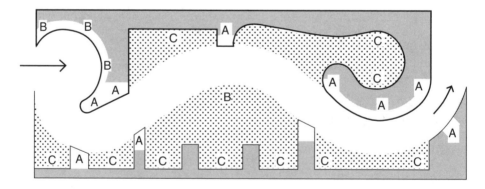

A: Constant flow
B: Crowd stoppage
C: Variable

Figure 18.1 Rates of flow illustrated by Stephan de Borhegyi's design for 'Hall of Life and Earth Processes', Milwaukee Public Museum

Ease of movement

Some general circulation guidelines for the blind have been established through experiments in the city of Victoria, BC, Canada (Moore 1968). Such guidelines should be applied more generally, as they also apply to the handicapped and the elderly, as well as providing insight into circulation for galleries in general. The criteria include the following:

- Changes in elevation should be by means of ramps.
- Adequate space should be allowed for wheelchairs, including adequate turning radii.
- Changes in direction generally should not be abrupt.
- Variations in floor textures are useful to denote changes in division of subject content.

Levels of interest

Although not necessarily applicable to all galleries, one basis for the organization of circulation is a path system which enables visitors whose interests vary in range and intensity to follow somewhat different paths through a gallery (Zetterberg 1968: 27). The most casual visitor would take the quickest route, and the more interested visitor could take a more comprehensive route. Figure 18.2 illustrates a series of paths for varying interests.

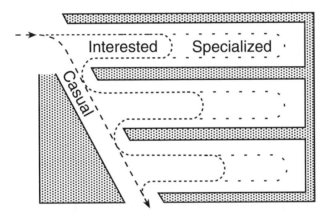

Figure 18.2 Paths for varying levels of interest

These general principles should be considered in relation to those factors unique to each gallery. These include the following:

- the shape of the gallery space
- the locations of entrances and exits
- the degree of direction or random browsing which is intended

There are no ideal solutions nor any typical arrangements that can be selected and applied to a gallery. However, some examples of circulation patterns and applications of some of the principles just outlined will help to illustrate these issues more clearly.

Typology of circulation patterns

A useful typology of circulation patterns has been evolved by Lehmbruck (1974). He suggests five basic patterns: arterial, comb, chain, star (or fan), and block. Although these are somewhat abstract versions of circulation patterns, they do illustrate some of the organizational considerations.

Arterial: This refers to a circulation pattern in which the main path is continuous and no options exist for the visitor; the path can be straight, curving, or virtually any shape. This type of pattern can be used where the presentation of material is dependent upon a fixed sequence. The major limitation is the rigidity which confronts the visitor (Figure 18.3).

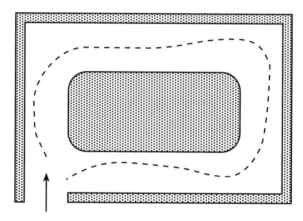

Figure 18.3 Arterial circulation pattern

Comb: This refers to a circulation pattern in which there is a main circulation path and optional alcoves which a visitor may enter or by-pass (Figure 18.4).

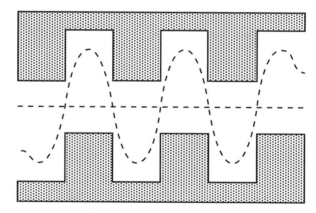

Figure 18.4 Comb circulation pattern

Chain: This refers to a circulation pattern in which the main path is generally continuous (as in arterials) but the path leads to a series of self-contained units which may have a more varied path within them (Figure 18.5).

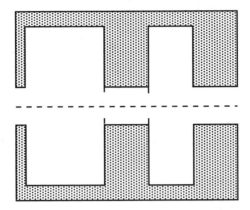

Figure 18.5 Chain circulation pattern

Star or Fan: This refers to a circulation pattern which presents a series of alternatives to a visitor from a central area (Figure 18.6).

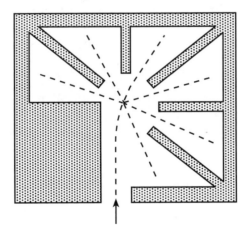

Figure 18.6 Star or Fan circulation pattern

Block: This refers to a circulation system which is relatively unconstrained and can be as random or as self-directive as desired by the visitor (Figure 18.7).

These circulation patterns give some indication of the possible variety. When they are connected with the principles previously described, some useful points become apparent. Some examples of the application of these principles are illustrated in Figure 18.8.

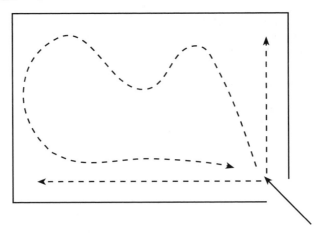

Figure 18.7 Block circulation system

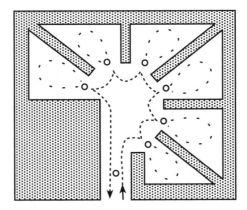

Figure 18.8 Circulation system with orientation information points

Figure 18.8 is an example of a circulation system in which every decision point is provided with orientation information which enables the visitor to select a path through a gallery easily (Lakota 1975). Orientation information can also be provided at the entry and summary information at the end.

The following examples (Figure 18.9) illustrate the application to door placements of the right-turn tendency and the exit gradient phenomenon. (These are based on the work of Coleman (1950).) The placement of doors in an axial relationship can result in visitors moving straight through one side of an exhibit as in the illustration (Figure 18.10).

An application of one of the principles previously outlined is demonstrated by a gallery design (Figure 18.11) at the Milwaukee Public Museum, incorporating a deflector to counteract the tendency to move to the right. This tendency 'results in a slow and disrupted traffic flow and the visitors' information retention factor is at a minimum. This problem can be solved by routing the viewers to the left with the aid of a "deflector" exhibit at the entrance to the hall. Visitors will now move from left to right and read the labels in each display case in the preferred order' (de Borhegyi 1965).

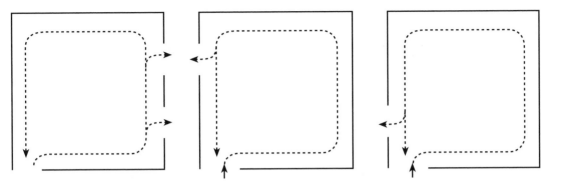

Figure 18.9 Door placements, the righthand turn tendency and the exit gradient

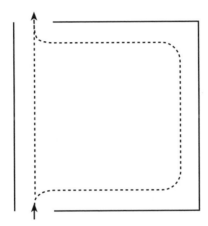

Figure 18.10 Doors in an axial relationship

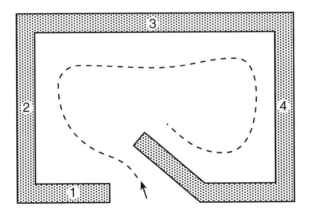

Figure 18.11 Effect of a deflector exhibit

The overall spatial organization of a gallery should consider all of the three major foregoing considerations: the existing spatial context, the use of that space in a way which will support and enhance the presentation of subject-matter, and the effect that circulation paths have on how the visitor moves through the space and comprehends what is presented.

This chapter first appeared in (1976) Communicating with the Museum Visitor: Guidelines for Planning, *Toronto: Royal Ontario Museum, 97–113.*

REFERENCES

Bernardo, J. R. (1972) 'Museum environments for communications: a study of environmental parameters in the design of museum experiences', PhD dissertation, Columbia University, NY.

Brawne, M. (1965) *The New Museum,* New York: Praeger.

Coleman, L. V. (1950) *Museum Buildings: a Planning Study,* Vol. I, Washington, DC: American Association of Museums.

de Borhegyi, S. F. (1963) 'Space problems and solutions', *Museum News* 42 (Nov.).

de Borhegyi, S. F. (1965) 'Testing an audience reaction to museum exhibits', *Curator* 8 (January).

Glicksman, H. (1972) 'A guide to art installations', *Museum News* 50 (Feb.).

Kimmel, P. S. and Maves, M. J. (1972) 'Public reaction to museum interiors', *Museum News* (Sept.).

Kischkewitz, H. (1975) 'New techniques in displaying traditional objects', *Museum* 27.

Lakota, R. A. (1975) *The National Museum of Natural History as a Behavioral Environment,* Part I, *An Environmental Analysis of Behavioral Performance,* Washington, DC: Office of Museum Programs, Smithsonian Institution.

Lehmbruck, M. (1974) 'Psychology: perception and behaviour', *Museum* 26.

Moore, G. (1968) 'Displays for the sightless', *Curator* 11 (April).

Neal, A. (1963) 'Gallery and case exhibit design', *Curator* 6 (January).

Parker, H. W. (1967) 'New hall of fossil invertebrates, Royal Ontario Museum', *Curator* 10 (April).

Parr, A. E. (1964) 'Remarks on layout, display, and response to design', *Curator* 7 (February).

Shettel, H. H., Butcher, M., Cotton, T. S., Northrup, J. and Clapp, D. (1968) *Strategies for Determining Exhibit Effectiveness,* technical report AIR-F58-11/67-FR, Pittsburgh, PA: American Institutes for Research.

Silver, Stuart (1976) interview (28 January).

Zetterberg, H. L. (1968) *Museums and Adult Education,* Paris: Evelyn, Adams & MacKay for the International Council of Museums.

19

The exhibition development process
David Dean

Many of the issues that need to be discussed in relation to museum communication are approached from a theoretical perspective. But museum workers are faced with the prospect of relating those theoretical issues to practical activity within museums. What are the actual things that people do when developing exhibitions? It is not possible to relate theoretical matters to matters of daily practice unless these processes are clearly understood.

This chapter describes one model for developing museum exhibitions. The model can be critiqued. How close is it to the simple model of communication discussed in Chapter 2? Does it need one or more feedback loops?

The model presents the various stages that take place in time. How is the audience integrated into these stages, and which of the activities listed are important in making exhibitions that communicate effectively?

APPROACHES TO PLANNING

Institutions and organizations such as museums are much like the proverbial iceberg. Most of the substance lies below the surface, hidden from view. Nearly all museums depend upon public use and approval to justify their places within society, so there is a real need for demonstration of the richness of those hidden depths. Exhibitions and programmes are the principal public expressions of the heart of museums: the collections.

The popular understanding of exhibitions does not recognize or appreciate the inner mechanisms required to prepare and present them. Like Athena leaping full-grown from the head of Zeus, there is a mythical quality to the ease with which exhibitions appear in public. However, as with any project, exhibitions require much planning and management to realize the end product. Over time, the sequence of events and efforts that produce public exhibitions has become established. The procedural elements in planning and executing any project are universal, regardless of the end product. The main difference between creating an exhibition and preparing a sales strategy or building an automobile is the mission of the organization undertaking the project.

In commercial affairs, accomplishing tasks is a highly organized operation. The system-atized approach used by businesses to manage their projects can be quite valuable if related to exhibition development. That is because any course of action with a product as its final goal is a project. As the process used in producing commercial products

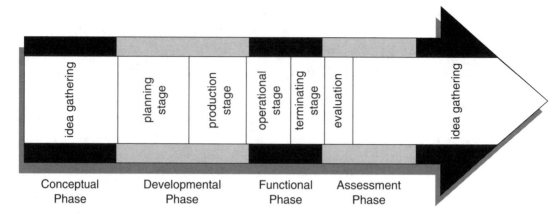

Figure 19.1 Exhibition project model

has proven to be effective, museums have adopted the methodology, and even the terminology, of business to describe the equivalent developmental steps in making exhibitions. Understanding the process is easier when outlined as a series of phases and subordinate stages.

All projects, regardless of their beginning or intended outcome, share common traits. The time it takes to plan, develop and execute the project is limited. Projects are cyclical. They have beginnings that arise from ideas generated from former activities, and after running their courses, they generate new approaches and ideas for future projects.

As Figure 19.1 shows, a project may be illustrated as a series of events along a line of time. This is called a project model.[1] It is easy to see how an exhibition's development fits into such a model.

The progressive, sequential nature of the project model works well with museum exhibition development. The sequential arrangement of phases and stages may be outlined to make types of activities and specific tasks more easily discernible. Throughout development, and in each phase, there are three principal tasking areas. They are:

- product-oriented activities – efforts centred on the collection objects and their interpretation
- management-oriented activities – tasks that focus on providing resources and personnel necessary to completing the project
- co-ordination activities – keeping the product- and management-oriented activities working toward the same goal

OUTLINE OF EXHIBITION DEVELOPMENT

Conceptual phase

- Product-oriented activities:
    collecting ideas
    comparing ideas with audience needs and the museum's mission
    selecting projects to develop

- Management activities:
  assessing available resources to do the project
- Results:
  a schedule of exhibitions
  identification of potential or available resources

Developmental phase

Planning stage

- Product-oriented activities:
  setting goals for the exhibition
  writing the storyline
  designing the physical exhibition
  creating an educational plan
  researching promotional strategies
- Management activities:
  estimating costs
  investigating sources and applying for funding
  establishing resource budgets
  appointing tasks
- Results:
  an exhibition plan
  an educational plan
  a promotional plan

Production stage

- Product-oriented activities:
  preparing the exhibition components
  mounting and installing the collection objects
  developing the educational programmes and training docents
  implementing the promotional plan
- Management activities:
  overseeing the availability and use of resources
  tracking progress and co-ordinating activities
- Results:
  presenting the exhibition to the public
  using the educational programmes with the exhibition

Functional phase

Operational stage

- Product-oriented activities:
  presenting the exhibition to the public on a regular basis
  implementing the educational programmes
  conducting visitor surveys
  maintaining the exhibition
  providing security for the exhibition
- Management activities:
  settling accounts

administration of personnel and services
- Results:
  achieving the exhibition goals
  preventing deterioration of collections

Terminating stage

- Product-oriented activities:
  dismantling the exhibition
  returning objects to the collection storage
  documenting collection handling
- Management activities:
  balancing accounts
- Results:
  the exhibition is ended
  the collections are returned
  the gallery is cleared and repaired

Assessment phase

- Product-oriented activities:
  assessing the exhibition
  assessing the development process
- Management activities:
  creating an evaluation report
- Results:
  an evaluation report
  suggested improvements to the product and the process

The application of the models and the outline to the actual process of exhibition development will be clearer if each part is examined separately. It is important to note that, although dissecting the process provides useful handles to grasp ideas by, the real activities are not always so clearly delineated. Often activities flow together and mix with each other as the project progresses.

Conceptual phase

To embark upon a detailed exploration of exhibition development, we must begin with its inception. Exhibitions start as ideas that come from many sources. Listed are some frequently encountered:

- audience suggestions
- board members or trustees
- collections management personnel
- community leaders
- curators
- current events
- director
- educators
- staff and volunteers

Ideas for exhibitions are not always conceived in an orderly fashion and often arrive with a variety of personal agendas attached. A patron, staff or board member may see an exhibition at another museum, watch a programme on television, or read a magazine, and thus become motivated to propose an exhibition topic. The experiences of individuals, the assessed needs of a community, or a new collection acquisition may provide the impetus for exhibiting. In some cases, the need to replace other exhibitions will prompt the search for new ideas and themes.

In all cases, the motivations to exhibit should emanate from a prevailing predisposition toward serving the public. Museums should be like leaky vessels or sponges in their communities. Ideas should seep in from all directions and be sifted constantly, searching for those that fulfil the criteria of public service and education. It is not appropriate for exhibitions to arise solely as outlets for self-aggrandizement by staff or board members. Often an initiator's exuberance for his or her idea leaps ahead of thoughtful consideration or careful planning. Failure to channel enthusiasm into a co-operative organizational process may lead to a chaotic and frustrating mixture of conflicting communication and confused goals. The outcome will be lack of focus, disaffection, dissatisfaction, and inferior exhibitions.

To avoid such a regrettable condition the administration needs to place the role and function of the museum foremost. Responsible collection care and properly assessing the needs of the museum's public are at the heart of conscientious exhibitions and interpretive programmes. However and wherever ideas may arise, a phased development plan permits everyone involved to see their part in the process with clarity.

Though ideas arise in many ways from multiple sources, there must be decisions made as to which to pursue or discard. Organizations develop approaches to decision-making that work for them. These approaches have many variations rendering a single set of criteria too restrictive to be useful to all organizations. However, it is vital that decisions be made based upon a well-defined sub-set of public-oriented criteria, rather than on personal biases.

Ideally, short- and long-range plans that incorporate the museum mission, constituency needs, educational goals, scope of collections and available resources are a part of the organizational documentation arsenal. Established standards ensure that choices are responsible. At the administrative level, a regularly reviewed written exhibition policy should be a priority. Appointing a committee to do initial research and provide advice can be helpful as well. Formulating exhibition strategies using foundational instruments will meet constituency needs. Lack of definition in planning exhibition programmes will lead to a museum being driven by the demand to fill space, rather than by ethical purpose and educational design.

The current consensus on the role of museums in their communities rests upon twin cornerstones: accountability to a constituency, and adherence to accepted professional museum standards. Arbitrary, unilateral choices in exhibition topics are not acceptable to a public with other leisure options. Personal preferences of staff or board members are not adequate foundations upon which to build an exhibition programme. Even in small museums, where staffs are small and often voluntary, the decision-making process needs to be clearly set down and the development of an exhibition programme founded upon a recognition of community needs and professionalism.

An understanding of community needs and expectations comes from audience assessment. A serious and common mistake is basing decisions about exhibition programmes on internal assumptions about community needs, rather than on information gathered from the community itself. Obtaining such knowledge requires time, skills and energies both to collect and to keep it current. These resources are often unavailable to largely volunteer governing boards. Professional consultants or staff members versed in the methodologies and techniques of community assessment are the proper parties to develop and apply exhibition assessment criteria. In many communities, chambers of commerce have already done visitor surveys, and demographic and psychographic studies. They are usually quite willing to make such information available to public-oriented institutions.

Having gained a working knowledge of community needs and expectations, and armed with the museum mission statement and exhibition policy, the task is to evaluate the suggested exhibitions. Using the knowledge and documents as filters and guides, a slate of exhibitions can be generated that demonstrates sensitivity toward constituency needs and expectations, while adhering to institutional goals and standards.

Conceptual phase activities can be viewed as product- and management-oriented, although not as clearly as the later phases. Conceptual phase product-oriented activities can be summarized as:

- gathering ideas
- assessing the ideas within the framework of the museum's mission, its policies and community needs
- selecting an exhibition for development

Management-oriented activities include:

- approving and scheduling the exhibition for development
- assessing available or potential resources

The results of conceptual phase activities should be the scheduling of the exhibition and the identification of the resources needed to present it.

Developmental phase

Exhibition development is a process aimed at realizing an idea – giving it flesh and bones. Much of the energy of a staff will be directed toward product-related goals. However, management activities are essential as well. Management duties centre upon procurement, distribution and regulation of resources. This involves the following:

- time management
- money management
- quality control
- communication
- organizational control – assigning tasks

Neither product- nor management-oriented activities can function properly without the other. It is the combined efforts of those people active in both areas of endeavour that produce the result: the exhibition.

After the decision to develop an exhibition is made, ideas need to be translated into actions moving toward realizable goals. The director decides whom to include in the planning process based on the requisite disciplines and skills. Whether the project is accomplished by a team of several people, or by only one or two individuals, the essential tasks remain the same. Only the scope and breadth of the job change based upon the time available to accomplish it. In some instances, only one or two people are available, and tailoring the size of the project to fit resources is necessary.

196

Normally, those roles required in product-oriented tasks include the curator, educator and designer. The curator or expert in the exhibition's subject does research, provides scholarly information, and selects and curates the appropriate collection objects. To guide interpretive planning and presentation, a team member with an educational background and training is needed. The educator advises about educational needs related to the design, develops information for tours and programmes, and provides training for docents and guides. Another member is needed to translate the subject, objects and ideas into visual form: the designer. The designer takes the information provided by other team members and creates a plan for presenting it to the public.

From the management side, a person is needed to oversee and co-ordinate planning and resources: a project manager. His or her purpose is to act as a person who facilitates – who encourages communication, sees that information and resources are available as needed, calls meetings and assigns tasks as required, and acts as a mediator when necessary. Most often, this task is not painful or stressful. However, the project manager needs to be an experienced professional to handle difficulties if they arise. Attached to the project manager's job may be periodic progress reports to the director or governing authority.

Technical advisors may be required for complex or specialized activities. Conservators may be consulted for collection management purposes. Marketing specialists may be employed depending upon the scope of the exhibition and the target audience. In effect, the exhibition planning team should be configured to fit the need. The larger the team, the more complex communication and consensus become. On the other hand, appropriate levels of expertise should be included to do the job properly.

Planning stage

The planning stage sets the standards for building the final exhibition. Without the spending of appropriate time and effort at this point, the rest of the development process stands a good chance of being confusing at best, and at worst resulting in a poorly executed exhibition lacking in content and direction.

Exhibition developers draw upon constituency surveys to determine the exhibition's target group or groups. Developing and setting down exhibition goals based upon a target audience will help clarify objectives. From these goals flow an identifiable set of criteria against which later to rate exhibition effectiveness.

After exhibition goals and objectives are established, the more concrete, object-oriented work of research, script-writing, designing and formulating educational and promotional plans may proceed.

During the planning stage, management activities are critical and centred around budgeting. Budgeting refers to the 'Big Three': time, personnel and money. These are essential to realizing exhibition goals. For example, giving someone a task carries with it the responsibility to provide available time by setting deadlines. When staff members are working in one place, they cannot be elsewhere. In most museums, there are more jobs to accomplish than people to do them. This makes time-budgeting an imperative for efficiently employing skills and energies. However, without funding and procurement, work cannot go forward. Cost estimates must be compiled, funding sources located and secured, budgets set, and an accounting system created to keep track of funds in a consistent and timely manner.

The result of all these activities is a plan of action for producing the exhibition. The exhibition plan should include a timeline, a working budget, the storyline, a conservation and maintenance schedule, design drawings and schematics, the education goals and plans, and promotional or marketing strategies.

Production stage

The production stage is the time in an exhibition's cycle that involves the greatest amount of activity, and requires the most co-ordination of efforts. At this stage there are several product-oriented activities to be completed. They include:

- an assessment by the curator or collection manager setting forth the level of preliminary conservation required
- a statement of requirements for the type and degree of support required and what environmental parameters are acceptable (light levels, relative humidity, temperature, etc.)
- a schedule for rotating collection objects off exhibition, and a maintenance plan
- negotiating and making arrangements for loans and contracts
- documenting the condition of the collection and its movement during the objects' transfer from storage to exhibition
- making transportation arrangements for some objects or people as required
- writing, checking and preparing label, text and title wording for production
- fabrication activities – preparing mounting structures for collection objects, preparing gallery space and environmental controls to meet specifications, producing printed materials and graphic images, and the construction of exhibited cases and vitrines
- development of educational and public programmes, including the preparation of printed instructional materials for the gallery or as pre- or post-visit educational supplements. Other tasks might include preparing materials and training docents, and co-ordinating with speakers and demonstrators
- promotional activities such as writing press releases, issuing press packets, co-ordinating with media for press conferences or special photographic sessions. Other activities might be designing and implementing publicity strategies such as renting billboards, distributing posters or pamphlets, or arranging for paid advertisements.
- installing the exhibition – the act of actualizing or executing the exhibition design. This includes erecting display structures such as walls and panels, installing environmental monitoring devices, and placing support elements and collection objects in the gallery space. Positioning wayfinders, labelling objects, installing barriers, and providing instructions to security and maintenance personnel for the proper care of the exhibition are necessary as well.

Management activities during the production stage centre on controlling the availability of resources and keeping track of their use. This involves:

- budgetary control and account maintenance during fabrication – making purchases of construction materials and paying for services such as construction and conservation activities
- progress control, requiring periodic checks, meetings and reports as necessary to determine the status of the project
- quality checks to ensure that predetermined standards are met
- administrative activities, including expenditure approvals, approval and monitoring of changes, and providing appropriate personnel management

The results of production stage activities should be:

- an exhibition open to the public of the quality and scope initially set forth as desirable
- instructions for proper care and maintenance of the exhibition, which should be available and disseminated to the proper departments and persons
- functional programmes such as school tours, guided tours and public events, which should be ready to be implemented

Functional phase

After the exhibition is open to the public, it enters the functional phase. Under this heading are two stages. The first is the operational stage, which includes the daily activities of running and managing the exhibition.

Operational stage

Product-oriented activities include:

- operating the exhibition, which might involve ticketing and admissions procedures. Also of major importance are the maintenance of the gallery and collections, seeing to the security and safety of staff and visitors, and monitoring conservation factors.
- implementing the programmes, tours, lectures, demonstrations, and any extra-museum activities such as trunk exhibits and outreach programmes
- evaluation activities such as visitor surveys, pre- and post-visit questionnaires, informal observations, and related tasks. These need to be generated while the exhibition is functioning to provide data so that the exhibition's success or failure can be assessed at a later date.

Operational stage management activities include:

- settling accounts
- administration of personnel and services

The result of the operational stage should be the accomplishment of the educational objectives set forth during planning. The prime outcome from a collection management standpoint is to ensure that no significant deterioration occurs in the collection objects while they are on exhibit.

Terminating stage

Following the operational stage and concluding the exhibition's public life are activities that may be called the terminating stage. Product-oriented activities include:

- dismantling the exhibition
- documenting the transfer of collection objects back to storage
- packing collection objects for return to lending institutions or for sending on to the next venue

Terminating stage management activities involve:

- balancing accounts to assess the proper use of funds and for reporting to granting agencies

The results are that the exhibition is ended, collections are returned to their proper places, and galleries are cleared and made ready for the next exhibition.

Assessment phase

The final phase, and an extremely important one in exhibition development, has to do with assessment. Evaluation is increasingly useful to museums for determining whether or not goals set early in the process were indeed accomplished. The process of assessment also serves to point the way to future exhibitions, improvements in methods and technologies, strategies, and goal-setting. Evaluation, too, is both product- and management-oriented.

Product-oriented activities are:

- assessment of the exhibition from a product point-of-view. Determining how well the exhibition accomplished the educational and public goals set for it, how extensively it was visited and utilized, and whether or not the maintenance activities were adequate to protect the collections
- determining the success of the process in planning and executing the exhibition, or process assessment

Assessment management activities include:

- the production of an evaluation report that sets down the findings of the product and process assessments
- the preparation of an evaluation report – some granting agencies require such a report to assess the proper use and effectiveness of their funding

The outcome of the assessment phase is to document the evaluation with a written report. However, the real value of assessment is improving the product and process for the next exhibition, and the engendering of new ideas for the future.

This chapter first appeared in (1994) Museum Exhibition: Theory and Practice, *London: Routledge,* 8–18.

NOTE

1   Vehaar, Jan and Meeter, Han, *Project Model Exhibitions* (Netherlands: Reinwardt Academie, 1989), 4.

20

Combating redundancy: writing texts for exhibitions

Margareta Ekarv

Margareta Ekarv writes easy-to-read books for adults and here describes how she applied lessons from this style of writing to exhibition texts. Most people find reading in museums difficult after a few minutes, often because of simple physical factors. The easy-to-read style often does not mean that language or subject-matter must be simplified.

Sentences are short, normal word order is preferred and lines are about forty-five characters long. The end of a line of text coincides with the end of a natural phrase. Subordinate clauses and unnecessary adverbial modifiers are avoided.

This style of text writing, based on this article, has been tried out in some museums in England very successfully.

Is there really any need for words in a museum? Aren't pictures, exhibits, labels and sets enough? Aren't our modern museums so loaded with messages of various kinds that visitors can learn all they need from the exhibits without the written word?

Far from it. By using written material for other purposes than mere labels and summaries we can put words on a par with the other exhibition material. We can use words to give a new, deeper dimension to our visual experience. Words make us think, and our thoughts conjure up pictures in our minds. Is it not through mental pictures like these that we discover the world around us?

When I was asked to write the texts for the Postal Museum's permanent exhibition 'A Letter Makes All the Difference' I was confronted, together with producer Elisabet Olofsson and designer Björn Ed, with a number of questions. Elisabet and Björn knew about these problems and they were agreed that in this exhibition the texts were to have the same status as the documents and other exhibits, that it was worth devoting time and energy to this written material rather than turning out something slapdash at the last minute.

An exhibition text has to put up with more competition than most other written material. It has to compete for people's attention with all the other material and tends to be the last thing to catch their eye when they stand in front of the exhibits. They have to read the text *standing*, probably after a tiring walk on hard stone floors. The light is poor compared to their reading lamps at home, and it is impossible to vary the reading angle as with a book or newspaper. We are up against great odds, and the only way to overcome these obstacles is to make the text *easy to read*.

'EASY READING FOR ADULTS'

When the Postal Museum approached me I had just finished writing an easy-to-read book for adults. It was therefore natural for me to use the easy-to-read method for this project. I believe this method can be a great help, and also an inspiration, to those who write exhibition texts for museums.

Ever since the 1960s the National Board of Education has given grants for the publication of easy-to-read books for adults. A condition for financial support for the publication of these books is that the writers must write simply and straightforwardly. However, this does not mean simplification either of the language or the subject-matter. The sentences are short, normal word order is preferred and the lines are about forty-five characters long. In dividing the text into lines the principle is to let the end of a line coincide with the end of a natural phrase. Subordinate clauses, complicated attributive constructions and unnecessary adverbial modifiers are avoided. To take an example of the sort of text you might see in a museum: 'Most of the manure was spread during late winter when there was still snow on the ground, but some of it was also spread in the summer.' A corresponding easy-to-read text would be phrased as follows:

> The farmers spread manure
> in late winter and in summer.

Does the reader miss anything essential in the latter version? Not as far as I can see. The information given in both cases refers to the time when the manure is spread. The easy-to-read version favours the active form of the verb, the subject confronting the reader with the natural order of things. Moreover, there is no division into syllables when an easy-to-read text is printed. Museum material, on the other hand, often contains syllable division, which is neither easy to read nor very attractive to the eye. In the following example it seems the length of the line was the decisive factor:

> The trade from the coastal districts of Northern Swe-
> den and Finland went through the country's capi-
> tal, Stockholm, which consequently became an im-
> portant transshipment centre.

A STEP-BY-STEP PROCESS

I was asked to write the texts about five months before the exhibition was to be opened. The exhibition concept had already been decided on, and also the arrangement by rooms, but not the final appearance of the rooms. Work had just started on the building of the exhibits. Documentation for each room was in the pipeline. My first task was to read up on the subject so as to be able to make judgements of my own. The factual information was to be provided by others.

The work of writing the texts took a little over two months. My texts were based on the data compiled by various museum officials and on the conversations I had at regular intervals with the producer and the designer *in the room where a particular text was to be shown*. It was important to relate to the exhibition room in each case.

Thus I began writing the texts long before the rooms themselves were finished. My first efforts were rough drafts. Elisabet and Björn read them and gave their views, which was not so easy since we did not yet have a definite idea of how the rooms would look. To start with I just wrote to get acquainted with my subject, and the reactions I got gave me inspiration and a sense of direction. I went home and rewrote the texts. My collaborators read through the new texts and we again had discussions together. Each new version and discussion resulted in significant changes. The spirit of these dialogues was open and critical, and the texts also provided ideas for the design of the exhibition rooms. This method of writing the material may sound time-consuming, but it worked. Choosing the subject-matter, putting it into words, rejecting some parts and altering others is a process that takes time. It was important to try the texts out, and my job was made easier by the fact that Elisabet and Björn had very definite ideas about what the exhibition was to convey.

The factual information in the texts was checked by those who had written the documentation. After altering and making clean copies of the texts we had them enlarged and taped them in place in the exhibition itself. Although I tried to keep in touch with each exhibition room while work was in progress, I was aware of the risk of producing armchair material. The texts must be an integral part of the exhibition environment, and we had to delete and change parts that we had already approved when we saw that reading the texts in the exhibition room gave a different impression from that intended. We typeset the texts with the typography we had decided on, we tested different sizes for readability and mounted the texts in frames to get as clear an idea as possible of what the finished results would look like. We were, however, aware that the finished result always has one or two surprises in store, since the overall impression depends on a combination of so many elements.

In the exhibition 'A Letter Makes All the Difference' the historical process is illustrated in fragments, by the lives and work of certain people. Some of these people are represented by full-scale wax figures. These figures were made at the same time as the texts were being written, and when their faces were being completed the texts were already in the typesetting state. If I had seen these faces first I would have been able to make some of the texts more authentic. This is just one example of the fact that the writer should always keep in touch with what is going on in the exhibition room, and of course the problem becomes increasingly acute in the final stages when everyone is pressed for time.

CONCENTRATING THE TEXT

When writing texts for exhibitions we constantly have to condense the material and delete everything superfluous until there remains a bare minimum necessary to convey the essential content. This situation makes great demands on style. The words must be well chosen and precise and each phrase must be concrete and clear to enable the reader to absorb it rapidly. This does not mean that a factual text must be dry as dust; the language can be full of associations and provide food for thought. I believe that you can concentrate such texts to an almost poetic level, though the object is not to write poetry. But you should be attentive to the sounds and rhythm. Even in a factual text you should bear in mind that the language depends on interaction between the different sounds of the language, especially the vowels. The melody produced by this interaction can be turned to account for rhythmical purposes, and a suitable rhythm makes a text easier to read.

We know from studies that have been carried out that few visitors, if any, read all the texts accompanying an exhibition. My goal in writing the exhibition texts was that if a visitor starts reading one of the texts, it should be so easy to read and interesting that he or she reads to the end of the paragraph. This is one of the reasons why the texts are divided into independent paragraphs, the other being that this division is made necessary by the content. I also hope of course that a visitor who reads one such paragraph with appreciation will go on to the next one.

In my view the language of these texts should match the subject, according to the time-honoured principle of harmony between form and content. So if I am writing for a historical exhibition I might use some words with an archaic ring. We should not forget our linguistic heritage: words like betide, regal and chattels help to create an atmosphere, and if the meaning of a word is not immediately apparent the context may offer a solution. At the same time, the text should also be addressed to the reader. There may seem to be a contradiction here, but in fact this is quite natural. Visitors reading a text in a museum should have the feeling that a knowledgeable guide is standing right beside them and talking to them. The tone and conversational expressions will help them to understand. I also think that these texts should be stimulating, conjure up pictures and make the reader feel 'this is really terribly interesting', as the Swedish writer Bengt Anderberg has said about just about everything in life and literature. It is true that the museum repertoire is 'classical' but as in the theatre it is the performance and the production that still bring the old truths home to us. The selection of historical facts, real life in fact, can be produced in a museum in such a way as to make us sit up and think. An important part is played in the production by the written material.

CAPTIONS, CATALOGUE?

This exhibition had no captions in the rooms. This was not because we had forgotten them, we simply could not find a satisfactory solution to the problem. It is difficult to produce captions which do not limit your scope or oversimplify. Perhaps we will find a solution when we evaluate the exhibition and make additions. No exhibition should be so permanent that it remains completely unchanged year after year.

What about a catalogue? How should it be written and what should be the relationship between catalogue and exhibition texts? The texts for the exhibition 'A Letter Makes All the Difference' are intended as a brief introduction, an inspiration to the visitor to find out more about the subject somewhere else, in a comprehensive catalogue for example. Such a catalogue would give us a chance to fill in the details, such as the material we had to exclude from the documentation provided by the museum officials. There is no reason why we should not write the catalogue in an easy-to-read style too. We have not yet started on this task, however.

Words certainly have an important function in a museum. Let us give them the chance to fulfil this function by broadening the visitors' experience while stimulating their interest. Don't we owe this to the museum visitor?

This chapter first appeared as a paper in Exhibitions in Sweden 27/8 (1986/7): 1–7.

21

Writing readable text: evaluation of the Ekarv method

Elizabeth Gilmore and Jennifer Sabine

In the first edition of this Reader I included an account by Margareta Ekarv of how she wrote texts for exhibitions (it is included in this second edition as Chapter 20). The ideas in the chapter have been discussed extensively with students on the Museum Studies course at the University of Leicester, and these ideas have accompanied students on their work-placements and back to their places of work.

These two case-studies show how the Ekarv method has been used in different ways in two exhibitions. The key to both approaches is the acknowledgement that reading text in an exhibition is not the same as reading text in a book. The reader is standing up, at a distance, in public, and frequently unfamiliar with the material to be read. Writing for such reading conditions demands special skills. These are two excellent examples.

EKARV'S THEORY

Margareta Ekarv developed her theory while writing exhibition texts for the Swedish Postal Museum. She based her method on experience gained during an earlier commission to write books for adult literacy classes.

Observing how museum visitors read texts – often in poor light, while standing up, and in a distracting, sometimes noisy environment – she recognized difficulties of concentration and comprehension similar to those experienced by people with low literacy skills. She experimented with the very simple format of the books to express the much more complicated information contained in the museum exhibition.

Ekarv recommends a structured and organic style of writing (Figure 21.2). She encourages the use of words 'to give a new, deeper dimension to our visual experience' (Ekarv 1987). She emphasizes the importance of close co-operation between the writer, curator and designer of the exhibition, so that each understands the others' objectives and the texts become an organic part of the whole display.

She believes it is possible to write museum texts which are so easy and attractive that readers will both enjoy and learn from them. Recent evaluations of her method by Jennifer Sabine at Swansea Museum and Elizabeth Gilmore at Nature in Art have endorsed most of her claims and shown a positive response from museum visitors.

SWANSEA MUSEUM

Jennifer Sabine used Ekarv's method to write texts for a new Egyptology gallery and evaluated the results for her MA dissertation at the University of Leicester.

Theory into practice

The new gallery at Swansea Museum contains an Egyptian mummy and a coffin which, after over 100 years on display, has recently undergone conservation. The mummy's absence and return excited local interest not only in Egyptian history and the identity of the mummy, but also in the conservation work itself. This prompted our decision to include information about museum conservation alongside the historical interpretation of the mummy.

The texts had to be appropriate to readers ranging from primary school children studying Ancient Peoples to adults with an amateur or specialist interest in Egyptology. When writing these texts, I followed Ekarv's guidelines faithfully (Figure 21.2). The information was divided into themed sections about the mummy, its provenance and historical background, and the conservation work it had undergone. I enjoyed the discipline of writing so precisely, searching for the one word which is both expressive and simple. Critical editing and the collaboration of my colleagues helped to avoid confusion and ambiguity; reading the passages aloud to them helped to catch the flow and rhythm of natural speech.

Evaluating the texts

Questionnaires given to visitors before the gallery opened asked them to compare a text written according to Ekarv with a more traditional one (Figure 21.1), and to

TRADITIONAL TEXT	EKARV TEXT
BISHOPSTON BURCH BARROW	**BISHOPSTON BURCH BARROW**
At Fairwood Common, Gower, Excavated by Mrs Audrey Williams in 1941. A.942.1.1 Ref: Arch. Camb. 1944, pp. 52–63	This barrow is on Fairwood Common in Gower. It was excavated in 1941 when Fairwood Aerodrome was being built.
The primary burial was found in a pit which had been cut two feet deep into the subsoil. This contained the cremated remains of a child (a) of 10–14 years of age, covered by an inverted urn (b). Over the base of the urn a thin slab of limestone, roughly 22 ins. square, had been placed. A cairn 40ft. in diameter covered the pit. This cairn was concealed by a mound of mixed clay and turf. It contained traces of secondary burials. Fragments of four cinerary urns (c), all of 'overhanging rim' type, were found towards the centre of the cairn.	The first body buried on the site was a child about 10 to 14 years old. It was placed in a small pit under a cinerary urn. Over the urn was a slab of limestone covered by a circular mound of stones. At a later date this was covered by a larger mound of clay and turf. When the barrow was excavated, the archaeologist found traces of other burials and pieces of four cinerary urns.

Figure 21.1 Examples of texts used for evaluation

indicate their preference from a variety of layouts. In each case, the text written in Ekarv's style proved the more popular. Responses showed that readers had understood these texts and in the main approved of their unconventional layout. They also found them easier to read. The age groupings of respondents showed that a majority of adults enjoyed Ekarv's style. Among younger age groups, teenagers mainly preferred traditional formats but young children liked the Ekarv text; possibly because teenagers usually read more traditional material, such as textbooks and novels, while young children's books are designed primarily for ease of reading.

The most engaging part of the project was studying visitors' reactions to the new gallery after it opened, using qualitative research methods. Focused observation of visitors' behaviour in the gallery, using the museum's CCTV security monitors, showed that 75 per cent of visitors read some of the texts, an unexpectedly high proportion. Of these, over half read for more than two minutes and almost all referred back to the texts while viewing the objects. This suggested that if people find reading easy they will continue to read and will use texts to interpret objects.

A more precise and detailed assessment of visitors' reactions was gained from interviews and written comments. These were largely favourable: only eight of the 52 respondents were positively critical and 11 mildly critical or neutral. A few identifiable themes emerged:

- The short lines, complete in themselves, and the well-separated blocks of text seem to facilitate reading. Some people had not noticed the unusual format used, others referred to it as 'like a poem': some liked this, but a few found it odd, even irritating
- In general, readers liked the informal and rhythmic quality. Several said they did not usually read museum texts but had read these, and enjoyed them
- The simple wording was not considered to be patronizing, and many visitors appreciated being able to read the short lines and paragraphs without much effort – this was particularly true of older people, 'I could read without my glasses' was a frequent comment.

The texts were also translated into Welsh in line with Swansea Museum's bilingual policy. Two native speakers and a Welsh learner, who were asked to read the translations with Ekarv's guidelines in mind, confirmed that her principles could be successfully maintained in translation.

Conclusion

Ekarv's style of texts has proved successful in Swansea Museum. In 1996 the Egyptology gallery won the Museums

- ◆ Use simple language to express complex ideas
- ◆ Use normal spoken word order
- ◆ One main idea per line, end of line coinciding with natural end of phrase
- ◆ Lines of about 45 letters, text broken into short paragraphs of four to five lines
- ◆ Use the active form of verbs and state the subject early in the sentence
- ◆ Avoid: subordinate clauses, complicated constructions, unnecessary adverbs, hyphenating words at the end of lines
- ◆ Read texts aloud and note natural pauses
- ◆ Adjust wording and punctuation to reflect the rhythm of speech
- ◆ Discuss texts with colleagues and consider their comments
- ◆ Co-ordinate the text writing with the design of displays
- ◆ Pin draft texts in their final positions to assess effect
- ◆ Continually revise and refine the wording
- ◆ Concentrate the meaning to 'an almost poetic level'

Figure 21.2 Guidelines for the Ekarv text method

and Galleries Commission Award for Communicating Conservation, and was also commended in the Interpret Britain Award 1996. But the strongest endorsement of Ekarv's method is that visitors can be heard reading the texts aloud to one another, quite comfortably, and quoting from them in conversation.

NATURE IN ART

Elizabeth Gilmore used Ekarv's principle to produce text for a display of ceramics during her work placement at Nature in Art at Gloucester in 1996. She evaluated the results as part of her MA research dissertation at the University of Leicester.

Pilot study

Nature in Art is an independent museum, attracting approximately 35,000 visitors each year. Retired people and school groups form a significant proportion of visitors, but the museum, housed in an eighteenth-century mansion within large secure grounds, is also particularly suited to the needs of family groups. The museum operates a policy of frequent redisplay to help promote repeat visits. Texts therefore have to be inter-changeable and in a standard size and format. Their language is typically formal and lines are justified left and right (recently, the museum has adopted more explanatory texts in a larger format, but my study preceded these changes).

The pilot display, entitled Representing Pottery, explored three themes: Pottery Politics, Marking Time and Pottery in Motion. The aim was to assess the learning potential of Ekarv's method and its impact on visitors' knowledge, memory and experience. The pilot texts were targeted at family groups, but took account of the needs of older visitors. Features of the text included:

- Conversational language
- Information presented in simple steps
- Deliberate attempt made to draw attention to the subjectivity of a curator's inter-pretative role
- Questions to encourage interaction between visitors, objects and text.

Interpretation was assessed through a combination of non-participant and focused observation, tracking studies, semi-structured interviews/focus group sessions and a visitors' comments book. I was particularly keen to compare my perceptions of visitors' experiences with their own interpretations. Semi-structured interviews were therefore carried out immediately after observing and tracking each visitor group.

Evaluation methods can record only selected memories and experiences, and this limits the extent to which the effect of the text on visitors can be assessed. Despite these limitations, the pilot study identified several patterns of reaction from which some useful lessons can be drawn.

Findings

The research findings can be grouped into four main themes: physical access; intel-lectual access; visitors' interactions with objects and texts; and group interaction – the contribution of the texts to the development of visitors' interpersonal skills.

The large print size (up to 38 point) and simple form of the pilot texts noticeably helped older people and those with impaired vision to read them more easily. The bold, physically accessible writing also subverted traditional role relationships between family members, enabling children and adults to read and learn through each other. Children were able to read aloud to accompanying adults, often gaining pleasure in misreading some of the text headings (on several occasions, for example, 'pottery politics' became 'potty politics'). The easy-to-read style resulting from Ekarv's methods enabled accompanying adults to quickly find answers to children's questions, and possibly helped to make their visit less stressful and more pleasurable.

Some visitors drew analogies between the characteristics of the pilot texts and leisure activities such as pub quizzes. Such comments suggest that the texts were perceived in terms of recreation, pleasure and informal learning and, most importantly, endorse Ekarv's claims that matching the verbal style of presentation with that of the visitor, can enhance the meaning, enjoyment and perhaps the quality of the visit.

Visitors' interpersonal meanings were developed pleasurably through interactions between texts, objects and group discussions. The conversational language encouraged visitors to talk to the texts, repeating words and phrases. In their conversations and thoughts they brought the texts to life. Some visitors related the contents of the text to their own experiences. For example, in response to the Ekarv style pilot text 'Boxing Hare' (Figure 21.3), a boy said, 'I've seen hares near my gran's house.' Apparently trivial exchanges of information are reminders that the way in which the texts are used socially (among the visiting group), is not necessarily apparent in the structure of a text itself. Visitors bring non-textual factors such as experience and memory with them to the process of making meaning. This indicates that there is not necessarily any connection between the preferred meanings intended by text writers and the meanings constructed by visitors.

Jan Sweeney, 1990

Jan captures the spirit and 'boxing' movement of a 'mad March hare'.

Imagine the male hares
as they bound,
kick,
and stand on their hind legs
to box with each other.
Pow!
Would you be attracted to this
   show,
like the female hares?

Jan used stoneware clay
to mould this sculpture by hand.
Stoneware clay is solid and
versatile.
A clay sketch is often completed
by sculptors
before casting in bronze.
It allows initial ideas to be tested
and revised.

Look for Jan's fingerprints
in the clay body!

Figure 21.3 Boxing Hare

CONCLUSIONS

The notion of pleasure, particularly that derived through empowerment, is intrinsic to visitors' responses and learning outcomes. It has been suggested[1] that successful communication depends on the sender and receiver sharing the same concepts – even the same passions.

Visitors' pleasure derived from empowerment is perhaps one way of arousing and instilling these passions. Ekarv's method certainly appeared to empower visitors and can perhaps be considered as one way of reconciling the needs of diverse visitor groups.

However, the pilot project also indicated some practical limitations on the use of Ekarv's method in a museum environment, including:

- The extra time taken to write text following Ekarv's guidelines compared with writing 'traditional' narrative text
- The intrusiveness of the larger text panels needed to accommodate the elongated layout of text in short lines, particularly for displays of small objects.

Perhaps the most important lesson to be drawn from Ekarv's method is the need for text to be in print large enough for everyone to read and in language that can be readily understood.

This chapter first appeared as a paper in Museum Practice *5 (2/2): 72–5 (London: Museums Association).*

NOTE

1 Hooper-Greenhill, E., *Museums and their Visitors* (London: Routledge 1994).

REFERENCES

Ekarv, M. (1987) 'Combating redundancy: writing texts for exhibitions', first published in *Exhibitions in Sweden* 27/8 (1986/7): 28–38, reprinted in Hooper-Greenhill, E. (1994) *The Educational Role of the Museum*, London: Routledge, pp. 140–3.

Ekarv, M. (1991) summary of contribution to *Smaka på Orden*, Stockholm: Carlsson Publishing with Riksutstatmuseum.

Gilmore, E. (1996) 'Pleasure through empowerment: enhanced and enjoyable learning through museum text', MA dissertation, University of Leicester, unpublished.

Sabine, J. (1995) 'An assessment of Ekarv's easy-to-read method of writing museum texts', MA dissertation, University of Leicester, unpublished.

22

How old is this text?

James Carter

Readability tests can help ensure that texts can be understood. The Fry and the Cloze tests are described. Although these measures can be useful, some caution is suggested in their use. Neither of them has been specifically designed for museum use.

Do your readers really understand you? Readability – the measure of how easy a text is to read and comprehend – depends on many factors. The reader's motivation is a major one. For example, an 8-year-old will work hard to understand a complex or poorly translated computer game instruction book, but wouldn't attempt a financial report of the same complexity. Typeface and layout also affect how fluently you can read text. But the complexity of the language is a factor too, and reading age tests can be a useful check on whether your writing is likely to be understandable or not.

They have been developed in the education sector, where it is obviously important to match the abilities of children who are learning to read with the style and complexity of the books their teacher gives them.

There are many different methods, some of which rely on involved mathematical formulae. The Fry test is easy to do and relatively quick.

1 Select at random three passages of 100 words. If your text isn't this long (and often it shouldn't be!) use just one passage.
2 Count the total number of sentences in each passage and take the average of these numbers.
3 Count the total number of syllables in each passage and again take the average. It's easiest to do this if you go through the text writing the number of syllables in pencil above each word.
4 Plot these two averages on the graph (Figure 22.1).

If you want a benchmark to aim for, try writing for a reading age of 12 for panels in an exhibition for the general public. If that seems low, just think about your readers. You can't rely on their being highly motivated: most interpretation is about provoking interest, not satisfying a desire for detailed knowledge. They're likely to be standing up, perhaps outdoors, with distractions including wandering children, low-flying jets and ice-cream stalls. It's not that you're writing for people who have a reading age of 12, just that you need to make your text as easy to read as possible.

It's important to recognize that reading age is not related to physical age or mental age. The method above is simply a measure of how complex the word and sentence structure is, and therefore of how easy it is to read. A recent test on a copy of the *Sun*

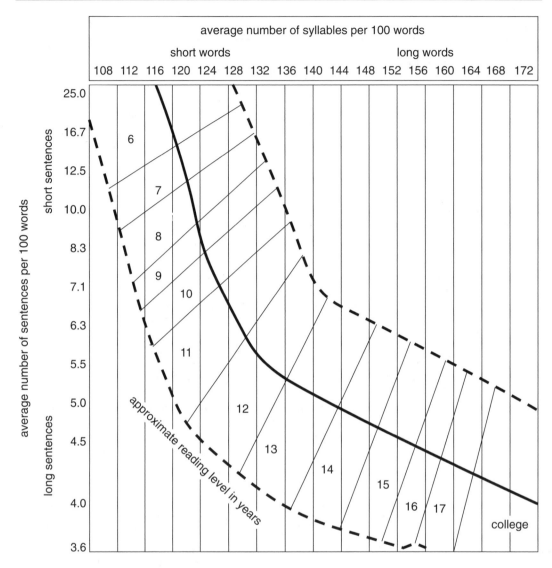

Figure 22.1 The Fry test for reading age: this graph has been redrawn from the *Journal of Reading*, April 1968; the dotted lines indicate the boundary of the region of maximum reliability of the test

and on a feature in the *Independent on Sunday* magazine gave reading ages of 11/12 and 15/16 respectively. The *Sun* isn't written for people who are stupid, just for those who prefer something easy to read (whatever else you may think about it!).

MIND THE GAP

The Fry test only measures complexity of language. It's quick and easy, but it can't tell you whether your intended audience actually understands what you've written. The

Cloze procedure gives an indication of how your readers interact with your text, and how much they really understand it.

The name comes from *closure*, a concept in Gestalt theory which suggests that we will mentally complete any incomplete pattern. For example, a diagram of a circle with gaps in it will still be perceived as a circle. As applied to readability and comprehension tests, the procedure has many possibilities and variants, but the version which follows is appropriate for interpretation intended for adults.

1   Select a passage from your text and prepare a version of it in which every fifth word is replaced by an equal-sized blank. The passage should start at the beginning of a paragraph. A length of about 250 words is recommended, but not essential. Leave the first and last sentences intact, and ensure that you don't remove proper nouns unless they have already occurred.
2   Show this prepared text to a representative sample of your audience, and ask them to guess the missing words. Allow as much time as necessary. The equal-size blanks prevent guesses on the basis of word length.
3   Calculate the score as a percentage. Count an answer as correct only if it is exactly the same word as in the original, though you can allow minor mis-spellings. Numbering the gaps interferes with the readers' flow, and makes it more difficult for them, so find some other method of checking the completed passages.
4   Scores below 40 show that your readers may have real difficulty with your text. The table in Figure 22.2 shows the relationship between Cloze scores and comprehension.

Comprehension level	Frustration	Instructional	Independent
Cloze score	0 . . . . 40	60 100	

Figure 22.2 Correlation between comprehension and Cloze scores: good interpretation should give a Cloze score above 40. From Rye (1982)

These comprehension levels indicate how well readers might do in a multiple-choice questionnaire based on a full version of the text.

'Independent' is equivalent to a score of 90% or better – complete understanding. 'Instructional' means a score of between 75% and 89% – in a classroom setting, enough for full understanding with some assistance. This should be acceptable for most interpretation: you're not aiming to equip visitors for an exam. Visitors are often in groups, and their companions will fill in gaps in any individual's understanding. They can also pick up clues from other text, or from objects on display.

'Frustration' level, however, means that the text is too difficult even with some help. It's time to go back to the drafting stage!

PASS THE SALT

There are many other tests for readability, some of them available as computer programs. But perhaps they all need to be taken with a healthy pinch of salt. They can mask real difficulties – a poorly written short sentence can be less comprehensible than a well-written long one. They can draw attention to apparent faults which would cause no difficulty, especially if they involve comparing text with lists of 'familiar' words. One computer package, for example, rejects 'Brighton', 'Royal' and 'dragons' in a children's guide to the Royal Pavilion in Brighton. It's worth remembering that some 'familiar words' lists were compiled in the United States in the 1930s!

Above all, tests like these are no substitute for writing with feeling and power. Writing solely to match a particular reading age could easily be dull: the trick is to write simply, but with an enthusiasm that makes your writing worth reading.

This paper first appeared in Environmental Interpretation *(Feb. 1993): 10--11.*

REFERENCES

If you want to know more about readability, try these books:

Gilliland, John (1972) *Readability*, London: Hodder & Stoughton.
Rye, James (1982) *Cloze Procedure and the Teaching of Reading*, Oxford: Heinemann Educational.

23

Museum text as mediated message

Helen Coxall

How does language work to construct meaning? Museums and their texts are active agents in shaping opinion and identity. Language is socially determined and therefore articulates ideologies, generally through the assumptions which underlie texts. Museum writers need to be aware that this is happening in order to identify the assumptions that texts will be built upon.

The writer demonstrates with examples from museum labels how linguistic variables such as the agentless passive, naming devices, and evalutive adjectives construct meanings which contain assumptions (which may be racist, sexist or biased in other ways) that the writers are unaware of and would probably not want to support.

My Ph.D. research into museum language is an exploration into how language means, that is, the process by which language conveys meanings. A large part of the research consists of linguistic analyses of texts from selected galleries and museums, with regard to social and ideological implications.

The following passage from the introduction to Gerda Lerner's book *The Creation of Patriarchy* highlights, both directly and indirectly, two very important issues that are relevant to my investigations. First, the significance of gaps in textual information and second the issue of discrimination:

> Until the most recent past historians have been men, and what they have recorded is what men have done and experienced and found significant. They have called this History and have claimed universality for it. What women have done and experienced has been left unrecorded, neglected and ignored in interpretation. Historical scholarship, up to the most recent past, has seen women as marginal to the making of civilisation and as unessential to those pursuits defined as having historical significance.

> Thus the recorded and interpreted record of the past of the human race is only a partial record, in that it omits the past of half of humankind, and it is distorted in that it tells the story from the viewpoint of the male half of humanity only.

If history is only a partial record of the past it follows that one way of looking at history is in accordance with the omissions in the text. In other words the world-view of the historian can be understood in relation to what the account does not say, because a way of saying is also a way of seeing. In this case the gap in the information suggests a particular stereotypical attitude to the role of women in society. However an omission in this quote itself foregrounds the fact that different ways of seeing the world are not limited to female or male perspectives alone. Here is an example to explain what I mean.

Dr Jeanne Cannizzo wrote an article, 'How sweet it is: cultural politics in Barbados', about the Museum of Barbados whose collection was (until recently) not a record of the history of the black Barbadian people, who form the majority on the island, but a record of the predominantly white Barbadian merchants and planters and their adoption of European culture. She makes the point in her article that:

> Museums and their displays are often active agents in shaping all kinds of identity. By not displaying the cultural heritage of the majority of the population, the museum has taken from them, by implication, their role as history makers, as active participants in their own past.

Thus, not only do the gaps in this museum's collection reveal the writers', and in this case the museum directors', ideological stance, they imply a meaning that is communicated to whomever reads the text. In other words, the writer is perpetuating and reinforcing their own ideological bias: the mediated message in this case being that the black Barbadians are not worthy of historical record. The responsibility that this implication places on any writer involved with educational institutions, such as museums, is obvious.

Mark Leone puts this point very forcefully in his article 'Methods as message: interpreting the past with the public'. 'Reading, writing, telling and performing history are *active* and *form* modern opinion, modern nationality, modern identity, class interests and social position' (my italics). Thus, assumptions that are embedded in language are all pervasive and cannot be ignored. My interest is in the way the avoided subjects in the text and the language itself transmit both the personal world-view of a writer of museum texts and the official policy of the museum itself.

In their book *Language as Ideology* Kress and Hodge make the following observation: 'The world is grasped through language. But in its use by a speaker, language is more than that. It is a version of the world offered to, imposed on, enacted by someone else.' They go on to make the claim that the grammar of a language itself is a theory of reality. Which perhaps sounds a little far-fetched to start with. Nevertheless, social structures not only determine discourse but are themselves produced by discourse. Subsequently, if you think about it, our system of communication (our language) is already in existence before our children learn it and in learning this language they learn words that appear to stand for value-free, common-sense concepts but are actually socially determined ones. For example, they learn the name of the person who delivers their letters every morning as 'postman' which seems straightforward enough until you stop to think that implicit in this name is the fact that all such people are men.

This does not mean that because our language is socially determined we are unable to escape the unconscious articulation of underlying ideologies. But it does mean that we must become clear about what these underlying assumptions are if it is not our wish to perpetuate them. Therefore, if the grammar of a language is indeed its theory of reality it should be possible to uncover its hidden agenda, for if writers are saying things they are unaware of, critical linguistic analysis can serve as a valuable means of exposure and therefore of consciousness-raising. Furthermore, it should be possible for an aware writer to draw on other discourses in order to create a new perspective. And this applies as much to historians as to writers of museum texts.

I will return to this issue later when the implications contained in selected museum texts will be examined. To return for now to Gerda Lerner's book; she does obliquely acknowledge that gender discrimination is not the only kind of discrimination found in historical records. She says:

> As formerly subordinate groups such as peasants, slaves, proletarians, have risen into positions of power, their experiences have become part of the historical record. That is the experiences of the male group; the females were, as usual, excluded. The point is that men and women have suffered exclusion and discrimination because of their class. No man has ever been excluded from the historical record because of his sex, yet all women were.

However, although Lerner explicitly acknowledges only gender and class discrimination, it seems to me that racial discrimination is also implied in her reference to slaves. By concentrating upon awareness of gender discrimination it is possible to overlook the fact that the same insidious discriminatory process is being perpetuated by methods of recording histories of many groups of marginalized peoples on the grounds of race, class, religion, politics and age.

In his essay 'Belief and the problem of women', Edwin Ardener refers to women as a *muted* group when opposed to the male dominant group. This is a particularly appropriate term as it not only refers to the process by which women have been written out of history but the process by which they are rendered inarticulate, as they are forced to communicate in male-orientated language. Thus the term muted indicates a problem both with language and with power.

However, women are not the only group that is effectively muted by the constructed language of the dominant group. Let us look at some texts that illustrate the problem for writers of text in social history museums who seek to redress the balance contained in previous historical accounts. Not everyone, of course, does seek to redress the balance, and it would not be surprising to find that there are some museums staff (as indeed there are historians) who, according to historian John Tosh 'reject theory and remain blissfully unaware of the assumptions and values which inform their own selection and interpretation of evidence'. But this position is difficult for staff to defend in the light of the fact that museums are regarded by the public as centres of excellence and knowledge that are automatically endowed with authenticity. However, is it possible to give an authentic historical account? John Tosh goes on to say: 'The record of recent centuries is so voluminous and varied that contradictory results can be obtained simply by asking different questions.'

Surely, therefore, it is the questions that are being asked that provide the key to differing interpretations of history? After all, it is possible to provide a completely one-sided version of any event, past or present, by simply avoiding certain facts, as we have already acknowledged, or, to put it another way, by avoiding certain questions. By examining the lexical and syntactical choices (that is the choice of words and grammar) in a text it is possible to find, first, evidence of the position of the writer; second, what they were saying; third, what they were choosing not to say and why; and last who they appeared to be addressing. It is also appropriate to enquire whether or not the information was both relevant and accessible to the potential audience. The purpose, as I mentioned at the outset, is to raise awareness about the ways that language choice can reflect a pre-determined way of seeing and to suggest alternative ways of saying that avoid unintentional bias.

The writers of museum texts have a responsibility to the public and therefore have to be very careful that they do not convey implicit, unintentional meanings. Thus museum writers are not justified in being familiar only with their own subject but must also concern themselves with their mode of communication.

Linguistic variables can create meanings that are at first glance not apparent. For example, the use of the passive as opposed to the active form can create problems for writers if they are unaware of the effect of using this particular language construction. A writer who uses the passive form is able to avoid naming the perpetrators of an event and simply make a statement about the end result. For example, the newspaper headline that says simply 'Three passers-by were shot during riots'. Now, if the journalist had used the active instead of the passive form s/he would have had to identify who did the shooting and the heading would therefore have implicated somebody, for example: 'The police shot three passers-by during riots' or 'Rioters shot three passers-by'. Of course from a journalist's point of view, if there were some confusion about who did the shooting this method of reporting is convenient; however, the same practice is used deliberately by politicians to avoid uncomfortable facts.[1] It can also be used quite innocently by writers with unfortunate results. Here is an example taken from the Georgian section of a social history museum.

> Under the influence of the Adam brothers furniture was simple, refined and strongly classical in form and ornament. . . . Hepplewhite designed oval and shield shaped backs to many of his chairs and both he and Sheraton, the other great furniture designer of this time, emphasised lightness of construction and elegance of treatment.

Note the specific naming of the individual designers and the use of the active formation. Compare this with the updated version of the same exhibit label:

> Neo-classical shapes and motifs were popular, like the lyre shape on the back of the music stand. This style of furniture is now often called Hepplewhite and Sheraton.

Here the furniture is named by the abstract noun *style*, the agentless passive is used, and when the designers are named it is only in reference to the name of their style of work which has miraculously detached itself from themselves as creators. It is like referring to a Shakespearian style of writing and denying the existence of Shakespeare himself. It does not take much imagination to guess that the writer did not intend the latter interpretation to be communicated; however, it does demonstrate the problems that can arise when adopting this 'impersonal' academic style of language.

The effect of the agentless passive here is twofold. First, it avoids telling the reader who exactly performed the work referred to. Second, the writer avoids identifying her/himself at all and therefore apparently remains objective. The facts being recorded acquire that aura of authenticity as they cannot be seen to be subjective. Thus the writer's choice and combination of lexicon and syntax control the meanings that can be read into the text by the museum's visitor. Let us look at a few more examples.

The various uses of nouns can mediate the meanings. We have already seen how the use of proper nouns (the specific naming of the designers in the last text) conferred status upon them. We have also already come across the use of an abstract noun (style) which contributed to the text's vagueness. Abstract nouns used frequently can create complexity. There is another type of noun that is used frequently by politicians which is called a noun construction. This is a noun that has been constructed from a verb which, like the use of the passive, usually has the effect of avoiding identifying the agent of the sentence.

George Orwell wrote a fascinating essay entitled 'Politics and the English language' in which he attacked political language or 'the institutional voice' as it is called nowadays. Although written in 1945 it still applies today: this is how he defined it.

In our time political speech and writing are largely the defence of the indefensible . . . political language consists largely of euphemisms, question begging and sheer cloudy vagueness. [And he gives the following example] Defenceless villages are bombarded from the air, the inhabitants driven out into the countryside, the cattle machine-gunned, the huts set on fire with incendiary bullets: this is called *pacification*. [Pacification is a noun construction – he continues –] Such phraseology is needed if one wants to name things without calling up mental pictures of them.

To demonstrate how this can be applicable to museum texts here is another example taken from the late eighteenth-century section of a social history museum.

The family here would have had three or four servants whose life would have been a lot less comfortable. They would have done all the shopping, cooking, cleaning and household chores, including looking after the children, in return for their keep.

The use of the generic noun 'servant' under-values the status of this group of workers. Presumably this generalization is intended to cover parlour maid, chamber maid, kitchen maid and perhaps nanny and governess too. We can only guess as we are not told. Such a generalization suggests an attitude to this kind of worker but does this originate in the mind of the writer or was it intended to reflect the class-conscious attitudes of the period?

As we have already observed, naming workers as 'designers' identifies them as individuals by virtue of their trade. In this passage, however, it is only the work that the servants performed that is given significance. The activities are described by noun constructions: 'cooking', 'cleaning', 'shopping', 'looking after children'. In other words a noun has been created out of a verb which deflects importance from the doer to the work itself. Thus the verb *to cook* is transformed into the noun *the cooking* and the necessity to refer to the doer, in this case the cook and her occupation, is avoided in favour of a description of the activity itself. Thus the cooks are demoted by the writer. Such terminology suggests that the people themselves who were probably mostly women were not important and that anyone could have done the job. It is also interesting that the children are parallelled linguistically with household chores which is a strange attitude for a social historian to take unless this was indeed the attitude to children at the time, in which case this surely warrants an explanation.

In the following text slaves are parallelled with mahogany, cotton, tea and spices.

London was a huge port and trade centre and London's merchants were wealthy. Of all the trades, the slave trade was perhaps the most profitable for London merchants and bankers, and many of them kept black slaves in their London homes. Trade with the British colonies provided the raw materials for the many luxury goods now found in British homes. Mahogany was imported from Jamaica and Cuba, tea, cotton and spices from India, sugar from the West Indies, as well as porcelain from China. London was a cosmopolitan city attracting skilled workers from many parts of the world. Many of these like the French Huguenot silk weavers who had settled in Spitalfields, influenced the look of furniture and furnishings in Britain.

The writer makes no linguistic differentiation between the trade in people and inanimate objects: both are referred to as commodities of contemporary trade. It is quite clear from the claim that 'rich merchants and bankers kept black slaves in their London homes', that this was a status symbol. The text reinforces this by the barely differentiated possession of slaves and luxury goods in the home.

It is well known that slave traders did not treat their 'commodities' as human beings; however, it seems rather strange that a text written in the 1980s should attempt to perpetuate, even condone, that view, for, by not mentioning the attitude to slaves at that time, this is the impression given. By using the verb to keep, in 'kept black slaves in their London homes', the parallel with a domestic animal is conjured up. After all, one *keeps* a dog but *employs* a cook. The *Oxford English Dictionary*'s definition of 'kept' is 'financially supported and privately controlled by interested persons'. This may have a bearing on the fact that servants were given such little status in the previous passage quoted if they were also black slaves. If the museum considers history to be part of an ongoing process of social development which embraces past, present and future, this issue should surely be addressed, or at least acknowledged, as failure to do so actually influences social attitudes.

The passage itself reads more like a promotion for London in a holiday brochure than an historical account. It commences with the name London and ends with the name Britain. In only six sentences London is repeated five times and British/Britain three times. Repetition is a linguistic technique used frequently in advertising. Although a certain amount of repetition is unavoidable and even desirable, for purposes of clarity, the repeated use of the name London in this text is a good example of linguistic redundancy: 'the slave trade was perhaps the most profitable for *London* merchants and bankers, and many of them kept black slaves in their *London* homes'. As the reader is aware right from the start that London is the subject of the paragraph, neither of these repetitions is necessary.

Also the choice of evaluative adjectives adds significantly to the impression that London is being promoted, thus: *huge* port, *profitable* (trade), *wealthy* (merchants), *luxury* goods, *British* homes, *cosmopolitan* city, *skilled* workers. *Huge, profitable, wealthy* and *luxury* are being used as maximizers to emphasize one very specific aspect of London life in the eighteenth century. *British* homes, without the qualification of 'some' or 'certain' before it, is very misleading as it implies that all homes in Britain possessed luxury goods, which is very far from the truth.

> London was a cosmopolitan city attracting skilled workers from many parts of the world. Many of these like the French Huguenot silk weavers who had settled in Spitalfields, influenced the look of furniture and furnishings in Britain.

Although the *OED*'s definition of cosmopolitan is 'belonging to all parts of the world', the word has assumed other, more exotic, connotations through its frequent use in travel brochures. Also the choice of the verb 'attracting' is interesting. Historians will know that the French Huguenots were driven from their own country by the religious persecution that followed the revocation of the 1685 Edict of Nantes. Therefore, as the Huguenots were refugees, the suggestion that they were part of a body of skilled workers that London attracted from all over the world is not only misleading but historically questionable.

The choice and combination of words contribute significantly to the mediation of versions of events. An alternative to 'attracting' for example, could be 'employing', and to 'French Huguenot silk weavers', 'immigrant refugee workers'. The text would have given a very different impression if these words had been altered. It is also interesting that the black slaves are parallelled linguistically with inanimate trade commodities whereas the white Huguenots are named specifically and thus given status on three counts, one by virtue of their nationality, 'French', two, their religion, 'Huguenot', and three, their trade, 'silk weavers'. Thus, the choice and combination of language represent not just a way of talking about the world but also a way of seeing it.

220

To return to Jeanne Cannizzo whom I quoted earlier, it would be difficult to contest her assertion that 'museums are carefully created, artificially constructed repositories; they are negotiated realities'. It is fair to add, however, that those involved in writing museum texts are often unaware of the implications of the language they use. Indeed, some would be very surprised to discover prejudices that they were unaware of appearing in the words they have written. It is clear that all discourses are socially constructed and museum staff are not exempt from the articulation of this process. Until authors of museum texts become more aware of the underlying ideological construction of their own world view, their personal angling of historical events will continue to mislead visitors because: 'the world is grasped through language. But in its use by a speaker, language is more than that. It is a version of the world offered to, imposed on, enacted by someone else' (Kress and Hodge 1974).

Thus we have looked at texts that discriminate against women and race. The last example relates history from a classist perspective:

> Whole suburbs sprang up in a matter of years; most of Holloway appeared in the 1860s and 1870s. The commuter had arrived. He made his money in the City, but could escape city life.

> Others were not so lucky. Commuter railways cut through vast slum areas; pools of cheap labour, used and yet avoided by the suburban resident. . . . At a time when everyone was supposed to 'know their place', where you lived was very important. Really wealthy and fashionable people lived either in the West End, in the country (or both).

Those people living in the suburbs are named by this text as commuters. Those living in the West End are named 'really wealthy and fashionable people', but those living in the slum areas are given no human status at all; instead they are indicated with the metaphor 'pools of cheap labour'. The noun pool is the name of something from which water can be drawn, the anonymous people being the water which could be drawn from the pool. In other words the working classes are named linguistically as a resource for the better-off and have no title, sex or trade.

The two verbs in the following clause, qualifying pools of cheap labour, are very significant: 'used and yet avoided by the suburban resident'. This is clearly written from the point of view of the suburban resident, not the slum resident. The fact that these people are being *used* as *cheap labour* indicated quite clearly that they were being exploited. If the writer had used the verb 'employed' instead of 'used' he or she would not have appeared to be condoning this practice. Also, the fact that these people were to be avoided indicates that the text is written from the point of view of the suburban resident. To elect to describe people and their homes from the point of view of those who exploited and avoided them, can hardly be claimed as an unbiased perspective.

I am not trying to suggest that it is possible for museum staff to produce exhibitions that are completely impartial and value-free. This would not be realistic and there is even a case to argue that it would not be desirable. However, it would be possible to raise the consciousness of writers in order that they are more aware of the process by which meanings are constructed and communicated. If this could be achieved they would have more control over the unconsciously mediated messages in their texts.

This chapter first appeared as a paper in Women, Heritage and Museums (WHAM) *14 (1990): 15–21.*

NOTE

Helen Coxall works as a freelance museum language consultant and teaches at the University of Westminster.

1 For more on this see C. L. Learman, 'Dominant discourse: the institutional voice and control of topic', in Howard Davies and Paul Walton (eds) *Language Image Media* (Oxford: Blackwell, 1983).

REFERENCES

Ardener, Edwin (1978) 'Belief and the problems of women', in S. Ardener (ed.) *Perceiving Women*, New York: Hammond.
Cannizzo, Jeanne (1987) 'How sweet it is: cultural politics in Barbados', *Muse*, Winter.
Kress, Gunther and Hodge, Robert (1974) *Language as Ideology*, London: Routledge & Kegan Paul.
Leone, Mark (1983) 'Methods as message: interpreting the past with the public', *Museums News* 62(1): 35–41.
Lerner, Gerda (1986) *The Creation of Patriarchy*, Oxford: Oxford University Press, 4–5.
Orwell, George (1946) 'Politics and the English language', in David Lodge (ed.) (1972) *20th Century Literary Criticism* (first published in *The Collected Essays, Journalism and Letters*), Harlow: Longman, 361–9.
Tosh, John (1982) *The Pursuit of History*, London: Longman.

24

Increased exhibit accessibility through multisensory interaction

Betty Davidson, Candace Lee Heald and George E. Hein

An evaluation study of a natural history gallery at the Boston Museum of Science resulted in the installation of multisensory consoles which developed the gallery audience and enabled much greater retention of information. Different learning styles were observed. Although people with disabilities were a major target audience, the changes made improved the experience for everyone, except those wanting a very quiet, solitary visit.

In 1985, the Boston Museum of Science conducted an accessibility audit, a self-evaluation of the physical and intellectual accessibility of its programmes and exhibits. It proved useful to the museum for exhibit design, long-range planning, and staff development. As one result of this self-evaluation, the museum sought and obtained funding from the National Science Foundation to modify one exhibit hall. The intent of the modifications was to make both the environment and the content more available to all visitors, including those with disabilities. This article describes the evaluation of those changes and suggests how these findings can be applied in a variety of museum settings.

Before modifications, the New England Lifezones Hall consisted of a large U-shaped gallery, approximately 30 by 60 feet [9 by 18 m], containing six dioramas of wild animals native to New England. Each animal species was depicted in its natural habitat: presentations of deer, bear, moose and beaver, and two dioramas of birds (those that frequent a sandy shore and others native to a rocky coast). The dioramas consisted entirely of visual material. Text panels were backlit, in small print, at adult shoulder height. The exhibit was similar to ones found in many natural history museums.

Our evaluation consisted of studies before, during and after modifications (baseline, interim and final). The gallery continued to function with a steady stream of visitors throughout the redesign activities. Since the major goal of the project was to make the hall more physically and intellectually accessible, one of the primary audiences for our evaluation was the disabled visitor. However, the total inaccessibility of the original dioramas to visually disadvantaged visitors and the lack of accommodation of the exhibit to other disabled populations precluded any studies on this population of visitors before modifications: we would not be able to collect any baseline data on responses to the gallery for visually impaired visitors, and we felt that it would be inappropriate to ask other disabled visitors to tour a gallery that could provide them with little or no satisfaction. We did carry out case-studies of special-needs audiences during the changes for formative feedback to exhibit developers. We also looked at the behaviour of 'ordinary' visitors before, during and after modifications. The term 'ordinary' is placed in quotation marks for three reasons.

1 One in six people in the United States population is classified as having some form of special need (*Disabilities Studies Quarterly* 1990), either physical or mental. Thus it is safe to assume that the general museum public includes a significant number of members with a range of special needs or disabilities.

2 The differences between those characterized as belonging to one group or the other cannot be sharply drawn but represent a continuum, a finding that became evident as we studied visits by both the general audience and special-needs groups.

3 The need for and benefits of accessibility extend to the entire museum public; the consequences of limited accessibility are the same, regardless of the cause. If a museum visitor cannot read a label because he or she has (a) vision impairment, (b) limited reading capability, or (c) limited understanding of English, the net result will be the same: the visitor will not understand the exhibit message. Similarly, benefits of accessibility are shared by multiple groups; for example, tactile elements placed low are accessible to visitors in wheelchairs and children.

EXHIBIT CHANGES

The modifications represent a new approach to accessibility: the intention was to make the exhibit more accessible to all visitors, not just to provide some form of substitute accessibility to those with handicaps. For example, visually impaired visitors have utilized guides or tapes to provide auditory access to dioramas in the past, but these have not been co-ordinated with other exhibit modifications. Audible descriptions alone do not provide access for visually impaired people, nor do multisensory experiences provide access without audible explanations and interpretations of them. As a visually impaired consultant for the New England Lifezones project commented (Bloomer 1987) on the use of auditory descriptions alone, 'Just send me the tapes, I'll stay home'. The modifications in the gallery consisted of three major components, plus additional materials.

Labels

All the dioramas received new and expanded sign panels. The old labels were all mounted at the side of each diorama at approximately shoulder height. The new 'signs' included information that could be accessed in several modes. The original labels were modified, rewritten, and the manner of their display altered, so they were easier to read and easier to understand. In addition, each diorama had constructed before it, approximately 2 feet [60 cm] off the ground, a console that contained an audiotape with descriptive material about the diorama and a 'smell box' that, when turned on, fanned an aroma associated with the animal or its habitat to the visitor. Two of these consoles also included something to touch; one had a pair of deer antlers, the other had a moose hoof.

The two bird dioramas originally had buttons on a panel mounted on the wall to the left of the diorama. When the buttons were pushed, a light shone on the species identified. The buttons were small and positioned so that it was not possible to hold the button and see the light in all instances. The buttons for each diorama were replaced with larger ones, easier to manipulate, and moved to a console in front of the exhibit.

Animal mounts

Three-dimensional representations of some of the species in the diorama were added in the gallery. These included a mounted specimen of a beaver and one of a black bear positioned near their respective dioramas. Two bird models, made of bronze, were also displayed. Each of the animal models could be touched.

Interactive exhibits

Three free-standing hands-on displays related to animal adaptations, the theme of the exhibit, were installed. They were animal coverings to touch and to view through a microscope, a comparison of animal features with human tools (e.g. claws and a hand cultivator), each of which had model animal parts and human tools that could be touched and wooden pieces from which various mock animals could be constructed. All three new components illustrate a feature of animal adaptation. Also, all of them are deliberately relatively 'low-tech', easily constructed and installed in any museum setting.

Exhibit introduction

A triangular kiosk explaining the exhibit was provided in the open entrance of the gallery, and some materials on the floor unrelated to the exhibit's theme were removed.[1]

During the interim period, some but not all of the new components were installed. The additional components were also tried out in several versions. For example, some labels were altered after visitors were observed to have difficulty seeing them; the structure of the free-standing components was modified after it was noted that visitors in wheel-chairs had difficulty using them, and the placement of components was modified.

An important feature of the final renovations was that all descriptive components were installed consistently in parallel locations; for example, earphones were always placed at the right-hand edge of the panels and free-standing exhibits. In addition, label and recorded message information contained considerable redundancy; repeated material was one of the various forms used to provide the visitor with access.

EVALUATION PLAN

We carried out three separate but related activities:

1 formative feedback to the exhibit designers as components were added to the gallery. This work was carried out throughout the period of the modifications; it consisted of discussions with exhibit designers based both on the structured observations and interviews used in the summative evaluation and informal observation of general visitors and visitors with special needs.
2 case-studies of groups of special-needs visitors who were invited to use exhibits after some or all of the modifications were complete.
3 observation of general visitor behaviour and interviews (a) before modifications, (b) approximately halfway through the modifications, and (c) after all the changes had been made. This paper reports primarily the results of the third evaluation component.

For the structured observations, visitors and visitor groups were chosen at random and observed from one position in the gallery. Since the entire exhibit was contained in a single large room with no major obstructions, there was no need to track visitors as they proceeded through the gallery. The first person (or group) who entered the exhibit area was selected for observation. When one observation was finished, the next person (or group) to enter was observed, and so on. One visitor group was defined as one unit of observation. The dates of observations, number of visitors observed, and composition of groups are recorded in Table 24.1.[2]

Table 24.1 Numbers and percentages of visitor groups observed and interviewed

Composition of groups	Observations					
	Baseline 7–27 Aug. 1987		Interim 20 Apr.–14 May 1988		Final 7 Feb.–5 May 1989	
	No.	%	No.	%	No.	%
Adult-only groups	36	53	25	25	13	16
Mixed groups	25	37	69	68	57	70
Children	7	10	8	8	12	15
Total number of groups observed	68	100	102	101	82	101

	Interviews		
	18 Aug.–3 Sept. 1987	8–13 June 1988	5–20 Apr. 1989
Total, all groups	37	29	31

For the interviews, the first available person (or group) exiting the exhibit when the interviewer was ready after completing the previous interview was selected and questions were directed to the group. Multiple responses were encouraged and tabulated as separate opinions. Therefore, the total number of answers to any one question can exceed the sample size. Interviews were conducted at approximately the same time as observations and included primarily open-ended questions. The interview form used for the first 10 baseline interviews was modified for all subsequent interviews. Quantitative comparisons reported in this paper are for questions that were consistent for the two forms. Not every respondent answered each question.

The interview sample included all three categories of visitors – adults, mixed age groups, and children – as did the observations. Since the interview sample was gathered by the same method as was the observation sample, at comparable times, the two samples are likely to have the same composition.

RESULTS

The observation study provided information on visitor composition and behaviour, primarily on length of time in the gallery and flow patterns. The interview study provided information on visitor attitudes and learning. All data in the following tables and figures refer to the sample sizes indicated in Table 24.1.

1 Audience composition

The data in Table 24.1 illustrates that as the exhibit changed to include more interactive materials, so did the composition of the audience who viewed it. The proportion of children and family groups increased. In the same period, there were no significant variations in the composition of the Museum of Science audience that could account for this change.

2 Time in gallery

Visitor time in the gallery has gone up dramatically following the modifications. This is true both for average time and the fraction of visitors who spend more than three minutes there. Conversely, and illustrating the same trend, the number of in-and-out visitors has decreased dramatically (Tables 24.2 and 24.3, Figure 24.1).

Table 24.2 Time in gallery

Average time in gallery	Baseline Minutes	Interim Minutes	Final Minutes
Children	1.0	3.0	2.6
Mixed groups	3.0	3.9	5.3
Adults	3.3	2.9	6.1
All visitors	3.1	3.6	5.3

Table 24.3 Percentage of all visitors in gallery

	Baseline %	Interim %	Final %
3 minutes or more	50	52	73
1–2 minutes	31	38	23
Less than one minute	19	10	4

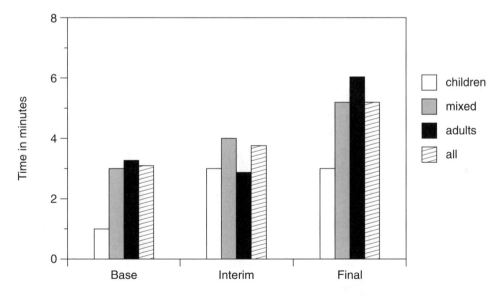

Figure 24.1 Average length of time spent in the hall by groups of visitors

3 Visitor flow patterns

In the baseline data, the predominant patterns observed among all visitors were groups who stopped and looked at several displays, those who browsed through the gallery in constant motion, and a high proportion of visitors (approximately one-third) who walked into the gallery and straight out again or walked in, looked at the moose exhibit and perhaps the beaver lodge, and then turned and went out.

In the interim data, and more clearly in the final evaluation, when all the components were on the floor, a number of other patterns emerged. As the quantitative data demonstrate, the number of in-and-out visitors had decreased. In addition, the new components filling the centre of the gallery encouraged movement between them, particularly for the groups with children. There was also a physical dialogue, movement back and forth between activity stations and diorama windows. This was particularly evident around the bear and beaver mounts and their related exhibits.

Finally, many children and some special-needs groups showed a preference for a particular sensory modality. They made a circuit of the smell boxes, the touch models, the auditory labels (earphones), and even the bird lights.

The net result of these varied visitor flow patterns was that the visitors, when viewed as a whole, appeared to engage in random motion through the exhibits; but this randomness resolved itself into purposeful paths when individual visitors were observed.

4 Attracting power

The attracting power of each exhibit component – that is, the fraction of the total visitors who stopped before that component – could be determined from the observation data. For this study, attracting power is defined as any instance in which there is an indicator in the field note that the visitor has had some observable interaction with the exhibit component. The results for the original dioramas and after modification are provided (Table 24.4, Figure 24.2).

Before the modification, there was clearly a major difference in attracting power for the various dioramas; the moose, with almost 66 per cent of visitors stopping before it, was more than four times as popular as the deer, which had only 16 per cent attracting power. After the changes, the difference between the various dioramas decreased; all of them fall in a band of attracting power at 60 per cent ± 10 per cent, with the difference between the most popular and the least only 19 per cent. In addition, most of the new free-standing components also attract up to approximately 60 per cent of the visitors.

The qualitative observations and the interviews support these results. A teacher who entered the room asking his students if they wanted to see the moose got sidetracked at the microscope. The class never did get to the moose. In another group, Cub Scout leaders tried to get their group away from the microscope by talking about the moose. When they failed to move the group into the gallery, the leaders asked if the scouts wanted to see the lightning show. The group moved on. Parents often surveyed the gallery and spotted the build-a-beast as something for their children to do. 'Here's something for Jamie to do.' Groups of kids were most animated by the activity stations and called back and forth between them, 'Come, see this.'

When visitors were asked 'Which of the exhibits in this room do you like the best?' the moose was most frequently mentioned in the baseline data. In the summative data the bear was the most popular exhibit, and the deer, the beaver and the 'touching' things all were mentioned more frequently than the moose.

Table 24.4 Attracting power of exhibit components (per cent of visitors who stop and interact with exhibit)

Component	Baseline %	Interim* %	Final† %
Coastal birds	37	19	61
Beaver	41	56	68
Moose	66	48	70
Shore birds	43	32	59
Deer	16	22	59
Bear	32	21	59
Smell box†		25	–
Build-a-beast		27	37
Microscope		41	54
Tools			34
Beaver mount			59
Bear mount			63

* As the exhibits were modified, the number of components increased. Some components were present during both interim and final evaluation phases, others were added after the interim observations.

† During the interim period, a smell box was installed as a separate component. In the final phase, smell boxes were incorporated into the panels in front of each diorama.

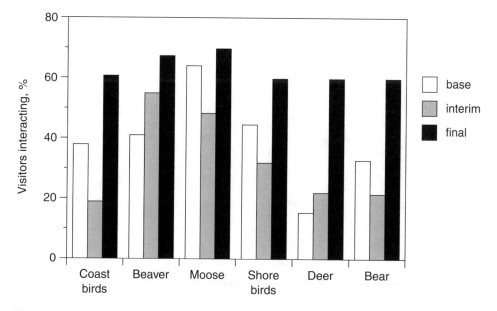

Figure 24.2 The attracting power of dioramas at three stages

5 Label use

Both observations and interviews indicated that after changes visitors interacted more with the labels, both written and recorded. (See samples of labels on pages 231–3.) The recorded labels were particularly popular; after modifications, more than twice as many visitor groups (72 per cent compared to 34 per cent) were observed using the recorded labels as compared to the written labels.

In the interviews, visitors were specifically asked about their use of labels. The responses to the question 'Did the labels provide you with any information?' are summarized in Figure 24.3. They indicate that the exhibit modifications increased the use of labels both in the amount and in the diversity of information obtained.

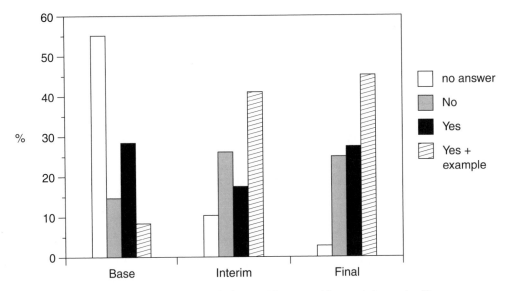

Figure 24.3 Responses to 'Did the labels provide you with any information?'

In the baseline data, half the sample did not answer this question, and an additional 15 per cent said that they didn't read the labels. Only 7 per cent of the visitors could give specific new information. In the final data, 45 per cent of the respondents gave some piece of information, including references to reading about the mounted animal specimens, and bird and place identification. Those who reported new information included some who cited examples from both the recorded tapes and the activity stations, as well as from the printed labels. Identification of birds was the most frequent animal-related information, followed by reference to the bear label on hibernation.

In general, the level of information and knowledge in the final data interviews and observations (from conversations overheard) showed an increase from baseline to the interim data, and from interim to final data, although the acknowledged reading of labels decreased for the interim data, compared to the baseline data. This combination of results suggests that information increasingly came from sources other than the written diorama labels; visitors knew more, and they gained that knowledge in a variety of ways. For example, when asked if he read the labels, one visitor said, 'No', but when asked to give an example of some new information, he repeated the recorded beaver label almost verbatim. Another 'no' response to the question about reading labels was coupled with the response to the question about gaining new information 'reading about the tool things'. Visitors also cited 'the smells' and 'that beaver fur feels soft' as new information they had learned from the exhibits – information obviously gained through means other than reading.

Whitetail Deer Diorama: Labels for the original, interim and final whitetail deer diorama and audio script for the final exhibit.

Original Label: Left of diorama

WHITETAIL DEER
Odocoilius virginianus

SQUAM LAKE, NEW HAMPSHIRE

WHITETAIL DEER, OFTEN CALLED "VIRGINIA DEER," ARE THE MOST PLENTIFUL AND BEST KNOWN OF AMERICAN BIG GAME MAMMALS. THEY LIVE IN OPEN WOODLANDS, USUALLY NEAR WATER, EATING GRASS, TWIGS AND LEAVES. WHEN STARTLED, THESE DEER BOUND AWAY, THEIR WHITE TAILS RAISED AS A SIGNAL OF ALARM.

THE DOE (FEMALE DEER) AND FAWNS SHOWN IN THIS EXHIBIT SPEND THE SUMMER TOGETHER; THE BUCK STAYS ALONE. WHITETAILS LIVE ABOUT TWELVE YEARS.

FAVORITE FOODS Many of the plants shown are favorites on the deer menu; blueberry, wild cherry, sensitive ferns, wild rose, lichens, and swamp grass. Can you recognize them? In the fall they gorge on acorns.

THE DEER'S YEAR The deer's mating season is in November. The fawns, usually twins, are born in June, and are concealed from enemies by their spotted coats which resemble the sunflecked forest floor. In winter, a small band of bucks, does and half grown fawns yard up in a sheltered place, trampling the snow to make feeding easier.

ANTLERS Only the buck has antlers, which are shed in January. New antlers begin to grow in April or May and are first covered with sensitive skin, or "velvet." In August, the antlers are fully formed and the velvet is rubbed off, leaving hard, sharp spikes for battling other males during the mating season.

HISTORY Whitetail deer were valuable game animals to the Indians and early settlers. The slaughter was so great that whitetails almost became extinct but under protection of the law they have now increased to an estimated four million in the United States. In some areas the food supply is not sufficient to last through the winter, and many deer would starve if hunters did not reduce the numbers.

RACES There are several races of whitetail deer, varying in weight from 35 to 400 pounds, ranging over most of North America. Related forms are found in South America.

SEE THE LABEL TO THE RIGHT FOR INFORMATION ABOUT THE LOCATION OF THIS GROUP.

Original Label: Right of diorama

ENVIRONMENT OF THE WHITETAIL DEER GROUP

THIS EXHIBIT SHOWS ONE OF NEW HAMPSHIRE'S MOST TYPICAL SIGHTS — WOODED LAKE SHORE WITH MOUNTAINS IN THE BACKGROUND. THE SCENE IS SET AT SQUAM LAKE IN CENTRAL NEW HAMPSHIRE, ON THE AFTERNOON OF A BRIGHT JUNE DAY. THIS KIND OF HABITAT IS PERFECT FOR DEER. THE OPEN WOODS ALLOW LIGHT TO REACH THE FOREST FLOOR SO THAT PLANTS AND SHRUBS CAN GROW WITHIN THE DEER'S REACH. SUCCULENT PLANTS GROW AT THE WATER'S EDGE, AND THE DEER ENJOY LYING IN THE SHALLOWS AND SWIMMING IN THE LAKE. THE BREEZES OF THE OPEN LAKE SHORE BLOW AWAY FLIES AND MOSQUITOES.

THE COMMON LOON is the water bird that startles summer visitors with its wild ringing cry. This large submarine-like bird is a strong diver, and uses its wings and feet for swimming under water after fish. Its range is eastern North America from Labrador to the Gulf of Mexico.

THE EASTERN CHIPMUNK is an industrious hoarder, gathering great quantities of fruits, seeds and nuts, which it carries in its capacious cheek pouches to its underground nest. During cold weather it hibernates in its burrow, occasionally nibbling on the food stored under its bed. It lives in the eastern United States and Canada.

THE DOWNY YELLOW LADY'S SLIPPER and the STEMLESS LADY'S SLIPPER (MOCCASIN FLOWER) are rare native orchids and *should not be picked*. The large pouch contains nectar which attracts insects, who pay for their meal by carrying fertilizing pollen from one flower to another.

THE PAINTED TRILLIUM and the NODDING TRILLIUM, JACK-IN-THE-PULPIT and BUNCHBERRY are other flowers on the *do not pick* list.

SQUAM LAKE lies in a lowland formed by the erosion of mountains made of soft rock by streams before glacial times, over two million years ago. The glaciers scraped and rounded the mountains still more. When the ice melted, it deposited masses of rocky debris that it had carried along with it. This dammed many of the valleys so that water could not drain out of them, and lakes were formed. The surrounding mountains are composed of more resistant rock that was not worn down as much by the streams and glaciers. The prominent Rattlesnake Mountains and Mount Morgan are made of such resistant rock. More information about the geology of central New Hampshire can be found in the Black Bear environment label.

SEE THE LABEL TO THE LEFT FOR INFORMATION ABOUT THE DEER.

Interim Label: Left of diorama

IT IS A JUNE AFTERNOON AT SQUAM LAKE, IN NEW HAMPSHIRE. THESE WHITETAIL DEER, A MOTHER AND HER TWO FAWNS, HAVE COME TO DRINK. THEY WILL SPEND MOST OF THE DAY BACK IN THE WOODS, RESTING QUIETLY, OUT OF SIGHT OF THEIR ENEMIES. IN A MOMENT,

THE SWIMMING LOON WILL DISAPPEAR UNDERWATER. THESE BLACK AND WHITE BIRDS ARE EXPERT UNDERWATER FISHERMEN.

THE DEER – Deer are plant eaters, not hunters. In New England, their chief enemies are people, dogs and coyotes. You could walk in the woods for hours and never see a deer, even if there are many around. WHY? A deer hears you, smells you and leaves, long before you get close. Its keen senses are the deer's best defense. Deer can run fast; about 35–40 miles per hour, but they tire quickly at that speed. Dogs run more slowly, but they can keep going. Often, dogs catch up with a deer when it becomes too tired to move on.

• Look at the deer. How do its long legs and large ears help it to live in its environment?

A hungry coyote might pass within a few feet of a fawn, and never notice it. WHY? These speckled fawns are too small to escape by running, but they have other defenses. They are born knowing how to lie as still as a stone. Their speckles make them hard to see. And newborn fawns have no deer odor at all.

The deer are in their tan summer coats. Their winter fur is different.

You can see and feel a deer's winter coat, at the activity station on your left.

Interim Label: Right of diorama

THE HABITAT – Squam Lake is surrounded by white pine trees (evergreens). There are also alders, wild cherry and other broadleafed trees. The forest floor is covered with early summer flowers.

• Look on your left for daisies, orange Indian paintbrush, and pink trillium. Look on your right, for the chipmunk sitting on a rock. It is surrounded by white bunchberry, pink lady's slipper, Indian paintbrush, striped Jack-in-the-pulpit and pink wild rose.

Final Label: Left of diorama
Whitetail Deer at Squam Lake

IT IS A JUNE AFTERNOON AT SQUAM LAKE, IN NEW HAMPSHIRE. THESE WHITETAIL DEER, A MOTHER AND HER TWO FAWNS, HAVE COME TO DRINK. THEY WILL SPEND MOST OF THE DAY BACK IN THE WOODS, RESTING QUIETLY, OUT OF SIGHT OF THEIR ENEMIES.

THE DEER − Deer are plant eaters, not hunters. In New England, their chief enemies are people, dogs and coyotes. You can walk in the woods for hours, and never see a deer, even if there are many around. WHY? A deer smells you, hears you and leaves, long before you get close. Its keen senses are the deer's best defense.

A hungry coyote might pass within a few feet of a fawn, and never notice it. WHY? These speckled fawns are too small to escape by running, but they have other defenses. They are born knowing how to lie as still as a stone. Their speckles make them hard to see. And newborn fawns have no deer odor at all.

• Look at the deer. How do its long legs and large ears help it to live in its environment? A deer's coat is tan in summer and brown-grey in winter. Naturalists refer to the summer coat as "red phase" and the winter coat as "brown phase."

OTHER ANIMALS − In a moment, the swimming loon will disappear under water. These black and white birds are expert underwater fishermen.

Final Label: Right of diorama

THE HABITAT − Squam Lake is surrounded by white pine trees and a variety of broadleafed trees. Near the shore, alders and wild cherry trees are growing in the moist soil. The forest floor is covered with early spring flowers. There is enough water and sunlight for many plants to grow here.

• Look on the left side of the diorama, for daisies, orange Indian paintbrush and pink trillium. Look to the right, for the chipmunk sitting on a rock. It is surrounded by white bunchberry, pink lady's slipper, Indian paintbrush, striped Jack-in-the-pulpit and pink wild rose.

Deer Audio Script

SOUND (birds, spring calls) Listen . . . It is almost summer at Squam Lake in central New Hampshire. The animals are active again, and the woods are bright with the color of new leaves and late spring wildflowers. Especially around the lakeshore, where sunlight and water are abundant, you can see daisies, orange and yellow hawkweed, ladyslippers, blue flag, white bunchberries and wild roses. You might, on this warm afternoon, notice the aroma of wild rose. Perhaps the breeze will bring a faint odor of deer.

SOUND (birds, green frog) The songs of the birds, the twang of the green frog, and the nighttime choruses of other frogs − all are aimed at attracting potential mates. Spring is mating season for all these creatures. Three whitetail deer, a doe and her two spotted fawns, have come to drink and browse the new growth along the shore. They spend most of the day resting quietly in the woods, hidden from their greatest enemies − people, domestic dogs and coyotes. Nighttime is safer: at dusk, the deer begin to move towards food and water.

SOUND (loon) The loon is alarmed. It is warning its mate of danger. Perhaps something is approaching their nest. These black and white water birds will not nest or live on a lake which has too many people. As New England's lakes and ponds become more congested, fewer and fewer of these beautiful birds can be seen. In many places, they are now only a memory.

6 Audience understanding of exhibit themes

An important goal of the modifications was to increase all visitors' understanding of the fundamental organizational concepts of the dioramas; that each diorama represents a typical New England environment (in fact, an actual place in New England), that these environments show diversity, and that the plants and animals in each diorama are typical of that environment and adapted to do well in that particular habitat.

(a) Connections between exhibits

The general conceptual organization of the gallery was apparent to visitors before modifications; in the baseline data, 50 per cent of the respondents could connect at least two out of the three ideas associated with New England Lifezones, but only one answer mentioned all three aspects. In the final data, 33 per cent of the visitors interviewed could connect all three aspects. Both the observations and the interviews provide direct evidence of the impact of the new interactive components on the topic of exhibit themes. For example, when asked about a connection between the dioramas in the final interviews, 9 per cent of the respondents said that they 'all smelled'. In the notes from the observations, one woman said to a child, 'Each one has the smell of a habitat ... where the animals live, and they got its smell.'

(b) Knowledge of adaptation

Visitors were asked before and after exhibit changes whether they could give examples of animal adaptation. The responses changed dramatically after the exhibit included the additional components. This can be illustrated by the visitors' responses to a specific question concerning the moose and the beaver. Visitors were shown a picture of a moose and a beaver and asked, 'Can you think of any part of this animal or things about it which might make it good at living where it does or how it does?' Respondents were encouraged to give as many answers as they could. In the baseline interviews, more than half the visitors could give no response to this question. At the time of the final evaluation, all visitors could give at least one adaptive feature for these animals, and the range of different adaptations mentioned had increased from only 6 for the two animals in the baseline data to a total of 25 (Figure 24.4).

The change in the knowledge about adaptation becomes especially clear when the kinds of responses that visitors gave during the various phases of the exhibit are compared. Table 24.5 provides this information. Visitors were shown pictures of the beaver and the moose and asked to name a specific adaptive feature of these animals after they had viewed the exhibit. In the baseline interviews, few visitors (under 10 per cent) could name any one feature, and the different adaptive features mentioned are small and encompass only the most obvious characteristics of these animals. After the modifications, a much larger percentage of visitors can think of adaptive features, but even more striking is the range of features that they suggest. It is evident that this longer list includes attributes that were noted through interaction with the beaver mount, from information on the recorded messages, or through other interactions in addition to reading the labels.

In the final evaluation, all the visitors who responded could name at least one adaptive feature for the beaver or the moose as compared to 89 per cent in the interim data; 88 per cent named more than two features for each, contrasted with only 32 per cent in the interim data.

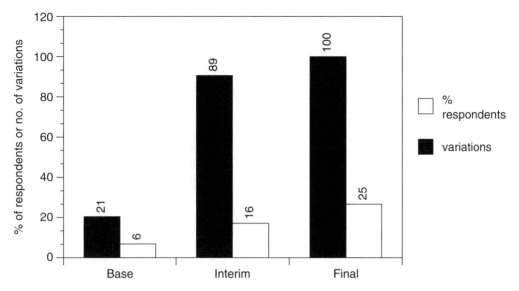

Figure 24.4 Percentage of visitors who can name at least one adaptation feature for beaver and moose, and number of different features cited

DISCUSSION

The modifications in the exhibits in the New England Lifezones Hall at the Boston Museum of Science have produced a significant alteration in visitor behaviour patterns. The time that visitors spend in the gallery has increased, the manner in which they interact with the exhibits has become more active, and they learn more from their visit to the exhibit. The quantitative data support these findings, but in many ways the qualitative are more revealing of the new feeling in the gallery.

The gallery has changed from a rather quiet, secluded place favoured by adults to a livelier hall populated by families and children. The noise level has increased, and the mood has altered. During the collection of baseline data, we observed many adult couples in the gallery who appeared to appreciate the relative seclusion and quiet of the gallery at least as much as the exhibits. This population does not appear as frequently after alteration. Museums may want to consider the potential negative impact of modifications on some audience segments before they remove all of the quieter galleries.

Before the changes, it was possible to observe many visitors as they walked through the gallery in traditional museum style, circling by the exhibits at the periphery of the room in clockwise or counterclockwise direction. After the modifications, the general visitation pattern appeared much more random. At any moment, the overall behaviour of visitors in the gallery seemed unsystematic. Some visitors went from diorama to diorama, others wandered across the room, and still others shuttled back and forth between particular sensory components.

However, when groups were tracked, it became clear that individuals followed purposeful paths. Just as adult couples, intent on reading labels, had been the predominant group before modifications, children who followed particular sensory modes

Table 24.5 Adaptive features mentioned for beaver and moose. An 'x' indicates a feature mentioned by at least one visitor. Per cent frequencies are given for features mentioned by more than 10 per cent of visitors

	Baseline		Interim		Final	
	No.	%	No.	%	No.	%
Beaver						
Teeth	x		x	71	x	82
Tail	x		x	43	x	84
Fur	x		x	25	x	41
Claws/paws			x	11	x	44
(Webbed) feet			x		x	22
Fat			x	11	x	
Colour			x		x	
Mouth			x			
Oil in fur					x	
Shape/body					x	
Nose					x	
Ears					x	
Membrane over eyes					x	
Soft					x	
Lungs					x	
Moose						
Antlers	x		x	39	x	66
Size	x		x	21	x	38
Hooves/feet	x		x	14	x	25
Fur			x	14	x	22
Long legs			x	11	x	22
Snout/nose			x		x	13
Fat			x		x	
Colour			x		x	
Ears					x	
Big heart					x	
Teeth					x	

became predominant after modifications. Children went from smell box to smell box, from earphone to earphone or from one hands-on activity station to the next. Analysis of the data suggests that children are making rational choices, indulging in preferred sensory learning modes (Gardner 1983), consistent with the general recognition that children's thoughts and actions are usually purposeful (Duckworth 1990; Hein 1988) when appropriate choices are available to them. This analysis suggests that the criticism often levelled at interactive exhibits – that they encourage aimless wandering from one exhibit to another – may need to be re-examined.

The data on attracting power are particularly rich in their implications. The addition of interpretive panels giving visitors the opportunity to learn about the dioramas using a wider range of senses has increased the attracting power of even the least popular dioramas. This suggests that traditional museum displays can be made interesting to a larger fraction of visitors with relatively minor modifications. The addition of hands-on components has added to the visitor time in the gallery; it has not detracted from the power of the dioramas to attract visitors. Visitors now stop both to look at the deer, moose and bears and to peer in the microscope or to build-a-beast. The persistence of approximately 60 per cent as a maximum attracting power for all the dioramas, as well as for the other components, suggests a natural upper limit for exhibit components regardless of modifications.

This robust interest in traditional museum cases suggests that museums may wish to consider adding interpretive panels, materials and activities to extant exhibits to allow for more physical and intellectual involvement by visitors, rather than eliminating the traditional cases in favour of only hands-on interactive exhibits. In some science museums, the actual artefacts are increasingly being replaced by videoscreens, models and other components that make hands-on interaction easier for some visitors, but the new galleries lose the flavour of the original collections. These interactive galleries are often thin on actual museum objects. Also, videoscreens as an interactive component exclude blind visitors and, depending on placement, may not be accessible to wheelchair users. Our results suggest that an alternative and inexpensive strategy may be to preserve the more traditional cases and exhibits but to increase access by adding multisensory interpretive components.

Our questions to visitors concerning label use provided surprising results. When asked what they had gained from the exhibit, it became clear that visitors responded with information they had obtained from many sources: reading, listening, smelling and touching. As educators and exhibit designers, we are conditioned to believe that conscious acquisition of information by visitors comes from written information. Our studies indicate that under the right circumstances, visitors are clearly able to synthesize information from many different sensory modalities into personal learning that they can articulate to an interviewer.

Redundant information provided by the variety of modalities was clearly of value for both the general public and special-needs groups. In addition, consistency of placement was noted as an important component leading to accessibility. During the interim modification phase as the placement of exhibit components changed, the gallery did not have the unified, consistent pattern finally achieved. The impact of this variation was noted especially with the handicapped visitors. For example, blind visitors simply would not find an earphone if they had discovered it at the left-hand side of one panel and it was placed at the right-hand side of the next panel they encountered. But all visitors responded in some way to this lack of consistency. If the second smell box they tried was not working, visitors would stop trying to use other smell boxes. The need for consistent basic design features and functioning exhibits is usually acknowledged, but the desire for interactive exhibits sometimes leads exhibit designers to disregard redundant labelling and mechanical consistency. This results in an increased physical and intellectual strain on visitors, making the exhibits less accessible.

A final point is the value of accessible exhibit design and content for all audiences. We think of making accommodations for people with special needs, but what we consistently saw is that these modifications constituted significant improvement in length of time spent and learning outcomes for *all* visitors. Multisensory learning opportunities not only provide a way to reach challenged audiences, but also provide an appropriate challenge for all visitors.

This chapter first appeared as a paper in Curator 34(4) (1991): 273–90.

NOTES

1 A full description of the exhibit modifications is contained in the final project report (Davidson 1991).
2 At the request of the museum staff, the second set of observations was carried out on both school visitation days and non-school days, although the original evaluation design had focused only on non-school visitors. Because schoolchildren were not a specific target audience for developing the new components, there is no comparable school visitation time in the baseline data. However, observation of school groups did help us to understand the patterns of this audience segment with the installation.

REFERENCES

Bloomer, R. (1987) private communication.
Davidson, B. (1991) *New Dimensions for Traditional Dioramas: Multisensory Additions for Access, Interest and Learning*, Boston, MA: Museum of Science.
Disabilities Study Quarterly (1990) special issue, 'Disability Demographics' 10(3).
Duckworth, E. (1990) 'Museum visitors and the development of understanding', *Journal of Museum Education* 15(1): 4–6.
Gardner, H. (1983) *Frames of Mind*, New York, NY: Basic Books.
Hein, G. E. (1988) 'How do children behave in museums?', *La Investigació de le'educator de museus*, Barcelona: Ajuntament de Barcelona (ICOM/CECA Conference Proceedings), 243–50.

Part IV
Thinking about museum audiences

The final section is the longest. It begins with two chapters that examine core assumptions about museum audiences, both in the past and at the present time. Tony Bennett's Chapter 25 offers a valuable analysis of patterns of museum use in Australia and contextualizes this within one view of museum history. Chapter 27 is a fascinating case-study of how the prior preconceptions of visitors influenced their interpretations in an exhibition and how these varied from the intended aims of the curators.

Chapters 28 and 29 discuss issues that are specific to certain audience groups. Both are concerned with barriers to access: physical access and cultural access.

The next six chapters 30–35, describe a range of approaches to evaluation in museums and galleries. Together, these give information on appropriate methods for small-scale studies, which are the type of studies most likely to be undertaken by students.

Finally, broad issues concerning the experience of the visitor from the perspective of environmental psychology are raised in the context of the museum as a whole.

25

That those who run may read

Tony Bennett

Evaluation and visitor research has developed very quickly in Australia. One of the museums involved in this development is the Powerhouse Museum in Sydney. This chapter comes from a paper delivered at a conference there in 1995. The writer is not a museum worker, but writes from a background in cultural studies.

Important issues are raised. Taking as his starting-point a statement from Henry Pitt Rivers in 1891, Bennett asks how far museums have come in increasing people's access to them in the intervening hundred years.

In answering this question, Bennett offers an overview of the pattern of museum use in contemporary Australia, and relates this both to the development of museum visitor studies and to current questions in cultural politics. The review of important sources in discussing the relationship between the museum and the public is extremely useful, although it must be pointed out that the model of the museum underpinning Bennett's argument is that of the large metropolitan art museum, 'The Museum' as I call it in the Introduction to the Reader.

Bennett's approach and conclusions are well researched and contentious. His central conclusion, for more effective learning opportunities, finds an echo in many of the other chapters in this Reader.

I have taken my title for this presentation from a somewhat obscure reference to Henry Pitt Rivers,[1] the founder of the typological method of museum display. In arranging the cultural materials of colonized peoples as the early stages of evolutionary sequences leading from the simple to the complex, from so-called 'primitive' to 'advanced' European standards of civilization, this method governed how many museums exhibited their ethnological collections from the 1870s through to the 1950s. A social Darwinist of sorts, Pitt Rivers thought that ethnological collections should be arranged to convey what he saw as the central message of evolutionary theory: that change, in societies as in species, came about slowly as a result of gradual and slow adaptations. The political import of this message was that attempts to force the rate of social change through revolution were doomed to failure. In extolling the virtues of the typological method, Pitt Rivers became a prominent advocate of the role which public displays of ethnological materials might play as a counter to socialist agitation among the working classes. He accordingly paid a good deal of attention to the question of how best to arrange such materials for this purpose. Summarizing his aim as being that of constructing a museum environment 'in which the visitors may instruct themselves' in the lessons of progress (Pitt Rivers 1891: 115), he argued that this goal could be realized only if collections were 'arranged in such a manner that those who run may read' (ibid.: 115–16).

There is little doubt as to whom Pitt Rivers has in mind here. 'The working classes', he says in the next sentence, 'have but little time for study; their leisure hours are, and always must be, comparatively brief' (ibid.: 116). And it is for this reason that he recommends that great care be exercised in determining the object lessons museums should aim to communicate and in choosing clear and distinct methods of display to ensure that those messages could be fully understood by working-class visitors in the brief snatches of time available to them. But why he uses the term 'those who run' to refer to the working classes was something of a mystery to me until recently when, quite by accident, I happened on the solution. However, if only to add a little narrative suspense to my paper, I shan't divulge this until later.

I can, however, be less mysterious about my reasons for wanting to call Pitt Rivers to mind for this occasion. For my purposes in this paper are twofold. First, I want to summarize the findings of three recent studies of the social and cultural characteristics of those who do, and those who do not, visit museums and art galleries in contemporary Australia.[2] In doing so, I shall identify the light these studies throw on the degree to which access to museums and art galleries is impeded by cultural factors as well as on the steps that might be taken to remove or minimize the effects of such cultural barriers to access. But I want also to anchor these debates in the longer history of museum visitor studies. Detailed and systematic statistical surveys of museum visitors are, of course, a relatively recent phenomenon. A concern with who goes to museums, why, and what they do when they get there, however, can be traced right back to the period of the modern museum's early formation – back, that is, at least as far as the 1830s. More to the point, while there are important differences, there are also striking continuities between the concerns which motivated those early inquiries and those which inform more recent studies. The evolutionary message Pitt Rivers was concerned to communicate can, today, count only as a negative model. Yet it is not difficult to see in his concern to design museum displays so that 'those who run may read' a forerunner of the concerns that would nowadays be brought under the heading of intellectual access policies. By tracing parallels of this kind and so placing modern access surveys in a historical perspective, my purpose is to identify the constraints which have proved systemic in limiting access to museums, and especially art galleries, with a view to suggesting what measures might be necessary to overcome those constraints.

CULTURAL BARRIERS TO ACCESS

Let me come first, then, to the three studies referred to earlier and the light these throw on the social and cultural characteristics of museum and art gallery visitors and non-visitors. The first comprised a survey, administered on site, of 510 visitors at three social history museums run by the History Trust of South Australia (see Bennett *et al.* 1991). The second asked a related set of questions of 518 visitors at three art galleries in South Australia and was, again, administered on site at each of those galleries (see Bennett and Frow 1991). The third comprised a telephone survey of 403 non-goers defined as those who had not visited either an art gallery or a museum over the previous five years or more (see Bennett 1994). In each case, the questionnaire was designed to allow correlations to be established between (1) patterns of visiting (or non-visiting), (2) a range of demographic indicators of social position (age, income, occupation, gender, education, etc.), (3) attitudes toward art galleries and museums, and toward different kinds of art or history, and (4) the respondents' broader cultural tastes and preferences as evidenced by the extent of their participation in other cultural pursuits.

The theoretical approach was derived from the work of Pierre Bourdieu and Alain Darbel whose now classic 1969 study *The Love of Art* showed that, at least in the European context, the most important barriers to more broadly based patterns of participation in museums and art galleries were cultural rather than economic (see Bourdieu and Darbel 1991). Bourdieu and Darbel found, that is to say, that level of educational attainment and occupational status had a more direct bearing on museum and gallery attendance than level of income. This is not to say that income had no role in such matters. Its role, however, was an indirect one, mediated through the part it plays in helping secure the forms and levels of education and professional status associated with, in particular, art gallery usage.

Let me put the point another way by (if it's still allowed) taking issue with a Prime Minister. In the midst of the Thai-teak table saga, Mr Keating, at the point where his fondness for wildlife prints had been called into question, ripped into the Opposition as a bunch of nouveau-riche philistines who failed to realize that 'You can't write a cheque for taste'. To which Bourdieu and Darbel might well have replied: 'True, but you can write a cheque for education' – through private education, for example, but, more generally, though the ability of the middle classes to support the long educational careers involved in the acquisition of higher secondary and tertiary qualifications – and it is education, as the most frequent route to high occupational status, that provides those cultural trainings, abilities and interests that are most frequently associated with high levels of involvement in art galleries, museums and other high-cultural pursuits.

It is necessary to add, however, that, for Bourdieu, the connection between class, education, occupation and culture which such correlations point to is not an accidental or merely empirical one. Rather, he argues that there is, in most advanced western societies, a systematic connection between their educational systems and the institutions of high artistic and intellectual culture which works to ensure that cultural tastes, interests and abilities are selectively transmitted along class lines in ways which help to perpetuate existing class differences (see Bourdieu 1984). This is done, Bourdieu suggests, by organizing contexts (art galleries) and activities (visiting them) which, to the extent that they tend to be used mainly by the professional middle classes, serve as a means of marking a cultural distinction, of drawing a symbolic dividing line, between those classes – who alone seem to have cultivated tastes – and the rest of the population. That boundary line, it needs to be added, works in two directions, distinguishing the cultivated classes from rich philistines as well as from the 'vulgar' working classes.

In what is now a substantial body of argument and evidence, similar tendencies have been observed in other national contexts although often, as is suggested by American studies, the distinctions associated with art gallery usage are not as pronounced as those which Bourdieu has chronicled in the French context (see, for example, Dimaggio and Useem 1978 and Lamont 1992). There is little room for doubt that the same is true in Australia. The cumulative weight of the evidence provided by the three studies I referred to earlier makes it clear that museums, and art galleries in particular, are at the heart of a powerful social dynamic that is driven by relations of class and culture. This is not the place to review the statistical evidence in detail. However, it will prove useful to look briefly at a few selected indicators which suggest both that

Table 25.1 Income distribution (%)

Household Income	Non-Goers	Museum Visitors	Art Gallery Visitors
$20,000 and less	26	26	30
$20,000–$30,000	22	26	17
$30,000–$40,000	15	21	16
$40,000–$50,000	13	10	8
$50,000–$60,000	4	6	4
$60,000 or more	6	7	12
Refused	8	–	6
Didn't know	7	4	8

the major barriers to access are cultural and that those barriers are organized very much in class terms.

Table 25.1 shows that there are differences of income between art gallery and museum visitors on the one hand and non-goers on the other. Moreover, these differences are most pronounced at the uppermost level of the income range with the art gallery sample having a significantly higher proportion of its members in the $60,000-plus category than the other two samples. However, it is also clear that these differences are not sufficient, in and of themselves, to account for the differences in patterns of visitation. Within both the visitor samples, for example, rate of visitation showed little tendency to vary with income and there was little difference between the income profiles for visitors at institutions where entrance charges were levied compared with those at which admission was free. It is, then, safe to assume that few Australians are prevented from making greater use of museums and art galleries solely on economic grounds. However, it should be noted that the relatively high number of low income earners among the art gallery visitors is due to special factors: the high percentage of students (18%) in this sample.

When it comes to education, however, the differences are pronounced. History museum visitors exhibited considerably higher levels of educational attainment than the non-goers and the educational profiles of the art gallery visitors were higher still. Those with only primary and lower-secondary schooling accounted for 39% of the non-goers, 30% of the museum visitors and only 18% of the art gallery visitors (see Table 25.2). Conversely, while only 13% of the non-goers had tertiary qualifications, this was true of 35% of the museum visitors and 42% of the art gallery visitors, a further 18% of whom were students. Just as important, there was a discernible and strong connection between level of educational qualification and rate of visitation. For example, 71% of those with tertiary qualifications in the museum visitor sample were regular visitors – defined as having visited five times in the past five years – whereas this was true of only 39% of those with only primary or junior-secondary schooling. The comparable figures for the art gallery sample were 84% and 62%, this last figure including the student portion of the sample.

Similar patterns were evident in the occupational structures of the samples. As Table 25.3 shows, professionals accounted for only 13% of the non-goers compared with 27% of the museum visitors and 38% of the art gallery visitors. Conversely, 27% of the non-goers were in manual occupations compared with 20% of the museum visitors and 15% of the art gallery visitors. These differences are likely to be more magnified if account is taken of the very high percentage of students (18%) in the art gallery sample and the

Table 25.2   Educational attainment (%)

Level of attainment	Non-Goers	Museum Visitors	Art Gallery Visitors
Primary school	7	11	1
Secondary to Year 10	32	19	17
Completed high school	38	25	33
TAFE, diploma, etc.	10	8	8
University, CAE, degree	11	26	32
Postgraduate	2	9	10
Refused/not known	0	2	–

Table 25.3   Occupation (%)

Occupation	Non-Goers	Museum Visitors	Art Gallery Visitors
Professional	13	27	38
Clerical, sales or other white collar	16	14	11
Manual worker (skilled)	15	12	10
Manual worker (other)	12	8	5
Student	3	6	18
Homemaker	16	16	8
Unemployed	6	1	3
Retired	17	13	7
Other	1	3	0

relative youthfulness of art gallery visitors (39% under 29) in view of the likelihood that many of these would later move into professional occupations. Finally, as with education, rate of visitation increased with occupational status: 69% of the professionals in the museum visitor sample were regular visitors compared with 61% of clerical workers, 51% of skilled manual workers and 21% of semi- or unskilled manual workers.

The picture is much the same when we move to consider the other interests, tastes and activities of the different samples. These issues were explored through questions asking about general cultural and leisure pursuits, TV station and programme preference, ownership of art objects and literature, aesthetic tastes and preferences, and so on. Three general tendencies emerged. First, art gallery visitors were considerably more likely to have high rates of participation and involvement in activities invested with a high cultural status than were museum visitors who, in turn, had higher rates of involvement in such activities than the non-goers. Second, within each of these samples, participation in such activities varied directly and significantly in accordance with frequency of visitation. And third, such participation correlated positively with the educational and occupational markers of social class we have already reviewed. Table 25.4 throws some useful light on these matters in showing the degree to which art gallery visitors have a higher rate of preference for ABC and SBS viewing than history museum visitors who, in turn, are much more likely to view these stations than non-goers. A breakdown of the figures for the art gallery sample shows how this pattern of preference is reinforced with regularity of visitation: 69% of regular visitors reported a preference for ABC viewing and 34% a preference for SBS.

Table 25.4 TV station viewed most regularly (%)

Station	Non-Goers	View Most Regularly Museum Visitors	Art Gallery Visitors
Commercial	68	64	38
ABC	23	60	63
SBS	4	12	28
None/rarely	5	6	7

However, perhaps the best way of highlighting the interactions of class and culture these figures attest to is by considering the relations between demographic and cultural indicators suggested by the cluster analyses. Table 25.5, in juxtaposing a selection of the clusters produced for the art gallery and non-goers samples, vividly illustrates the systemic nature of the interconnections I am concerned with. It does so by bringing together the two extremes produced by the three samples and two intermediate clusters. Thus the confirmed non-goers had the highest non-visitation rates of the non-goers sample (60% had not visited a gallery in over ten years) and, in the attitudes they expressed, showed themselves quite determined to continue not going to art galleries. The members of this cluster, in other words, didn't just happen not to go to art galleries but rather actively chose to stay away. By contrast, the art apprentices had the lowest non-visitation rates of the non-goers sample (36% had not visited in over 10 years) while also showing an active interest in visiting more regularly. The third column gives the averages for the art gallery visitors sample as a whole while the final column summarizes some of the key cultural and demographic indicators for the art enthusiasts. These comprised the cluster in the art gallery visitors sample that visited galleries most regularly: 87% had visited a gallery on at least five occasions over the previous five years compared with a sample average of 63%.

What is most remarkable about these figures is the consistency of the correlations to which they attest. As, in moving from left to right, we encounter an ascending involvement in art galleries so we also encounter an ascending involvement in other high-cultural pursuits and tastes as well as ascending demographic indicators of class status. And so we also encounter, it is worth noting, an increasing representation of women – from only 38% of the confirmed non-goers to 65% of the art enthusiasts. This merely displays, in an exaggerated fashion, a tendency evident throughout the data: that of women's higher overall rates of participation in museums and art galleries. Women thus accounted for 59% of the museum visitor sample and for 63% of the art gallery visitor sample.[3]

It is possible, on the basis of these figures, to propose an identikit for each of the extremes represented. The archetypal gallery devotee thus emerges as a highly educated professional and relatively young woman with high degrees of involvement in other art and high-cultural activities who is likely to want art galleries to be more innovative and progressive both aesthetically and politically. By contrast, the confirmed non-goer is likely to be an ageing, poorly educated man in a manual or clerical occupation with little or no involvement in other artistic or high-cultural pursuits and relatively conservative aesthetic and political attitudes.

How should the implications of findings like these be assessed? It is a difficult question to answer in view of the often conflicting considerations which have to be taken

Table 25.5 Comparative characteristics of art gallery visitors and non-goers (%)

	Confirmed Non-Goers	Art Apprentices	Art Gallery Visitors (sample averages)	Art Enthusiasts
Percentage with practical experience of art	20	41	72	90
Percentage who have original works of art at home	22	50	80	87
Percentage who own art books or magazines	10	48	82	94
Percentage who own art postcards	11	20	70	81
Percentage who regularly participate in live theatre/classical music/opera	2	9	27	43
Percentage who prefer TV arts programmes	12	43	53	72
Percentage more likely to visit art galleries if they showed more:				
art by women	18	28	58	74
Aboriginal art	49	58	61	71
experimental video	16	37	57	70
ethnic/migrant art	19	53	64	83
Percentage aged < 29	21	32	36	40
Percentage aged > 50	45	32	17	11
Percentage with higher education degree	4	15	41	60
Percentage professional	5	17	38	53
Percentage female	38	45	59	65

into account in arriving at any concrete policy mix. There are good reasons why, in terms of their public educative functions and their capacity to reform public attitudes and values, art galleries should properly resist the suggestion that they should show more aesthetically and politically conservative art in order to tempt confirmed non-goers through their doors. And there may also be, at least for the present moment, good reasons for welcoming the fact that at least one significant cultural institution is proving to cater more to the interests of women than those of men. Yet such arguments can too easily slide over into unacceptable ones resulting in a complacency which sees merely the perpetuation of those aspects of art gallery practices which continue to inscribe the gallery as a key institutional player in the social processes through which class relations are culturally marked and organized. If this is not to be so, careful attention needs to be paid to those aspects of the art gallery's ethos which make it complicit with such processes. And it is in order to unravel these matters that I need, now, to return to those earlier debates, from which I took my initial bearings, intended to ensure that 'those who run may read'.

THE WRITING ON THE WALL

Why, then, to return to my earlier question, did Pitt Rivers use this term to refer to the working classes? And what was coded into this reference? I happened on an answer to these questions when reading John Barrell's account of John Barry's theories of painting and the part these played in late eighteenth and early nineteenth-century English debates regarding the role which art might play in forming a public and schooling it in the virtues expected of citizens. For Barry, himself a prominent painter, art's function was both to create a democratic republic of taste which would include all men and women and then to school this universal citizenry in the virtues and requirements of citizenship. It was to do so by serving as a vehicle for communicating the abstract moral and intellectual ideas required for effective citizenship, especially the need for individual wishes to be subordinated to the interests of the social whole. This resulted, Barrell suggests, in two slightly contradictory attitudes toward painting on Barry's part. In the first, by taking fables for their subject, paintings should aim to be 'immediately intelligible to the "unlettered"' (Barrell 1986: 188). In the second, however, paintings were to represent fables which, rather than being immediately intelligible, would need a further contextualizing commentary from 'the knowing' if their significance and value were to be communicated to 'the ignorant'. Here is how Barry puts the point in suggesting that the fable in a painting should not be 'so brought down to the understanding of the vulgar, that they who run may read: when the art is solely levelled to the immediate comprehension of the ignorant, the intelligent can find nothing in it, and there will be nothing to improve or to reward the attention even of the ignorant themselves, upon a second or third view' (ibid.).

Barry's target here is Sir Joshua Reynolds whose aesthetic theories drew a rigid distinction between, on the one hand, the liberal public, comprised essentially of landed and propertied men, and, on the other hand, women and those whom Reynolds called mechanics: members of the artisanal classes involved in manual or merely mechanical occupations. Only members of the liberal public, Reynolds argued, could become members of the republic of taste for only they possessed those capacities for abstract and disinterested reasoning required to distil from the particular details of the work of art those abstract and general moral qualities which would be of service in forming civic virtue. Women were denied this capacity for abstract thought, and they were denied it absolutely on the basis of their sex. Mechanics were also judged to lack this ability albeit that, in their case, this incapacity was viewed as a contingent one arising from the fact that the pursuit of mechanical occupations did not require the exercise of generalizing intellectual abilities.

For Reynolds, then, the proper administration of artistic institutions required that they rigorously reinforce the logic of these distinctions by excluding all those judged incapable of meeting the intellectual and cultural requirements of the liberal ideal of art. He therefore recommended that a charge be levied for admission to exhibitions at the Academy 'to prevent the room from being fill'd by improper Persons' (cited in Barrell 1986: 77). For Barry, by contrast, all are to be admitted to the public contexts in which art is exhibited: not in the expectation that, as he variously called them, the 'ignorant' or the 'vulgar' would spontaneously understand the civic value of the art displayed but, rather, in order that this might be explained to them by means of supplementary texts of one kind or another.

By the time, some fifty or sixty years later, we reach Pitt Rivers the museum is thought of as an automated learning environment – his aim was to organize displays in which 'the visitors may instruct themselves' – but one in which that same division of the public is still evident in the very attempt to bridge it. Unlike Barry, Pitt Rivers is concerned to organize a context in which 'those who run may read', and do so unaided, without textual supplements. But that those who run are still thought of in the same terms proposed by Reynolds becomes clear when Pitt Rivers further elaborates their characteristics. 'The more intelligent portion of the working classes', he says, 'though they have but little book learning, are extremely quick in appreciating all mechanical matters, more so even than highly educated men, because they are trained up to them; and this is another reason why the importance of the object lessons that museums are capable of teaching should be well considered' (Pitt Rivers 1891: 116).

But if Pitt Rivers's proposals echoed the earlier concerns of James Barry, they were also an advance on them, reflecting the experience of the intervening fifty or so years during which the museum and the art gallery – in the course of 'going public' – had emerged as highly formalized spaces of social observation. Much has been written about the emergence of prisons and asylums as specialized spaces in which the conduct of the criminal and the insane might be observed. Paralleling these developments, the museum and the art gallery also emerged as new kinds of social space, and ones which were regularly and intensely monitored with a view to throwing as much light as possible on the composition and conduct of their publics. The sophisticated statistical and observational techniques that are used in modern visitor studies were, of course, not in evidence. Nor was there any suggestion that it was important to know about these things to establish whether museums and art galleries were equitably meeting the cultural needs and rights of all sections of the population.

Yet, although not bound up with notions of cultural rights, questions of access did predominate in the earliest attempts to establish who used museums and art galleries and to find out how such visitors conducted themselves. Given that the policy rationale for opening such institutions to the public was governed by the conviction that exposing the general population to the improving influence of art and high culture would help to civilize that population – to wean it away from the bad habits of excessive drunkenness, gambling and debauchery and lead it to adopt more refined and elevating customs and manners – reforming opinion was ever-anxious to know whether, indeed, the working classes were visiting museums and art galleries and whether, whilst there, they behaved in ways which suggested the experience was having an improving influence on them. Francis Place, the prominent radical, presaged later developments in compiling statistics showing that attendance at London's art galleries increased on bank holidays, inferring from this their capacity to appeal to the working classes whose occupations made it difficult for them to visit at other times. By the end of the century, this kind of statistical monitoring had become routine with most major museums regularly reporting on their numbers of visitors over the weekends and bank holidays as evidence of their extensive use by the working classes (see Greenwood 1888).

The limited value of such purely quantitative indices was clearly identified by William Stanley Jevons when he noted, in 1888, that although the turnstiles at the South Kensington Art Museum were able 'to record the precise numbers of visitors' and so could calculate 'to a unit the exact amount of civilising effect produced in any day, week, month, or year', they were unable to say how many of those visitors were really gaining value from the experience or how many of them were from the social classes who most stood in need of the museum's 'civilising effect' (Jevons 1883: 55–6). How many of the museum's visitors, Jevons asked, were the children of the local well-to-do sent to run off their energies through the galleries on rainy days? Motivated by these concerns, the municipal museum in Liverpool, in one of the first visitor surveys conducted in Britain, found that 78% of its visitors came without any clearer purpose than to see the museum while 20% were children or 'loungers' (see Lewis 1989).

A similar set of concerns, albeit given a slightly different political twist, informed the later development of social science techniques in visitor surveys. The formative initiatives here were taken in America in the 1920s and 1930s. In a period when – at least in the United States – the language of museum administration was increasingly borrowed from that of scientific management, social science surveys were seen as necessary management aids if museums were to discharge their civic responsibilities effectively. Neil Harris has argued that this period of museum administration was governed by an ethos of what he calls 'authoritarian experimentalism'. The visitor, viewed in the terms of this ethos, was seen less as a citizen endowed with rights than as a citizen in need of the kinds of training in the nature and duties of citizenship which the museum could uniquely provide (see Harris 1990). Viewed from this perspective, the detailed knowledge of visitor behaviour provided by the social science survey was to guide museum managers in designing the museum environment in such a way as to enhance its ability to transmit civic virtue to the citizen. Yet these managerialist orientations could also be combined with radical populist sentiments as was most notably the case with John Cotton Dana, the Director of the Newark Museum. Dana thought that art galleries had degenerated into institutions for elite gazing, mere fashion centres for the idle rich. In his concern to transform art galleries into 'institutes of visual instruction', Dana attributed a crucial role to social science surveys to ensure that museums would achieve 'returns for their cost' in terms of civic benefits that would be 'in good degree positive, definite, visible, measurable' (Dana 1920: 13).

A similar mixture of authoritarian managerialism and radical populism is evident in T.R. Adams's classic 1937 text *The Civic Value of Museums*. Stating, quite unashamedly, that the duty of the art gallery in a democracy is to determine both what the public shall regard as art and the nature of the civic benefits to be derived from it, Adams sees their role in this regard as being limited by the fact that the 'crowds that wander through museum halls, looking where they like and conversing as they please, are as foot-loose as the street philosophers of ancient Athens' (Adams 1937: 13). He therefore looks to surveys of visitor habits for guidance on how to design the museum space in ways which, in regulating the conduct of the visitor in greater detail, will allow the museum to fulfil its civic role more effectively. Here is how he puts the matter:

> The larger and more richly stored the museum is, the greater the need for an effective plan of guidance for the average visitor. Otherwise, invisible barriers are put up against the general public. Though the physical doors of the museum remain open, the uninformed visitor finds himself at loose in a labyrinth of culture to which he lacks the secret. The minority who come armed with previous knowledge receive too great a proportion of the benefits of museum education.
>
> (Adams 1937: 31)

What interests me about this passage are the respects in which it stretches both forwards and backwards, suggesting a substantial continuity of critique of the art gallery on the part of reforming opinion from the mid-nineteenth century into the present, even though the political valency of that critique has varied. On the one hand, Adams's remarks stretch back to James Barry's conception of the need for clear written messages to supplement the paintings displayed in order that 'those who run may read'. They also connect with a whole tradition of museum reform in the nineteenth century, influential in both France and Britain, which aimed to refashion the space of the art gallery – through the introduction of the chronological hang, via streamlined displays which ended the baroque clutter of earlier arrangements in clearly separating individual works of art from one another, and through the provision of descriptive labels – in order to allow it to function more didactically for working-class visitors. Yet they also connect forward to the diagnoses of Pierre Bourdieu and Alain Darbel who, in explaining why modern art galleries appeal mainly to a restricted middle-class clientele, suggest that this is partly because most art galleries make little effort to contextualize the art they exhibit. They thus note that working-class visitors typically respond most positively to the provision of descriptive labels, guidebooks, or directions as to the best route to take through an art museum and that the cultivated classes are the most hostile to such attempts to make art more accessible. Bourdieu and Darbel suggest that this is because such pedagogic props, in implying that an appreciation of art is something which can be acquired through training, detract from the art gallery's capacity to confer a social distinction on those who, through the cultural capital they have acquired in association with their class status, stand in no need of such assistance. Although not sharing Bourdieu's theoretical stance, Adams similarly suggested that, by the 1930s, most American art museums arranged their exhibits as though the 'right to appreciate aesthetic qualities' were 'a privilege of wealth and leisure', arguing that, rather than spreading art, they had 'set up barriers against the proper diffusion of improved standards of taste throughout a metropolitan area' (Adams 1939: 62).

There is, then, a substantial continuity of concern in a body of argument which, stretching from James Barry to Pierre Bourdieu, from the late eighteenth to the late twentieth century, has stressed the need for the public display of art to be accompanied by a range of contextualizing and pedagogic props if – for whatever purpose – it is to be made intelligible and accessible to the generality of the population. The fact that this is so – the fact, that is, that there is a continuing observable correlation between the socially exclusive composition of art gallery publics and the relative paucity of the contextualizing materials that most art galleries offer their visitors – is ample evidence of the countervailing weight of the other factors which have fashioned the history of the art gallery. These are numerous and complex. On the one hand, it seems clear that, from around the 1870s and 1880s, the ethos of 'bringing art to the people' which had characterized the earlier nineteenth-century development of public art galleries was increasingly overridden by strategies of gentrification in which art galleries increasingly served as marker institutions for exclusive residential areas and were, in effect, captured by both local and national elites for their own socially exclusive purposes. As we have seen, both Dana and Adams argued that this had happened in the American context and Sherman paints a similar picture in his discussion of the establishment of provincial art museums in late nineteenth-century France (Sherman 1989). Side by side with these social tendencies, however, the development of modernist conceptions of art and the influence of these on display practices have tended to construct the gallery as a self-enclosed and self-referring space which, in the name of attending to art for its own sake, has warded off the inclusion of contextualizing materials.

But what is the point of this history lesson? A part of my purpose has been to suggest that the evidence of *The Reluctant Museum Visitor* regarding the social composition of Australian art gallery and museum visitors should really occasion no surprise. Indeed, my own motivation in the project was substantially driven by a concern to challenge what I took to be a policy complacency in this area. When I first tried to initiate inquiries of this kind, I was told by a number of influential policy-makers that they thought such work would be of little value in view of their experience that

Australian museums and art galleries did not conform to the northern hemisphere experience. The value of the studies I presented earlier in the chapter consists in the degree to which they demonstrate – and I think incontrovertibly so – the respects in which Australian museums, no less than their American and European counterparts, are involved in a similar dynamic of class and culture and for much the same reasons. The key practical question this poses is: what might be done to lessen the role that art galleries play in such dynamics? This is a question which we shall be able to answer only if we recognize that the existing social exclusiveness of the art gallery is not an accidental feature, an incidental but fortunate by-product, but an essential aspect of the modern art gallery's constitution.

The history of the modern art gallery, I have suggested, is governed by a systematic contradiction between its conception as a public cultural resource to which all citizens have an equal entitlement and which is to be administered for the benefit of the citizenry as a whole, and its social capture by elite social strata. This is not simply a matter of what goes on in art galleries. It concerns equally what goes on in the relations between art galleries and other cultural spheres or institutions, especially the education system. It is, accordingly, this broader context that needs to be borne in mind when considering policies which might assist in opening up art galleries to more generally representative publics. There are, I think, at least in so far as these issues concern questions of social class, three general areas that would repay attention.

First, and here I join hands with the tradition that runs from James Barry to Pierre Bourdieu, the writing is on the wall that there should, so to speak, be more writing on the walls of art galleries. The argument that the proper business of the art gallery is to display works of art without any kind of contextualizing information – whether it be stylistic, historical, or cultural – has now to be recognized as entirely bogus. The practices of art for art's sake themselves constitute a particular cultural and historical context for art, and one that has been shown to be culturally disenfranchising for large sections of the population. Of course, there can and should be vigorous debate about how particular works of art might best be contextualized. There is, however, now more than enough evidence to make it a reasonable policy requirement that art galleries develop a range of contextualizing strategies for enhancing the intellectual accessibility of their exhibits.

That said, unless greater public accessibility is to be purchased at the price of an increased aesthetic and political conservatism, it needs also to be recognized that art galleries are not the only institutions with a responsibility for developing visual literacy. The role of schooling in the production and distribution of cultural trainings and competences has also to be taken into account. Bourdieu and Darbel suggested as much in attributing to the education system the responsibility 'of mass-producing competent individuals endowed with the schemes of perception, thought and expression which are the condition for the appropriation of cultural goods' (Bourdieu and Darbel 1991: 67). Issues of this kind are scarcely on the policy agenda. Yet they need to be if art galleries are to assume a population with certain levels of visual literacy – and I would include in this a skill in interpreting popular audio-visual media – that they might then build on.

Finally, I believe that the balance of evidence should now tilt us in favour of admission charges being levied at art galleries and museums. Recognizing that special provision needs to be made for repeat users, especially students, it seems clear that few people are now inhibited from using museums and art galleries for economic reasons. The barriers, as I argued earlier, are cultural and I would suggest that – if seen as part of a greater commercialization of the museum and art gallery spaces – the introduction of charges would actually help to remove some of those barriers in making museums and galleries more like commercial centres of entertainment. Historically, of course, the principle of free entry has been an important part of the conception of museums and galleries as public institutions committed to the service of a democratic citizenry and it is clear, if we recall Sir Joshua Reynolds's remarks, that there have been good historical reasons for defending those principles. A question that might now be asked, however, is whether or not the continued defence of this principle serves merely to deliver added benefits to the art gallery's largely middle-class clientele while also, and paradoxically, serving as cultural barrier to access for other classes. We need, in other words, to consider whether the historical circumstances which initially prompted free admission policies have passed away so that now, paradoxically, they serve as impediments to access.

This chapter first appeared in the papers of the conference held on 16–19 March 1995 at Powerhouse Museum, Sydney, Australia, published as Evaluation and Visitor Research in Museums – towards 2000, *ed. C. Scott.*

NOTES

1   When arranging for his ethnological collections to be exhibited to the working classes in the Bethnal Green Museum in east London, Henry Pitt Rivers stated that he had arranged his collections so that 'those who run may read'. By this he meant that he had devised display principles intended to make the message of the exhibits readily intelligible to the working man. His thinking in this matter was shared by many of his contemporaries in the late nineteenth century when there was a widespread commitment to making the lessons of museums and art galleries more easily accessible to the working classes. How far have museums and art galleries succeeded in addressing these problems of intellectual access and what part have museum evaluation studies played in this process?

2   In Tables 25.1 to 25.4, the figures for the Non-Goers column are derived from Bennett (1994), those for the Museum Visitors column from Bennett, Bulbeck and Finnane (1991), and those for the Art Gallery Visitors from Bennett and Frow (1991).

3   Gender proved to be a barrier to access only when connected to specific age or life-cycle circumstances. Widows and homemakers – most of whom were women – thus proved to be particularly low users of both kinds of institutions.

REFERENCES

Adams, T. R. (1937) *The Civic Value of Museums*, New York: American Association for Adult Education.

Adams, T. R. (1939) *The Museum and Popular Culture*, New York: American Association for Adult Education.

Barrell, John (1986) *The Political Theory of Painting from Reynolds to Hazlitt: 'The Body of the Public'*, New Haven, CT and London: Yale University Press.

Bennett, Tony (1994) *The Reluctant Museum Visitor: A Study of Non-Goers to History Museums and Art Galleries*, Redfern: Australia Council.

Bennett, Tony, Bulbeck, Chilla and Finnane, Mark (1991) *Accessing the Past*, Brisbane: Institute for Cultural Policy Studies, Griffith University.

Bennett, Tony and Frow, John (1991) *Art Galleries: Who Goes? A Study of Visitors to Three Australian Art Galleries, with International Comparisons*, Sydney: Australia Council.

Bourdieu, Pierre (1984) *Distinction: A Social Critique of the Judgement of Taste*, London: Routledge & Kegan Paul.

Bourdieu, Pierre and Darbel, Alain (1991) *The Love of Art: European Art Museums and their Public*, trans. Caroline Beattie and Nick Merriman, Cambridge: Polity Press. (First published in French in 1969.)

Dana, John Cotton (1920) *A Plan for a New Museum: The Kind of Museum it Will Profit a City to Maintain*, Woodstock, VT: Elm Tree Press.

Dimaggio, P. and Useem, M. (1978) 'Social class and arts consumption: the origins and consequences of class differences in exposure to the arts in America', *Theory and Society* 5(2).

Greenwood, Thomas (1888) *Museums and Art Galleries*, London: Simpkin, Marshall.

Harris, Neil (1990) *Cultural Excursions: Marketing Appetites and Cultural Tastes in Modern America*, Chicago and London: University of Chicago Press.

Jevons, W. Stanley (1883) *Methods of Social Reform*, New York: Augustus M. Kelley.

Lamont, Michèle (1992) *Money, Morals and Manners: The Culture of the French and American Upper-Middle Class*, Chicago and London: University of Chicago Press.

Lewis, Geoffrey (1989) *For Instruction and Recreation: A Centenary History of the Museums Association*, London: Quiller Press.

Pitt Rivers, Henry (1891) 'Typological museums, as exemplified by the Pitt Rivers Museum at Oxford, and his provincial museum at Farnham', *Journal of the Society of Arts* 40.

Sherman, Daniel J. (1989) *Worthy Monuments: Art Museums and the Politics of Culture in Nineteenth Century France*, Cambridge, MA: Harvard University Press.

26

Audiences: a curatorial dilemma
Eilean Hooper-Greenhill

Focusing specifically on art museums, this chapter discusses the claim that in order to change the audience for art galleries it is necessary to change the art museum into something completely different. It is suggested that such radical measures are not really necessary. Museums have always been capable of enormous change while retaining the central objective of representing ideas through displaying objects.

Art museums (especially large, national institutions) have lagged behind other museums in their audience-related strategies. Their visitors remain more highly educated, more wealthy and of a higher social class than the visitors to other museums. They are not well used by families.

This chapter discusses some of the strategies used by smaller art galleries, or by non-art museums, to work towards a more democratic visitor profile. Many of the methods used are relevant to the development of a critical museum pedagogy. Some art museums have some hard questions to answer.

INTRODUCTION

Museums and galleries are at a time of enormous change. In the United Kingdom, both central government and local government are demanding greater accountability combined with an emphasis on quality and provision, while at the same time funds and resources for museums are being reduced. During the 1960s and 1970s, museums in Britain were seen as deserving public support because they represented a civilized society, and contributed to a public culture. During the 1980s, these attitudes were overriden by the ideology of the free market. Today, museums and galleries must increasingly earn their own livings and at the same time demonstrate social relevance to justify those public funds that they do still receive. These circumstances are not peculiar to Britain, but are familiar in many parts of the world.

The briefing papers for the conference Art Museums and the Price of Success, at which a shorter version of this chapter was delivered, suggested that the most frequent response to this situation in art museums was the mounting of blockbuster exhibitions to bring in the crowds. If this is indeed the case, I would suggest that this response brings with it a number of problems. The emphasis on mega-exhibitions leads to a tremendous strain on resources, increases competition between art museums, leads to an emphasis on commercialism and entails planning based on revenue-generation. This emphasis may result in a serious neglect of the permanent collections and displays.

This approach is also likely to lead to a lack of consideration for the needs of audiences. The audience for the museum is seen in terms of *visitors*, those who will actually come, rather than in terms of *audience*, all those who might come, if the experience were judged (by them) to be worthwhile. Visitors themselves are conceived in extremely narrow terms, judged more in terms of what they will spend rather than what they might experience.

The emphasis on mega-exhibitions with their intention to draw in large numbers can also lead to conceptualizing the museum experience in terms of tourists. Tourists tend to visit once only, ticking off the art museum on a long agenda of places that merely need to be seen to be experienced. The demands of tourists are satisfied by just walking through the galleries for an hour or so; a greater engagement with the collections is not often required. Other approaches to audiences are obscured by this assumption of the visitor as tourist. These other approaches might mean developing the museum to appeal to local residents, might concentrate on methods to broaden the audience base, or might emphasize reviewing and improving the experience that visitors to the art museum might have.

In the past, art museums have been notorious for precisely this lack of attention to the needs of their audiences. Where other types of museum, such as science museums or science centres, history museums and children's museums, have researched how they might make relationships with their actual and potential visitors, art museums have tended to remain aloof. Where other types of museum have begun to explore the *quality* of the experience of the visitor, art museums have concentrated on increasing the *quantity* of visitors.

I would like to suggest that it is time for art museums to shift the emphasis from quantity to quality, and that lessons on how to do this can be learnt in part from other types of museums, but also from some new ideas being developed in art galleries themselves. Paradoxically, it is likely that as the quality of the experience is raised, visitor numbers will also increase, whereas if effort is put into merely increasing numbers, the quality of the experience is likely to fall.

How can the attention be shifted from quantity to quality? There are two important areas that need to be addressed.

First, the nature of audiences should be considered very seriously. What type of people go to art museums and why? What are their needs, and how can art museums respond? In Britain, recent attention to the marketing of museums has led to new, more in-depth ways of conceptualizing audiences.

Secondly, policies and practices of exhibitions need to be reviewed to consider how both permanent displays and temporary exhibitions can be improved to enable a better experience for all visitors. Where displays are easy for people to relate to, local and repeat visitors will increase. Where the experience of the art museum is comfortable, enjoyable and personally extending, people will seek it out.

ART GALLERY AUDIENCES

Who goes to art galleries? Very many studies over the last ten years have shown the gallery audience to be more affluent and better educated than the general population (Hooper-Greenhill 1994). Eckstein and Feist summarize the British data, and point out that 'recent surveys have repeatedly demonstrated that museum visiting in the UK remains primarily a white upper/middle class pastime' (Eckstein and Feist 1992: 77).

Schuster (1995) usefully summarizes the data from several countries, including Britain, North America and Europe, and concludes that despite the fact that there are major differences between countries in the management, administration and funding of art galleries, audiences consist of a small, highly educated, wealthy, upper/middle-class élite. This he proposes rather ruefully as an essential aspect of art galleries, concluding that the institutional form itself necessarily entails this type of audience. He suggests that in order to achieve an audience with different characteristics an entirely new type of institutional form or a completely new type of public policy will be necessary.

Curators and directors of art galleries have had access to information about the nature of their public for some time. Some have also become aware that, short of changing the entire institutional form, modifications to the 'product' change the nature of the 'customer'. For example, at Leicester Museum and Art Gallery (the New Walk Museum), a policy to broaden the ethnic mix of local visitors led in the early 1980s to the establishment of a staff position with specific responsibilities to develop relevant collections and exhibitions. Over the years, exhibitions have been held that have targeted various sections of the local community. An art exhibition 'Caribbean Expressions in Britain' was mounted in conjunction with an exhibition about Caribbean history. The local Afro-Caribbean community made up a large part of the audience. An exhibition of Chinese jewellery attracted the Chinese community. 'Traditional Indian Arts of Gujarat' appealed to the Asian community in Leicester, many of whose families had come to Leicester from Gujarat, in north-west India, via Uganda (Smith 1991). Relating the exhibitions to the interests of different audience segments of the local population in Leicester resulted in new audiences for the museum.

A further example expands this point and shows how this method of broadening audiences has been used strategically by one art museum.

Walsall Museum and Art Gallery held an exhibition exploring Sikh culture, history and religion from February to April 1992. Entitled 'Warm and Rich and Fearless', and originally curated by Bradford Art Galleries and Museums, this exhibition was taken as an opportunity to develop links with a section of the population of Walsall to whom the gallery had previously been irrelevant. It was decided to expand the skills of the gallery curators by appointing a community events co-ordinator whose task was 'to promote the exhibition to local Sikh communities and to consult them regarding appropriate participative links; to translate their needs into creative projects which might include live performance, practical workshops, demonstrations, involvement in displays and interpretation; to be involved in the planning and implementation of these projects, to a given budget' (Walsall Museum and Art Gallery 1992a).

This was a new way of working for the gallery, and has been described as 'one of the most exciting and rewarding ventures in which the staff have been involved' (Walsall Museum and Art Gallery 1992b). Strong links were made with the Sikh community through the events co-ordinator, who was himself a Sikh able to speak Punjabi. The process was not without its difficulties, and success was largely achieved through the skills and knowledge of this temporary member of the gallery staff.

This project did not mean that the art museum was completed reinvented. The institutional form remained, with the exhibition looking much like any other. The methods for public programming were not in themselves very different from methods that museum educators have developed over the years. What was different was the specific targeting and the employment of an appropriate expert. Again this is not so very unusual – experts are often employed by art galleries to work with exhibitions. Usually these are collection experts. This expert, however, was an expert in the needs of the target audience. Being able to speak Punjabi was a major advantage in building the links between the artefacts and the culture from which they had come. The exhibition was slightly modified and relevant public programming introduced through working with the agenda of the target group, negotiating their needs in relation to the possibilities and constraints of the museum.

Exhibitions over the last ten years at Leicester, Bradford, Kirklees, Walsall and in other places too, have demonstrated conclusively that people who are not regular visitors will visit art galleries if there is something there that they find of relevance. This is particularly the case if advisory groups drawn from the relevant communities have been established, as has been the case in Bradford and Leicester (Smith 1991) and Walsall. The process of negotiation of interests and values itself partly creates the new audience.

As these examples demonstrate clearly, opening up the experience of the art gallery to specific cultural groups expands the nature of the audience. This has been achieved through accumulating relevant collections, by borrowing from other museums or members of the community on a temporary basis, and also by active collecting in the local area and in the relevant country of origin. In addition, as exhibitions and collections were developed, advice has been sought from the relevant community experts, short-term project workers have been appointed, and in some instances permanent advisory groups which meet on an annual basis have been established (Smith 1991).

Targeting specific sections of the gallery audience has successfully enabled some art galleries to develop that section of the audience. That this success is not always noticeable in broad audience statistics is explained by the fact that these targeted exhibitions are generally temporary exhibitions, and if museums target different sections of the community from year to year, overall figures will be low. In addition, most statistics on museum and gallery audiences are necessarily drawn from the published reports of work generally carried out by governmental bodies or market research firms. These on the whole have tended to produce large-scale quantitative accounts that obscure detail at the local level. The paucity of research in the museum and gallery field ensures that there are very few written accounts of how specific exhibitions have been developed and new audiences recruited, and therefore few reports of innovative work that researchers can turn to. As a result, much good practice is lost, barely recorded in the museum archives, let alone opened to critical interest, and the overall large-scale picture remains undisturbed. This does not serve the art museum world well. Until reports of the work are written and made readily available, museums and galleries will remain open to the charge of doing nothing to change their élitist image, in spite of the fact that some individual institutions have been working very hard to do so, with considerable success.

My examples so far have considered target groups drawn from a range of ethnic communities. Target groups can, however, be defined in a number of ways, and it should be recognized that most individuals will fall into more than one group. Groups can be identified in terms of life-stage, which would include families, school groups, young retired, elderly people; or level of educational achievement – beginning learners, some knowledge of the subject-matter, or scholars. Target groups should include those with special needs, with visual, physical, auditory, or learning impairment, or with young children, or with elderly members in their party. Gender, class, race and religion are other dimensions that are useful. Demographics (age, gender, education) and psychographics (life-style characteristics) are both regularly used by market researchers outside museums and galleries to identify target groups for niche marketing.

The number of examples of exhibitions with specific target groups is growing very rapidly and, as they develop, good practice can be logged. In January and February 1994 at the Herbert Museum and Art Gallery, Coventry, an exhibition of nineteenth-century prints and drawings was set up in one gallery space with a target audience of Key Stage 2 children. With the English National Curriculum, both programmes of study and attainment targets are structured according to four key stages: Key Stage 2 (KS2) consists of children aged 7–11 years. At the research stage of the exhibition, the material to be displayed was reviewed and selected with an eye to the National Curriculum documents, particularly in history and art, and teachers were interviewed as to how they could use the material with this age of student. The exhibition when mounted was divided into five themes – one displayed on each wall and one based on material in a display case in the middle of the room. A teachers' pack was prepared at the same time using the same themes: the division of the space and material meant that teachers could use the room easily with five groups of children, who were expected to visit in class-groups of about 30. Material on a nineteenth-century Coventry school was included to enable the children to think about what their peers would have experienced 100 years before (Adler 1993).

The exhibition was of course open to other visitors who would have seen something that looked remarkably like most other art gallery exhibitions – smallish prints and drawings on white walls, perhaps hung rather lower than usual. The only overtly unusual feature was a child-sized silhouette based on a photograph of a pupil from the nineteenth-century school, who welcomed visitors to the gallery and whose face was repeated on additional labels. These (rather small) labels, which were placed next to the standard art gallery labels, used a very discreet text bubble to ask one question of each of the items on display.

During the running of the exhibition, a programme of visits to the schools that used the exhibition was carried out as an integral part of the exhibition plan. Teachers and children were interviewed, children's drawings and writings were examined, and other results of the visits to the gallery were discussed. Such an evaluation provides a huge amount of material that demonstrates the way the gallery has been used. For funders and governing bodies, this represents the true value of the gallery.

This form of detailed audience-related planning enables accurate provision for researched needs, provides the information required for focused marketing, and enables the collection of qualitative data that demonstrate the use value of the institution. The development of an exhibition policy that considers which audiences will be targeted, how, when and how often audience research will be carried out, and what evaluation will be done, greatly assists the management of this process.

The concept of targeting has become built into the forward planning of museums and galleries (Ambrose and Runyard 1991; Ambrose and Paine 1993: 20–5). In many museums and galleries, the idea of 'the general public', or 'the museum visitor', as a large amorphous mass, has been replaced by the concept of target groups. The concept of target groups facilitates audience research into particular needs and actual interests. In addition it enables each exhibition to be reviewed in relation to the requirements of specific groups. The exhibition programme as a whole can be planned to provide for the needs of different groups or communities over a period of time.

THE INTRODUCTION OF MARKET RESEARCH

The introduction of qualitative research, including the notion of target groups, into museums and galleries has partly come about with the development of marketing in museums and galleries. In the past, many museums have carried out visitor surveys looking at how many people visited the museum or gallery, where they have come from, with what level of education, and so on. Government departments and other bodies such as tourist or leisure authorities have conducted participation studies among sample populations, looking at what percentage of a population visits museums how often (Hooper-Greenhill 1994: Ch. 3). Both of these forms of research tend to produce quantitative data in the form of statistics. Once the needs of a range of target groups are considered in relation to museum provision, a different focus for research becomes necessary. It becomes important to know what the experience means to people. How do visitors make sense out of their visit? How do they interpret the visit and what perceptions do they have of museums in general? Qualitative data, which reveal and illuminate attitudes and perceptions, become necessary.

A museum that genuinely wants to provide a service that is relevant to its audience has to go even further than this; it must ask those who do not at present visit museums what their perceptions are, and then consider how far either the perceptions, or the museum experience, can and should be changed.

Work in the area of qualitative research has begun in both Britain and the United States. In the United States the work of the Getty Center for Education in the Arts (1991) has involved using focus group research methods with groups of non-visitors, first-time art gallery visitors and gallery staff. Focus groups are groups of people with similar characteristics who are gathered together with a trained researcher to discuss in an open and free-flowing way what they feel about a particular product, or, in this case, an experience. The Getty research was a large-scale project, with profound and important results, involving eleven art museums across America. A market research company familiar with the leisure and heritage industry worked with the art museums to identify staff expectations and assumptions about the museum visitor's experience. Public expectations and actual experiences were also analysed and compared with the expectation of museum staffs.

The project report contains a great deal of fascinating material which is very difficult to summarize. The museum participants in the project clearly enhanced their professional knowledge of visitors and the joys and problems of museum visiting. Major gaps between staff expectations and visitor experiences were manifested in relation to orientation, information and direction. Both repeat and first-time visitors wanted more support in deciding what to look at and in knowing what was significant about specific objects. More information about the events, activities and services that were available was felt to be needed, and many visitors, especially first-time visitors, found the buildings very confusing and intimidating (Getty Center for Education in the Arts 1991: 44–5).

Perhaps even more important than concrete findings such as these was the change of philosophy that the project engendered in the museum participants. Listening (through a two-way mirror) to visitors talking about their experiences in art museums, one director concluded that art museum priorities had shifted; the centrality of the object had been replaced by the centrality of the encounter, and that quality, once defined solely in terms of the object and connoisseurship, has come to refer also to the visitor's experience (Getty Center for Education in the Arts 1991: 111). Along with this has come the realization, at least for some participants, that directors of art museums had failed to take account of the visitor's experience, leaving this to the education department, while the main emphasis of the museum was concentrated on acquisition and care of collections. 'Acquisition and presentation [were seen] as the chief priorities of the museum, overshadowing education, appreciation and interpretation.' In a 'post-collecting' age, this had to change, with more of an emphasis on *using* rather than increasing collections (Getty Center 1991: 46).

This long-term, large-scale research project, with an excellent project report and accompanying video, demonstrates the commitment in some sections of the American art museum world to broadening audiences and to improving the experiences of visitors. It also demonstrates an availability of research funding which is rare elsewhere in the world.

A project also using qualitative research methods, in Britain, illustrates a similar desire to expand the relevance of museums and galleries, but has been limited to one museum. The project grew out of individual convictions, and although an excellent report has been produced, it remains an internal management document and is not therefore easily available, except by writing to the museum.

The London Borough of Croydon appointed a curator in 1989 to open a new museum, based on small social history and art collections. The museum was to be part of a larger arts centre based around the library, and would open after five years. This lead-time has been crucial in the planning of the new museum, as it has enabled the curator and (gradually) her staff to carry out considerable market research before the design of the museum was completed. The market research has in fact influenced the entire concept of the museum (MacDonald 1995).

A market research firm was employed to investigate, by using focus groups, the perceptions held about museums by people who traditionally have rarely visited them (Susie Fisher Group 1990). These groups were identified through demographic research, which clearly indicates which sections of the population tend not to visit. Researchers talked to Asian and black teenagers, elderly men, mothers with very young children, and other groups who are generally conspicuous by their absence in museums and galleries.

Among the barriers to museum visiting to emerge from the research were feelings that the arts and museums were irrelevant, 'too virtuous', that 'do-gooders' were the sort of people who went to museums, that you had to have specialist knowledge to understand the displays, that it would be a luxury, that other things were more important. The overall atmosphere of museums was felt to be one of 'keep off'. People believed that they would be physically uncomfortable, cold, on their feet all the time, peering to see depressing old relics whose significance could only be understood through a great deal of hard work deciphering complicated wordy explanations (Susie Fisher Group 1990: 21–2). It was discovered that both museum visitors, and those who did not visit, thought all museums were quite boring, and that visitors went largely from a sense of duty.

From this early research, the plans for the new museum evolved. It has been decided not to use the word museum in order to avoid preconceptions. Displays will include ideas about the present and the future as well as the past. In order to represent sections of the community that are not represented in the existing social history collections, new collections are being built up. Short-term contracts have employed an Irish and an Asian researcher, two cultural groups that have a strong presence in the local area.

Members of the Chinese community have been consulted over the redisplay of the existing Chinese porcelain collection. Trial exhibitions have been held in the local shopping precinct, partly to experiment with modes of display and partly to meet and talk to people. In the drawing up of the budgets for the new museum, an exhibition budget will include a sum for evaluation. Audience research, including concept testing, will also be allowed for (MacDonald 1995).

The introduction of market research methods into museums and galleries has provided methods that curators and directors can use to begin to get closer to their actual and potential audiences. By exploring attitudes and values and beginning to understand the problems that many people have with art galleries, it is becoming possible to modify the policy and resource priorities to enable a closer fit with the everyday world of both new and repeat visitors. When museums and galleries are seen as a normal part of the lives of ordinary people then the audience will consist of more than the élite.

IMPROVING DISPLAYS FOR VISITORS

The market research studies discussed above indicate that many people find that art (and other) museums have little relationship with their interests and experience. Most people lead fairly parochial lives and their interests centre round their families, their work, their hobbies. Essentially these interests are small-scale, domestic and personal. Museums that represent the world through large-scale universal themes do not speak to those people who do not experience the world in this way. Many non-visitors and rare visitors feel that museums have nothing to do with daily life (Merriman 1991: 64).

It might be argued that it is a function of museums and galleries to offer the opportunity to transcend the everyday world and to forget the trials of the trivial. This *is* an important aspect of the museum experience, but visitors will find it difficult to achieve if feeling intimidated, not sufficiently knowledgeable and uncertain of how to behave. Educational psychology reminds us that we need to feel welcomed and comfortable before we can allow our mind to escape to higher realms and new learning.

Most art museum staff do not spend much time thinking about how the exhibitions can be made of relevance to people who know nothing of art. On the other hand, many non-art museums are beginning to find ways of linking their collections with everyday life. In Hull, in Yorkshire, for example, the new history gallery presents the history collections in relation to the life-stages of people rather than to a municipal history of Hull. Display themes are 'Childhood', 'Marriage', 'Death', rather than 'Eighteenth-Century Hull', or 'The Development of Local Industries in Hull' (Frostick 1991). A similar approach is taken in Birmingham to the redisplay of the ethnographic collection: themes such as 'Eating and Drinking', 'Making Music' and 'Symbols' are used in a cross-cultural approach (Peirson Jones 1992). A similar ethnographic theme was used some years ago at the Museum of Popular Arts and Traditions, Paris in an exhibition entitled 'La France et La Table'.

Most themes used in art galleries are very predictable – the artist and his (sometimes her) work, an art-historical school or period, a style. This type of approach requires the visitor or potential visitor to recognize and value significant artists, styles, art-historical periods and schools. Why is it always seventeenth-century Holland and nineteenth-century France? The geography of art history is bizarre! Without the basic structuring of concepts that is informed by a knowledge of art history, the themes of

262

many exhibitions are remote and incomprehensible. Theming according to everyday categories and classifications has been very successful with other types of collections. Would exhibitions of paintings on the themes of, say, 'Eating and Drinking', 'Making Music', 'Children', broaden the audience?

Exactly this approach has been taken at Walsall Art Gallery in the re-display of the Garman Ryan collection. Paintings and sculptures in this small but outstanding collection of work by artists such as Rembrandt, Picasso, Constable, Modigliani, have been grouped in themes of 'The Family', 'Work', 'Leisure', 'Children', 'Animals', 'Trees' and 'Birds'. Guides to the collection introduce a new set of themes – 'Working Women in the Garman Ryan Collection', 'A Guide to Clothing in the Garman Ryan Collection', and others all focus on specific ways of reading the collection that can relate to interests visitors might either already have, or might even develop in the gallery.

Efforts to relate collections to people are often scorned by art curators, either (overtly stated) because they 'talk down' to people, or (actually meant) because these efforts to appeal to non-specialist visitors do not reveal the extensive expert knowledge of the art curator. These attitudes are no longer appropriate. Leaflets such as those described above open up ideas in relation to the objects, they make interesting connections between them, and they enable links to be discovered between what visitors already know and what they can find out. This is the real stuff of learning and engagement.

It is now generally recognized that people learn in a variety of ways; that there is a range of learning styles. Some people take in information best through reading; some through discussion; some through doing something actively and then thinking about the experience; some learn best through other people (Gardner 1983; Hooper-Greenhill 1994: 140–70). Different types of question are asked by different types of learner: these include 'why', 'how' and 'so what' questions. People typically process information best when able to learn in their own way. In many museums, therefore, a mix of types of learning opportunity is offered: looking and thinking; object-handling; interactive exhibits; demonstration; reconstructions; drama; film. Many non-art museums are developing ways to enable people to enter an active process of exploration and discovery that has the potential of becoming personally meaningful to them, recognizing that it is only when experiences are personally meaningful that they are truly valued. Most art museums limit the mode of learning to looking and reading, a physically passive yet intellectually demanding form of learning. People who are more comfortable learning in more active and concrete modes are disadvantaged.

Discovery centres which enable the handling and exploration of collections have become enormously popular, and some museums are integrating the potential for active engagement into their glass-case displays (Frostick 1991). Some art museums have found ways of enabling handling and interaction with fine and decorative art collections. The Victoria and Albert Museum, for example, has placed two large Chinese jars in its new Tsui Gallery of Chinese Art. At the Museum of Civilisation in Québec an exhibition on the art and culture of Tunisia was supported by a small discovery room where perfume vessels could be handled and the perfume smelt, simple musical instruments could be played, music could be listened to, large leather cushions could be sat upon, a short film about aspects of women's lives could be viewed. The extremely successful Discovery Room at the National Museum of Scotland has led to the development of a travelling Discovery Room with Japanese material, where visitors can set a table for breakfast, wrap presents, try on a kimono and so on (Statham 1993). Exhibitions specifically targeted at people with visual handicaps have been familiar in galleries in Britain for some years. These enable handling of art works, some of which have been specially commissioned (Nottingham, Leicester), and some of which have been chosen from the permanent collections (British Museum).

Exhibitions which enable the use of more than just the visual sense are always enormously popular. One of the great pleasures of working in museums and galleries is the very special opportunity to work very closely with objects of all sorts. Visitors enjoy this just as much as curators! The feeling of privilege in being able to get very close to real, old and rare things is very seductive, although little research has been carried out to explore precisely why. Ongoing evaluation research into learning from objects revealed that quite young children thought that looking at an object 'makes you feel more important than looking at a postcard' (Barnes 1994).

Exhibitions that allow the play of the imagination and memory through enabling people to make personal links, and which enable the intellect to operate in its preferred way through offering a range of ways of accessing information, will broaden the numbers and types of people that can enjoy art museums. This in itself, however, will not entice infrequent visitors to art museums. Effective marketing, interesting press coverage, outreach workshops and other methods must present the museum as a desirable and comfortable place to go.

WHOM ARE ART EXHIBITIONS AND MUSEUMS FOR?

A case-study shows some of the ways in which one art museum has researched the needs of visitor target groups and has created a new permanent gallery which takes account of the findings.

The Laing Art Gallery, Newcastle-upon-Tyne, is a traditionally imposing museum building with a classical façade. The gallery is funded by the local authority, and is a local art gallery in an important and historic regional city (Millard 1992). The museum director, John Millard, and his staff were aware that the gallery was seen as irrelevant and intimidating by very many local people. They set out to re-display some of the permanent collections in such a way as to change this perception. The permanent exhibition 'Art on Tyneside' opened in the summer of 1991. It aims to show aspects of the history of the fine and decorative arts on Tyneside since the sixteenth century.

The exhibition team included the education officer and a social historian as well as fine and decorative arts experts. The exhibition had two main target groups: schoolchildren aged 9–12, and people with disabilities. Experts such as teachers and disability advisers were consulted throughout the process of the development of the exhibition and specific provision is made for these groups. The exhibition team also wanted to avoid gender stereotypes.

The displays mix fine art objects such as paintings and prints with decorative art objects such as glass, furniture and ceramics. The display approach offers opportunities for a range of learning styles, and the use of many senses. Figures are used in reconstructed contexts like room-settings. There are opportunities for touching, such as scraps of silks and brocade next to a case showing an eighteenth-century dress. Interactive devices enable active participation: for example, a magnetic board with adhesive shapes based on the stylistic features of classical façades enables visitors to experiment with architectural design. Appeals to senses other than the visual are to be found with smells, such as the smell of coffee, and the sounds of the coffee-drinkers talking, in the coffee-house reconstruction.

Specific provision for people with disabilities is made. For people with visual impairment, provision includes a raised track, clear and raised room numbers, things to touch, non-reflective glass, tape guides and thermaforms (sculpted versions of a painting mounted on a bat). Subtitles on video screens and notes accompanying the displays help those with hearing impairment. The exhibition is accessible throughout for wheelchair users.

The other target group for the exhibition, children of primary school age, are provided for in a number of ways, which include the interactive and tactile devices; information provided especially for them in the form of cartoons, with two cartoon characters to follow through the exhibition; and very clever worksheets that take the user through the exhibition in role as either a craftsperson, an artist, or an architect.

This exhibition has revitalized the gallery and given it a new and dynamic local presence. During the first two years after opening, the visitor numbers increased by 60 per cent, from 86,238 to 139,059 in 1992. Most of these visitors are local people. About a year after its opening, a regional newspaper printed a guide to museums in the north-east of England with the Laing Art Gallery being the only museum to get a top score for its appeal to both adults and children (Millard 1994).

'Art on Tyneside' represents one way of presenting art-historical themes so that those without specialist knowledge can appreciate them. It is an introductory show, giving glimpses of classicism, eighteenth- and nineteenth-century silverwork, glass engraving, nineteenth-century British painting, and so on. The methods used here include reconstructions, period rooms and full-size figures. These methods are not appropriate for all types of art work, but can be particularly suitable when fine and decorative arts are combined. Other ways of making exhibitions that make no assumptions about the level of knowledge of the visitor should perhaps be developed for other types of collection. It is also useful to balance introductory shows with shows that demand more from visitors.

Interestingly, one of the very few negative responses to the exhibition has come from an art critic. The *Daily Telegraph* reported that the exhibition was a 'vile accretion':

> poor in design and vacuous in content 'Art on Tyneside' proved to be the most abysmal museum installation I've ever encountered. But it was clear from the visitors' book that, with some sectors of the public, 'Art on Tyneside' has been popular. I suppose one must accept this. If some visitors are so unimaginative that they need such half-baked gimmicks to make history come alive, then by all means let them have them. But not in a museum.
>
> (Dorment 1993; quoted in Millard 1994)

The vehemence of the language is surprising, revealing a strong degree of scorn and distaste for the pleasure that the general public have found in paintings. The comments raise interesting and difficult questions for art galleries, the most important of which is whom do we make our exhibitions for? Non-specialist audiences or art critics? In many art museums the answer will most definitely be art critics. Many art exhibitions are mounted with a very sharply focused 'weather eye' on the reputation and career possibilities inherent in the exercise. This raises ethical and moral imperatives which are rarely discussed with the seriousness they demand.

Why are art exhibitions made? The main reason in many cases is a specific passion on the part of the curator. Often this relates to developing knowledge about an artist, an art form, an art movement. Clearly one of the most important roles for art museums is to explore and promote art of the past, the present and the future. Art museums have a responsibility to society to care for art and make it available through exhibitions, writing and good scholarship. I would argue that they also have the challenge to introduce art to those who do not yet understand why they should be interested. In art museums such as those in Britain which are very largely funded out of the public purse, this becomes a social responsibility. In times of recession, it becomes a matter of survival.

At the present time, art museums serve a small well-informed audience that is relatively satisfied with what is on offer. This audience need not be compromised by making additional provision for new audiences that need more information, more introductory frameworks and more reasons for becoming involved with art.

The extent to which different galleries are willing or able to consider the interests and needs of new visitors will depend on a variety of matters, including the strength and vision of the director, the composition of the governing body, the level of the revenue budget, the philosophies of individual members of staff. Although there are examples of new ways of working in galleries, as we have seen, the older ways, which tend to exclude the vast majority of the population, have the power of inertia behind them. In addition, the lack of written project reports of good practice, and the failure to write up successful approaches to building links between galleries and communities, mean that much excellent work is completely unknown.

The development of an exhibition policy which is planned to take account of the characteristics of a range of target groups enables galleries to assess and resource their provision according to the needs and interests of their audiences. This has proved easier both to understand and to achieve in Britain in art galleries funded by local authorities, rather than in national art museums. At city or county level, institutions are smaller, and the links between the gallery and its audiences are perhaps easier to define and research than in the national gallery, where arguably the audience is both national and international. Local art galleries are very often part of a museum complex where new ideas can be shared between all sections. The effectiveness of working with local communities in the social history museum, for example, may lead to the adaptation of these techniques in the art gallery. It is also at local authority level that budget reduction has been felt most acutely. At the present time in Britain, while most national museums and galleries are flourishing, local museums and galleries need to demonstrate their relevance to local audiences in competition with other local amenities such as swimming pools, day-care for the elderly and nurseries. The on-going reorganization of the local authority structure across England and Wales poses a further threat for many local art galleries. Local galleries are seeking to strengthen their political position by broadening the audience base, establishing strong links to named groups and centres, working in partnerships with a network of agencies, and improving professional practice through audience research and evaluation.

Although many things have changed for national museums and galleries in recent years, the size of the institutions, the arms'-length management structure of trustees, and the much higher level of resources combined with much larger and more diffuse audiences means that national galleries can survive comfortably while asking fewer questions about the experiences or expectations of their audiences. Where innovation is to be identified in the national galleries, it is frequently in the outstations rather than in the central gallery.

In addition, national art galleries exist within a network of social relations where powerful interest groups are able to use their power, wealth and status to maintain their own class positions. Powerful sponsors, influential friends, critics that command large audiences – these and other factors create strong influences that work towards keeping art museums free and untainted by the 'hoi polloi', those 'unimaginative people' that need 'gimmicks to make history come alive', and which perhaps are needed to take the place of higher education, an elevated social status and specialist knowledge about art. Vision, courage and determination are required by those art museum staff who wish to jolt the forces that maintain this élite position on to a different and more democratic track.

There is in Britain a vast pool of interest in the arts. The Report of the National Inquiry into the Arts and the Community (1992) quoted a survey carried out on behalf of the Arts Council, and pointed out that 79 per cent of the population say that they attend at least one type of arts or cultural event nowadays. In addition 53 per cent of the population of Great Britain take an active part in at least one arts or craft activity. Although 48 per cent visit all exhibition and museum venues on a regular basis, only 18 per cent visit galleries of painting and sculpture (RSGB 1991). There is an extraordinarily large drop between participation in the arts in general and the visiting of galleries of fine art. This gap is created and sustained, perhaps unknowingly, by those who work to support the continuation of art exhibitions that ignore the needs of their publics.

Art galleries do not have to become completely new institutions to broaden their visitor profile. They need to develop empathy towards their audiences both actual and potential, increase their knowledge of what is recognized as contemporary good practice in exhibition design and, most important of all, shift their resource and policy priorities from objects to people.

This chapter first appeared as 'Giving people what they want: quality or quantity in art museums?', a paper given at the conference Art Museums and the Price of Success, which was organized by Boekman Stichting, Amsterdam, Netherlands, 10–11 December 1992.

REFERENCES

Alder, C. P. (1993) 'Creating effective exhibitions', unpublished MA thesis, Department of Museum Studies, University of Leicester.

Ambrose, T. and Paine, C. (1993) *Museum Basics*, London and New York: Routledge.

Ambrose, T. and Runyard, S. (eds) (1991) *Forward Planning: A Handbook of Business, Corporate and Development Planning for Museums and Galleries*, London and New York: Routledge.

Barnes, C. (1994) 'Evaluation project. Outline report one', unpublished research report, Museum Education Evaluation Project, Department of Museum Studies, University of Leicester.

Dorment, R. (1993) 'Are galleries losing art?', *Daily Telegraph* (9 September): 14.

Eckstein, J. and Feist, A. (1992) 'Attendances at museums and galleries', in *Cultural Trends 1991*, London: Policy Studies Institute, 70–9.

Frostick, E. (1991) 'Worth a Hull lot more', *Museums Journal* 91(2): 33–5.

Gardner, H. (1983) *Frames of Mind*, London: Paladin Books.

Getty Center for Education in the Arts (1991) *Insights: Museums, Visitors, Attitudes, Expectations*, J. Paul Getty Museum.

Hooper-Greenhill, E. (1994) *Museums and their Visitors*, London: Routledge.

MacDonald, S. (1995) 'Changing our minds – planning a responsive museum service', in E. Hooper-Greenhill (ed.) *Museum: Media: Message*. London: Routledge, 165–74

Merriman, N. (1991) *Beyond the Glass Case*, Leicester: Leicester University Press.

Millard, J. (1992) 'Art history for all the family', *Museum Journal* 92(2): 32–3.

Millard, J. (1994) 'Hands on art', *Museum Visitor* 10 (British Association of Friends of Museums): 49–54.

Peirson Jones, J. (1992) 'The colonial legacy and the community: the Gallery 33 project', in I. Karp, C. M. Kreamer and S. Lavine (eds) *Museums and Communities: The Politics of Public Culture*, Washington, DC: Smithsonian Institution Press, 221–41.

Report of the National Inquiry into Arts and the Community (1992) *Arts and Communities*, London: Community Development Foundation Publications.

RSGB (1991) *Report on a Survey on Arts and Cultural Activities in G.B.: Research Surveys of Great Britain Omnibus Arts Survey*, London: Arts Council of Great Britain.

Schuster, J. Mack Davidson (1995) 'The public interest in the art museum's public', in S. Pearce, (ed.) *New Research in Museum Studies*, Vol. 5, London: Athlone Press, 109–42.

Smith, N. P. (1991) 'Exhibitions and audiences: catering for a pluralistic public', in G. Kavanagh (ed.) *Museum Languages: Objects and Texts*, Leicester: Leicester University Press, 119–34.

Statham, R. (1993) 'Getting to grips with Japan', *Journal of Education in Museums* 14: 8–10.

Susie Fisher Group (1990) *Bringing History and the Arts to a New Audience: Qualitative Research for the London Borough of Croydon*, London: Susie Fisher Group.

Walsall Museum and Art Gallery (1992a) Brief for community events co-ordinator for 'Warm and Rich and Fearless', unpublished document.

Walsall Museum and Art Gallery (1992b) Evaluation report for 'Warm and Rich and Fearless', unpublished document.

27

Cultural imagining among museum visitors

Sharon Macdonald

A great deal of museum communication theory suggests that people make their own meanings, and that these do not necessarily conform to those that the museum intended or expected them to make. This chapter describes some of the results of an in-depth study that examined the ways in which visitors responded to one exhibition.

Macdonald takes an unusual approach from the point of view of visitor studies as currently undertaken within museums. She works from a base informed by cultural studies, and she asks questions about the broad cultural meanings that visitors construct. The conventional approach to visitor studies, especially in America, works from a positivist perspective and limits the questions asked to those internal to the study in question.

Working from a constructivist paradigm, Macdonald shows how the cultural imaginings of visitors to the 'Food for Thought' exhibition (Science Museum, London) were constructed through those sections of the exhibition that they used (which may relate to their preferred learning styles), and also through the messages about food that they brought with them to the museum. These had come from other media of mass communication.

INTRODUCTION

A museum exhibition can, I suggest, be regarded as a 'technology of imagination'. It is an ordered site where the sensory and the cognitive are brought together; and where, through experience, visitors may extend and reinforce or reshape their knowledges. This process, however, is not one in which visitors can be seen simply as passive, more or less resistant, recipients of the knowledge disseminated. Rather, they themselves come with their own visions and predispositions for particular imaginings. My aim in this paper is to illustrate something of this visitor activity through specific case-study material and to discuss some of its consequences.

Research on the understandings of visitors in museums (particularly science museums) has tended to focus on questions of what visitors learn. Within these cognitive approaches, the work of Minda Borun on 'naive conceptions' has been a significant advance.[1] Her approach is to look at ways in which visitors may misunderstand the nature of the exhibition because of the prior conceptions with which they come to an exhibition (e.g. 'naive conceptions' about gravity). However, visitors inevitably come to any exhibition laden with cultural preconceptions which shape the nature of their visit and affect their responses to it. This is a much bigger issue, then, than one of individual and specific 'naive conceptions'. Indeed, the kinds of social and cultural conceptions which people may hold are often difficult to detect because far from being 'naive' they are embedded in everyday life and make a good deal of sense within it. The kinds of cultural conceptions under consideration may also be of various orders, and about more than cognition alone. They may entail, for example, emotive attraction towards or avoidance of certain kinds of representations; tendencies to make particular classifications or order sense-data in specific ways; or the creation of personal stories, say, or the instigation of group activities in response to some kinds of exhibits. A good deal of the response to an exhibition may well be individually variable, but within this there will be certain recurring, though not necessarily universal, patterns. These patterns – cultural imaginings – are imaginative in that they involve creative interaction between visitors and the exhibition; and they are cultural in that these interactions are influenced by all kinds of expectations and ideas about the nature of museum visiting, science and so forth. Things could be otherwise. Let me give just one example. Most of the visitors interviewed in the case-study described below were British. But imagine how differently a visit would be both conceived and acted by a member of the Igbo people of Nigeria for whom the very preservation of material culture is anathema and a danger to social continuity,[2] and for whom 'science' does not traditionally exist as an even notional explanatory system. Their reaction would be quite other, I think, from that which I shall describe here.

THE STUDY: 'FOOD FOR THOUGHT'

The detail of this chapter is based on a study of visitors to 'Food for Thought: the Sainsbury Gallery', an exhibition which opened in the Science Museum, London, in 1989.[3] The study was principally qualitative, its central aim being to encourage visitors to talk about their experience of the exhibition rather than to enumerate responses to closed format questions. The methodology was devised around an intention of looking at the kinds of readings of the exhibition which visitors would make; and it entailed semi-structured interviews with families – the main target audience of the exhibition – in the groups in which they visited. Responses were all recorded and transcribed and the negotiations and occasional arguments recorded are an important part of the data.[4]

As its name implies, 'Food for Thought' is an exhibition about food. It is a large (810 m²) permanent exhibition, expected to be in place for about ten years. It cost approximately £1.2 million, excluding staff costs. It is a mixed media exhibition, containing a high proportion of interactive exhibits. The exhibition was specifically designed to be as accessible as possible to the layperson, and it uses a number of specific strategies, such as simple, multilevel text, to be so. The following account does not by any means cover all dimensions of the exhibition, or of the visitor study. Instead, it takes three examples of ways in which visitors bring their own, patterned, input to bear on the exhibition.

Example one: readings of the exhibition

The first example concerns the overall readings of what the exhibition is about. The overall theme devised by the exhibition-makers was 'To help people understand the impact of science and technology on our food'. Perhaps surprisingly, given that the exhibition is in the Science Museum, few visitors mentioned science or technology in their answers to our questions about the theme of the exhibition. Instead, visitors predominantly verbalized the theme in two main ways – both relevant to the makers' intentions – though not, perhaps, quite as they would have anticipated. These were: (1) 'history'; (2) 'healthy eating'.

Readings of the exhibition: some examples.

'History'
'It's got to do with food through the ages hasn't it?' (I. 2, p. 2)[5]
'History of foods in the shops and what it's like, or in the home' (I. 9, p. 1)
'It's how the way we approach food's changed through the years I suppose' (I. 13, p. 2)

'Healthy eating'
'I support it's trying to promote healthy eating' (I. 11, p. 2)
'Food and health – healthy living' (I. 32, p. 3)
'It seems to be geared towards healthy eating which is good' (I. 41, p. 2)

More interesting than the fact that they give these as the themes, however, is that they reconstruct the gallery in terms of them. In interviews the first thing that visitors were asked to do was to talk about where they went and what they saw in the exhibition. The idea here was to try to get visitors to generate their own accounts of the visit. One thing that happens in many of these accounts is that visitors link together particular exhibits into patterns of 'history' and 'healthy eating'. What happens in the case of 'history' is that visitors link together some or all of the following exhibits: 1920s Sainsburys, larders and nippy and kitchens (occasionally, also the street seller and snacks section), marked by * on the exhibition plan (see Figure 27.1). They talk about these one after another as though they form a continuity. For 'healthy eating', visitors join together some or all of: additives, the mirrors and scales and the exercise bikes and the nutritional puzzles and food pyramid (marked on the plan by +).

There are, I suggest, factors both external to the exhibition and unintended suggestions within it which play a part in promoting these particular readings. Within the exhibition it seems that a key to the linking of these sections by visitors may be the media used. The 'history' sections that visitors join together are all historical reconstructions and most also contain a model of a person or persons. The 'healthy eating' sections, on the other hand, all involve interactive exhibits, and it is these which visitors seem to pick up on in their accounts.

One external factor involved in these particular linkages and the identification of them as themes may well be experience from other types of exhibition. (Our study suggested that the majority of the visitors seemed to be general museum-goers rather than specific Science Museum aficionados.)[6] The 'history' theme may be one that is particularly expected from heritage-type reconstructions, while the 'healthy eating' theme may have derived from health education-type exhibitions. More generally, of course, both historical narratives and messages about health are extremely prevalent within the general culture from which the visitors come, and perhaps these – rather than ideas about sciences and technology – are dominantly associated with the subject-matter of the exhibition, namely food. Certain exhibits, because of their contextual location outside the exhibition, may act as particularly dominant triggers for specific readings. Scales, exercise bikes and mirrors, for example, seem to spark off a personalized discussion of self, of body shape and of a concern with health.[7]

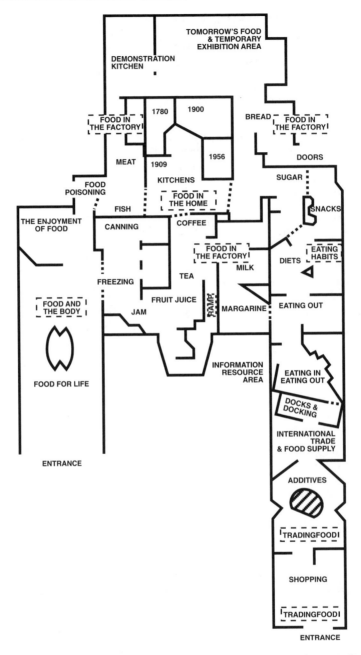

Figure 27.1 Schematic groundplan of 'Food for Thought: the Sainsbury Gallery' at the Science Museum, London (adapted from the museum's education resource pack). Intended to help people understand the impact of science and technology on our food, the displays were opened in 1989

Example two: 'good' foods and 'bad' foods

The second example of visitors bringing their own messages to the exhibition concerns the subject-matter of the exhibition still more directly, and continues the 'healthy eating' theme. When visitors talk about healthy eating they very frequently claim that the exhibition is telling them which foods are 'good' and which foods are 'bad'.

'Good' foods and 'bad' foods: some examples.

[Do you think that there is a theme to the exhibition?]
'Good foods and bad foods' (I. 26, p. 2)
'I suppose in a way ... showing you what's right to eat and what's not right to eat. Round here it had the Mars – what was in the Mars – and what was in the carrot and things like that' (I. 28, p. 3)
'Telling you more about food than just eating it. It tells you more about it. What's good for you and what's bad for you, ain't it?' (I. 40, p. 2)

However, this was a point which the exhibition-makers had not wanted to make and indeed at one point the text of the exhibition directly states: 'Most scientists agree that no one food in isolation is "good" or "bad".' Despite this, the neat discrimination between good and bad foods is prevalent among visitors. What is more, although the exhibition-makers had hoped to avoid being narrowly prescriptive about diet – favouring notions of balance and choice instead – visitors nearly always themselves phrase the exhibition's message in terms of 'being told' or shown what is right and wrong, what should or should not be eaten.

Again, there is a culturally dominant assumption involved here. Classifying foods into 'good' and 'bad' is one of the main ways in which food is thought about in the cultural contexts from which the majority of visitors come.[8] For an exhibition to give a message counter to such a deeply-rooted notion it would clearly have had to do so in a very much more direct way. Secondly, however, there are elements in the exhibition which can be read in terms of right and wrong, and good and bad. In particular, this applies to some of the interactive exhibits. When visitors talk about good and bad foods they never mention the text panels but instead talk about some of the interactive exhibits. In this particular case they talk especially about the scales and the exercise bikes and about the food pyramid, an exhibit which involves constructing a healthy diet by fitting different types of foods into different sections of a wire-mesh pyramid.

Interactives and prescription: some examples.

'We did ... the pyramid and found out what we should be eating and what we shouldn't' (I. 7, p. 1)
G2: '... and in the pyramid the sugar was at the top and I put all mine in the bottom. That's not right'
G1: 'About the same really – I'm eating all the wrong foods!' (I. 26, p. 4)
'We weighed ourselves too didn't we? To see if we were the right weight and height. And to find out how many calories we used on the bicycle' (I. 22, pp. 1–2)
'I know that the bikes were to get fit if you ate too much fat things' (I. 16, p. 4)

This raises a number of more general points for exhibition-making. The first is that of from where in an exhibition visitors are going to get their 'messages'. This research suggests that – in this type of exhibition and this type of visit – messages come principally from the three-dimensional exhibits rather than from the text itself. There are relatively few instances in the interviews overall where visitors mention things which they read in the exhibition. It may be the case, of course, that this tendency to 'read' messages into, or off from, three-dimensional exhibits rather than the text is something which is particularly likely to be the case for the family group visitors, who were the subject of this study. However, even if this is not a tendency which necessarily occurs among all types of visitors, it is nevertheless clearly significant and something which exhibition-makers need to take into account. This example shows that written messages which contradict visitors' preconceptions may even be ignored, a possibility which suggests that careful investigation of preconceptions and careful co-ordination of countervailing messages is essential to successful exhibition-making.

The second point here concerns the *nature* of the messages which can be conveyed by three-dimensional exhibits, or, in this case, specifically by interactive exhibits. There are two cases to be made here which seem to pull in different directions. One is that any non-text exhibit is especially capable of being read in diverse ways. This means that exhibition-creators need to be especially attentive to alternative possible readings. The second, however, concerns the use of puzzles more specifically. Puzzles invite visitors to 'get it right' and, inevitably, to possibly 'get it wrong'. The very fact of right and wrong answers to the puzzles seems to set up a more general expectation of right and wrong answers throughout the exhibition, and as such may be difficult to use alongside more subtle messages of balance and choice.

Example three: making science everyday

This example provides further material on which to reflect about the nature of interactive exhibits. It concerns the exhibition-makers' intention of countering the distant and difficult image of science and technology and instead introducing ideas about them via the familiar and everyday. The aim was to break down that vision of science as a separate domain from ordinary everyday life.[9] This was tackled on many levels in the exhibition design. Interactive exhibits were a key part of this in that they physically allowed visitors to participate rather than be debarred from the world of science; a strategy of introducing science and technology via familiar objects and experiences, e.g. shopping, piles of food, was used throughout the exhibition, and the exhibition avoided the use of unexplained technical jargon.

Visitors themselves frequently voiced approval of the fact that the exhibition is comprehensible and that there is a hands-on element. Whether the exhibition managed to alter preconceived views about science is the more important issue, however, and more difficult to determine. In the study, one of the questions asked was: 'Did it strike you as a scientific exhibition?' There were three main types of response to this:

Science is something else

A minority of respondents simply said that the exhibition did not strike them as 'scientific' and was not 'scientific' – sometimes saying that 'science' was about subjects like physics and chemistry as studied at school. These interviewees see the exhibition, realize that it does not accord with their preconceptions, and respond by dismissing it and retaining their previous definition unchanged.

Science is everyday

Another minority held a view that science was, of course, thoroughly concerned with the everyday and so, of course, the exhibition was scientific.

There are types and levels of science

The majority of respondents, however, seemed to be rather ambivalent and the question generated discussion. They often replied to the effect that the exhibition had not struck them particularly as a 'scientific' exhibition – and here they identified 'science' as distant and difficult, as anticipated by the exhibition-makers. However, they also recognized that it must be scientific because of its location in the Science Museum. This power of the Museum to say what counts as science, to define and legitimate science, is very important here. What then happens for these visitors is that, faced by this challenge to their preconceptions, they try to resolve the mismatching visions. And they do so either by moving towards the boundary-less vision, or – more often – by partitioning science into *levels* or *types*. In some cases this has the effect of shifting 'real science' elsewhere.

Challenges to images of science: some examples.

[Does this strike you as a scientific exhibition?]
> 'No ... Studying science at school – physics and chemistry and so on – it doesn't really come into it in my view' (I. 13, p. 3).
> 'I just didn't think that food was very ... was *science*. I just didn't think food was science, but now I know' (I. 12, p. 4)
> M: 'Not really, no ... It doesn't go into that great an analysis – it's ...'
> W1: 'No, not substantially'
> M: 'Science is everyday and if that is the case then, yes, but ...'
> W1: 'Not in the sense of pure science as it were ... There's levels of scientific thought ...' (I., p. 3 and p. 10)
> 'Well, it has to be – it's in the Science Museum' (I. 17, p. 4)

CONCLUSIONS

Visitors bring to any exhibition particular preconceptions – particular tendencies towards certain imaginings. Clearly, the more that exhibition-makers can manage to detect of these predispositions, the better they will be able to work with them. As we have seen from the example of the explicit and multi-pronged challenge to expected public images of science, exhibitions can at least shake preconceptions which visitors may hold.

Exhibition messages may be more likely to be made through three-dimensional media – at least in an exhibition of this type and with a family-group audience – than through the text-panels. However, the media of an exhibition may give rise to readings which had not been anticipated by its makers. There have, of course, been doubts raised about the efffectiveness of interactive exhibits to further public understanding of science. For example, Diane Saunier, a French museums' consultant, has cautioned against assuming that presenting science *as* accessible is the same as actually making it accessible: 'the presentation of science and technology as spectacle leads to a belief in the accessibility of knowledge, yet knowledge remains concealed'.[10] Understanding of scientific principles or of scientific processes is misleadingly conveyed – or not conveyed at all – by interactives, she claims.

However, although many of these arguments clearly deserve attention, we must be wary of seeing 'understanding' in too narrow a fashion. The understanding of scientific principles and processes may well be difficult to convey – and museums *might* not be particularly good at it in any media – but they may be very good at something rather less narrowly cognitive. That is, less at getting across scientific facts and details, than furthering understanding through more general images and messages about the nature of science, its possibilities, its relevance *and* its limitations.

The same arguments might be made about other kinds of museums and exhibitions, such as social history and ethnographic exhibitions. The kind of research into visitors' likely preconceptions which this paper calls for is particularly crucial where the subject-matter of exhibitions touches on politically and socially sensitive topics: and these days that seems to encompass more and more exhibitions. Although this paper is based on research carried out subsequent to the opening of the exhibition, formative evaluative research could be based on the same principles and methodologies.[11] More generally, this kind of research should be adopted alongside a more thoroughgoing development of broadly semiotic techniques for understanding the kinds of implicit 'messages' which may be inadvertently written into exhibitions. It has already become widely regarded as inadequate for exhibition-makers to ignore their potential visitors altogether, but there is still a long way to go before they are taken fully into account in exhibition-making.

This chapter first appeared as a case-study in Management and Curatorship *11(4) (1992): 401–9.*

ACKNOWLEDGEMENTS

This research was supported by the Science Policy Support Group/Economic and Social Research Council under the 'Public Understanding of Science' programme. It was directed by Professor Roger Silverstone, Sussex University, to whom thanks for comments on the paper are especially due. Thanks are also due to Gilly Heron for carrying out the interviews and preliminary analysis; and to staff at the Science Museum, London, and in particular the 'Food for Thought' team for so generously allowing the exhibition to be studied. I would also like to express my gratitude to participants at the 'Museums and the Public Understanding of Science' conference held at the Science Museum in April 1992 at which I presented a version of this paper. In particular I would like to acknowledge comments from Steve Allison, Jane Bywaters, John Durant and Roy MacLeod.

NOTES

1 See, for example, Minda Borun, *Measuring the Immeasurable*, 3rd edn (Philadelphia, PA: Franklin Institute of Science, 1982).
2 See, for example, James Clifford, *The Predicament of Culture* (Cambridge, MA: Harvard University Press, 1988), 206–9.
3 The study was devised by myself, Roger Silverstone and Gilly Heron, and largely carried out by Gilly Heron. The 'Food for Thought' team (especially its leader Jane Bywaters) and other Science Museum staff with an interest in visitor research in various ways were extremely helpful to us in devising this study, and much of the focus was designed to tie in with questions which had been raised during the making of the exhibition. For an account of the making of the exhibition see Sharon Macdonald and Roger Silverstone, ' "Food for Thought: the Sainsbury Gallery": Some issues raised by the making of an exhibition in the Science Museum, London' (London: Centre for Research into Innovation, Culture and Technology, Brunel University, 1990).
4 Forty-two family groups were tracked through the gallery and interviewed. This entailed 123 subjects in total. Interviews began by asking subjects to describe their visit to the exhibition ('Could you describe where you went and what you saw?') and continued to ask open-ended questions on a number of subject areas. The mean length of time of interviews was 19.5 minutes. For further details see Sharon Macdonald, ' "Food for Thought": Visitors to a Science Museum Exhibition' (Department of Sociology and Social Anthropology, Keele University, 1992).

5 Abbreviations used in quotations, which are taken from transcriptions of recorded interviews with groups of visitors, are: I = the number of the interview; G = girl; B = boy; W = woman; M = man.

6 The great majority of the visitors interviewed had visited other museums or other related institutions during the past year and these ranged from the National Gallery to Madame Tussauds.

7 For a discussion of the embodiment of visitors in the exhibition see Sharon Macdonald, 'Un Nouveau "Corps des Visiteurs: Musées et Changements Culturel"'; (*Publics et Musées*, 3, 13–29).

8 For some further anthropological reflections on the classification of foods in the USA and the UK see Marshall Sahlins, *Culture and Practical Reason* (Chicago: University of Chicago Press, 1976) and Rosalind Coward, *The Whole Truth* (London: Faber & Faber 1989).

9 For further discussion of this strategy in the exhibition see Sharon Macdonald, 'Authorizing science: public understanding of science in museum exhibitions', in Brian Wynne and Alan Irwin (eds) *Misunderstanding Science? The Public Reconstruction of Science and Technology* (Cambridge: Cambridge University Press, 1996).

10 Diane Saunier, 'Museology and Scientific Culture', *Impact of Science on Society* 152: 332–53.

11 To some extent this is happening with qualitative style techniques, e.g. focus group research, being used increasingly in many museums. See, for example, R. S. Miles *et al.*, *The Design of Educational Exhibits*, 2nd edn (London: Unwin Hyman, 1988).

28

The disabling society
Rebecca McGinnis

One of the central recommendations of all theorists, both cultural and museological, is that museums need to get closer to their audiences.

As this chapter points out, the biggest barrier to the participation of some audience groups is the lack of awareness and knowledge among museums workers of their characteristics and needs. The chapter offers demographic and other information that relates to disability issues in Britain, and presents some small case-studies.

We are all aware of the need for improved access to museums for people with disabilities, but most of us regard it as a vague and abstract issue which barely affects our work. When access is addressed, it is often in the limited terms of a ramp, a toilet for wheelchair-users, or perhaps a touch-tour for visually impaired people. So how well do we actually understand the issue of access for people with disabilities and its relevance to all areas of museum work?

In recent years, disability has come to be understood as a condition imposed by an able-bodied society rather than the inevitable consequence of impairment. Barriers of attitude can be as impassable as physical and sensory barriers and there is no single disabled audience. There are blind and partially sighted people, deaf and hearing-impaired people, people with mobility difficulties, people with learning difficulties and people with hidden disabilities such as back pain and epilepsy. Together, people with disabilities make up a larger audience than is generally recognized. There are about six million people in the UK with a disability; that is, one in ten. In fact, six million is a conservative estimate based on a narrow medical definition. One in four may be a more realistic figure.

Very often we find misconceptions about the relative size of groups of people with particular disabilities. Only about 2% of these six million people use wheelchairs. Therefore 98% are ignored when disability is equated to the use of a wheelchair. Although there are one million people who could be registered blind and partially sighted in the UK, and an additional 750,000 people with severe visual impairments, only about 1% of museums offer information in braille and only about 2% provide information in large print.

CONSULTING DISABLED AUDIENCES

Each group of disabled people must be located and targeted carefully. And this should be done by museums before they develop their programmes and facilities. Groups of disabled people should be consulted from the planning stage right through to the evaluation of the finished product. A good example of the importance of consultation concerns a large museum in the USA which planned a series of sign language-interpreted events on Friday evenings. No one turned up for the evenings. When evaluating what went wrong, the organizer found that Friday was the one evening each week when several television programmes were sign-language interpreted. One brief chat with a well-informed member of the deaf community would have prevented this disaster.

Many museums in the UK are now forging links with local societies of and for disabled people. However, this is still done haphazardly, usually on a one-off basis and relying on the initiative of one person rather than any museum policy. The Museums and Galleries Commission (MGC) Guidelines on Disability clearly state that 'regular consultation with disabled people and disability organizations [should be undertaken] in order to assist in designing, improving and developing the provision of services and the recruitment and employment of disabled people'. The guidelines also say that such consultation should be an integral part of a museum's disability policy.

Consultation develops in different ways according to the culture of an institution. Local authority museums may find it more natural to draw on links with local agencies and societies, whereas national museums, which cannot rely on a pre-existing network, may have to work harder to find sources of potential user groups. In the USA, the consultative process has become an official procedure and is virtually standard practice. Committees called advisory boards, consisting of members of the target audience, are established and maintained.

Once programmes and provisions have been put into place, the audience must be informed about what the museum has to offer them. Museums do not have a good reputation for their accessibility, or for programmes for disabled people, so getting a positive message across can be a daunting task. People's mobility difficulties or their need for information in alternative formats may, in turn, slow the dissemination of information. For example, people with mobility difficulties may not get out as much as others and may therefore miss much of a museum's advertising. Blind and partially sighted people may not have access to information about a museum unless it is available in large print, braille, or on tape or computer disk.

Museums must make it clear what they have to offer and what assistance can be given. Some of the most valuable contacts for marketing facilities and services are the press officers of organizations representing disabled people – they can advise on appropriate specialist disability publications that reach other organizations and societies, and on other methods of communication with the target group. The talking newspaper network, for instance, is an invaluable method of spreading information to visually impaired people.

Many of the suggestions listed below would benefit all visitors, not just people with disabilities. Everyone appreciates clear print on labels, good lighting and good signs for directions. And certain facilities will also help children, people for whom English is not a first language, those with children in pushchairs, older people and those with minor or temporary disabilities, such as cataracts or broken legs.

What can museums offer people with disabilities?

General services for disabled people:

- access brochure
- advertising
- staff trained in disability awareness
- staff assistance

Services for visually impaired people:

- taped guides
- pre-visit information
- touch tours
- handling gloves (only if absolutely necessary)
- handling sessions
- tactile plans
- tactile drawings of objects
- workshops
- braille information
- large-print information
- objects for touch by all
- legible labels
- braille labels
- large-print handouts of labels/text panels
- shop items
- tactile postcards
- good lighting
- clear signs
- guide-dog access into the museum
- water for guide-dogs

Services for deaf and hearing-impaired people:

- sign language-interpreted tours
- print transcript of taped tours and information
- staff trained in British Sign Language and deafblind alphabet
- fire alarms with flashing lights
- sympathetic hearing scheme (contact Hearing Concern, London)
- hearing-dog access into the museum
- water for hearing dogs

Services for people with mobility difficulties:

- ramps of a regulation slope near all steps
- public lifts (not goods lifts)
- accessible lavatories
- signs, labels and displays, as well as doorhandles, information counters and public telephones, at an appropriate height for people using wheelchairs (these facilities will also benefit children)
- doorways wide enough for wheelchairs
- wheelchairs for use in the museum
- stools for use on guided tours
- adequate seating in all galleries and public areas offering back-rests and different heights and degrees of hardness

- set-down point at the entrance to the museum
- maps showing seating
- ramped routes marked clearly on a map
- numbers of steps indicated in the brochure
- sessions where objects (possibly from handling collections) are brought to one place.

Services for people with learning difficulties:

- clear labels and signs
- large print
- specially tailored taped tours

GETTING ON GOOD TERMS

Appropriate language is vital when talking with, or about, people with disabilities. Terminology surrounding disability has become increasingly problematic and politically charged in recent years. Knowing which of the many descriptions for various types of disability to use without giving offence can confound the best-informed person. Phrases can be cumbersome and awkward. Words move in and out of favour quickly and there is also a wide diversity of personal preferences but you can avoid resorting to stereotypes. Usually there is a comfortable middle ground. Indeed, understanding how to communicate, how to behave and how to assist disabled visitors are the first hurdles museums must face.

A vital first step is to address the person – the individual and not the disability. Avoid saying things like 'there are two wheelchairs on the first floor'. To say 'there are two people using wheelchairs on the first floor' conveys a more positive message. Disability awareness training or disability equality training for all members of staff, particularly those who provide a first point of contact with the museum, is an essential first step towards accessibility.

The term 'access' itself should be clarified. Access means not only physical access, but conceptual, intellectual and multi-sensory access as well. A lift will not help a person with a learning difficulty or a partially sighted person to understand a museum's collection; but clearer layout and large print on labels and signs will. Another important aspect of access is the employment of people with disabilities in museums. This side of the equation is almost always forgotten. In all, consultation between museum departments on issues relating to access must be developed and maintained. A committee consisting of curators, conservators, designers, educationalists, exhibition organizers, fundraisers, health and safety officers, personnel officers, press and public relations officers, printers and warders, would be an invaluable forum for these issues. Such a committee should draw on the expertise of disabled people, perhaps inviting representatives of different groups to the meetings.

LEGISLATION AND EQUAL OPPORTUNITIES

There is no anti-discrimination legislation for people with disabilities in the UK. Until this changes, enforcing access and preventing active and passive discrimination in employment and visitor services will be impossible. Many museums have equal opportunities policies, but these usually vague policies tend to rely on the goodwill of personnel departments. These policies are rarely tested, since few people with disabilities are employed by museums. They are not enforceable by law and there are no clear mechanisms of recourse for dissatisfied employees.

Anti-discrimination legislation does exist in the USA. The Americans with Disabilities Act of 1990 (ADA) has been a tremendous catalyst to the development of physical and psychological access to museums in the USA. In addition to anti-discrimination legislation, the ADA requires that public, commercial and government premises and services be made 'readily accessible'. This means that, for instance, access through the kitchen is unacceptable. Measures include everything from major structural alterations, such as widening doorways, to minor additions, such as legible signs, good lighting and braille labels on lift controls. Of course, these regulations are relatively easy to follow in the USA, where most buildings are often quite new and there is lots of space. But historic houses enjoy no exceptions – they have to provide for people with sensory impairments and many have come to realize that loop systems, legible signs, information in large print, braille and on tape, good lighting and the like need not be defacing or expensive to implement. Though there are alternative minimum requirements for historic structures, one accessible route through the publicly used sections of the premises is still required.

In the light of this legislation, museums have had to address access and equal opportunities seriously and coherently. Many museums have access advisers and ADA committees designed to exchange ideas and air problems in every aspect of the museum's activities. In New York City, seven large museums have recently formed the Museums Access Consortium. It is hoped that this sort of structured communication between museums will spread to other cities and regions throughout the country. Although the UK has no such formal links between museums where access is concerned, area museum services could and sometimes do perform similar functions. The Museums and Galleries Disability Association is another channel for exchanges of information and discussion.

The MGC Guidelines on Disability give excellent recommendations for developing access and equal opportunities within museums, but the guidelines are problematic. As they are not requirements, they are often seen as extras rather than as an integral part of museum activities. They do not give any ideas about incorporating the recommendations into pre-existing structures and regulations. For example, equal access will contravene the fire regulations which recommend that only a limited number of wheelchair-users may be above ground-floor level in a building that does not have adequate lift access or a fire-safe lift. No solutions to such problems have been found.

The guidelines provide no practical help with creating a disability policy and action plan, nor with setting up mechanisms for consultation with groups of disabled people, developing evaluation procedures, or implementing equal opportunities policies and positive action on employment of disabled people. All of these, none the less, are recommended in the guidelines. The MGC has recently published its Disability Resource Directory for Museums, which, for the first time, provides a thorough central point of reference to information pertaining directly to museums and disability. This document is a valuable tool for creating an accessible experience for all museum visitors. It is also a vital step in the process of informing everyone in museums of the needs and rights of disabled people.

As the Universal Declaration of Human Rights (article 27) states: 'Everyone has the right freely to participate in the cultural life of the community, to enjoy the arts and to share in scientific advancement and its benefits.' Only when these rights are recognized, understood and reinforced by legislation, can people with disabilities be empowered to take full advantage of all that museums can offer.

CASE-STUDIES

Listen with MoMA

Rebecca McGinnis: the ground-breaking work of the Museum of Modern Art in New York

The Museum of Modern Art (MoMA) has a long history of providing programmes that encourage visitors with disabilities to participate in museum activities. Efforts to integrate these programmes into mainstream MoMA policy and services were initiated in 1944 with the museum's collaboration with the War Veterans' Art Center which offered one of the first art therapy programmes in the USA. Since 1972, touch tours have been offered by trained education staff, enabling visually impaired visitors to experience a selection of sculptures from the museum's permanent collection through touch. Braille and large print brochures are prepared for special exhibitions and the Museum Access Project, begun in 1979, continues to offer programmes, gallery talks and courses for deaf people through sign-language interpretation. When the museum facilities were expanded in 1984, lifts, ramps and other features were incorporated to make all galleries, theatres, offices and the library accessible. Plans are now under way to modify the film theatres to permit wheelchair-users to sit with friends rather than in a segregated area. In recognition of these activities MoMA has received the New York State Governor's Art Award for amplified film screenings and, in June 1992, one of the first annual Access New York awards from the Manhattan borough president's office.

The museum is also working to develop a larger community sensitive to the needs of visitors with disabilities. In 1988, its ties with community-based organizations such as Hospital Audiences and the Jewish Guild for the Blind led to two well-attended seminars exploring the possibilities of tactile exhibits. And four years later MoMA contributed to the Hospital Audiences' symposium Access to Art.

Perhaps the most challenging project has been that aimed at expanding access for blind and partially sighted visitors. The touch tour has been extremely popular. But since it opened up only a very small selection from the museum's vast collection, the education department convened a focus group to investigate further possibilities. This study found that people who are visually impaired wanted access to all parts of MoMA's collections, preferring to be integrated into regularly scheduled programmes such as gallery talks, rather than being segregated with special programmes. They wanted descriptions of two-dimensional works of art available in a variety of formats, such as taped or live lectures with high-contrast black and white photos or raised-line drawings. Following work with the focus group, the museum has been exploring ways of composing accurate verbal descriptions and developing tactile representations of works of art. The group Art Education for the Blind (AEB) has, for several years, created three-dimensional tactile models based on objects in MoMA's collection. Founded to provide access to art through multi-sensory tools suitable for use by educational institutions, museums and independent learners, AEB has developed an introductory art-history textbook on tape with raised diagrams to explain works of art and concepts such as perspective. Using computer-generated, raised-line drawings, models, audio-tapes and other descriptions, it has created a system specially designed for visually impaired people.

With the support of the National Federation for the Blind, AEB has become expert in the field of verbal description. And, backing this expertise, MoMA's education department recently completed a one-year study which assessed audience comprehension, with and without the auxiliary aids.

Friends to call upon

Chris and Geoff Howarth: an outreach project run by the Friends of the Whitworth Art Gallery

In October 1990 the Friends of the Whitworth Art Gallery organized an outreach project to bring people with special needs into the gallery. Since then the Whitworth has been visited by many people with special needs, including those in stroke support groups, residents of nursing homes and epilepsy centres and children with learning difficulties. Last year the outreach project attracted 33 groups of people with special needs.

The Whitworth is a bright, spacious, accessible gallery where staff are determined to create a friendly relaxed atmosphere. To complement this, volunteers from the friends organization can provide an informal atmosphere in which visitors can enjoy the collections.

The average visiting group includes ten disabled people and is met by five volunteers. A typical visit lasts about an hour and a half including 30 to 40 minutes spent looking at a particular exhibition, often with a curator present. Half an hour is taken for light refreshments, which facilitates general conversations among volunteers and visitors. For the remaining time, the volunteers accompany small groups of visitors as they look at whatever interests them in the gallery.

Visitors appreciate a lightness of touch and the odd spark of humour and the curators and volunteers encourage a two-way discourse. Some visitors tire easily and prefer to sit with a volunteer and discuss the pictures, the memories they evoke, or their own lives and interests. Others like to tour the gallery alone or with a volunteer. Many respond with pleasure to the tapestries, wallhangings, garments and domestic textiles, often recalling their own career in textiles or interest in needlework. Many of those who come from day centres and stroke support groups use art as a therapy and a visit to the gallery often gives them fresh ideas for their own work.

People with very little or no sight enjoy having pictures described to them, responding with imagination and wit. They also have the pleasure of touching and discussing certain sculptures with the help of a volunteer and with a curator present. Magnifying glasses have helped all kinds of visitors (and volunteers) to appreciate detailed work, especially that in finely hatched etchings.

In all these ways the personal and adaptable approach of the volunteers has helped to make the Whitworth more accessible to a wider range of people.

The layered approach

Nicholas Dodd: 'access' means more than just physical access

The exhibition 'Godiva City: 1,000 Years in the Making', which opened at Coventry's Herbert Art Gallery and Museum in June 1994, represented five years' work to research and explain the story of Coventry in an accessible, interesting, educational and stimulating way.

From the beginning of the planning process museum staff were committed to improving facilities for people with disabilities by integrating their needs and desires into the content and structure of the exhibition. To do this we wrote an information strategy that had at its heart the issues of access. The question of intellectual access is very important. It was one of the main reasons for Godiva City's 'layered' approach. As people have a range of intellectual needs and abilities, providing different levels – things to do, to play with, to hear, to see and to touch – is crucial to bringing more people to museums. This policy was borne out by consultation which confirmed that in being creative with access for people with disabilities, the exhibition would benefit all users.

The strategy aimed to create a meaningful exhibition that clearly and succinctly intro-duced the main historical stories and provided a breadth rather than a depth of infor-mation. Different layers of interpretation allow people to choose their own journey of discovery via either text or objects, animation, interactive exhibits, audiovisuals, handling stations or touchable objects.

The storyline had to be strong, simple and compact and we had to take difficult deci-sions on the amount and complexity of text, the type and sort of object, the style of display and the places for interactivity. These decisions were based on the reading level and learning abilities of the average visitor, and the needs of the national curriculum, but also flowed from a desire to place comprehensive access first. The approach recognized that visitors wish to inform and entertain themselves in a varied and unstructured way.

Deciding what access should be included involved discussions between a number of people who used wheelchairs, had learning difficulties, or were deaf, blind, or partially sighted. The talks included the project manager, the council's disability officer, the marketing officer, the education officer, a disability consultant (William Kirby) and Redman Design Associates (RDA).

A 'feelie' model was produced, which allowed the group of disabled people to try out the design. This acted as the centrepiece for a two-month public consultation programme which allowed staff the opportunity to walk or wheel people around the empty space and to generate ideas. A list of practical improvements compatible with the space was compiled and we arrived at an understanding of the varieties of intel-lectual access that were possible.

With designers John and Laurie Redman, the group looked in detail at text sizes and location, tonal contrasts, colours, textures, finishes, aisle widths, display tolerances, heights, lighting and ease-of-use and safe zones. These were all low- or no-cost elements that could make all the difference to the enjoyment of the finished product.

At the same time, the more complex and expensive suggestions of the consultative group, such as the audio tour, the tactile pathway and location posts, the touchable relief map, the 'feelie' objects, glare-free glass and the sounds of the city, were costed so that we could approach sponsors and charities for funds.

Courtaulds Amtico seized the idea that their tiles could become the tactile pathway through the exhibition. The pathway was developed and tested with the help of a local man, Eric Sayce, who is blind and who uses a guide dog. The trial pathway not only includes a walkway, which was narrowed after trialling, a contrasting guide strip for canes and a textured 'warning' surface at the walkway junctions, but also carried the exhibition's colour scheme, a different logo for each display section to improve location awareness and a scuff strip. It had tactile location posts at the beginning of each section, sponsored by Courtaulds Advanced Materials, which carried a logo and sequential numbers. The whole package was linked to an audio tour designed specifically for blind and partially sighted people.

Coupled with the tape-track package were six cases with non-reflective glass, three 'living paintings' of two pictures and a banner, and a 1:50 tactile relief map of the exhibition layout made of wood, perspex and metal, with a roller indicator for the fire door, and buttons marking the activity areas. Training the deaf-signing staff at the local technical college enabled them to become regular guides at the gallery.

The exhibition also used a local resource centre for the blind to produce a talking newspaper on the scheme, and some braille labels, and to provide large-print text and audio information on the displays for those thinking of a visit.

As part of the commissioning and evaluation of the exhibition, the consultative group was to return to test the interactives, the 'feelie' objects and access provisions, and to make minor improvements. For the future, the exhibition could call on a two-year funding scheme with Courtaulds, and a £9,000 ten-year maintenance budget.

Providing insights

Marista Leishman: disability equality training

Disability equality training (DET) is not about feeling sorry for disabled people. It is about discovering that disabled people are no different from anyone else. They are able, talented, slow-witted, responsible, enlightened, careless, or lazy in equal measure. DET is about changing attitudes that project disabled people as less than capable, heroic, the subject of tragic misfortune, needing help, or miserable.

For most people, relating to disabled people in the same way as everyone else takes more than simply reading about how to do it. In turn, disabled people regularly experience the uncertainty and embarrassment of others who, for example, make a remark and then immediately think that they must have said the wrong thing. Often people compensate for their uncertainty with over-the-top helpfulness; for example, propelling the blind girl over the road she did not intend to cross, talking loudly the while as though she was also deaf.

DET is about being free to relate to disabled people in an ordinary way. It is the starting-point for every initiative to increase access to the museum. Disability is not, after all, the result of a particular impairment but the effect of trying to function in a world designed for others.

A wheelchair user may be disabled in relation to the museum he or she likes to visit because its front entry has five stairs, the service lift is not for public use, and the exhibits are displayed and labelled so that they are only seen from underneath. In that particular case DET introduced flexibility to the museum. While a moveable ramp was being made, access was agreed through the service entrance, which was already ramped. Display and labelling levels were discussed and the stacking chairs were stored away from the disabled toilet.

Awareness of disability is a two-way process. When a museum becomes known for its readiness to receive all comers without fuss and bother, its reputation for access quickly grows and the number of disabled visitors and their helpers increases.

In return, disabled people learn to change habits of dependency and passivity which they may experience simply because they have not got what it takes to face the world.

In-site DET is provided by trainers who are themselves disabled. Lively communicators can provide a positive role model that defies the tragic mould. The training programme enables participants to listen, think, face their own consternation and learn from people whose physical or sensory impairments contribute to changing attitudes. A rigorous programme of exercises centred on discussion groups and videos aids understanding, encourages self-questioning and stimulates people to review their own attitudes. People soon realize that any division between disabled and able-bodied is of their own imagining because they are all disabled in some way. Trainees go away with information and some experience of facilities for access as well as practical ideas for complementing audio material with visual, and visual with audio. They also consider tactile and braille signs, audio loops and the gradients and measurements of ramps.

DET is about taking responsibility. Disabled people need to enlarge their opportunities and museums need to increase their audiences. Museums, with their interest in opening up their buildings and their staff, are set to challenge stereotypes. They and their disabled visitors can only stand to gain.

This chapter first appeared as an article in Museums Journal *94(6) (1994): 27–33.*

FURTHER READING

Designing for Accessibility (London: Centre for Accessible Environments (CAE), 1993); available at £7 from CAE, Nutmeg House, 60 Gainsford Street, London SE1 2NY.

Disability Resource Directory for Museums (London: Museums and Galleries Commission, 1993); ISBN 0-948630-24-8; loose-leaf binder, available free to those museums in the UK which are eligible for MGC registration; available with a charge of £6 to cover postage and packing to museum support organizations recognized by the MGC; from 16 Queen Anne's Gate, London SW1H 9AA.

Disabled People Welcome! Meeting People: Acceptable Language and Behaviour (Museums and Galleries Disability Association, 1993), available from Kathy Niblett, MAGDA Secretary, City Museum and Art Gallery, Stoke-on-Trent ST1 3DW.

Jayne Earnscliffe, *In Through the Front Door* (London: Arts Council of Great Britain, 1992), £9.95, available from AN Publications, FREEPOST, PO Box 23, Sunderland SR1 1BR.

Museums Without Barriers: A New Deal for Disabled People (London: Routledge, for ICOM and Fondation de France, 1992), £20 (pbk), £40 (hbk), available to Museums Association members through the booklist, £17.50 (pbk,) £37.50 (hbk).

The Accessible Museum: Model Programs of Accessibility for Disabled and Older People (1992), ISBN 0-931201-16-0, $40, available from AAM Bookstore, 1225 Eye Street Northwest, Suite 200, Washington, DC 20005, USA.

29

Museums and cultural diversity in contemporary Britain

Eilean Hooper-Greenhill

In Britain many minority groups find museums irrelevant or intimidating and, in some cases, offensive. The report from the Museums and Galleries Commission on Cultural Diversity (Desai and Thomas 1998) discussed in the introductory chapter to this Reader, confirms and extends our knowledge in this area.

This chapter examines some of the reasons why this might be the case, reviews the expression 'cultural diversity', and places the discussion within an analysis of the museum in modern culture. Some long-established museum techniques are analysed to show how black people and culture are positioned as inferior. Some recent examples of attempts to respond to these historical injustices are described.

WHAT IS CULTURAL DIVERSITY IN BRITAIN?

The range of cultures, religions and ethnicities in a society is specific to that society's history. The present-day diversity of culture in Britain has a broad spectrum that includes but is not limited to Europe. In common with many other European countries, Britain has been a site of transition over many centuries: people coming to Britain have included 'the Celts, Romans, Anglo-Saxons, Vikings, Normans, Jews, Huguenots, Poles, Ukrainians, people from Africa, from Asia, and from the Caribbean. An even greater number has migrated from Britain, for example to the USA, Canada, New Zealand and Australia' (Webb 1993: 4). Much of the mix of people in Britain relates to Britain's history of Empire and colonialism.

At the present time,[1] those living in Britain who have been born outside Britain make up 7.3% of the population: of these the largest group is Irish people,[2] who comprise 1.5% of the total population. Other European groups[3] make up 0.9% of the total. Of the total population of Britain 3.1% were born in New Commonwealth countries (which includes the Caribbean, South and South-East Asia, and Africa).

On the whole, when the expression 'cultural diversity' is used in Britain, it refers to those who bear visible marks of difference; in other words, people from the Indian subcontinent, Africa and the Caribbean. Sometimes Chinese people are also included. Many of these groups have come to Britain relatively recently, but many cities, such as Liverpool and London, have their own long-established black communities that are (generally) living alongside, but not always part of, the local neighbourhood groups. 'Ethnic diversity' might be a more accurate expression, and in many ways the term 'cultural diversity' succeeds the term 'ethnic minority', which is currently seen as tending towards the pejorative.

At the time of the 1991 census, 5.5% of the population of Britain was described as not white; of this figure 1.6% belonged to an ethnic group described as black, 2.7% were from South Asian groups, and 1.2% were Chinese and others. Nearly half of these black and Chinese people live in Greater London, where the proportion of the population that identify themselves as belonging to a major ethnic group of non-European origin is approximately 20%[4] (Merriman 1997: 147).

It is difficult to talk about 'cultural diversity' without very quickly acknowledging issues to do with perceptions of 'race', class and gender. British society is deeply divided along these lines, and over the last fifteen years, if some limited gender barriers have been broken, many of those to do with race and class have become more strongly established. For many black communities, both those born in Britain and those who have arrived since the Second World War, life is not easy. Stephen Small points out that, measured by just about every major economic and social indicator, black people are at a disadvantage: they are more likely to be unemployed or to be lowly paid, to be living in rented accommodation, and to be less well educated than their white counterparts (Small 1997: 54).

Small uses the expression 'racialized' inequality, to indicate that 'race' is not a biological given, but is a socially constructed set of beliefs and ideas created historically during the colonization of the Americas (Small 1994: 29). That 'racialized barriers' exist for black people in Britain is documented in statistics and reports such as the recent government (OFSTED) report which shows how, in Birmingham in 1994, 4.6% of black 5-year-olds were performing at levels expected of 6- or 7-year-olds, compared with 3.6% of white children. African-Caribbean 5-year-olds out-performed their white peers in both 1992 and 1994 (the only years that figures are available for), and yet, by the age of 16, African-Caribbean children are six times more likely than other children to be excluded from school, and in their GCSE exams are on average about five points lower than white pupils (Gillborn and Gipps 1996). This grim picture of disadvantage is confirmed by research by the Scarman Centre, University of Leicester, that confirms trends at a local level. It further states that a high proportion of black children do not enjoy or like school, and one of the reasons is that there is little material about black history or culture. As one child said when interviewed: 'There's nothing about black people in any of the lessons. I think that is wrong especially as we have to learn things about everyone else' (Lyle *et al.* 1996: 16).

Very many African-Caribbean and Asian youngsters face a future of unemployment, especially in some of the inner cities. Many of the older generation are angry and disillusioned. Although the picture is not entirely bleak, many people, both black and white, have been distressed over the last fifteen years to see the implementation of social policies in education, law and order and by the police that have led to a deterioration of race relations. The government's involvement in the 1997 European Year against Racism was viewed with suspicion both by anti-racist organizations and by individuals (Bennetto 1997; Boggan 1997).

Largely as a result of the social and political situation described above, 'cultural diversity' in British museums is perceived as an issue that focuses almost exclusively on black communities and that is a response to concerns over their position within British society. At the same time, to talk about 'cultural diversity' is to use a language that glosses over the realities of unequal social relations and life-opportunities through focusing on culture rather than economics and on diversity rather than disadvantage. There is a further problem with the expression: to refer to something or someone as 'diverse' suggests that there is a 'norm' which is being diverged from. Although I have used the expression myself (Hooper-Greenhill 1997), I am not happy about this aspect of it, although one alternative, 'cultural difference', is also problematic.

BRITISH HISTORY AND CULTURE

In the middle of the nineteenth century, when the National Portrait Gallery was founded (in 1856), the intention was to draw together a collection of 'likenesses of celebrated individuals' . . . 'whose names stood for the maintenance and development of the whole national tradition' (National Portrait Gallery 1949: ix). The first portrait to be collected was William Shakespeare's. The 'whole national tradition' was in the event limited to royalty and upper-class and aristocratic men, those who had either ruled the country through political involvement, or been prominent in the arts. This attempt to construct a monolithic and singular view of the world can now be seen as one facet of the modernist project, one of the metanarratives that were called upon to underpin and validate positions of dominance.

This modernist world-view is still very much in evidence, although on all fronts it is under attack. It permeates British culture, and is still in many places invisible, even though it is written into the buildings and environments that form our cultural monuments. Clandon Park in southern England is an archetypical British country house. It stands as an example of a cultural tradition that is venerated for its taste, sophisticated architecture and erudite classical references. It belongs to the National Trust. One of its most celebrated features is the ceiling of the Great Hall, described in glowing art-historical terms in the guidebook (the National Trust 1994: 7–10): 'extraordinary feats of foreshortening' give us relief sculptures of slaves that are contrived to fall from the ceiling, making a reference for those who can read it to Michelangelo's work in the Sistine Chapel. Over the east and west doors are what the guidebook calls 'busts of negroes', which are thought to refer to the Jamaican origins of the Onslow family fortune. The guidebook is not specific as to precisely what activities in Jamaica the family was engaged in, and further research would be needed to find out, but it is well known that many English fortunes were made in the eighteenth century from the profits of slavery. The main point to make here is that this casual architectural comment on the processes of colonialism goes largely unremarked today but is mute testament to the deep-seated relations of advantage and disadvantage on which present-day British society has been built. It is precisely these relationships that begin to explain the figures of black school failures quoted above, and it is partly through culture that these relationships are forgotten.

Traditional museum techniques of display tend to decontextualization, drawing objects out of their untidy and confused contexts in the real world into new purer relationships in the museum where they tell large-scale stories, stories of imagined communities and of invented pasts, stories, which, like Walter Benjamin's angel of history, stand over the wreckage of history, looking into the past but which are hurled into the future, drawing the past and the future together into a compelling narrative of progress that writes out those who because of the emptiness of their pockets, their gender, or the colour of their skin, cannot take part (Benjamin 1970: 259). Authoritative, large-scale, frequently celebratory, these museum narratives are difficult to contradict; there is no named author, they are legitimized by the power of the institution, their labels and texts state facts rather than suggest interpretations.

Traditional museum display techniques seem designed to isolate the past, to sever the connections to the present and to efface the symbolic references of things. Placing objects in glass cases cuts them off physically from the observer, sets them apart as things to be seen but not understood, and in the minimal labels that name and date the object, its stories are lost. In the absence of the object's own narrative, it is susceptible to incorporation into the fiction of the observer.

To take a specific example, a 'Ghost Dance' shirt from Glasgow Museum's collection is merely a curiosity, susceptible to being seen as belonging to the days of 'cowboys and Indians' and 'the Wild West'. The film genre of the 'Western' and children's stories and games perpetuate a romantic myth that conceals the unsavoury processes behind the construction of American democracy. The object's own story, however, once brought to light, reveals a more poignant and brutal set of events that, while appearing to be lost in the past, in fact affect us globally today. The garment in question is a Ghost Dance shirt, thought to protect its wearer from death, but looted from a body at the Battle of Wounded Knee in South Dakota on 29 December 1890; it was used as part of late nineteenth-century 'Wild West' exhibitions and performances, and was given to the museum following Buffalo Bill Cody's Wild West European tour of 1891. It was displayed at Kelvingrove Museum in the ethnography gallery alongside other artefacts from Wounded Knee (a necklace of hide, a pair of buckskin moccasins embroidered with beadwork, and a Sioux cradle). In 1992 the Ghost shirt was lent to the exhibition 'Home of the Brave', in Glasgow, where an American lawyer, John Earl, a Cherokee descendant, recognized it. On returning home, he contacted the Wounded Knee Survivors Association, and currently the museum is engaged in a prolonged discussion over the restitution of this artefact, with many Scottish people feeling that it should indeed go home, along with the necklace and other items (Maddra 1996; Brown 1991).

This small case-study serves as a good example of processes that museums are engaged in across the world, and curators in Britain are well aware of events in Canada, Australia, New Zealand and elsewhere. Artefacts that have previously been silent are being made to speak again, but to tell stories from new perspectives, to make the connections between the past and the present explicit and to expose the contradictory elements that the pure universalist modernist discourse concealed. The deep-seated cultural diversity of British history and society is coming into view as a result.

MUSEUMS AND 'CULTURAL DIVERSITY'?

There are a range of issues that emerge when considering how museums in Britain have responded to the challenge of cultural diversity. One of the most crucial is staffing. Some few museums over the last few years have employed staff from specific local communities,[5] and where this has happened excellent and long-lasting links have been built. Cartwright Hall in Bradford is a particular example, where, with an Asian curator of art, relationships with a range of Asian communities are of long establishment. In Liverpool, an outreach officer from the African-Caribbean community has been appointed to work with a new permanent display on 'Transatlantic Slavery'.

A second issue is the membership of the board or committee, where much museum policy is decided. Few have members of different ethnic groups on their strength.

A third issue is how objects are displayed. Some curators are exploring new approaches to displaying objects. At the National Portrait Gallery in London, a small temporary exhibition uses the familiar celebratory approach to celebrate the life of Ignatius Sancho. Very traditional display techniques are used – objects are placed in cases, with small amounts of information given for each of them. However, the choice and juxtaposition of objects are used to make unusual points, as is the choice of words to contextualize the objects.

The contrast between Sancho's birth on board a slave-ship and his later acceptance as a writer and composer in British eighteenth-century society is made evident by the conjunction of slave shackles placed next to a harpsichord. As the visitor contemplates this real but surreal relationship, she hears Sancho's harpsichord music being played.

The information given with a portrait of the Duchess of Portsmouth, used in the temporary exhibition on Sancho, highlights the eighteenth-century custom of having black pages and servants. In the permanent NPG display the label names the sitter, and the artist, but ignores the child in the painting.

A coffee cup is displayed, with comments made on the transfer print, which shows a couple being served by a black servant. Further label text refers to the importance of sugar in British (and European) social life, and the origins of this in the slave plantations in the Caribbean. This places the cup in a social and political context. Such a cup would 'normally', through references to ceramic techniques such as 'creamware', be placed within the context of the history of design. Objects are susceptible to multiple interpretations, many of which in the museum context are constructed through the accompanying text, which illuminates some aspects of the object, but, by doing so, conceals others. The choice of which aspect to bring to light is ultimately a political one.

The exhibition is being used by schools, and is linked to the BBC Black History project through the internet. The exhibition has its own website (the NPG's first) accessible through http://www.npg.org.uk/sancho.htm. The *Times Educational Supplement* has been used to alert teachers to the potential of the exhibition.

In this exhibition familiar display techniques have been used to reveal previously ignored links between the present and the past, to give new information about some episodes of black history; new technologies have been used as a strategy to broaden the audience and to introduce the project to children.

A number of exhibitions in recent years have been based directly on researching and acknowledging the diversity of British culture. Three such are 'Transatlantic Slavery: Beyond Human Dignity' in Liverpool, 'The Peopling of London' at the Museum of London, and 'Warm and Rich and Fearless' in Bradford.[6]

At the same time, many museum education departments have been working for many years with school groups from inner city schools which are nearly always made up of ethnically mixed groups. Much of the work has been planned with an awareness of the needs of children who may not speak English as a first language, who may live in one culture in school and another at home, or who may have come to Britain as refugees from ethnic struggles. Working in South London, the education department of the Horniman Museum, for example, is sensitive to the environments from which many of their smallest customers come.

This sensitivity has led to some innovative methods of using collections. Vivien Golding, one of the education officers, has used natural history specimens to illustrate a West African dilemma tale, and I would like to conclude with an example of this (Golding 1997). The museum 'lesson' consists of the telling of the story, and the ensuing discussion with the children of the dilemma over differences that the story poses. This is an abbreviated version of the story:

One day it rained and rained. The water made bigger and bigger puddles, and rose higher and higher. Squirrel was happy that she had made a nest high up in a tree and was safe. Then she saw her friend Hedgehog. He couldn't swim, and he didn't have a nest, so Squirrel helped him by letting him come into hers.

That night the friends were very tired and went to sleep exhausted. Hedgehog rolled into a ball, because hedgehogs like to sleep like that, but he took up all the nest, so that Squirrel couldn't get to sleep. Next morning she told him she didn't like this, and he promised to try to be more careful. The second night Hedgehog tried to sleep on the other side of the nest, but he rolled over and pricked Squirrel so she couldn't sleep again. This went on for some time until finally Squirrel said to Hedgehog that he would have to leave, but Hedgehog said if he did he would die because he couldn't swim. They decided to build a bigger nest together.

What would you have done?

This chapter was written as a conference paper (unpublished) in March 1998 for the conference 'Cultural Diversity in Contemporary Europe', Cultural Traditions Group, Belfast, 8–11 April 1997.

NOTES

1 Figures from the 1991 census, quoted in Brown and Hanna (1996: 38–9).
2 This includes those born in Northern Ireland (245,000 people) and in the Irish Republic (592,000).
3 Excluding those from Scandinavia EFTA.
4 Figures taken from a 1993 survey by the Association of London Authorities, quoted in Merriman (1997: 147, note 1).
5 In local authority museums, Section 11 posts (Local Government Act 1966, and see Hooper-Greenhill 1994: 146), additional to the core museum budget, were used in this way, and the V & A employs a Chinese and a South Asian Liaison Officer.
6 There are accounts of all these exhibitions in Hooper-Greenhill (1997) where many of the issues raised in this chapter are discussed further.

REFERENCES

Benjamin, W. (1970) 'Theses on the philosophy of history', in his *Illuminations*, London: Fontana/Collins, 255–66.
Bennetto, J. (1997) 'Initiative to combat problem derided', *The Independent* (20 February): 6.
Boggan, S. (1997) 'Where racism is not simply a black and white issue', *The Independent* (20 February): 6.
Brown, D. (1991) *Bury my Heart at Wounded Knee: an Indian History of the American West*, London: Vintage.
Brown, M. and Hanna, J. (1996) *Roots of the Future: Ethnic Diversity in the Making of Britain*, London: Commission for Racial Equality.
Gillborn, D. and Gipps, C. (1996) *Recent Research in the Achievement of Ethnic Minority Pupils*, London: HMSO.
Golding, V. (1997) 'Meaning and truth in multi-cultural museum education', in E. Hooper-Greenhill (ed.) *Cultural Diversity: Developing Museum Audiences in Britain*, Leicester: Leicester University Press, 204–25.
Hooper-Greenhill, E. (1994) *Museum and Gallery Education*, Leicester: Leicester University Press.
Hooper-Greenhill, E. (ed.) (1997) *Cultural Diversity: Developing Museum Audiences in Britain*, Leicester: Leicester University Press.
Lyle, S., Benyon, J., Garland, J. and McClure, A. (1996) *Education Matters: African Caribbean People and Schools in Leicestershire*, Leicester: Scarman Centre for the Study of Public Order, University of Leicester.
Maddra, S. (1996) 'The Wounded Knee Ghost Dance shirt', *Journal of Museum Ethnography* 8: 41–58.
Merriman, N. (1997) 'The Peopling of London project', in E. Hooper-Greenhill (ed.) *Cultural Diversity: Developing Museum Audiences in Britain*, Leicester: Leicester University Press, 119–48.

National Portrait Gallery (1949) *Catalogue of the National Portrait Gallery 1856–1947: with an Index of Artists*, London: National Portrait Gallery.

National Trust, the (1994) *Clandon Park, Surrey*, London: National Trust.

Small, S. (1994) *Racialised Barriers: the Black Experience in the United States and England in the 1980s*, London and New York: Routledge.

Small, S. (1997) 'Contextualising black presence in British museums: representations, resources and response', in E. Hooper-Greenhill (ed.) *Cultural Diversity: Developing Museum Audiences in Britain*, Leicester: Leicester University Press, 50–66.

Webb, E. (1993) *The Peopling of London: Fifteen Thousand Years of Settlement from Overseas*, resource pack with notes for teachers, London: Museum of London.

30

A *beginner's guide to evaluation*
Phil Bull

What is evaluation? What does it entail for exhibition producers? Front-end analysis, formative evaluation and summative evaluation are each explained with an example.

The attitude of exhibition designers towards evaluation (and its professional practitioners) has traditionally been ambivalent. While recognizing the potential of evaluation to draw the attention of a design team to imperfections in their work, they have none the less tended to regard any adverse criticism as a slur upon their professional integrity. But suspicion of evaluators often stems from an ignorance of their function, their methods and their terminology. Professional evaluators have been accused of seeking to legitimize their prejudices behind a smokescreen of quasi-scientific jargon. This article attempts to provide a general introduction to the subject and to demystify some of its key concepts.

The evaluation of exhibitions usually falls into one of three categories:

> front-end analysis
> formative evaluation
> summative evaluation

These categories refer to when the evaluation takes place in relation to the design and construction of the exhibition. Generally speaking the earlier it takes place the more cost-effective it is likely to be.

Front-end analysis takes place during the pre-planning and planning stages. It is conducted with the intention of identifying potential problems before the exhibition goes into production. Strictly speaking, it cannot be classified as evaluation at all since it takes place before there is anything concrete to evaluate.

In an article in *Museum News* (1988), Dr Giles Clarke of the British Museum (Natural History) describes how front-end analysis assisted in the planning of an exhibition on arthropods – a group of animals comprising insects, spiders, crustaceans and centipedes. Having decided that such an exhibition was necessary, the key question became 'How much do potential visitors know about arthropods already?' It is of paramount importance that the ideas and terminology of an exhibition should be neither so advanced as to confuse and alienate visitors nor so simplistic as to appear patronizing. A short multiple choice questionnaire was circulated to a representative sample of 145 visitors and its findings were helpful in determining the academic level at which the exhibition should be pitched. It was also considered necessary to assess the level of public enthusiasm for the subject and this was done by means of a series of four discussion groups in which visitors were invited to give their views on ideas for material to be included in the gallery. These discussions revealed that public attitudes towards arthropods tended to range from apathy to outright hostility. Rather than deterring the exhibition team from going ahead, this alerted the team to the need for an accessible, high-profile exhibition which would stimulate and maintain visitors' enthusiasm. The Natural History Museum now conducts front-end analysis as a matter of routine before embarking upon any major new exhibition.

Formative evaluation takes place during the implementation of plans with the intention of providing directional guidance while work is in progress. Often it takes the form of 'developmental testing' which involves the testing of mock-ups of proposed exhibits on a random sample of museum visitors. Their reactions can provide valuable insights into the effectiveness of a particular exhibit in communicating its intended message. But developmental testing is restricted to assessing the impact of content rather than presentation since a crude mock-up will inevitably be less visually appealing than the finished exhibit. The Natural History Museum's evaluation coordinator, Jo Jarrett, has published a paper entitled 'Learning from the developmental testing of exhibits' in which she gives an account of a recent programme of developmental testing in the 'Inheritance and Variation' section of the museum's *Origin of Species* exhibition. It had become apparent that this particular section of the exhibition was failing to communicate its message clearly because it assumed too great a knowledge of the subject in visitors. A new set of exhibits was designed with the intention of explaining the concept of genetic mutation in layperson's terms and developmental testing was conducted on these.

The testing was done in two stages: a pilot stage to identify any major problems and a second stage to evaluate the amended mock-ups. At each stage the methodology was the same. Visitors were allowed to peruse the exhibits in their own time and were then given a semi-structured interview which was intended to establish how well they had understood the message being conveyed in each exhibit. Pilot testing revealed that one exhibit in particular was being misconstrued by an unacceptably large proportion of visitors. This exhibit, entitled 'Odd One Out', explained the effects of genetic mutation, using the Ancon breed of sheep as an example. Pilot testing identified a number of problems, the most serious of which was the tendency of visitors to interpret the exhibit too literally. Visitors construed the exhibit to be exclusively concerned with sheep-breeding and failed to realize that the principle of variation and mutation can be applied to any species of living organism. The exhibit also failed to rectify the commonly held belief amongst visitors that mutation is always a bad thing.

The findings of pilot testing led to a new exhibit entitled 'Everybody Makes Mistakes', which provides an explanation of mutation without making reference to any particular species, being substituted for 'Odd One Out'. The superiority of this new exhibit was well illustrated by the second stage of developmental testing. There was a substantial improvement in the proportion of visitors who were able to paraphrase the message. Developmental testing does not provide solutions to problems of ineffective communication but it can often draw the attention of the exhibition team to unsuccessful exhibits at mock-up stage. This is important because the cost of making changes after an exhibition has been constructed are often prohibitive.

Summative evaluation takes place after an exhibition has been opened to the public, by which time it is usually too late to be thinking about alterations. Its purpose is to establish how successful an exhibition has been rather than to see how it could be improved or how it might have been done better in the first place. Just as a doctor might diagnose an illness without necessarily being able to cure it, summative evaluation might conclude that an exhibition has been a failure without being able to suggest how it might have been done better. Most summative evaluation takes the form of visitor surveys conducted by questionnaire. Surveys of this kind do not normally pose any complex methodological problems although there are certain golden rules to be obeyed when designing a questionnaire or obtaining a representative sample group. (See Miles *et al.* 1982: Ch. 16.) Another form of summative evaluation is 'observational study'. This does not involve any direct contact with the visitor but simply entails observing visitors as they walk around the museum. Observational study can be very useful in gauging the attracting and holding power of each exhibit. But it can be fraught with methodological difficulties since it necessitates following visitors around. If visitors become aware that they are being 'spied upon' this may affect their behaviour. Where possible it is better to conduct observational study by means of closed circuit video cameras since these tend to be less obtrusive.

In the present economic climate with many budgets frozen or curtailed, there is a growing preoccupation with cost-effective exhibitions. Against this scenario, the professional evaluator seems destined to become an increasingly integral member of any exhibition design team.

This chapter first appeared as a paper in Environmental Interpretation *(July 1989): 20–1.*

REFERENCES

Clarke, G. (1988) 'Front-end research: essential preparation in planning an exhibition', *Museum News* 43 (Winter 1988/89).
Jarrett, J. E. (1986) 'Learning from the developmental testing of exhibits', *Curator* 29(4): 295–306.
Miles, R. S., Alt, M. B., Gosling, D. C., Lewis, B. N. and Tout, A. F. (1982) *The Design of Educational Exhibitions*, London: Unwin Hyman.

31

Monitoring and evaluation: the techniques

G. Binks and D. Uzzell

A very practical outline of the strengths, weaknesses and likely costs of questionnaire surveys, in-depth interviews, structured interviews and behavioural mapping.

Most of the techniques used are established ones in the field of marketing, social survey and educational psychology, which are applied and modified to suit the particular situation about which the interpreter, interpretive planner or facility manager is concerned.

Regrettably there is not yet a British handbook of evaluation techniques for interpretation facilities and services. There are, however, useful guides to recreation site surveys and accounts of surveys and evaluation studies of individual interpretive media and facilities which are worth consulting. They offer valuable information; for example, on planning and designing surveys, using questionnaires, observation, group and depth interviews and some deal with techniques of measuring learning and attitude change. Many of them include examples of questionnaires which provide a useful basis for devising your own.

It is possible with the help of some of the key references described on page 301 to devise, carry out and analyse your own survey. Alternatively you may decide to use an off-the-peg survey, some of which have been devised for museums, or you may decide to bring in outside help. It usually all depends on the size and complexity of the evaluation you wish to undertake and your budget. Market research companies, university and polytechnic marketing, tourism and social science and educational psychology departments and individual recreation and interpretation consultancy firms can usually offer tailor-made surveys and evaluation packages on a consultancy basis. Many polytechnic and university departments have staff who are willing to advise you informally on aspects of your survey if you decide to do it yourself. Some may supply student help and there are some computer services departments that also offer help with questionnaires, design and processing.

The sections below describe the main techniques, with their strengths, weaknesses and likely costs.

QUESTIONNAIRE SURVEYS

Strengths
- Lots of experience around among people who have carried out questionnaire surveys in other nearby museums, visitor attractions, etc. You may be able to use, with minor modification, questionnaires they have designed – provided they answer the questions you want answered. Be careful!
- Quite cost-effective. You can produce a large number of questionnaires for the price of the print run. However, the more you produce, the more you will have to analyse. Also a larger sample may mean a more accurate sample.
- Again easy to train people to give out questionnaires, or administer them.

Weaknesses
- While there may be expertise available locally in the design and production of question- naires, it doesn't mean that it's going to be good expertise! There are many badly designed questionnaires around. Poorly designed question- naires give you inaccu- rate, unreliable and therefore useless results. Questionnaire design is a skill.
- Large sample needed for reliable and representa- tive results.
- May require the use of computer to analyse results: see comments on structured interviews.

Likely costs
- Considerable staff time to plan, supervise and analyse.
- Specialist advice as necessary £200–£300 per day.
- Printing of questionnaires – depending on length and print run.
- Off-the-shelf question- naires e.g. DRS Museum Scan around £400 per 500 standard question- naires printed and processed; or £2,000 for 3,000 questionnaires designed for your site, with analysis and customized report.
- Interviewers' fees – ranging from student rates, staff time or professional interviewers. 20–40 questionnaires per interviewer per day depending on length.
- Computer processing costs.

IN-DEPTH INTERVIEWS (with a small sample of people)

Strengths
- Detailed qualitative information, very revealing and 'true'.
- Enables exploration of issues both guided and in response to respondents' concerns and agenda.
- Useful for initial explo- ration of issues prior to a more representative survey.
- Does not require sophisticated technology to analyse data, although there are advanced computer programs which will, after content analysis, analyse the findings.

Weaknesses
- Time-consuming.
- Typically only feasible with a small sample, therefore difficult to make representative. This may not matter – depends on purpose.
- Needs skilled interviewer.
- Difficulty of interpreting information – content analysis is typically used.

Likely costs
- Staff time to plan, supervise and analyse.
- Specialist advice (training of interviewers as necessary) £200–£300 + per day.
- Skilled interviewers' fees £100–£200 per day – maybe 4 interviews per day per interviewer.
- Interviewers' travel costs if interviews are home based.
- Costs of computer processing if appropriate.

STRUCTURED INTERVIEWS

Strengths
- Can deal with a larger sample than in-depth interviews.
- Allows respondents to elaborate their answers, perhaps unlike a questionnaire.
- Not too difficult to train interviewers.
- Can also be useful for initial exploration of issues prior to a more representative sample survey.
- Can use data in a qualitative or quantitative way.

Weaknesses
- Labour-intensive and therefore expensive.
- Large sample needed, (like a questionnaire survey) if they are to be regarded as representative of a larger population.
- May require the use of computer to analyse results, with consequent necessary understanding of statistics and computer programs. There are now many 'off the shelf' computer programs available, but they still require an understanding of the statistical analyses, and the assumptions on which the statistics are based.

Likely costs
- Staff time to plan, supervise and analyse.
- Specialist advice £200–£300 per day.
- Printing costs of interview schedule/ questionnaire.
- Interviewer fees ranging from student rates, £30–£50 per day to professional market research interviews, £50–£100 per day. 15–20 interviews per interviewer day.
- Computer processing.

BEHAVIOURAL MAPPING OR OBSERVATION

Strengths
- Direct measure of the public's behaviour. What the public say they do and what they really do are often two very different things. Enables you to see how they actually use your exhibition, country park, etc.
- Useful complement to other techniques such as questionnaires or interviews, as it enables you to check or corroborate responses.
- Low technology – pencil and paper.
- Inexpensive.

Weaknesses
- Time-consuming. Following or observing one person around an exhibition may take 30 minutes, therefore limited number can be completed in a day.
- Doesn't provide you with the visitor's account of what they were doing or why. You have to interpret their actions: in some cases it is not always clear what people are doing. They may spend 5 minutes looking at an exhibit – this could be because it is fascinating, or because they are having great difficulties understanding it.

Likely costs
- Staff time to plan, supervise and analyse.
- Specialist help if necessary.
- Observers' fees: student rates or equivalent staff time.
- Computer analysis as appropriate.

This chapter first appeared as a paper in Environmental Interpretation *(July 1990): 16–17.*

REFERENCES

Lee, T. R. and Uzzell, D. L. (1980) *The Educational Effectiveness of the Farm Open Day*, Countryside Commission for Scotland. In a series of visitor surveys at Farm Open Days in Scotland, questionnaires were devised to elicit visitor attitudes and to establish the extent of attitude change as a result of what visitors had learnt or seen at the Farm Open Day. As with the Forestry Commission package this provides useful examples of sampling process, questions and analysis procedures.

Miles, R. S., Alt, M. B., Gosling, D. C., Lewis, B. N. and Tout, A. F. (1982) *The Design of Educational Exhibits*, London: Allen & Unwin. This book gives detailed guidance on the design and evaluation of educational exhibits based on the experience of designing exhibitions at the Natural History Museum. It is a manual of good practice and essential reading for anyone planning an exhibition, however small. In particular it discusses techniques for formative evaluation (the testing of various approaches to presenting material before final choice of content and media) and summative evaluation (the visitor response to the material and media that were used). It includes a useful explanation of sampling techniques.

Stansfield, G. (1981) *Effective Interpretive Exhibitions CCP 145*, Countryside Commission. This booklet draws together the conclusions and recommendations for good practice which have emerged from a wide range of research into interpretive exhibitions in a range of museums and visitor centres in Europe and North America.

Tourism and Recreation Research Unit (1983) *Recreational Site Survey Manual: Methods and Techniques for Conducting Visitor Surveys*, London: E. & F. N. Spon. This manual provides comprehensive advice on survey planning, design and implementation at recreation sites. It covers sampling procedures, recruiting and training staff and administration of the survey, data preparation and analysis, as well as providing detailed guidance on mechanical methods of recording and counting visitors, observation methods and a range of questionnaire techniques.

Uzzell, D. L. and Lee, T. R. (1980) *Forestry Commission Visitor Centres: an Evaluation Package*, report to Forestry Commission, Edinburgh. This report describes the evaluation package which was devised for the Forestry Commission to test the role of the commission's visitor centres in attracting visitors, communicating with them, providing an enjoyable experience and encouraging them to explore the forest as a result. The package, designed to be administered by Forestry Commission staff, has several elements: a visitor centre interview using a questionnaire designed to elicit visitors' attitudes and opinions about the centre and particularly about the exhibition and their preferences for different media in use; a forest use questionnaire designed to elicit views of visitors using the forest, car parks and picnic areas about facilities and their knowledge/use of the visitor centre (primarily to test the role of the visitor centre in encouraging people to explore the forest); a brief postal questionnaire for distribution in the visitor centre or in car parks and picnic sites, designed to elicit information retrospectively on visitors' activities and routes taken in the forest recorded by them on a map. The purpose of the package is to provide relatively simple sets of interviews and observation techniques which can be administered by staff, and easily modified and updated over time. The data are readily analysed on computer to provide tables showing frequency counts of the answers to each question and cross-tabulations of answers to one question set against another.

32

Small-scale evaluation

Tim Badman

This chapter describes a specific evaluation project in a historical setting. The objectives of the programme to be evaluated were clarified in terms of messages to be conveyed and the feelings that staff hoped visitors would have. A change in attitude to the historical theme was hoped for and this formed the subject of the evaluation. The methods used, which involved questionnaires used on site, the results and the lessons learnt are discussed.

Quarry Bank Mill at Styal, Cheshire is owned by the National Trust and run by the Quarry Bank Mill Trust with the purpose of interpreting the development of the factory system at the end of the eighteenth century. The Apprentice House aims to contribute to this theme by giving a glimpse of domestic apprentice life in the 1830s. The approach taken combines living history with an informal guided tour. The general public are accompanied around the house by costumed demonstrators, who aim to maintain an informal atmosphere in the group – visitors are encouraged to pick up and touch artefacts, to question and to chat. The emphasis is on learning through experience rather than taking in large amounts of historical fact.

AIMS AND OBJECTIVES

The first thing to be clear about in an evaluation is exactly what is to be evaluated. This means knowing definite objectives for the interpretation: 'What are we trying to say or do?' These should hopefully be written down in some sort of plan or statement, but if not then it will be necessary to sit down and clarify them. This is an important exercise in its own right. At the Apprentice House the aims of the interpretation divide into two categories which can be termed *messages* and *visitor experience*.

Messages

The messages basically revolve around creating empathy with the apprentices and portraying the institutional way of life in the Apprentice House. Within this framework a series of specific factors were identified. Examples included:

- awareness of the lack of individuality of the apprentices
- awareness of the strict routine of apprentice life

Visitor experience

Visitor experience relates to the feelings which staff at the House hoped that visitors would have about the interpretation itself. Specific objectives included:

- feeling entertained and at ease
- feeling the house had an atmosphere of activity
- feeling that the portrayal of apprentice life was honest

At the Apprentice House the principal aim of the survey was to assess attitude change and a questionnaire survey was decided upon as the appropriate method. The detailed work of designing the questionnaire needed to take into account a number of external factors. The main one of these related to time. It is essential that any questionnaire is not too long. People are normally very happy to take time to answer questions but this can quickly become an imposition. The nature of the site may also impose constraints. At the Apprentice House most people arrived for their tour between five and ten minutes before it began – giving a maximum possible time for each interview. It is also useful at this stage to have an idea about the number of results required. This will reflect the amount of time available for data collection. Collecting data is hard work and time-consuming, a reasonable expectation for a questionnaire survey is twenty results per person per day.

SAMPLE SIZE

A certain number of results are needed before data can be considered to be reasonably representative of any group of visitors. This is essential for the definite results which can be produced by statistical analysis. There are several techniques for estimating sample size, but a useful rule of thumb is that at least fifty results are needed for each *group* of data (e.g. 50 results before the visit, 50 results after). This is particularly important if you plan to analyse results according to different types of visitor. Detailed information about visitors may be irrelevant if you are planning to collect a small data set.

For the Apprentice House the finished questionnaire consisted of three sections. The first two aimed to gain basic information about the visitors themselves and about visitor attitudes to apprentice life. These were asked to visitors both before and after visiting the House. Interviewing can 'sensitize' people and affect the way they experience and react to interpretation. It was important, therefore, that people asked before were not interviewed afterwards. The third section of the questionnaire gained information about the visitor experience on the tour and was only asked to visitors who had already visited the House.

Trying to assess attitudes to apprentices presented difficulties; how do you measure empathy? The approach taken was that used by Lee and Uzzell in their work on assessing Farm Open Days. A series of fourteen statements were devised to tap into the attitudes which the interpretation tries to address, for example: 'The millowner exploited the apprentices' and 'Apprenticeship gave poor people a chance to improve their lot'. Visitors were asked to grade these on a numbered scale according to how much they agreed or disagreed with them. Giving numerical values to opinions in this way permits detailed statistical analysis. This analysis can seem quite daunting, but the maths is fairly straightforward and the results are worth the effort.

CONCLUSIONS

So what can result from evaluation? At the Apprentice House the basic conclusions showed that the interpretation was broadly meeting its objectives. The 'graded statement' technique worked and showed a clear difference in attitudes before and after. Changed reactions were observed for nine out of the fourteen statements, and six cases were statistically significant. The survey also showed that most of the aims set for visitor experience were being met. These results have been useful in encouraging staff and giving confidence in the approach that has been taken. The process of the survey itself has also focused the minds of staff on exactly what the interpretation is trying to achieve. The report also highlighted one area of weakness. A number of visitors didn't feel that the house had an atmosphere of 1830s activity. This was something which staff had expected might be the case. Thought is now being given to this aspect of the interpretation.

The total amount of time spent on the project amounted to about ten person days and almost half of this was spent collecting data. This provided about 100 responses. In some cases, a way of reducing the time involved is to use questionnaires or survey forms which can be taken away by visitors and filled in independently. This removes the time-consuming data collection stage but is not appropriate in all cases. An alternative, as was the case with this project, is to work with students. This sort of project can be useful to the site, reducing staff input to a supervisory or liaison role, and make a complete and fulfilling piece of work for the student. Possible places to approach about conducting a student survey include educational establishments which run courses in subjects such as tourism, countryside management, or leisure management.

This chapter first appeared as a paper in Environmental Interpretation *(July 1990): 20–1.*

REFERENCE

Lee, T. R. and Uzzell, D. L. (1980) *The Educational Effectiveness of the Farm Open Day*, Countryside Commission for Scotland.

33

Evaluation of museum programmes and exhibits
George E. Hein

The need for evaluation of programmes and exhibits is discussed, along with an outline of main theoretical approaches, indicating what the epistemological antecedents of these approaches are.

A practical approach is described which offers a useful methodology that is successful in the evaluation of museum education programmes. This relies on the collection of a wide range of data that enables a holistic picture to be obtained. Evaluation should be part of the on-going work of the education section, and an evaluation plan should form part of the museum education policy.

THE NEED FOR EVALUATION

During the last twenty years, museum staffs have become increasingly self-critical and self-inquiring about their programmes and their *raisons-d'être*. A number of factors have contributed to this self-examination. Most important has been the worsening world-wide economic situation. After a period of prosperity following the Second World War, an era of growth, rebuilding and renewal, museums, like other institutions, have had to ask some hard questions about priorities, programmes, audiences, and operating styles. There is clearly not enough money (and consequently insufficient staff and support services) to do everything that might be desired. So questions arise as to which activities are most essential, or most beneficial to the museum and to society.

As a result of the economic crisis, pressure on museums has increased to perform a variety of functions. As schools face cuts in staff, especially in the 'cultural' or 'humanities' areas, they turn to museums and other institutions to provide educational experiences in these areas for their pupils. Museums are asked to make up for discontinued art programmes, decreased material resources, and even for cuts in the science teaching previously carried out in the schools.

This pressure to provide services to the education community also forces museum staffs to question the activities of museums: which are useful, which help children to grow and learn, which efficiently use the museum resources? At the same time, museum audiences are growing. One result of the post-war expansion and prosperity and especially of post-war social changes, is that a much wider segment of the public makes use of public institutions, especially museums. New museums have opened, old ones have expanded, and larger numbers of individuals from a broader spectrum of the population visit them. This pressure of numbers on the institutions also raises questions about the efficient use and best distribution of resources.

Finally, the museum world is becoming increasingly professional. The inspired amateurs and government employees who staffed museums in the past are being replaced by people trained specifically for museum work, many of whom are making a life-time commitment to museum work, and even to museum education. This professionalization brings with it the desire to develop a cumulative review of practice, to document instances, to build on former experience: to establish a profession of museum work and museum education with accepted professional standards and shared procedures.

All these factors – economic constraints, increased museum use, and professionalization – create pressure on museum personnel to look more carefully at their priorities and programmes. The kinds of questions that are raised about museum programmes are of two types. First is a set of concerns about what actually happens in museum programmes: what occurs when children come to a programme, when classes view an exhibit, when the public wanders through the halls? Second is a need to determine if the things that happen are what was intended. Do visitors really learn more about the origins of humanity, do children begin to understand the baroque style, did the museum provide a replication of a 'hands-on' experience in family life of two centuries ago?

Both these types of questions are basic questions of *evaluation studies* – a careful documentation of what a programme is, and examination to see if it meets its objectives. In short, the increased pressures for 'accountability' in museums – both from external economic factors and internal forces leading to increased professionalization – result in greater need for evaluation activities.

THE RANGE OF EVALUATION

The increased need for evaluation in museums is not unique. Other institutions and professions have felt similar pressures in recent years. The spectacular rise in health care facilities (and the rapidly escalating costs!), the expansion of the criminal justice system, and (in the United States) the introduction of Federal funds into the education system starting after the passing of the Elementary and Secondary Education Act in the mid-1960s, have brought with them the need, and often the statutory requirement, for more evaluation.

At the same time, and partly in response to this need, the evaluation field has gone through a dramatic period of growth. This expansion can be seen in the establishment of professional societies of evaluators, the rapid increase in publications devoted to evaluation work and the development, by professional committees, of standards for evaluation. However, the most important change in the evaluation enterprise during this time has not been its considerable growth in size, but the widening of conceptual approaches to evaluation. As professionals have needed to look carefully at a very broad range of programmes and activities they have recognized that systematic inquiry into what happens in the world, how things occur and whether they take place as planned or intended, requires a wide range of approaches and methods.

Before this period of growth, formal evaluation work was confined largely (but not exclusively) to education in schools and was dominated by a scientific approach which took as its model the epistemology and style of the physical, laboratory sciences. Evaluation work was primarily an offshoot from educational psychology, a profession dominated by this quantitative, laboratory-based model. The best-known achievement of this type of evaluation is the now ubiquitous standardized test and the most common method is that of pre-/post-test experimental design.

306

More recently, a new range of evaluation strategies has been developed. Although these strategies use a variety of means, they share an approach which has a different epistemological base from the traditional 'experimental' model. They look to the field-based sciences – ethnography, anthropology and sociology – for their basic theory and rationale. Characteristically, these newer evaluation methods stress documentation, observation and in-depth interviews, and result in case-studies and 'thick' descriptions of practice. They tend to be qualitative rather than quantitative in method and to result in primarily narrative reports.

These two general approaches to evaluation have been repeatedly characterized in recent years, and their values and shortcomings discussed in the literature.[1, 2, 3] As the museum world has begun to examine itself more carefully, and more systematically, a variety of evaluation strategies are used. The more traditional evaluation mode, based on careful specification of desired outcomes and clear efforts to approximate controlled situations, is exemplified by the work of Shettel[4] and Screven,[5] among others. Anthropological and ethnographic approaches to studying museums have been used by a group in Berkeley,[6] while more strictly evaluative studies based on observation and interviews have been carried out, among others, by Wolf,[7] and my colleague Brenda Engel and myself.[8] I will describe our own approach to evaluation in a later section. First I want to make some generalizations about all evaluations.

SOME TRUTHS ABOUT EVALUATION WORK

1. All forms of evaluation can be useful. The styles of evaluation available may appear to be so different that they are contradictory, but each can be of use in certain situations. Each represents a different approach to knowledge, and each provides data and leads to conclusions. The choice of the form of evaluation that will be carried out depends on the problem that is being addressed, the audience to whom the work is directed, and the professional and personal inclinations of the people involved. That does not make one form 'right' and the other 'wrong'. Each must be assessed on its own merits and within its own frame of reference.

2. Under appropriate conditions any form of evaluation can address questions related both to what occurs and what the outcomes are, although the traditional form of evaluation is usually associated more with measuring predetermined objectives, while the field-based methods are better at providing descriptive information and documenting unanticipated outcomes. If both sorts of questions are of interest, it is important that museum professionals stipulate their needs and see to it that the evaluation addresses their concerns.

3. No matter what the form of evaluation chosen, it is crucial that museum programme staff be involved in the evaluation. There is a mistaken assumption that evaluation, like plumbing or accounting, is an activity carried out in isolation from other activities by outside experts. Most of us do call on professionals to repair the water pipes and leave the methodology completely up to them. But, many of us at institutions have learned that it is essential to work with financial experts in order to get an accounting system that meets our needs. It is even more important to work with evaluators because, unlike accounting, there is no standard system that can be applied in the absence of input from programme staff. Evaluation studies are useful only to the extent that professional staff are involved in every phase from planning to data collection and analysis. There is no such thing as evaluation in the absence of goals. These goals should be determined by the people who intend to use the information.

307

4. Evaluation activities should be an ongoing part of the programme itself. They should be carried out concurrently with the activities, not initiated after the programme or exhibit is only a memory for the participants. We and other evaluators are often asked to evaluate a programme after it is almost ended or already completed. This makes more work for everyone, leaves the conclusions nebulous at best, and drastically limits the usefulness of the whole process. An evaluation that occurs while a programme is going on has the following advantages over a retrospective evaluation:

(a) it forces participants to look at what they are doing in a formal and reflective way while they are doing it;
(b) it permits ongoing modification and correction of components that are not working well, or permits changes in later phases based on earlier experiences;
(c) it maximizes the use of normal programme components (records, interviews, observations, participants' products) as part of the evaluation, making it possible to carry out the evaluation with a minimum additional burden to anyone.

5. In the preceding paragraphs I have argued that evaluation is contextual: it happens in a setting. It is an applied task performed in the service of some larger organizational framework. There is no 'pure' science of evaluation independent of its purposes within the context of the institution that carries it out. Another way to say this is to point out that evaluation is political. The kind of questions asked, the sort of information determined to be useful, the means used to gather data, and the way the information is organized and presented will depend on the social views of those who carry out and direct the evaluation. This in no way diminishes the value of evaluation work. It is simply important to remember to ask why any particular study is carried out, what the authors' or sponsors' intentions are, and how the study is to be used.

The above point is only an extension of a more general point about museums. Exhibitions and educational programmes inevitably and necessarily illustrate some social/political point of view. We call them 'neutral' when from *our* point of view they reflect the prevailing socio-political norm. They appear to us apolitical when we cannot even imagine an alternative viewpoint.

PRACTICAL EVALUATION WORK

For the last six years, my colleague Brenda Engel and I have carried out hundreds of evaluation studies for museums and other cultural institutions. Many of these evaluations were of educational programmes developed as part of the effort to bring about racial integration in Massachusetts schools by involving cultural institutions with schools. In our work we have looked at programmes that include younger and older children, that take place in schools, museums or other settings, that are intensive (all day for a week or two) and extensive (once a week for an hour over a long period), that include children who know each other previously and those who don't, as well as programmes that include teachers, parents, and others. Much of our work has been of necessity quite limited: the funds available for evaluation are often only a small fraction of the total budget, and they are usually the first to be cut when, as happens so often, the programme is forced to carry on with a smaller than anticipated appropriation. In the course of this work, we have developed a careful, systematic approach that allows us to meet at least some of the needs of evaluation. We have described this work elsewhere in more detail.[9] What I wish to do here is to outline the essentials of our method, and to draw some conclusions from it for evaluation work in general.

We have found that it is absolutely essential that we meet with programme staff and hear, directly, their description of the programme: what they intend to have happen, and what they expect the outcomes to be. Written descriptions found in proposals or funding requests are usually inadequate and often out of date by the time a programme actually gets underway. At this meeting we match programme intentions and expected outcomes with means for collecting data. There are many possible sources for evaluation information including programme products and activities. The enclosed table (Table 33.1) lists a wide range of data sources that we have found useful. The match of programme issues or interests (whatever is important to the people who are responsible for the programme) with means for collecting data is done graphically in the form of a matrix, so that we can see what means will address each particular issue.

Table 33.1 General matrix and list of possible sources of data

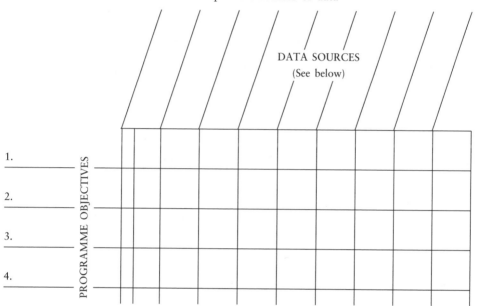

Sources of Data:

Logs and Journals
- personal journals
- records of meetings
- records of class activities
- journal from trip

Reports
- meeting notes
- staff evaluation form
- children's evaluation

Curriculum
- lesson plans
- description of activities

- resource book
- outline
- bibliography of resources
- slide/tape show

Observations
- in class
- on a trip
- of meetings

Interviews
- teachers
- museum staff
- administrators
- children (single or in groups)

Student Products
- pictures
- written work
- objects
- photos of products
- tests
- record of field trip

Other Products
- photos of trip
- children's interview

When we make up this matrix, we make sure that for any issue that we intend to investigate we have more than one means for collecting data. For example, if we are interested in programme impact on children, we may interview programme staff, the children, and their teachers, and look at some of the work produced by the children. If we are concerned with administrative co-operation, we may not only interview the people concerned, but look at meeting notes and a log of telephone calls or other correspondence.

After determining what data will be gathered, we decide on a schedule for these tasks and distribute responsibility for carrying them out among the programme staff and ourselves. Since much of the information comes from the ordinary activities of the programme (meeting notes, participants' products, curriculum produced, etc.) some portion of the documentation is always carried out by the staff. This has several advantages: it keeps down the cost of the evaluation, it provides a way for the staff to remain involved in the evaluation, and it takes much of the mystery out of the summary report written at the end. Our conclusions are based on the data that have been collected openly and are available to all the programme participants. No matter what other information we gather, at least one personal visit to the programme is essential to us if we are to write a report of our findings. There is no substitute for first-hand experience of a programme.

We have come to some generalizations from doing this work many times:

1. Unless we have worked together previously, our initial meeting with museum staff members to define the issues to be addressed in the evaluation is usually difficult and threatening for the staff. But it is also the most important part of the process. It is simply very hard to sit down with an outsider and describe in detail just what is going to happen in a programme, to justify the activities, to explain how the activities are related to the proposed outcomes, and to commit oneself to the kind of evidence that would constitute satisfactory results. But, this first step is crucial. It both provides the basic working contract for our relationship and helps everyone understand what is going to happen.

2. If we have taken the trouble to meet at the beginning of the programme and define issues important to the staff, we have never failed to obtain data that are relevant to the expressed concerns. Although the mountains of information which come in as the programme progresses often at first appear shapeless and vague, the data always contain information relevant to the questions that were addressed, after the data are organized and analysed.

3. It is as important to look at and to define what actually happens in a programme as it is to define what the expected results of a programme are going to be. Often just the fact that children from two different schools came together for two hours once a week for eight weeks is as important an achievement as that they learned something about different cultures. We have documented many instances where the trials and difficulties in simply carrying out a programme provided a strong endorsement of the activity. In other instances, documentation of the factors which prevented the programme staff from performing the activities they intended provided important information for the institution. In any case, the extent to which expected results were achieved must be examined in the context of what actually occurred, as well as in relation to what was proposed.

4. Inevitably, the evaluation process helps programme staff to think about what they are doing and to plan for the future. We find that the considerable interaction we

have with programme staff during the course of a programme often encourages modi-fication of the programme, either for the current sessions or for some future time.

5. The data invariably allow us to make generalizations that were not anticipated at the beginning of the evaluation. Whether it is communication between administrators and staff, problems with transportation, the physical condition of the galleries, or some other factor which had not occurred to any of us at the beginning, we always find something which is illuminated by the evaluation process, and for which the evaluation provides the solid data for addressing the issue. Even in cases where the deficiency or problem is obvious to all, the evaluation sometimes provides the documentation that is needed to convince a higher administrator that the issue is serious.

CONCLUSION

Thoughtful and careful museum professionals recognize the need to document their work and to ask serious and systematic questions about what they are doing. Many already carry out such inquiries as part of their daily activities.

In this paper I have argued that evaluation work should be an integral component of any museum education programme. By making evaluation a part of the activity itself, it can be carried out with a minimum of additional effort and can provide useful information to improve future activities. Appropriate evaluation styles exist to match the philosophical inclination of the programme staff and specific methods exist for any kind of programme.

A formal evaluation plan can help to strengthen museum education work. If it is carried out with the help of an independent consultant, this professional can provide a fresh perspective on the museum's work.

This chapter first appeared as a paper in Museum Education *(1982) Copenhagen: Danish ICOM/CECA: 21–6.*

REFERENCES

1 Guba, E. (1978) *Towards a Methodology of Naturalistic Inquiry in Educational Evaluation*, Los Angeles: Center for the Study of Evaluation.
2 Mitroff, I. I. and Kilman, R. H. (1978) *Methodological Approaches to Social Science*, San Francisco: Jossey-Bass.
3 Hein, G. E. (1979) 'Evaluation in open education: emergence of qualitative methodology', in S. Meisels (ed.) *Special Education and Development*, Baltimore, MD: University Park Press.
4 Shettel, H. H., Butcher, M. *et al.* (1968) *Strategies for Determining Exhibit Effectiveness*, Final Report, AIR E95–4168FR, ED 026718 ERIC Document Reproduction Service.
5 Screven, C. G. (1976) 'Exhibit evaluations: a goal referenced approach', *Curator* 19.
6 Laetsch, W. M. *et al.* (n.d.) 'Naturalistic Studies of Children and Family Groups in Science Centers', unpublished manuscript, Berkeley, CA: Lawrence Hall of Science.
7 Wolf, R. L. (1980) 'A naturalistic view of evaluation', *Museum News* 58, July/August: 39–45.
8 Engel, B. S. and Hein, G. E. (1981) 'Qualitative evaluation of cultural institution/school education programs', in S. N. Lehman and K. Inge (eds) *Museum–School Partnerships: Plans and Programs*, Washington, DC: Center for Museum Education.
9 ibid.

34

Pupils' perceptions of museum education sessions

Marilyn Ingle

The museum education service was at a point of change and in order to make informed decisions about the way forward decided to survey the opinions of a range of children of different ages to discover their thoughts after experiencing a visit involving the handling of objects.

The post-visit survey and its results are discussed in detail, with notes made on how changes have been made to the services offered.

The interpretation of museum collections for pupils offers much scope for museum educators. Rarely have the opinions of pupils been sought about their perceptions of museum education services. It seemed appropriate to canvass pupils' opinions about a museum education service which had diversified and developed in response to the educational changes of the 1980s. This article is based on research for an MA thesis for the University of York.[1]

THE MUSEUM EDUCATION SERVICE

The survey was restricted to the museum education sessions which took place in York Castle Museum. The education service, funded to work with the schools and colleges of North Yorkshire County Council, has many regular visitors. Large collections of military, textile and social history exhibits are displayed in two former eighteenth-century prison buildings constructed in the bailey of a medieval castle. The museum education department provides a service to interpret the museum's site and collections through object-based learning. Visitor pressure limits teaching sessions in the galleries, therefore the museum education sessions tend to take place in the education room. Teachers are requested to make preliminary visits to plan their pupils' sessions at the museum.

DESIGN OF THE SURVEY

An opportunity sample was taken of pupils visiting York Castle Museum Education Service during a five-week period from the middle of February until late March 1986. Unfortunately, the sample provided an age imbalance compared with the mean use for the education service. There were far more infant pupils (19.5 per cent of the total sample), and fewer secondary pupils (16.5 per cent of the total sample). However, age

---

Teachers' survey sheet

Date of the questionnaires' completion

Was this the first subject lesson after the
visit?
Yes or No

Date of the museum visit

Theme of the museum visit

Please name the school subject associated
with the visit

Does the museum visit form an integral part
of the pupils' current work?
Yes or No

With which subject theme is the museum
visit linked?

Since September 1985, how many times has
this class visited the Education Service?

Figure 34.1 Teachers' survey sheet

imbalance is not unusual over a half-term period. The sample had a reasonable spread of day and half-day visits.

On their return to school, the pupils were asked to complete questionnaires about the museum visits. Seven hundred and thirty-two pupils (an 80.5 per cent response rate) from thirty-four classes returned questionnaires. A brief survey sheet was given to each teacher for completion. See Figure 34.1 for the questions which the teachers were asked.

The sample provided classes which were frequent, infrequent or new users of the Education Service. History, science and textiles were the main subjects associated with the visits. All the teachers had helped to plan the museum education sessions for their pupils, so that the museum visits were extensions of the work in school.

As the pupils were aged from 4 to 18 years, the questionnaires had to be reasonably brief and easy to understand. The questions had been refined in a pilot survey. Most questions were open-ended which provided problems in categorizing the information. For greater reliability, the pupils' responses were coded into minor groups of reasons, which were later placed into broader categories of reasons.

The questionnaires, printed on coloured paper, were designed to be attractive to children. The questions, listed in Figure 34.2, were spread over three sides of A4 paper to provide sufficient space for pupils' handwriting. There was evidence that some of the younger primary pupils found the questionnaires too long as the response rate declined to 69.8 per cent for the last question. There was little evidence of teachers influencing the questionnaires' completion. For pupils spending a full day with the education service, an additional sheet was included about specific activities. Pupils were asked to comment

> ## The pupils' questionnaire
>
> *First page*
> Your age. Boy or girl?
>
> What did you like doing?
>
> Why did you like doing these things?
>
> *Second page*
> Which object interested you the most?
>
> Why were you interested?
>
> Since your visit, have you wanted to learn more about this object?
>
> If your answer is yes, what are you going to do?
>
> *Third page*
> What did you like doing the least?
>
> Why did you dislike this?
>
> What do you think you came to learn about at the Castle Museum?
>
> Has your Castle Museum visit helped you to understand the way people lived in the past?
>
> If your answer is yes, how has the visit helped?

Figure 34.2 Pupils' questionnaire

about their likes and dislikes of wearing costume, using drama, trying skills of the past and making models and pictures.

FINDINGS

Pupils liked to handle objects

The educational literature emphasizes the advantages of handling objects, yet many museum professionals have strong reservations about touching artefacts. All the pupils in the survey had had the opportunities to handle objects. It was hoped that useful insights into the pupils' opinions about handling objects would come from the replies to the open-ended questions of 'What did you like doing?' and 'Which object interested you the most?'

Of the categories of activities liked by pupils, 32.9 per cent liked touching and using objects. One 14-year-old pupil wrote: 'I liked how we were given objects. Being able to touch them was better than just looking at them through glass or at displays you can't touch.' The other categories of activities were looking at objects (28.0 per cent), recording objects (22.5 per cent) and past skills or drama (16.5 per cent). Pupils did not have the same activities, although all had had the opportunity to look at and touch objects. Therefore the percentages needed to be interpreted with caution; for example, of those who had experienced drama, 37.2 per cent had listed it as the favourite activity.

The secondary pupils studying history or textiles, were more likely to prefer the activity of handling objects than primary pupils. An 18-year-old's comment was: 'I prefer to be able to handle the garments, to see the construction and be able to measure the garment as I think this gives a greater realization of the sort of people who wore them and the extremes they went to fit into them, I like this activity because it makes drawing the garments a lot easier as seams, darts etc. are very clear.'

For the activities of touching and using objects, all pupils were much more likely to give historical reasons. The appearance and qualities of the objects were important to those who wrote about liking to touch the objects.

In response to the question 'Which object interested you the most?' 44.1 per cent had liked the less spectacular objects which they had handled in the education room. One-third of primary pupils and three-quarters of secondary pupils chose education room objects. Objects touched had appeal even if they were not as impressive as those displayed in the galleries.

Less than a fifth of the pupils chose as their favourite object one which was behind glass in the galleries, usually dolls and dolls' houses. There was a tendency for infant pupils to select large gallery objects such as the hansom cab, gypsy caravan, fire-engines, sweet shop and automaton clock.

Two-fifths of the pupils liked the gallery objects due to the appearance and qualities of the objects, whereas a quarter of pupils liked the education room objects for the same reason. Another quarter of pupils chose education room objects because they liked the involvement of being able to touch the objects in the education room. A 6-year-old boy, from the class where pupils worked the mechanism of the deadfall mouse-trap, liked the mousetrap: 'Because every mouse likes cheese they go for the cheese the rope goes up and the hard piece of wood goes down splat – one squashed mouse.'

Pupils were more likely to give historical and comparative reasons for liking objects which they had touched in the education room. 'The wheel of life was like a television', wrote one 8-year-old boy.

The choice of favourite objects may have been affected by the length of time which had elapsed before the completion of the questionnaires at school. Of the primary pupils who completed the questionnaires on the same day, 24.0 per cent selected objects which had been handled; whereas for those given the questionnaires to complete four or more days after the museum visit, the number who selected objects which had been handled rose to 49.0 per cent.

The pupils' opinions have been useful in selecting objects for the handling collection. As pupils had liked the opportunities to touch and work objects, more thought has been given to collecting objects with the potential for varied sensory experiences. The findings suggested that certain activities could be more relevant depending on the teachers' purpose; so touching objects would be a suitable activity if the intention was to focus the pupils' attention on historical and comparative understanding.

315

Pupils enjoyed wearing costume

A tenth of the 732 pupils had chosen wearing costume as the favourite activity, though only a half of the sample had had the opportunity to wear costume. A 10-year-old considered a soldier's uniform was 'heavy and prickly'. Pupils, used to modern standards of comfort and cloth textures, were unable to cope with the fit, style and discomfort of armour, uniform and civilian clothing.

Although much of the costume was reproduction, 27.1 per cent gave historical reasons for why they liked wearing costume, like this 10-year-old boy. 'Because somebody had worn it in the seventeenth century in a battle and I felt as if I was going back in time.'

Costume seemed to provide a tangible link with the past; as Radcliffe suggested: 'Instead of looking at stationary, inanimate objects and wondering about their place in history, visitors develop a greater perspective on the past. They can see the drape of fabric or the hindrance of a too-tight sleeve and watch living people in action.'[2]

A 13-year-old girl's comment was: 'Because you could see people try them on, and even you could try them on, it made it a lot more interesting than seeing a dummy dressed up. You could see the problems they had and experience them for yourself.'

Despite the difficulties of resourcing reproduction costume, the pupils highlighted the value of wearing costume. Perhaps, when trying on costume, more consideration should be given to explaining about the discomfort due to fit, fabrics and styles of historical costume.

PARTICIPATIVE EXPERIENCES WERE ENJOYABLE

Due to the teachers' planning, the opportunity to try former skills and drama was restricted to 45.2 per cent of the 732 pupils. All were primary pupils. Only one child out of the 47 pupils who experienced drama considered that the visit had not helped in her understanding of the past. For one class, on a series of visits, the favoured activity was taking part in the dramatic sessions, rather than the more recent activities of touching, recording and former skills. One 10-year-old wrote: 'It really made me feel like a Victorian girl in a Victorian street, which was great because I haven't been one before.'

More than half of the pupils gave reasons for liking the activities because of the personal involvement, with the second group of reasons being fun. Less than 6 per cent gave historical reasons for liking to learn former skills. 'I like turning the dolly peg round and I liked scrubbing on the rubbing board,' wrote one 6-year-old girl.

However, there were pupils who disliked taking part in participatory activities. Reasons given were associations, skills needed, repetitive tasks and discomfort. Some dislikes were inevitable and formed part of the experience as for this 7-year-old boy. 'I don't like cold water and I hate having a bath.' Writing with a quill pen had posed problems for a 10-year-old girl: 'I thought it was easy to write with and it was not. It kept dripping all over the paper.'

In teaching skills of the past, it seems necessary to offer a balance of different former skills, whilst considering their possible unpleasant associations and the historical purposes for teaching the skills. If to have fun and pleasure through former skills and drama will increase motivation to learn as O'Connell and Alexander suggested,[3] then these activities are of educational value. However, care should be taken to prevent the learning experiences from being too shallow.

Regular visitors preferred participatory experiences

Regular and infrequent users of the museum education service appeared to have different requirements. For first-time visitors, it was found that more than half the pupils selected gallery objects and more than half the pupils chose looking as the favourite activity. By contrast, 'We can touch things and we like doing things rather than being told things,' wrote a 9-year-old boy from a school which made regular visits.

Since the survey, first-time visitors to the museum have been allowed more opportunity to browse in selected galleries. Secondary pupils have been given more practical activities because the regular visitors favoured this form of museum education experience.

Pupils intended to learn more

Two-thirds of the half-day visitors intended to learn more about their favourite objects, supporting the idea that museum visits are good for the motivation of pupils. However, more primary (72.3 per cent), than secondary (49.1 per cent) pupils intended to learn more about their favourite objects. Some secondary pupils considered the knowledge they had gained about their objects was finite. With increasing age, pupils were more likely to seek further information in libraries and museums.

Museum education visits promoted interests in further visits to museums. The pupils were not asked specifically if they intended to visit museums. Most of the 17.3 per cent of pupils, who intended to return to museums to learn more about their favourite object, named the York Castle Museum. However, most pupils were not thinking of museums as resources for further learning about objects.

Vary the recording experiences

The findings provided a considerable number, 19.8 per cent, who liked drawing and writing and a slightly lower percentage who disliked drawing and writing. 'It was fun. I met a real artist in Kirkgate. He helped me,' wrote an 8-year-old boy, whereas an 18-year-old disliked: 'Drawing in the museum when visitors are wandering round. Because these people are more interested in what you are doing rather than what is on show. Seats at the back of a room are better as visitors are unable to notice what you are doing.'

Since the survey, methods of recording have included the use of the computer and attempts have been made to diversify recording techniques. Older pupils have been made more aware of the purpose of recording in relation to their school work.

Differences in responses according to pupils' ages

The problems of understanding time language, mentioned by Vukelich,[4] were apparent in the pupils' responses, especially the vagueness of those pupils under 8 years of age. In general terms, four-fifths of all pupils recognized the historical link and if the pupils were studying history, a higher number thought the visits had helped in their understanding of the past. A 9-year-old boy wrote: 'It has put a picture in my mind what it would be like to live 100 years ago.'

Secondary pupils liked tactile opportunities. Preferences for looking declined with age, fewer fourth-year juniors preferred looking than did first-year juniors. There was evidence of the problems of working in a large building with young children. One tenth of primary pupils complained about climbing steps or walking long distances in the museum.

Different responses of boys and girls

Very few gender preferences existed. Twelve primary pupils, all below the age of 9 years, expressed dislikes because the activities or objects were thought to be more appropriate for the other sex. One 4-year-old wrote: 'I didn like the girls toys girls toys are not fo boys.'

There was a tendency for boys and girls to select different objects, and the differences were most noticeable for gallery objects rather than the education room objects which would have been touched. In the galleries, the most popular exclusively male exhibits were the fire-engines, compared with dolls and dolls' houses for the girls. However, where children had handled exhibits, fewer objects were chosen exclusively by one sex, perhaps because there had been the opportunity to find out more about the objects.

Further research would be useful taking subjects traditionally associated with one sex, such as warfare; for from the class of 10- and 11-year-olds where both military and domestic aspects were studied by both sexes, boys tended to ignore the domestic aspects, though only one girl failed to mention military objects for either the preferred activity or object. Although the favourite object was the close helmet because it had so many parts which moved, one 11-year-old girl put the military and domestic objects into relative importance: 'I liked trying on the helmets and best of all I liked looking at the embroidery patterns that the seventeenth-century girls sewed. I enjoyed trying on the helmets because I knew that people had actually maybe died or got injured in that helmet. I enjoyed the embroidery patterns because it fascinated me how they sewed things that small, and how the sewing had secret messages behind the pictures.'

Pupils should understand the purposes for the museum visit

Compared with school classrooms, museum galleries and education rooms contain a wealth of images and objects unrelated to pupils' current studies. Beer had found that more than half the displays in museums were likely to be ignored by visitors.[5] Problems in focusing attention to promote effective learning in the museum had been noted by Chase.[6]

In the York Castle Museum survey, it was found that there were noticeable differences in the pupils' responses where more than half the class were unclear about why they had been brought. When teachers and pupils were not sharing the same purposes for the visits, pupils expressed more dissatisfaction, preferred looking generally and were more attracted to objects and galleries irrelevant to the teachers' themes for the visits.

Clearly, at the start of each museum lesson, it is important to reinforce the links between the museum education sessions and the pupils' current work in school. During teachers' preliminary visits and on information sheets for teachers, it seems wise to inform teachers of the benefits of pupils and teachers sharing common purposes for the museum visits.

CONCLUSION

From the limited information a survey supplies, useful insights were obtained for developing the education service. In discussions with curatorial and conservation colleagues, pupils' opinions have been used to justify the provision of high-quality objects for the handling collection and for continued access to the reserve collections. At teachers' meetings and courses, knowledge of pupils' opinions has been useful in planning pupils' museum sessions: in particular, making sure the pupils are aware of the purposes of the museum visits.

More research concerning the needs of frequent visitors and the pupils' views of museums as learning institutions would be useful. On this survey's very limited evidence most pupils were not aware of the potential for learning in museums.

All ages of pupils confirmed the benefits of museum education provision which stressed tactile practical experiences. Relatively few dislikes were expressed. The museum visits had been positive, enjoyable experiences which had helped the pupils' understanding of the topics being studied.

The advantages of a museum education visit were summed up by a 10-year-old girl: 'I liked handling, touching, and trying on things better than looking round the museum. I liked especially trying clothes on, because you can't normally touch things and try things on when you go to a museum with your parents and it gives you an idea of what it was like then when the things were used.'

This chapter first appeared as a paper in Journal for Education in Museums *11 (1990): 5–8.*

NOTES

1 Ingle, M. G., 'Pupils' perceptions of museum education sessions planned by their teachers and the museum education officer', unpublished MA thesis (University of York, 1988).
2 Radcliffe, P. M., 'Period dress projects: considerations for administrators', *Curator* 30(3) (1987): 193–8.
3 O'Connell, P. S. and Alexander, M., 'Reaching the High School audience', *Museum News* 58(2) (1979): 50–6.
4 Vukelich, R., 'Time language for interpreting history collections to children', *Museum Studies Journal* 1(4) (1984): 42–50.
5 Beer, V., 'Great expectations: do museums know what visitors are doing?', *Curator* 30(3) (1987): 206–15.
6 Chase, R. A., 'Museums as learning environments', *Museum News* 54(1) (1975): 37–43.

35

Collaborative evaluation studies between the University of Liverpool and national museums and galleries on Merseyside

Terry Russell

It is not easy for a museum to begin in a serious way on evaluation and visitor research studies on its own. Specific expertise is needed. It is time-consuming. Partnerships with other institutions are a useful way forward.

This chapter describes a specific partnership, between a museum and a university. It goes on to discuss a range of possible methods and approaches and gives specific details of one or two.

Developing and using methods such as these will not only bring museums information about their visitors, it will also act as a stringent form of professional development. Assumptions will need to be examined, priorities clarified and decisions made.

The association between the University of Liverpool and National Museums and Galleries on Merseyside (NMGM) began with a research proposal to undertake formative evaluation and documentation of Interactive Technology Centres, at Liverpool and elsewhere in the UK. From the university's perspective, this work, which commenced in April 1986, encompassed studies at Techniquest in Cardiff, Jodrell Bank Science Centre and Liverpool's Technology Testbed. (See Harlen *et al.* 1986; Russell *et al.* 1987: Russell *et al.* 1988.) For NMGM, the collaboration centred on studies of visitors' reactions to Technology Testbed, one of the pioneering UK interactive centres.

At the time at which these studies commenced, very little systematic information about the use and potential of such learning environments had been collected. Not surprisingly, funding agencies were also interested in obtaining feedback about usage. In this instance, the one sponsor, the Gatsby Charitable Foundation, was funding both the exhibition and the evaluation. The nature of the proposed evaluation was formative, particularly aimed at the collection of information about the effectiveness of Interactive Technology Centre (ITC) exhibits and exhibitions while these were still in a fluid state. Any proposed modifications or recommendations arising from the evaluation studies could actually be implemented by exhibition development staff to extend the effectiveness of the exhibits. Evaluation was intended to be not judgemental but sympathetic to operational constraints, as well as informative. Reducing the 'mystification' and increasing the enjoyment of science should follow as a consequence.

The kind of information which was identified as being of particular interest to NMGM related to the learning outcomes of the interactions between visitors and exhibits. In this context, realistic expectations could not include *guaranteed* learning outcomes, for the visitor was seen as a free agent with any of a range of motives for being present. However, the view was adopted that developers have obligations to present to the public exhibits which are manifestly sensitive to visitors' needs. In particular, the way that the visitor might be helped to make sense of the information presented by an exhibit was a main focus of interest.

In the context of interactive centres, a constructivist view of learning was adopted. This assumes that visitors do not approach exhibits with a totally passive outlook, but with active (albeit 'un-schooled' or 'informal') theories of their own. Visitors, it was assumed, will tend to make their own sense of the information which the museum is trying to make accessible. The exact nature of the learning outcome will be the result of an interaction between each visitor's prior understanding and the new learning experience offered by the museum. Experience confirms that the outcome of interactions between visitors and open-ended exhibits is neither totally idiosyncratic nor unpredictable. Even inaccurate assumptions ('getting hold of the wrong end of the stick') occur with regularity and can be predicted as the result of the formative evaluation process. Rather like a survey which identifies the pitfalls and inaccessible reaches of a terrain, formative evaluation can be designed to indicate the most probable successful route to the intended destination. In the museum context, increasing the possibility of the visitor's achieving some enhanced understanding of the exhibit's content is the objective of the formative evaluation process.

Of necessity, expectations about learning outcomes must be couched in terms of probabilities rather than certainties. With most visits prompted primarily by recreational motives, the inclination to *learn* should be accepted as a variable and indeterminate factor possessed (or not) by each visitor, but one having a significant impact on the quality of the interaction. This characteristic of the learner playing a significant part in determining the quality of the interaction with an exhibit or exhibition is characteristic of learning in informal settings. It implies that the quality of the interaction is to a large extent under the control of the visitor, as much as with the exhibition developer. The expertise which should be expected of the developer would therefore include the principles that, as far as possible, every interaction exhibit should:

1 attract visitors' interest and motivate active engagement
2 embody a sensitivity towards the needs and preferences of visitors, in terms of the modes of activity and the manner of presentation of information on offer
3 be constructed so as to avoid the possibility of visitors developing or reinforcing commonly encountered misconceptions.

(An example of a failure to meet the third criterion is an exhibit which inadvertently confirmed a significant number of visitors in their belief that different materials have different intrinsic temperatures. This followed an invitation to touch a series of tiles made of wood, rubber, metal, etc. The *temperature sensation* tended to confirm the everyday intuition that the materials were at different temperatures: the scientific explanation which the exhibit was actually attempting to clarify was that this sensation was misleading. Although the tiles *felt* as though they were at different temperatures, they could not have been. The sensation of difference is actually attributable to the varying capacity of the materials to conduct heat energy away from the finger-tips. The exhibit tended to confirm visitors' intuitive but scientifically incorrect impressions and as such was dangerously counter-productive in that form.)

The old adage of taking horses to water is apt. The displays might be thought of as extending the invitation to partake of a feast which has been devised to be irresistible, skilfully anticipating needs and preferences, but with no certain expectation of being consumed.

A range of techniques is available to the researcher or evaluator who is interested in the nature of learning experiences in interactive centres. These fall broadly into two groups, behavioural and phenomenological.

BEHAVIOURAL TECHNIQUES

The implication in collecting behavioural data is that it is for the evaluator to attach meaning to the data which are collected. An example might be the use of video-recordings of visitor interactions at an exhibit. In playing back the recording, perhaps with the purpose of summarizing how a group of visitors reacted to a given exhibit, there is no expectation, perhaps no possibility, of discerning motives, feelings, reactions. These have to be inferred. It is always possible that two instances of apparently similar behaviour might have quite different underlying motives. In the interactive centres, the most frequent use of behavioural data was in the use of an observational checklist, as reproduced in Figure 35.1.

Such a checklist would be developed after some time observing behaviours. It is not an atheoretical construction, since it would focus on those behaviours considered to have relevance to the interpretation of the visitor's interactive experience. Each of the observational criteria might be examined against variables such as age, gender or prior knowledge (though this latter information is rarely available, especially in the kind of detail needed for it to be useful). Typically, a random or a stratified sample of visitors would be selected for 'tracking' through an exhibition space.

There are certain constraints on the tracking technique. It must be discreet without running the risk of appearing sinister, which implies an environment within which observation can take place unobtrusively. The duration of an average visit should be within the limits of time available for data collection. There should be boundaries to the exhibition area. Generally, the museum environment meets these conditions, interactive centres particularly so, since the exhibits tend to be large and involve a lot of movement which can be observed from a discreet distance.

PHENOMENOLOGICAL TECHNIQUES

Data collection procedures which call on visitors to reflect and comment on aspects of their interactive experience which cannot be directly observed are referred to as phenomenological techniques. Interviews and self-report (where the interviewee is invited to 'tell the story' from his or her angle) are the most commonly used methods of gaining feedback of this type. Clearly, when the objective is to gain information about visitors' understanding of scientific or technological concepts, direct dialogue is likely to be a favoured technique.

There is no reason why the two approaches should not be used together, since they offer complementary information. In the event, this frequently happened in the evaluation of interactive technology centres. For example, having collected behavioural data through tracking and observing the course of the visit, it was perfectly feasible to interview the visitor at the point of exit from the exhibition in order to add qualitative impressions to the quantitative profile of behaviour.

Date	Time	Target Visitor No.	Male or Female	Age	Or over	Collector's Name
					30 40 50 60	

TIME TAKEN

EXHIBIT NUMBER/NAME

Observed Actions	Tick Appropriate Column
Helper present/ in view	
Interacts after help	
Engages with helper	
Touches apparatus	
Moves part of apparatus	
Works alone	
Works with others	
Talks with others	
Watches others	
Questions helper	
Questions others	
Repeats action	
Has to queue or wait	

Figure 35.1 Example of observational checklist

Other refinements and particular methods could be described, but in principle the behavioural and phenomenological techniques encompass the possibilities. Putting these techniques in the framework of the exhibition developers' expectations, we arrive at the model in Figure 35.2. This figure shows a representation of the relationship between the visitor's experience, the evaluator's data collection options, and the feedback of

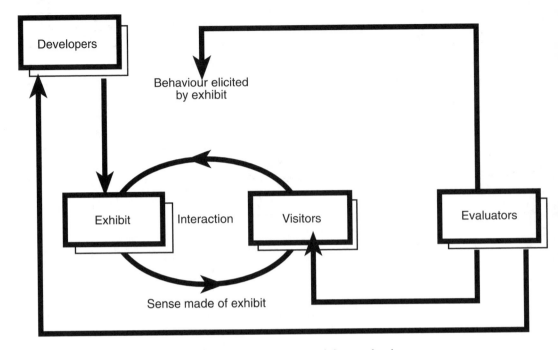

Figure 35.2 The formative evaluation process in exhibition development

this information to exhibit developers, as formative evaluation. An example of the kind of information which was passed back to exhibition developers is shown in Figure 35.3.

EVALUATION STUDIES IN THE LIVERPOOL MUSEUM

Expressed in the general terms of Figure 35.2, it should be apparent that such an approach can have a wider application than to interactive science and technology centres alone. By agreement, the display evaluation activities were extended into selected galleries of the Liverpool Museum. The first large study undertaken there focused on a gallery concerned with ceramics and the art of the potter. Some aspects of this study will be described so as to give some indication of the techniques and the general issues which it was possible to address.

One hundred visitors were tracked through the gallery: their movements between the ten display cases and an information station consisting of two computer terminals (with simplified keyboards) were recorded on a floor plan. Each tracked visitor was also interviewed at the point of exit from the gallery. The kind of information collected included the composition of the visitor population, visit duration, use of labels and use of computer databases.

Composition of the visitor population was described on the basis of the sample. The categories used were 'singleton', which was restricted to solitary adults; 'couples' described any pair of adults; 'families' was the category used for any combination of adults and children; 'adult group' was used for more than two adults without children present; 'children' was used to describe visitors appearing to be under the age of 16. The proportion in which each group was represented could be readily described at the end of the study. Such demographic information can provide an interesting baseline for comparisons between galleries. For example, far more family groups and children visited the science and technology interactive centre than visited the ceramics area. Such information should be of use to the museum in helping to identify likely visitor populations and their needs.

Duration of visit was another basic variable which could be very easily computed, and which could also be related to the number of display cases to which visitors gave their direct attention. In the ceramics gallery study, many visits proved to be cursory. Half the visitors examined less than half the display cases. It was possible to generate hypotheses as to why this might have been so; for instance, a certain number of visitors appeared to be simply 'passing through', virtually using the gallery as a corridor. Others examined only those cases closest to the direct route through the gallery. The average duration of visits was just five minutes, the most frequently measured time spent in the gallery (modal duration of visit) being between two and three minutes. It was evident from the bi-modal nature of the distribution of visit durations that a more committed sub-group was discernible within the sample. This was the 12 per cent who appeared to be demonstrating a special interest in spending between ten and twenty minutes in the gallery.

Again, the most basic data, such as those described, raise interesting questions. For example, should the *descriptive* data lead to any *prescriptive* messages for the structuring of special exhibitions? Should designers be thinking of a five-minute visit as being sufficient for the majority of visitors, with twenty minutes for the *aficionado*? Or should there be a 'rapid route' through an exhibition? Is it justifiable to attempt to slow visitors down, for example, by putting a dog-leg in the through-route? Empirical data can prompt a re-examination of basic assumptions, given a receptive frame of mind on the part of those with the power and responsibility to implement changes.

Labels are a perennial cause of concern and frequent anguish in museum environments. One third of visitors sampled in the ceramics gallery did not refer to any of the information panels set beside the display cases. In the course of the exit interviews it was possible to discuss labelling with visitors, with the result that some relatively low-cost adjustments were recommended.

Computer databases are becoming more common as a mode of supporting the information needs of a gallery with the advantage of avoiding unnecessary clutter and information overload. If the visitor feels comfortable in using the hardware, an extensive database can be made available. In the context of the interactive centre, it was striking that younger visitors were much more prepared to use the computers than were the adults who were escorting them; parents frequently looked on as their often more confident and experienced children used the computers. In the ceramics gallery, 40 per cent of the sample used the computer database.

Talking to visitors is an indispensable component of an evaluation and has been included wherever possible in the studies which have been undertaken. These interviews provide visitors with the opportunity to express a personal viewpoint and the offer of the chance to express an opinion is turned down very rarely. This invitation to comment was a fairly typical approach that had been adopted, usually prefaced by a brief explanation of NMGM's motive in setting up the evaluation. Feedback, it was explained to visitors, would help the museum staff in modifying and improving galleries and exhibitions. In the ceramics gallery study, suggestions for improvement were invited, but many comments were simply positive remarks about the quality of the

Exhibit Description: 'Brick Bond'

Photographs illustrating four types of brick are displayed on boards positioned on a table.

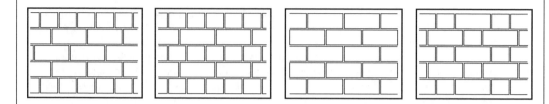

Forty-eight wooden bricks measuring 15 × 7 × 5 cm are available for visitors to use to build walls incorporating the various bond patterns.

Label:

> Firstly, look at the photos of different walls.
> Choose one and try to build it.
> Try another. Is it stronger?
> Why?

Museum Objective: Principles of wall construction and strengths.

Formative Evaluation

Two thirds of the visitors who were interviewed on this exhibit built one wall. This was either a copy of the 'stretcher' bond (see above) or they arranged the bricks in columns with no overlapping bonds. Very few of these visitors commented on, or tested, the strength of their wall.

Two or three walls were built by a quarter of the visitors interviewed. These visitors compared the strength of their walls by either pressing against them with their hands, removing a brick from the middle, or pushing the walls over.

Visitors' responses highlighted the potential of this exhibit as a scientific investigation. The comments were offered by three 14-year-old girls who worked collaboratively on 'Brick Bond'.

Visitor: *We're trying to see which is best. Which is strongest?*

Interviewer: *How could you find out?*

Visitor: *Use pressure or something. It'd have to be the same for each though.*

(They built four walls.)

Proposed Changes

(a) Visitors were reluctant to knock the walls over since they looked precarious on the table. It was recommended that the exhibit be placed on the floor against a wall.

(b) A projectile for the fair testing of two (or more) walls built with different bond types was suggested.

(c) The fabrication of more bricks from the same wood sufficient for visitors to build two substantial double thickness walls was recommended.

(d) In the interest of providing factual information and identification of each bond during collaborative activity, it was suggested that the photographs be labelled with the names of each bond type.

(e) It was recommended that the Centre should provide plan diagrams so that visitors might see the different types of bond from a different viewpoint.

Implementation

This exhibit was repositioned in a corner against a wall, on the floor. Although its basic appearance had changed little, much had been added. Each of the photographs was labelled with the bond names (i.e. 1 – Flemish, 2 – Stretcher, 3 – English Garden Wall) and the bond patterns were highlighted with white paint. The quantity of original sized bricks was increased to 84 and 15 half-bricks were fabricated. A projectile with a pointer and simple scale, to encourage fair testing, was also introduced.

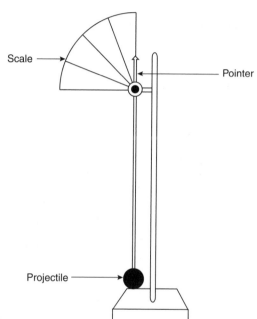

The label and museum objectives remained unchanged.

Visitor Responses Following Changes

The high quality of responses given by visitors indicated how worthwhile the changes to this exhibit had been. Visitors collaborated with far more purpose and the testing of walls and discussions which followed, concerning their strengths, were of a much higher quality. Highlighting the bond patterns facilitated construction, and communication in comparing walls was eased due to labelling each bond type. Purposeful testing was made possible by the introduction of the projectile and the increased quantity of wooden bricks.

The recommendations constituted a significant shift towards a process-based, investigative hands-on approach. One result was a highly significant increase in dwell time. The recommendations based on a straightforward evaluation resulted in what was a dramatic change in visitor response.

Figure 35.3 An illustration of formative evaluation

exhibits and their setting. It may be that the museum environment offers the chance of visitors giving feedback to the curatorial and design staff all too infrequently. Some very direct and telling comments may emerge from this source. For example, in relation to the database:

> If it told you about the computers at the beginning, it would be better. We walked half way round before we realised they were there.

This comment offers a reminder that a visitor's orientation within a gallery is an important consideration. Feedback of this nature was taken seriously and acted upon whenever possible. In the ceramics gallery, additional information about the database was provided and a subsequent small-scale empirical check confirmed that use of the computer increased by about 15 per cent. Effective changes do not necessarily depend on massive expenditure of time and resources; nor do they depend on huge samples. A perceptive comment and well-considered but simple intervention may have a significant impact on the visitor's experience. This is the strength of qualitative methodology which complements quantitative methods.

EVALUATION STUDIES WITHIN THE NATURAL HISTORY CENTRE

The Natural History Centre is situated within the Liverpool Museum, with the implication that, unlike the separate site of Technology Testbed, casual visitors were likely to drift in, almost as 'passers-by' without any pre-organized intent. The smaller, more intimate and more crowded setting offered different possibilities and different constraints in so far as data collection was concerned. For example, it was possible to monitor conversations between visitors, both adults and children, and demonstrators. Generally, the studies conducted in the Natural History Centre could be more detailed and intimate, focusing on the processes and quality of the interactions taking place. It was also possible to use audio- and video-recording to supplement the more direct data collection methods used elsewhere.

The role of the demonstrators and the adults who accompanied children in supporting children's understanding and interaction was examined in some detail. Enlarged images of specimens which visitors could themselves select by reorientating objects within the field of the macro lens of a video camera (objects included shells, fossils and insects) provided excellent stimulus for discussion which was closely monitored. The specimens, their magnified images and the conversations which accompanied their perusal were all accessible to monitoring by the evaluators. One particular interest was the extent to which *science process skills* were in evidence, i.e. hypothesizing, interpreting, generalizing and so on. It emerged that 'transfer of information' questions tended to be more prevalent than 'open' questions. This orientation was confirmed as being that which was also favoured by the demonstrators employed by the National History Centre. That is, demonstrators tended to view their function as being predominantly to provide information rather than to stimulate conjecture. There were important lessons here for the nature of the training which, it might be inferred, was required by the demonstrators.

Another important medium in the Natural History Centre which received a certain amount of attention was the use of videodisc technology. The opportunity for visitors to select audio and visual material to complement and extend their direct experiences in the museum environment is an area with enormous potential, not without attendant contrasting viewpoints and controversy. This is another museum issue in which empirically collected information can serve to inform the debate.

PRACTICALITIES OF FUNDING COLLABORATION

Collaboration between NMGM and the university has adopted several different patterns. The different models of funding collaboration can be summarized as follows:

1 Exhibition development and evaluation funded independently, but by the same donor.

This arrangement, as with the Gatsby Charitable Foundation funding of ITC exhibitions and evaluation, leaves each party with full responsibility to fulfil its particular functions. If the evaluation is to be formative, close collaboration is needed and resourcing conflicts may arise. For example, there is little point in the evaluators seeking to monitor the implementation of changes if the exhibition developers lack either the resources or the commitment to implement them.

2 Exhibition and evaluation work funded as a collaborative activity by an external funding agent.

Relatively small-scale funding has been provided for work carried out jointly between NMGM and the university. For example, the Committee on Public Understanding of Science of the Royal Society provided funds towards the development of videodisc material for experimental use in the Natural History Centre. BP has funded an investigation of public understanding in the area of earth sciences, together with curriculum guidance based on the information obtained.

3 Evaluation funded by NMGM in the form of salary costs for a researcher paid to the university.

This form of contractual arrangement shifts the balance slightly from the first model in that the priorities of the programme are under the control of the museum, while the technical and methodological considerations are determined by the evaluation agency.

4 Museum personnel identified in the evaluation role supported by consultancy to discuss methodology, instrumentation and analysis.

The fourth model is an attempt to shift the role and function of evaluation into the institutional structure of the museum, while retaining expert support from outside. In theory, costs should not differ greatly from model three. In practice, there may be other marginal savings made possible if the bulk of data collection utilizes available resources from within the museum environment. In effect, the initial role of the museum staff identified in the evaluation role is as a manager and co-ordinator of data collection. With time, experience and goodwill, it is conceivable that the total range of evaluation functions is taken on by the museum. However, this does require institutional commitment and appropriate resourcing.

5 University used by museum on a consultancy basis.

The fifth model is one in which the museum buys-in evaluation expertise for specific purposes, as and when required. This is akin to the common practice of buying-in market research consultants. The costs are justified by the fact that the museum buys the necessary expertise when it requires it, without the necessity of tying down staff to evaluation or data collection functions. The museum is then free to use its own resources and expertise in dealing with the identification of needs, problem areas and the consequences of evaluation exercises which specifically address those issues. Clearly, this option only exists where the necessary expertise is available and willing. It is only possible or likely when the relationship between the parties is well developed, for it must be more than a commercial relationship and has to be sustained by a common sense of educational purpose.

USING THE INFORMATION COLLECTED

The studies outlined above, and a number of others conducted at other NMGM sites, were of intrinsic interest in providing insights into how the visitor population was seen to behave in a variety of museum contexts. More importantly, the studies were designed to inform policy and practical action. The usual product was a short report summarizing the quantitative data; interpretations and recommendations based on the data were approached only tentatively by the evaluators. The reason for this was that any action resulting from the studies would have to have the commitment and support of the management, curatorial, education and design staff. The curators, wherever possible, had been involved in the process of defining the issues for empirical exploration. They would also be in the best-informed position in terms of awareness of impediments and possibilities with regard to change. This consideration is just one of the fundamental sensitivities which must be implicit in any evaluation study conducted by a third party.

In practice, the most satisfactory manner of proceeding from evaluation to implementation is through face-to-face discussion of the issues, the evidence collected, the implications and possibilities for action. In this way, blind spots stand a chance of becoming illuminated: differences in assumptions and the ways that different groups use the same words may be clarified; reasons for doing things in particular ways can be justified.

Good evaluation reports should read as being 'common sense'. For example, the evaluators and curators might agree that a 10-cm^2 label 30 cm from the ground is not helpful to the visiting public, but changes cannot be assumed to flow logically from such agreement. The logic of all parties is likely to agree that for a label to be placed thus is nobody's preference. Habitual constraints and habitual ways of operating sometimes lead to unacceptable outcomes being tolerated. Evaluators have to live with this possibility; in the museum context, it is for the curatorial staff to decide when more radical solutions are appropriate.

Without the commitment and resources for subsequent action, evaluation can become a sterile and frustrating exercise, like raising dust only to choke on it. In some cases (as with the modifications made to the labelling of the computer database in the ceramics gallery, reported above), it was possible not only to implement change suggested by a study, but to go further, carrying out a small-scale monitoring of the consequences of that change. It is all too easy when museum staff are under pressure to plan and develop the exhibition, 'to leave well-enough alone'.

This chapter first appeared in P. Sudbury and T. Russell (eds) (1995) Evaluation of Museum and Gallery Displays, *Liverpool: Liverpool University Press, 13–26.*

REFERENCES

Harlen, W., Russell, T., and Van der Waal, A. (1986) *Evaluation of the Pilot Phase of the Liverpool Interactive Technology Centre*, Liverpool: CRIPSAT, University of Liverpool.

Martin, M., Brown, S. and Russell, T. (1991) *A Study of Child–Adult Interaction at a Natural History Centre*, Studies in Educational Evaluation.

Russell, T., Van der Waal, A. and Whitelock, M. (1987) *Development Stage Evaluation of Interactive Exhibits at Jodrell Bank Science Centre*, Liverpool: CRIPSAT, University of Liverpool.

Russell, T., Van der Waal, A. and Whitelock, M. (1988) *Evaluation of the Pilot Phase of the Cardiff Interactive Technology Centre, 'Techniquest'*, Liverpool: CRIPSAT, University of Liverpool.

36

Sending them home alive

Anita Rui Olds

What ideas from environmental psychology can museums use to increase the enjoyment of a museum visit? 'Aliveness' and the resultant feelings of well-being and enjoyment can be achieved by designing an ambience with sufficient environmental stimulation to keep the brain at optimal levels of stimulation by meeting four basic needs: movement, comfort, competence and control.

Through the discussion of the ways in which people react in a range of different types of environment, we are made aware of the social, physiological and psychological factors that come into play during a museum visit. Ideally a balance between movement, comfort, competence and control is necessary for physiological and psychological harmony. In museums, where it is often necessary to restrict one or more aspects, special care should be taken to increase provision for the others.

Ideally, a museum visit is a memorable experience that affects a person's life beyond the museum's walls. To be changed in this way, however, people must be fully *alive* where they are; free to drop their self-consciousness, their roles and façades, their fears of knowing too little, or of needing to judge and analyse; free to allow the objects and events to become part of themselves. Over and above the design requirements and neutral architectural backdrop of an exhibit, there is the opportunity and challenge to make each space a more successful place of learning and creativity, where people get more in touch with who they really are and what they might be. The following summary of ideas gathered from research in the field of environmental psychology suggests that achieving such 'aliveness' depends on designing an ambience with sufficient environmental stimulation to keep the brain at optimal levels of alertness by meeting at least four basic needs: movement, comfort, competence and control.

MOVEMENT

The freedom to move about in space, assume different body postures, create one's own boundaries and enter diverse territories is a prime way in which people manifest health and power and fulfil their potential. Indoors, however, the presence of many bodies moving in unpredictable ways is often experienced as discomforting. And because motion is more apparent in small spaces and can make space feel more congested, it is not encouraged where square footage is limited or focused attention is required. In most museums and galleries, visitors are expected to be quiet, move carefully, and behave in a formal and subdued way. These restrictions tire the body and dull the mind.

People feel most alive, however, when they can move freely within a setting to explore its limits and facets, have access to needs (lavatories, telephones, lockers, food), and can vary the pace of their activities over time. Thus museum visitors, especially children, may prefer to give an exhibit a 'once over' at the outset to determine its physical and informational scope and then proceed to absorb its contents step by step. Some visitors are content to follow a given sequence, while for others the visit is enriched by a more random approach.

It is particularly helpful, therefore, for aspects of an exhibit to allow for fine and gross motor interaction with the materials (pushing buttons, ringing bells, using body weight to unbalance or relocate objects) and encourage different types of movements and body postures: sitting (on chairs, floor, loft with feet dangling); standing; climbing (on stairs, ladders, inclines); lying (under or inside something); encircling something; bending or stooping (through lowered doorways); reaching; looking up, over, or under; moving (through wide and tight spaces, forward and backward, on level or inclined ground, with clear or minimal visibility, and with some or no light at the end of the tunnel). Where participants cannot be permitted to interact with the materials, demonstration by a craftsperson or operator can still have the powerful effect of introducing movement and change into the setting.

Just as a brisk walk may clear the mind, a period of standing or sitting to look at something, if followed by an active experience of walking a distance, changing levels, or using the body vigorously, helps wake up the brain. If this motion takes one to a space with an entirely different configuration and mood, so much the better. In homes, living rooms, kitchens and bedrooms are distinct places involving different levels of activity, body postures, and degrees of privacy. Moving through such different rooms is often (as in the Pepsi ad) 'the pause that refreshes'. Similarly, moving through an exhibit in varied ways, through spaces with distinctly different moods and qualities, and using one's body (or someone else's) to make things happen in a display are all ways of creating movement, the *sine qua non* of life.

COMFORT

In addition to bodily movement, the senses also must 'move' and receive changing stimulation from the external environment. Our eyes see by scanning a visual field but are reduced to 'nonsight' when forced to stare at a stationary image. Our ears hear when soundwaves strike and vibrate the ear drum.

Dramatic fluctuations in stimulation level can be frightening and disorienting. But an environment that provides rhythmic patterns of predictable sameness combined with moderate diversity enables the senses to maintain optimal levels of responsivity and makes us feel 'comfortable'. Natural elements, such as blazing fires, babbling brooks, and gentle breezes exemplify this principle well. They are always moving in ways that are fairly predictable. Yet moderate variations – a flicker or flare, a new pitch, a cooler or warmer draft – prevent boredom or withdrawal by introducing a change that catches the attention and reawakens the nervous system.

The difference-within-sameness so exquisitely present in nature is difficult to create within the static built world. Clearly, in a museum one does not want the background to have such arousal levels that it detracts from the exhibit itself. Paradoxically, it is often the sensorial blandness of a museum's setting that makes it difficult for visitors to absorb the details of even a particularly wondrous exhibit. The old adage, 'Variety is the spice of life', is the best guideline for generating an ambience that supports aliveness and learning.

This guideline means, first of all, that all the senses should be moderately stimulated. If an exhibit is largely visual, a quiet background of pleasantly varied sounds, odours, textures and opportunities for movement will actually enhance the visual experience. Variety in physical parameters – scale, areas of light and shadow, floor levels and ceiling and partition heights, room size and number of occupants, degrees of intimacy, activities that are messy and clean – can also powerfully contribute to comfort and heightened awareness.

Attention to detail, especially to the finish materials used on floors, walls, ceilings, windows and furniture, can have a more powerful impact on users and on the overall 'feel' of a place than any other single factor. The textures, colours and forms applied (or not applied) to interior surfaces are the environmental qualities with which occupants come most closely in contact. These are 'read' continually as people experience any setting. Finishes and design details affect what is seen, heard, smelled and touched, and therefore how people feel in a space.

To the extent that a comfortable environment is aesthetically integrated and whole, it is also beautiful. Its physical wholeness and harmony transmit psychic wholeness and tranquillity, elevating the spirit and encouraging the senses to play with surrounding events and forms.

A powerful way to design for aesthetic richness is to conceive of all elements of a room (floors, ceilings, walls, horizontal and vertical supports, objects, forms, and architectural details) as interactive surfaces that can be sculpted, painted, draped and moulded, much the way artists sculpt, paint and mould wood, clay, canvas, fibres, colours and forms. An environment is most comfortable when there are varied moods throughout the facility, created by interesting things to look at, unexpected surprises of light and shadow, sound, warmth, and colour, nooks and crannies, and things that respond, smell, or feel inviting. Then the senses can play everywhere, not solely with the exhibits.

All environments affect people in at least two ways: they suggest a range of activities that can or cannot occur in a setting, and they evoke feelings. Thus environments are always both emotionally felt and mentally interpreted by each occupant. Exhibits tell people what they can do, whereas the beauty and aesthetic qualities of a facility affect people's emotions and convey messages about their self-worth. A context of wholeness that unites body, mind and spirit, thought and feeling, head and heart, invariably uplifts and transforms, helping people to learn and experience things they do not know and making them feel good about themselves and life. When the inner loveliness of the visitor meets the outer loveliness of an exhibit, then there is magic!

COMPETENCE

Aliveness also comes from being able to care for one's basic needs autonomously and from being successful at meaningful activities. Museum-goers often experience a sense of inferiority and submissiveness since they come to encounter the unfamiliar. They are unable to stake out territories over which they have jurisdiction or to control their activities and levels of social interaction in customary ways. To compensate for this loss of control and status, visitors should be helped to feel that they belong by being able to make their way easily through the facility and to participate in activities that grant them some control over territory, materials and social encounters. An interpretable physical layout, reinforced by good signage and graphics in lobbies, corridors, elevators, exhibit areas, and at critical junctures, can help people get to where they want to go. Facilities that enable them to fulfil basic personal needs without assistance – coat racks, coffee machines, water fountains, clocks, telephones, baby-changing tables, conveniently located lavatories – honour independence and personal power.

Where people of a variety of ages and physical conditions are present, adaptive facilities, as well as those scaled to meet a range of developmental and educational levels and interests, further affirm the inherent learning capacities of each participant. Dioramas and full-scale mock-ups of a setting, which create an environment or contextual framework for an exhibit, help all visitors make inferences that bridge the gaps between the familiar and the unknown.

A sense of competence is also boosted by an ordered space whose parts are distinguishable from one another. Areas or zones within a room can be set apart by the amount of physical space between them, distinctive lighting and pools of light, boundaries and dividers, and the use of colour – our most powerful visual organizer. With different colours on work surfaces and sitting surfaces at the visitor's eye level, even a visually chaotic environment becomes interpretable. Seeing a red, blue, or green space within a room communicates more powerfully than signage that where the colours begin and end, so do the activities.

There is another sense in which competence can be addressed. Studies of cognitive and personality styles suggest that people process information in different ways (left brain/right brain, screener/non-screener, reflective/impulsive) and primarily along one of three dimensions: visual, auditory, or kinesthetic. A kinesthetic learner, for example, will have a hard time absorbing information from a purely visual display where there is nothing to touch or manipulate. To ensure that no one is 'disabled', a successful exhibit presents the same information in at least these three modalities so everyone can approach and interpret the material in the way that suits him or her best.

CONTROL

Because we do not have eyes in the backs of our heads and cannot protect ourselves from attack from the rear, control and physical security depend upon having something solid at our backs, with the ability to see and hear what approaches head-on. Thus people move across beaches, fields and parks and stand still only when their backs are against a wall, a tree, or a bench. If protection at the rear is impossible, security may also be achieved by sitting or standing close to a wall, sitting or lying close to the ground, or attaining a position of height from which to survey the surrounding terrain. Most spaces have a zone (usually a corner) that is recognizably more protected than all other points in the room. It is there you will find the teacher's or doctor's desk, dad's favourite chair, and storage for precious items. People instinctively gravitate to a protected zone and like to stay there. Activities requiring a willingness to sit still and concentrate work best when placed in this location.

Physical security also depends upon being able to make predictions about territories and events beyond one's immediate spatial sphere. Broad vistas, rendered by an architecturally open plan, achieve this sense of security best. Interior windows or walls of glass, however, bold graphics, lighting that does not create mysterious shadows, and balanced acoustics can be intentionally employed in more enclosed settings to provide the 'extension of the senses' that is required.

A CONCLUDING THOUGHT

Psychological and physiological harmony depend upon the balance maintained among movement, comfort, competence and control. Whenever one factor is limited (when movement is restricted, for example, because an exhibit requires the visitor to sit), the value of the other factors must be increased (a more stimulating background ambience, more back protection, varied sensorial modes for approaching the information). Because museum environments often produce many limitations at once, including restricted movement, interaction with unfamiliar materials, and restricted territorial control, the comfort dimension is exceedingly important and requires far more attention than is often characteristic of exhibit design practice. But, when all four needs are met and balanced to complement the extremes of visitor and exhibit limitations and excesses, then the setting truly lives and people leave the museum renewed and more alive.

This chapter first appeared as a paper in Journal of Museum Education *15(1) (1990): 10–12.*

FURTHER READING

Alexander, Christopher (1979) *The Timeless Way of Building*, New York: Oxford University Press.
Alexander, Christopher *et al.* (1977) *A Pattern Language*, New York: Oxford University Press.
Bachelard, Gaston (1969) *The Poetics of Space*, Boston, MA: Beacon Press.
Fiske, D. W., and Maddi, S. R. (1961) *Functions of Varied Experience*, Homewood, IL: Dorsey.
Mehrabian, Albert (1976) *Public Places and Private Spaces: the Psychology of Work, Play, and Living Environments*, New York: Basic Books.
Walter, Eugene Victor (1988) *Placeways: a Theory of Human Environments*, Chapel Hill, NC: University of North Carolina Press.

Index